Schriften des Europa-Instituts der Universität des Saarlandes – Rechtswissenschaft

Band 101

Edina Márton

Violations of Personality Rights through the Internet: Jurisdictional Issues under European Law

HART
PUBLISHING

Nomos

Die Deutsche Nationalbibliothek verzeichnet diese Publikation in der Deutschen Nationalbibliografie; detaillierte bibliografische Daten sind im Internet über http://dnb.d-nb.de abrufbar.

at.: Univ. d. Saarlandes, Diss., 2015

The Deutsche Nationalbibliothek lists this publication in the Deutsche Nationalbibliografie; detailed bibliographic data are available on the Internet at http://dnb.d-nb.de

ISBN: HB (Nomos) 978-3-8487-2726-1
ePDF (Nomos) 978-3-8452-7070-8

British Library Cataloguing-in-Publication Data
A catalogue record for this book is available from the British Library.

ISBN: HB (Hart) 978-1-5099-0802-8

Library of Congress Cataloging-in-Publication Data
Márton, Edina
Violations of Personality Rights through the Internet: Jurisdictional Issues under European Law
Edina Márton
382 p.
Includes bibliographic references.

ISBN: HB (Hart) 978-1-5099-0802-8

1. Auflage 2016

Acknowledgements

This book is based on my doctoral thesis, which I successfully defended at Saarland University, Germany, in July 2015.

I owe my deepest gratitude to my supervisor, Professor Christian Kohler. Without him, it would not have been possible to begin this book. I am privileged to have benefitted from his scholarly guidance and wisdom, constructive comments, genuine kindness, and support over the years. He strengthened my interest in the fascinating European area of justice, and his scholarship continues to be an inspiration. I would also like to express my sincere thanks to Professor Helmut Rüßmann for his support and for writing the second evaluation report on my doctoral thesis. Likewise, I am grateful to the other members of the doctoral jury: Professors Annemarie Matusche-Beckmann and Thomas Giegerich.

In addition, I wish to thank a number of institutions for their generous financial support, which was key to the completion of my thesis and the publication of this book. Thus, I would like to thank the scholarship programme of The Hague Academy of International Law, which enabled me to attend the summer course in Private International Law in 2010. Thanks are also due to the German Academic Exchange Service (DAAD), Bonn, and the FAZIT-STIFTUNG Gemeinnützige Verlagsgesellschaft mbH, Frankfurt am Main, for partly funding my research project. Similarly, I am grateful to the Johanna und Fritz Buch Gedächtnis-Stiftung, Hamburg, for supporting the publication of this book.

Furthermore, special thanks go to the editors of the collection of academic series of the Europa-Institut of Saarland University for their decision to publish my thesis in their collection.

Moreover, I wholeheartedly thank my partner, Christopher, and my family, especially my mother, for their love, care, support, and companionship.

And, of course, I remember with much gratitude and appreciation those people and institutions that cannot be listed in this limited space but that have helped me, directly or indirectly, to complete my thesis and finalise this book.

Saarbrücken, December 2015 *Edina Márton*

Note on the Usage and Style Guidelines of this Book

The present book contains numbered chapters and sections. Sections are divided into up to four grades of subsections. The first Roman number refers to the chapter and the other numbers to the section and subsection(s). Thus, Ch. VII.B.II.1.a)aa) is a reference to the respective grade of subsection in the seventh chapter.

Cross-references are generally made to chapters and their respective grade of (sub)section but sometimes they also refer to footnotes.

Abbreviations, including short forms of European Union and national legislation, are commonly used and are explained in the List of Abbreviations on pages 19-26.

Throughout this book, the following terms are used with the following meaning, unless otherwise indicated or the text suggests otherwise:

- Brussels Regime/instruments: Convention of 27 September 1968 on jurisdiction and the enforcement of judgments in civil and commercial matters (OJ 1972 L 299/32) as amended by the four accession conventions (OJ 1998 C 27/1) (BC); Council Regulation (EC) No 44/2001 of 22 December 2000 on jurisdiction and the recognition and enforcement of judgments in civil and commercial matters (OJ 2001 L 12/1) (Brussels I) (repealed); Regulation (EU) No 1215/2012 of the European Parliament and of the Council of 12 December 2012 on jurisdiction and the recognition and enforcement of judgments in civil and commercial matters (OJ 2012 L 351/1) (Brussels Ia); Agreement between the European Community and the Kingdom of Denmark on jurisdiction and the recognition and enforcement of judgments in civil and commercial matters (OJ 2005 L 299/62) [EC/Denmark Agreement (OJ 2005 L 299/62)]; Agreement between the European Community and the Kingdom of Denmark on jurisdiction and the recognition and enforcement of judgments in civil and commercial matters (OJ 2013 L 79/4) [EC/Denmark Agreement (OJ 2013 L 79/4)].
- Brussels States: Member and Contracting States of the Brussels instruments.
- Brussels-Lugano Regime (cf. Layton/Mercer, European Civil Practice, paras 1.001, 11.001): Consolidated version of the Convention of 27 September 1968 on jurisdiction and the enforcement of judgments in civil and commercial matters (OJ 1972 L 299/32) as amended by the four accession conventions (OJ 1998 C 27/1) (BC); Council Regulation (EC) No 44/2001 of 22 December 2000 on jurisdiction and the recognition and enforcement of judgments in civil and commercial matters (OJ 2001 L 12/1) (Brussels I) (repealed); Regulation (EU) No 1215/2012 of the European Parliament and of the Council of 12 December 2012 on jurisdiction and the recognition and enforcement of judgments in civil and commercial matters (OJ 2012 L 351/1) (Brussels Ia); Convention of 16 September 1988 on jurisdiction and the enforcement of judgments in civil and commercial matters (OJ 1988 L 319/9) (1988 LC); Convention on jurisdiction and the enforcement of judgments in civil and commercial matters (OJ 2007 L 339/3) (2007 LC); Agreement between the European Community

and the Kingdom of Denmark on jurisdiction and the recognition and enforcement of judgments in civil and commercial matters (OJ 2005 L 299/62) [EC/Denmark Agreement (OJ 2005 L 299/62)]; Agreement between the European Community and the Kingdom of Denmark on jurisdiction and the recognition and enforcement of judgments in civil and commercial matters (OJ 2013 L 79/4) [EC/Denmark Agreement (OJ 2013 L 79/4)].

- Contracting States: parties of the Lugano Conventions and/or the Brussels Convention, as the case may be.
- Defamation: violation of the right to personal and professional (occupational) reputation. In England: libel. Violation of business reputation is principally excluded.
- EFTA countries: Iceland, Norway and Switzerland (excluding Liechtenstein).
- England: England and Wales.
- English law: principally refers to the legal system of England and Wales.
- European: refers to things belonging to the Brussels and Lugano States or to the persons established therein.
- Internet user: depending on the context, an online visitor, or an actor as a publisher.
- Internet: the diverse kinds of online communication services, such as WWW, social media sites (platforms) and other applications.
- Lugano Regime/instruments/conventions: Convention of 16 September 1988 on jurisdiction and the enforcement of judgments in civil and commercial matters (OJ 1988 L 319/9) (1988 LC); Convention on jurisdiction and the enforcement of judgments in civil and commercial matters (OJ 2007 L 339/3) (2007 LC).
- Lugano States: Contracting States of the Lugano Conventions.
- Member States: Member States of the EU, including Denmark.
- Online visitor: a person who connects to the Internet and requests online information.
- Personality rights: the right to reputation and the right to respect for private life, especially private information, image (likeness) and name.
- Previous Brussels-Lugano instruments: Brussels-Lugano instruments adopted or concluded prior to Regulation (EU) No 1215/2012 of the European Parliament and of the Council of 12 December 2012 on jurisdiction and the recognition and enforcement of judgments in civil and commercial matters (OJ 2012 L 351/1) (Brussels Ia).
- Publisher: legal or private person who publishes or places online its/his own content. In the case of a legal person, the term 'publisher' also covers the act or omission of its employee(s).
- Regime: see Brussels-Lugano Regime.
- Violation of personality rights: a dispute in which the victim seeks to establish the liability of the publisher for the allegedly injurious content cross-border published and distributed either online or offline and claims for compensation for his non-pecuniary harm caused by that content. Alternatively, the (potential) victim seeks to prevent the occurrence of such a violation.

Throughout this book, the following terms are used as synonyms, unless otherwise indicated or the text suggests otherwise:

- Causal event and jurisdictionally relevant event, act, activity and omission.
- Connecting factor, approach, test, criterion and concept.
- European Union, EU and Union.
- Non-pecuniary/non-material harm, damage and loss as well as damage, harm and loss.
- Parties and litigants.
- Pecuniary/material damage and loss.
- PIL rules and conflict of laws rules.
- Plaintiff and victim.
- Publisher and online/Internet actor.
- Right to privacy and right to respect for private life.
- Tort, delict, quasi-delict and non-contractual obligation.
- Tortfeasor, perpetrator and wrongdoer.
- Tortious liability and non-contractual liability.
- Victim, aggrieved person and person who considers that his personality rights have been violated or they are threatened to be violated.

Words importing the masculine gender also include the feminine gender and, depending on the textual context, the neutral gender as referring to a legal person.

Article and recital numbers without further detail or in respect of the Brussels-Lugano Regime shall be understood as references to the provision numbers and wording of Brussels Ia, unless otherwise indicated or the text suggests otherwise. A table in Appendix 3 illustrates the correlation between the provisions of the Brussels and Lugano instruments.

References to the case law of the European Court of Justice are indicated by using solely the name of one of the parties, generally the plaintiff, in italics. Opinions of the Advocates General are indicated as follows: 'AG in' and the reference to the case name in italics.

Conclusions drawn from individual cases of the European Court of Justice are generally applied to the Brussels-Lugano Regime.

References to national cases retain the name of the court in the original language in italics.

References to the decisions of the European Court of Human Rights are indicated by the name of the parties and the application number of the case.

Documents of the European Union are referred to with their number and their publication in the Official Journal of the European Union, except for some legislation, which is referred to with special terms, as listed on pages 19-26.

National legislation and cases are partly read and comprehended indirectly through an analysis or a summary prepared by a third person.

Websites referred to were last accessed on 30 March 2015, unless otherwise indicated.

Source materials found in this book are systematised at the end of the book. Reference numbers (i.e., numbers of pages and footnotes) are generally indicated.

Dates are referred to in the following format: dd.mm.yyyy.

The law is up to date as of 15 April 2015.

Table of Contents

List of Abbreviations

1971 Protocol	Protocol on the interpretation by the Court of Justice of the Convention of 27 September 1968 on jurisdiction and the enforcement of judgments in civil and commercial matters (OJ 1975 L 204/28) as amended by the four accession conventions (OJ 1998 C 27/28)
1988 LC	Convention of 16 September 1988 on jurisdiction and the enforcement of judgments in civil and commercial matters (OJ 1988 L 319/9)
2007 LC	Convention on jurisdiction and the enforcement of judgments in civil and commercial matters (OJ 2007 L 339/3)
AB	Alkotmánybíróság (Hungary)
Abs.	Absatz
AC	Appeal Cases (Law Reports)
acc. to	according to
AfP	Zeitschrift für Medien- und Kommunikationsrecht (Archiv für Presserecht)
AG	Advocate General
AG	Amtsgericht (Germany)
Alb. L.J. Sci. & Tech.	Albany Law Journal of Science & Technology
ALJR	Australian Law Journal Reports
All ER	The All England Law Reports
ALR	Australian Law Reports
Am. J. Comp. L.	American Journal of Comparative Law
Anm.	Anmerkung
Annales Univ. Sci. Budapest., Sec. Iur.	Annales Universitatis Scientiarum Budapestinensis de Rolando Eötvös Nominatae, Sectio Iuridica
APRANET	Advanced Research Projects Agency Network
Art / Arts	Article / Articles
Aufl.	Auflage
BC	Convention of 27 September 1968 on jurisdiction and the enforcement of judgments in civil and commercial matters (OJ 1972 L 299/32) as amended by the four accession conventions (OJ 1998 C 27/1)
BDT	Bírósági Döntések Tára
Be.	1998. évi XIX. törvény a büntetőeljárásról (Hungary)

BGB	Bürgerliches Gesetzbuch (Germany)
BGH	Bundesgerichtshof
BGHZ	Amtliche Sammlung der Entscheidungen des Bundesgerichtshofs in Zivilsachen
BH	Kúriai Döntések (BH)
BIICL	British Institute of International and Comparative Law
Brussels I	Council Regulation (EC) No 44/2001 of 22 December 2000 on jurisdiction and the recognition and enforcement of judgments in civil and commercial matters (OJ 2001 L 12/1)
Brussels Ia	Regulation (EU) No 1215/2012 of the European Parliament and of the Council of 12 December 2012 on jurisdiction and the recognition and enforcement of judgments in civil and commercial matters (OJ 2012 L 351/1)
Btk.	2012. évi C. törvény a Büntető Törvénykönyvről (Hungary)
BYbIL	British Yearbook of International Law
C.A. / CA	Court of Appeal
C.J.Q.	Civil Justice Quarterly
C.L.J.	Cambridge Law Journal
C.L.Pract.	Commercial Law Practitioner
c/C	contra
CC	Code civil (1804) (France)
Cf.	confer (compare)
Ch.	Chapter
ch.	chamber (France)
Charter	Charter of Fundamental Rights of the European Union (OJ 2012 C 326/391)
CILE	Center for International Legal Education
Civ	Civil
CJEU	Court of Justice of the European Union
CLIP	Center on Law and Information Policy at Fordham Law School
CLP	Current Legal Problems
CLR	Commonwealth Law Reports
CML Rev.	Common Market Law Review
Co.	company
COM	European Commission
Comm. L. & Pol'y	Communication Law & Policy
Comm. Law.	Communications Lawyer
Council	Council of the European Union

Court	see ECJ
CR	Computer und Recht
CRi	Computer Law Review International
CUP	Cambridge University Press
CZK	Czech koruna (crown)
D.N.D.	District North Dakota
dd.mm.yyyy	day – month – year
Doc.	Document
e.g.	exempli grātiā (for example)
E.L.Rev.	European Law Review
EC	European Community
EC Treaty	Treaty establishing the European Community
ECHR	European Convention for the Protection of Human Rights and Fundamental Freedoms (Rome, 4.11.1950)
ECJ	European Court of Justice (CJEU, former Court of Justice of the European Communities and Court of Justice of the European Economic Community)
ECL	European Current Law
ECtHR	European Court of Human Rights
ed. / eds.	editor / editors
edn.	edition
EEC	European Economic Community
EFTA	European Free Trade Association
EGTL	European Group on Tort Law
EJLT	European Journal of Law and Technology
EP	European Parliament
EPC	European Publishers Council
ERPL	European Review of Private Law
et al. / et a.	et alia (and others)
EU	European Union
EuGH	Europäischer Gerichtshof / Gerichtshof der Europäischen Union, see ECJ
EuGVÜ	see BC
EuGVVO	see Brussels I
EuLF	The European Legal Forum
EUR	euro
Eur. J.L. Reform	European Journal of Law Reform
Eur. L. Rptr.	European Law Reporter

EuZPR	Europäisches Zivilprozessrecht
EuZW	Europäische Zeitschrift für Wirtschaftsrecht
EWCA Civ	England and Wales Court of Appeal Civil Division
EWHC	England and Wales High Court
EWiR	Entscheidungen zum Wirtschaftsrecht
f. / ff.	following page / pages
F.Supp.	Federal Supplement
F.Supp.2d	Federal Supplement, Second Series
fn / fns	footnote / footnotes
Fordham Intell. Prop. Media & Ent. L.J.	Fordham Intellectual Property, Media and Entertainment Law Journal
FS	Festschrift
GA	Generalanwalt / Generalanwältin (EuGH)
GEDIP	Goupe européen de droit international privé / European Group for Private International Law
Gf.	gazdasági ügy, fellebbvitel
Gfv.	gazdasági ügy, felülvizsgálat
GG	Grundgesetz für die Bundesrepublik Deutschland (1949)
GLJ	German Law Journal
GmbH	Gesellschaft mit beschränkter Haftung
GMT	Greenwich Mean Time
GPR	Zeitschrift für das Privatrecht der Europäischen Union
GPS	Global Positioning System
GRUR	Gewerblicher Rechtsschutz und Urheberrecht
GRUR Int.	Gewerblicher Rechtsschutz und Urheberrecht, Internationaler Teil
GRUR-Prax	Gewerblicher Rechtsschutz und Urheberrecht, Praxis im Immaterialgüter- und Wettbewerbsrecht
H.L.	House of Lords
Harv. L. Rev.	Harvard Law Review
HCA	High Court of Australia
HCCH	The Hague Conference on Private International Law
HRA	Human Rights Act 1998
Hrsg.	Herausgeber
HUF	forint
i.e.	id est (that is)

I.P.Q.	Intellectual Property Quarterly
ibid.	ibidem (in the same place)
ICLQ	International and Comparative Law Quarterly
IECL	International Encyclopedia of Comparative Law
IEHC	Irish High Court
IESC	Supreme Court of Ireland
ÍH	Ítélőtáblai Határozatok
IIC	International Review of Intellectual Property and Competition Law
IJPL	International Journal of Procedural Law
ILRM	Irish Law Reports Monthly
Inc.	Incorporated (company)
incl.	including
Ind. J. Global Legal Stud.	Indiana Journal of Global Legal Studies
infra	below
Intr.	Introduction
IP	Internet Protocol
IPI	International Press Institute
IPRax	Praxis des Internationalen Privat- und Verfahrensrechts
IRIS	Database on legal information relevant to the audiovisiual sector in Europe (IRIS Merlin)
IRLCT	International Review of Law, Computers & Technology
J. Priv. Int. L.	Journal of Private International Law
JeMa	Jogesetek Magyarázata
jg	Jahrgang
JURE	Collection of relevant judgments regarding jurisdiction, recognition and enforcement of judgments in civil and commercial matters
jurisPR-ITR	JurisPR IT-Recht
JurPC	Internet-Zeitschrift für Rechtsinformatik und Informationsrecht
JuS	Juristische Schulung
JZ	JuristenZeitung
K&R	Kommunikation und Recht
KUG	Gesetz betreffend das Urheberrecht an Werken der bildenden Künste und der Photographie (1907)
L.Q.R.	Law Quarterly Review
Law & Contemp. Probs.	Law and Contemporary Problems

LB	See Legf. Bír.
LC	Lugano Convention
Legf. Bír.	Legfelsőbb Bíróság
LG	Landgericht (Germany)
LLC	Limited liability company
LMK	Lindenmaier-Möhring Kommentierte BGH-Rechtsprechung
Ltd.	Limited (company)
Masaryk U. J.L. & Tech.	Masaryk University Journal of Law and Technology
MMR	MultiMedia und Recht
MR	Medien und Recht
NCPC	Nouveau Code de Procédure Civile
NIQB	Northern Ireland Queen's Bench
NILR	Netherlands International Law Review
NJW	Neue Juristische Wochenschrift
N.N.	nomen nescio
Nmj.	A nemzetközi magánjogról szóló 1979. évi 13. törvényerejű rendelet (Hungary)
n°	number
no / nos	number / numbers
Nw. J. Int'l L. & Bus.	Northwestern Journal of International Law & Business
NWULR	Northwestern University Law Review
OGH	Oberster Gerichtshof (Austria)
OHADAC	Organization for the Harmonization of Business Law in the Caribbean
OJ	Official Journal (of the European Community and the European Union)
ÖJZ	Österreichische Juristen-Zeitung
OLG	Oberlandesgericht
ord.	ordonnance
OUP	Oxford University Press
p / pp	page / pages
para / paras	paragraph / paragraphs
PCMLP	Programme in Comparative Media Law and Policy (Centre for Socio-Legal Studies, University of Oxford)
Pf.	polgári ügy, fellebbvitel
Pfv.	polgári ügy, felülvizsgálat

PIL	Private International Law
Pp.	1952. évi III. törvény a polgári perrendtartásról (Hungary)
Prel. Doc.	Preliminary Document
Ptk.	1959. évi IV. törvény a Polgári Törvénykönyvről (Hungary)
QB	Queen's Bench
RabelsZ	Rabels Zeitschrift für ausländisches und internationales Privatrecht
Regulation No 44/2001	See Brussels I
RH	Rättsfall från hovrätterna (Sweden)
RIDA	Revue Internationale du Droit d'Auteur
Rome I	Regulation (EC) No 593/2008 of the European Parliament and of the Council of 17 June 2008 on the law applicable to contractual obligations (OJ 2008 L 177/6)
Rome II	Regulation (EC) No 864/2007 of the European Parliament and of the Council of 11 July 2007 on the law applicable to non-contractual obligations (OJ 2007 L 199/40)
RSS	Really Simple Syndication
Rt	Norsk Retstidende (Norway)
s. / ss.	section / sections
S.C.R.	Supreme Court Reports (Canada)
SCC	Supreme Court of Canada
St. Louis U. L.J.	Saint Louis University Law Journal
Stan. L. Rev.	Stanford Law Review
StGB	Strafgesetzbuch (Germany)
supra	above
SPEECH Act	Securing the Protection of our Enduring and Established Constitutional Heritage (SPEECH) Act (USA)
sz.	szám
szerk.	szerkesztő
SZIER	Schweizerische Zeitschrift für internationales und europäisches Recht
TEU	Treaty on the European Union (2009)
TFEU	Treaty on the Functioning of the European Union
TGI	Tribunal de grande instance
Treaty of Rome	Treaty establishing the European Economic Community (1957)

új Ptk.	2013. évi V. törvény a Polgári Törvénykönyvről (Hungary)
UK	United Kingdom
UKHL	United Kingdom House of Lords Decisions
Urt.	Urteil
US / U.S.	United States (of America) as a noun or as an adjective
USA	United States of America
UTC	Coordinated Universal Time
v. / v	versus
Va. J. Int'l L.	Virginia Journal of International Law
Vht.	1994. évi LIII. törvény a bírósági végrehajtásról (Hungary)
Vol.	Volume
W.L.R. / WLR	The Weekly Law Reports
WWW	World Wide Web
Yale J. World Pub. Ord.	Yale Journal of World Public Order
YbPIL	Yearbook of Private International Law
ZEuP	Zeitschrift für Europäisches Privatrecht
ZPO	Zivilprozessordnung (Germany)
ZSR	Zeitschrift für Schweizerisches Recht
ZUM	Zeitschrift für Urheber- und Medienrecht
ZVglRWiss	Zeitschrift für Vergleichende Rechtswissenschaft

Introduction: International jurisdiction of courts in the digital age - A bird's eye view

International jurisdiction is an 'adjudicatory authority' exercised by the courts and derived from the physical power of the political entity where the court sits.[1] Rules of international jurisdiction geographically localise and, in turn, nationalise trans-border legal disputes, and for this purpose, they usually comprise two basic elements: a subject matter and a connecting factor. The subject matter delimitates the scope of application of the rules. «The connecting factor is», as Frank Vischer explains, «the element forming one of the facts of the case which is selected in order to attach a question of law to a legal system.»[2] It is not solely a technical creature of a legal order that mechanically allocates adjudicatory authority to the courts to hear and decide upon disputes. Rather, it reflects and gives effect to several broad considerations, interests, and preferences of the legislator, the litigants, and the courts, and implies a selection of law applicable to the procedural and substantive issues of the controversies.[3] Connecting factors are basically designed, as Arthur T. von Mehren asserts, on two policies, namely, ease of administration of justice and predictability on the one hand, and litigational justice, fairness, and convenience on the other hand. Although it is desirable to employ both of them equally, he observes:

> «[U]sually these policy goals are in tension. To carry out the first, connecting factors that are singular and objective are needed; implementing the second, typically requires plural factors that include subjective elements and take into account the characteristics of the specific controversy to be adjudicated. It follows that normally a connecting factor cannot systematically advance equally both administrability and litigational justice.»[4]

As a consequence of technological advances, connecting factors may be founded or reshaped, and accordingly, the balance between the two

---

1 Cf. Justice Holmes as cited in von Mehren, Recueil des Cours 295, p 104 stating, «The foundation of jurisdiction is physical power ....» For details on adjudicatory authority, see von Mehren, Recueil des Cours 295.

2 Vischer, in: Lipstein, IECL, p 3 (s.4-I).

3 See Von Mehren, Recueil des Cours 295, pp 27 ff.

4 Von Mehren, Recueil des Cours 295, p 70.

policies may vary. Such a challenging technological advancement was the invention and wide-spread adoption of automobiles,[5] and currently, it is the Internet. This informational medium is often portrayed as an interactive, fluid, and dynamic medium, which has penetrated into people's everyday life and has revolutionised their social relationships as well as their methods of communication and news consumption. Due to its inherently global nature, it allows persons, regardless of their cultural or financial backgrounds, to consume or disseminate information around the world easily, instantaneously, simultaneously, permanently, and at a low cost. In Lawrence Siry and Sandra Schmitz's words:

> «Nowhere is the world smaller than on the Internet. Today, with a click of a mouse, people from across the globe can re-acquaint themselves with the old friends, research the unknown, and read newspapers from faraway places and far away times.»[6]

Mindful of these special features, two different views are crystallised among academics and legal practitioners on the application of contemporary physical world-oriented connecting factors to disputes arising out of the use of the Internet. Some of the scholars are of the opinion that the emergence of this technology suggests a need to adopt often complex, technology-specific connecting factors, while others claim that the traditional technology-neutral criteria based on the existence of the geographical boundaries of states are still applicable.[7] This dichotomy of views can also be perceived in judicial practice. Courts from different corners of the globe have established various connecting factors to localise disputes in which the victim seeks to establish the non-contractual liability of the publisher or brings an action to prevent the publication of such content as the following sampling of selected judicial decisions indicates.[8]

---

5 See e.g. EU: Jenard Report, p 26 as referring to the high number of road accidents as a ground for laying down a rule of jurisdiction in tort (see *infra* Intr. to Ch. IV); US: Norris, Arizona Law Review 2011, 1013, 1018 noting their impact on personal jurisdiction over individuals.

6 Siry/Schmitz, EJLT 2012, 1.

7 Cf. *infra* Ch. VI. See also academics and proposals as referred to in e.g. Norris, Arizona Law Review 2011, 1013, 1015-1016; Bigos, ICLQ 2005, 585, 601-603.

8 The sampling aims to show the array of various solutions solely on the basis of the author's selection. For details on jurisdiction in different states, see e.g. Svantesson, PIL and the Internet; Bertoni, in: Bertoni, Towards an Internet Free of Censorship; Hoare, C.L.Pract. 2004, 4-13.

The High Court of Australia's approach: the place of downloading

In the *Dow Jones and Company Inc v Gutnick*[9] case, the seven-member High Court of Australia unanimously dismissed the appeal of Dow Jones. The dispute arose between the plaintiff, Mr Gutnick, much of whose social and business life could be said to be focused in Victoria, where he was a resident, and the defendant, Dow Jones & Company Inc., a US company. The plaintiff sought damages against the defendant for defaming his reputation in Victoria by publishing an article in that state both in print and in Barron's Online, a subscription news site.[10] The court confirmed the traditional Australian approach whereby tort of defamation concentrates on publications causing harm to reputation.[11] That harm occurs where and when the listener, the reader, or the observer comprehends the defamatory publication.[12] Accordingly, publication is «a bilateral act - in which the publisher makes it available and a third party has it available for his or her comprehension.»[13] However, the court did not focus primarily on the defendant's conduct. Rather, it went on to hold that defamation is ordinarily to be located where the harm to reputation occurs, i.e., at the place where the allegedly defamatory material is available in a comprehensible form and the person defamed has reputation there. In the online context, the material is not available in a comprehensible form until the material complained of is downloaded.[14] Accordingly, the damage to reputation may be

9 [2002] HCA 56; 210 CLR 575; 194 ALR 433; 77 ALJR 255 (10 December 2002).

10 As is clear from paras 97 and 169 of this judgment, five copies were sold in Victoria and roughly 1,700 from 550,000 people «paid subscription fees by credit cards whose holders had Australian addresses.»

11 *Dow Jones and Company Inc v Gutnick* [2002] HCA 56; 210 CLR 575; 194 ALR 433; 77 ALJR 255 (10 December 2002), 25 (Gleeson CJ, McHugh, Gummow and Hayne JJ.).

12 *Dow Jones and Company Inc v Gutnick* [2002] HCA 56; 210 CLR 575; 194 ALR 433; 77 ALJR 255 (10 December 2002), 26 (Gleeson CJ, McHugh, Gummow and Hayne JJ.). Cf. Canada: *Breeden v. Black* 2012 SCC 19, [2012] 1 S.C.R. 666, 20.

13 *Dow Jones and Company Inc v Gutnick* [2002] HCA 56; 210 CLR 575; 194 ALR 433; 77 ALJR 255 (10 December 2002), 26 (Gleeson CJ, McHugh, Gummow and Hayne JJ.).

14 *Dow Jones and Company Inc v Gutnick* [2002] HCA 56; 210 CLR 575; 194 ALR 433; 77 ALJR 255 (10 December 2002), 44 (Gleeson CJ, McHugh, Gummow and Hayne JJ.).

done at the place where the person downloads the material.[15] Based on this finding, the court asserted that the tort of defamation was committed in Victoria.

The United States District Court, D. North Dakota, Southwestern Division's approaches: the sliding scale test and the effects test

In *Zidon v. Pickrell,*[16] the plaintiff Mr Zidon, a resident of North Dakota, alleged that Ms Pickrell, a resident of Colorado, created a website at the domain name indicating his name, where she posted allegedly defamatory statements. Furthermore, he also alleged that the defendant emailed a hyperlink to the website to persons in the area of Bismarck, North Dakota, as well as to the public at large. Therefore, he claimed for defamation and intentional infliction of emotional distress.[17] The United States District Court, D. North Dakota, Southwestern Division, had recourse to a five-part test from which it essentially examined the nature of the quality of the defendant's contacts for asserting its specific personal jurisdiction, which was disputed by Ms Pickrell.[18] This factor was examined on the basis of two rulings, which are predominantly applied for determining personal jurisdiction in Internet-related cases in the US.[19] First, it applied the Zippo's sliding scale test, which considers the level of interactivity of the website (i.e., 'active', 'passive', and 'middle ground') and the nature of its com-

15 *Dow Jones and Company Inc v Gutnick* [2002] HCA 56; 210 CLR 575; 194 ALR 433; 77 ALJR 255 (10 December 2002), 44 (Gleeson CJ, McHugh, Gummow and Hayne JJ.). See also Slane, Law & Contemp. Probs. 2008, 129, fn 75. Cf. Irish residual rule, i.e., rule applicable to cases which do not fall under the Brussels-Lugano Regime (on this, see also *infra* fn 431): *USA Rugby Football Union Limited v Ivan Calhoun* (*High Court,* unreported, 2002) as reported, and commented in Gallagher, Internet Defamation; English residual rule: *King v Lewis* [2004] EWCA Civ 1329, affirming: *King v Lewis* [2004] EWHC 168 (QB); ss.9-10 of the *Defamation Act 2013* and its accompanying Explanatory Notes (on these sections, see also Bennett, YbPIL 2012/2013, 173 ff.).

16 344 F.Supp. 2d 624 (D.N.D. 2004). Cf. *Broadvoice, Inc. v. TP Innovations LLC* 733 F.Supp.2d 219 (D. Mass. 2010) as referred to in Little, YbPIL 2012/2013, 181, 187-188.

17 *Zidon v. Pickrell* 344 F.Supp.2d 624 (D.N.D. 2004) (Background).

18 For the other factors (i.e., 'quantity of contacts, relation of the cause of action to the contacts, interest of the forum state, and convenience of the parties'), see *Zidon v. Pickrell* 344 F.Supp.2d 624 (D.N.D. 2004), 632-633.

19 For US court practice, see e.g. Bosky, St. Louis U. L.J. 2012, 587 ff.; Little, YbPIL 2012/2013, 181 ff.

mercial activities.[20] The court held that although Ms Pickrell's website was interactive, this was not sufficient to exercise jurisdiction over her[21] and thus, it turned to examine whether the effects test set out in *Calder v. Jones*[22] was met. After examining the defendant's activities, it was satisfied that the effects test was met, since «[t]he Web site reveals that the focus of the Web site was North Dakota. Pickrell knew Zidon was a resident of North Dakota, and knew the "brunt of the injury" would be felt in North Dakota. ... Pickrell particularly and directly targeted North Dakota with her Web site and e-mails, and specifically targeted North Dakota resident ... Zidon.»[23] Hence, the court asserted its special personal jurisdiction.[24]

---

20 *Zidon v. Pickrell* 344 F.Supp.2d 624 (D.N.D. 2004), 629. *Zippo Manufacturing Co. v. Zippo Dot Com, Inc.*, 952 F.Supp. 1119 (W.D. Pa. 1997). On this test, see Bosky, St. Louis U. L.J. 2012, 587, 591 ff.; Little, YbPIL 2012/2013, 181, 186 ff. Regarding the importance of the interactive nature of the website in the case law of the ECJ, see *infra* fn 874.

21 *Zidon v. Pickrell* 344 F.Supp.2d 624 (D.N.D. 2004), 630.

22 465 U.S. 783 (1984). The effects test requires an intentional action, which is expressly aimed at the forum state with knowledge that the brunt of the harm would be suffered in that state. The US Supreme Court also held in *Calder v. Jones,* 465 U.S. 783 (1984), 789 that the place where the plaintiff resides and works was «the focal point both of the story and of the harm suffered.» Note that the Yale Supreme Court Clinic, Petition, 2010 identifies two different standards adopted on the basis of *Calder v. Jones* 465 U.S. 783 (1984) by the US lower courts in respect of the due process test for personal jurisdiction in international tort cases through the Internet: (1) 'knowledge' test: «requiring the plaintiff to show only that the defendant engaged in an intentional tort involving the Internet knowing the plaintiff's State of residence.» (*Ibid.*, p 10); (2) 'knowledge-plus' standard: awareness of the plaintiff's residence is not sufficient; the plaintiff must show additional facts linking the defendant to the forum, such as his targeting activity (*ibid.*, p 11). For the dichotomy of standards, see also the majority and dissenting opinions in *William Roger Clemens*, Plaintiff-Appellant, v. *Brian McNamee*, Defendant-Appellee, No. 09-20625 (decided: August 12, 2010), U.S. Court of Appeals, Fifth Circuit. Cf. *Walden v. Fiore et al.* (certiorari to the United States Court of Appeals for the Ninth Circuit, No. 12–574, Argued November 4, 2013 – Decided February 25, 2014) in which the US Supreme Court although dealt with *Calder v. Jones* 465 U.S. 783 (1984) left «questions about virtual contacts for another day.» (*Ibid.*, fn 9.) For comments on *Walden v. Fiore et al.* in respect of Internet defamation cases, see e.g. Rhinehart, Internet Defamation Cases, 2014.

23 *Zidon v. Pickrell* 344 F.Supp.2d 624 (D.N.D. 2004), 632 (emphases omitted).

24 *Zidon v. Pickrell* 344 F.Supp.2d 624 (D.N.D. 2004), 633.

The German Federal Court of Justice's approach: an objective domestic connection

In the *New York Times* decision,[25] the dispute arose out of an article published both offline and online by the New York Times, which allegedly violated the right to the name and the reputation of the plaintiff, who was domiciled in Germany and ran a business there. He brought an action for an injunction against the publisher and the author of the article, who was established in New York. The *BGH* applied one of the limbs of its German residual jurisdictional rule in tort [i.e., place of the damage within Art 32 of the German *Code of Civil Procedure (Zivilprozessordnung; ZPO)*] to establish its own jurisdiction.[26] It explained that to assume jurisdiction, the statement complained of must objectively have a clear domestic connection to the forum state. Such an objective domestic connection exists if, in the light of the specific circumstances, particularly based on the content of the disputed statement, a collision of conflicting interests – the plaintiff's interest in respect of his right to protection of personality and the defendant's interest in forming his online appearance and news reporting – actually occurred or may occur domestically.[27] This is the case when, in the light of the circumstances of a specific dispute, notice of the statement complained of is significantly more probable than it would be with mere accessibility and when the alleged violation of the victim's personality right by the notice of the statement would (also) occur domestically.[28] After examining multiple factors,[29] such as the subject matter of the statement complained of, the number of registered users of the website alleg-

---

25 Case *New York Times* VI ZR 23/09 (2.3.2010), *BGH* (BGHZ 184, 313). Cf. Case *Seven Days in Moscow* VI ZR 111/10 (29.3.2011), *BGH* (GRUR 2011, 558); Case VI ZR 269/12 (14.5.2013), *BGH* (GRUR 2013, 751), II.1.a). For comments on these cases, see e.g. Jaeger-Fine *et al.*, Internet Jurisdiction, 2013, pp 7-9, 18-20; Thorn, FS Bernd von Hoffmann, pp 758-761; Weller, FS Athanassios Kaissis, pp 1039-1051; Gebauer, IPRax 2014, 513-520.

26 Due to the ubiquity principle (on this, see also Rüßmann, K&R 1998, 422, 423), the other limb of that residual rule is the place of acting. In an online context, it was held in case *Seven Days in Moscow* VI ZR 111/10 (29.3.2011), *BGH* (GRUR 2011, 558), 16 to be the place where the injurious content was written and put on the Internet (see also *infra* fn 836; cf. Thorn, FS Bernd von Hoffmann, p 760).

27 Case *New York Times* VI ZR 23/09 (2.3.2010), *BGH* (BGHZ 184, 313), 20. Cf. *eDate and Martinez*, 24, second question.

28 Case *New York Times* VI ZR 23/09 (2.3.2010), *BGH* (BGHZ 184, 313), 20.

29 See case *New York Times* VI ZR 23/09 (2.3.2010), *BGH* (BGHZ 184, 313), 21-24.

edly having domicile in Germany, and the nature of the website, the *BGH* overruled the decision of the *OLG Düsseldorf*.[30] It held that the article was of particular interest to the German Internet users, encouraging them to view that material, and in turn, the article may violate the personality right of the plaintiff.[31]

The European Court of Justice's approaches: the concept of the publisher's establishment, the concept of the victim's centre of interests, and the accessibility of the content test

The ECJ was faced with the interpretation of Art 5(3) of Brussels I in the *eDate and Martinez* joined cases. The former case concerned an action brought by Mr X, an individual domiciled in Germany against a company established in Austria for a Germany-wide order to refrain from using his full name when reporting about him on its Internet portal relating to a crime he had committed in the past. In the latter case, the plaintiffs, O. Martinez and R. Martinez, French nationals, contested the information and photographs posted online on a website published by the defendant, MGN Limited, a company governed by English law. The court essentially held that the person who considers that his rights have been violated by means of content placed online on a universally accessible Internet website has the option of bringing an action for liability in respect of all the damage caused in either of two states. Accordingly, he could bring the action either in the courts of the Member State where the publisher of that content is established or in the courts of the Member State where the centre of his interests at the time when the content was placed online is based. Alternatively, he could, «instead of an action for liability in respect of all the damage caused, bring his action before the courts of each Member State in the territory of which content placed online is or has been accessible. Those courts have jurisdiction only in respect of the damage caused in the territory of the Member State of the court seised.»[32]

---

30 Case I-15 U 17/08 (30.12.2008), *OLG Düsseldorf*.

31 See case *New York Times* VI ZR 23/09 (2.3.2010), *BGH* (BGHZ 184, 313), 21-25. In *ibid.*, 24, the *BGH* held that it is sufficient if only one person from the victim's social environment («Lebenskreis») comprehends the material. Contra: Case *Seven Days in Moscow* VI ZR 111/10 (29.3.2011), *BGH* (GRUR 2011, 558), 12. On this, see also Thorn, FS Bernd von Hoffmann, p 760.

32 *eDate and Martinez*, 52. For the factual and procedural background of the cases, see also *infra* Ch. VII.A. For localising the violation at the victim's forum, see

From a bird's eye view, it could be argued that the concept of the place of downloading; the sliding scale test; the effects test in the meaning of the 'knowledge' test; as well as the concepts of the publisher's establishment, accessibility of the content, and the victim's centre of interests, are more or less predictable, clear-cut, and non-specific connecting factors. On the other hand, the effects test in the meaning of the 'knowledge-plus' standard and the objective domestic connection approach are complex factors supposedly advancing litigational justice. In addition, these two latter connecting factors, together with the concept of the place of downloading and the accessibility of the content test, are technology-dependent criteria, while the other concepts can generally be determined in an Internet-neutral manner. Interestingly, irrespective of these differences, they were considered and discussed in the legal writing and in the European judicial practice as possible approaches for localising cross-border online (potential) violations of personality rights in Europe before the decision in the *eDate and Martinez* joined cases was delivered.[33] The present book contributes to and extends this academic discourse in the light of *eDate and Martinez*, the recent developments of the law of the EU (e.g. hierarchy and consistency of EU law, revised European rules on jurisdiction and the recognition and enforcement of judgments in civil and commercial matters), the latest case law of the ECJ (e.g. *Hejduk, Kolassa*), and the new and constantly changing characteristics of the Internet. It examines how the *eDate and Martinez*-approaches advance administrability, predictability, and litigational justice and assesses whether they are suitable jurisdictional grounds for disputes concerning (potential) violations of personality rights through the Internet in Europe, where common legal norms, interests, and

---

also US: 'knowledge' test (see *supra* fn 22); Argentina: *J.G.R v Google Inc, Federal Court of Appeal of Salta* [Cámara Federal de Apelaciones de Salta], July 4, 2011, LA LEY 7/19/01 (see Bertoni, in: Bertoni, Towards an Internet Free of Censorship, para II.B.I.a and para III, text to fn 106); Brazil: Superior Court of Justice, Recurso Especial no 1.168.547/RJ, Rel. Min. Luis Felipe Salomão, Quarta Turma, *DJe* 07.02.2011 as referred to in Mendes/Tiburcio, IJPL 2013, 223, 237-238 (domestic competence of courts in tort; «the place where the victim resides and works»); People's Republic of China: Svantesson, PIL and the Internet, p 233 identifies several People's Courts, such as the «People's Court where the plaintiff is domiciled», which may be competent for an action of Internet defamation.

33 See *infra* Ch. VI.

values strongly integrate and connect persons.[34] It concludes that they are not and recommends their possible reform.

To achieve this aim, the present book proceeds in eight chapters. The first two chapters function as background notes on the basic characteristics of the disputes concerned. In particular, Chapter I, without going into detail, sheds light on the protection of the different aspects of the personality and on selected measures that can be ordered for their actual or potential violations in four national legal systems. Chapter II addresses the revolutionary nature of the Internet by demonstrating its constantly changing and evolving characteristics and by comparing it to the traditional media, especially the press. In this way, these background notes establish common understandings of basic concepts and contribute to the assessment of the connecting factors adopted in *eDate and Martinez*. Chapter III maps the European jurisdictional landscape by outlining the legal regimes that regulate common European rules of jurisdiction and by giving their governing objectives and underlying principles as well as their basic features. Furthermore, it also lists the array of bases of jurisdiction among which the victim who considers that his personality rights are (threatened to be) violated might choose to sue the publisher, providing that certain circumstances are satisfied. Chapter IV further paves the jurisdictional way for an accurate critical analysis of the connecting factors adopted in *eDate and Martinez*. In particular, it looks at the peculiarities of the rule of jurisdiction in tort through the lens of the settled case law of the ECJ dating back to 1976, when the first judgment on that rule was delivered and with particular regard to violations of personality rights. Chapter V moves one step forward by placing in the limelight *Shevill*, concerning cross-border defamation through the paper-based press. This judgment, delivered in 1995, is of significant importance for two reasons. First, the different proposals put forward in legal theory and practice for localising online (potential) violations of personality rights under the common European rule of jurisdiction in tort outlined in Chapter VI are mostly based on this judgment. Secondly, the connecting factors established in offline defamation served as

34 Note that acc. to Commission Document COM(2014) 144 final (point 3/Mobility), «[t]here are currently nearly 14 million EU citizens residing in a Member State of which they are not a national». In addition Commission Document COM(2013) 627 final (p 2, point 1.1) proposes the establishment of a connected continent where «citizens and businesses can access electronic communications services wherever they are provided in the Union, without cross-border restrictions or unjustified additional costs».

sound bases for confirming or revising them in online (potential) violations of personality rights, as Chapter VII indicates. Besides examining and critically analysing the connecting factors established in *eDate and Martinez* and thus determining where the common European rule of jurisdiction in online (potential) violations of personality rights currently stands, Chapter VII recommends possible changes. The present author's proposal to reform the *eDate and Martinez* judgment and the virtues of that proposal are summed up in Chapter VIII. Finally, the present author's conclusions on the international jurisdiction of European courts in (potential) violations of personality rights in the digital age conclude this book.

Chapter I: Background: four national perspectives on violations of personality rights

The legal protection of the various aspects of the personality (i.e., personality rights) and the adjudication of their violations are deeply rooted in the national substantive laws reflecting the social, cultural, philosophical, and historic conditions as well as the moral expectations of each state.[35] This is true irrespective of the fact that the ECHR, an international convention on the protection of human rights and fundamental freedoms in Europe to which the Member States and the EFTA countries acceded, approximates these national practices to some extent.[36] Thus, after outlining the common understanding of a few of the basic concepts employed in this book, the present chapter directs a few rays of light onto the Hungarian, German, French, and English paths of civil legal protection of the personality and onto selected measures that can be ordered for their actual or threatened violations.[37] By doing so, these non-exhaustive background notes pursue a dual aim: they construct a narrative on the inherent nature

---

35 For initiatives to create common European rules on the protection of personality rights, see e.g. PEL/von Bar, Liab. Dam., Chapter 2, Art 2:203; von Bar/Clive, Principles, Definitions and Model Rules, Art 2:203; EGTL, Principles, Chapter 2, Art 2:102. Cf. statements and standards as summarised in IPI, Principles on Freedom of Expression and Protection of Reputation.

36 E.g. *Karakó v. Hungary* (no 39311/05), 23 [ruling on those aspects of the reputation that fall within the concept of private life (Art 8 of the ECHR)]; *Reklos and Davourlis v. Greece* (no 1234/05), 40, 43 [holding that the right to one's own image presupposes the right to control the use (incl. recording, conservation and reproduction) of the image]; *von Hannover v. Germany (No. 2)* (nos 40660/08, 60641/08), especially paras 104-113 and *Axel Springer AG v. Germany* (no 39954/08), especially paras 85-95 [on a number of factors encouraging national courts to apply uniform criteria when they determine the limit of protection of the personality rights by striking a fair balance between Art 8 (respect for the right to private life) and Art 10 (freedom of expression) of the ECHR]. On this issue, see also e.g. *Von Hannover v Germany (No. 3)* (no 8772/10).

37 For comparison of national laws, see e.g. works whose relevant parts served considerable bases of this chapter: Beverley-Smith/Ohly/Lucas-Schloetter, Privacy, Property and Personality; Koziol/Warzilek, Persönlichkeitsschutz; Ollier/Le Gall, in: Tunc, IECL, s.10-70–10-106. See also Brüggemeier/Colombi Ciacchi/O'Callaghan, Personality Rights; Rogers, Damages for Non-Pecuniary Loss; Mainstrat Study.

of the substantive legal matters concerned in this book, namely, violations of personality rights; in addition, since a connecting factor comprises elements of such violations, they might also contribute to a certain extent to the localisation of these violations, as is demonstrated in the following chapters.

A. Common understanding of basic concepts

The concept of personality considered in the entire book is regarded as a terminological umbrella that covers two values, namely, privacy and reputation, enjoyed by and inseparably attached to «an individual within a society of which he is a member».[38] These values differ in the extent of their dependency on the external evaluation of the society. While such an evaluation plays a decisive role in reputation, privacy issues are independent from it;[39] indeed, the right to privacy «consists essentially in the right to live one's own life with a minimum of interference.»[40] On the other hand, their common thread is that their violations result in non-pecuniary harm, such as injury to feelings, pain and suffering, loss of reputation, social discredit, mental distress and worry, or physical discomfort. The essential feature of this harm is that it is attributable to the victim's bodily, spiritual, and/or social-environmental sphere,[41] and it can be defined neither by employing objective criteria nor independently of the subjective feelings, views, and inclinations of the victim.[42] It is a loss other than physical or economic, and it is imbued with personal values.[43] These personal values serve as the bases of the argument according to which the monetary compensation for such non-material harm cannot be divided among the territorial borders of states, since its object, namely, the soul

---

38 Ollier/Le Gall, in: Tunc, IECL, s.10-70. Regarding legal persons, see *infra* Ch. VII.D.II.2.

39 See *Karakó v. Hungary* (no 39311/05), 23. The concept of privacy is also many-faceted covering various aspects of the personality, such as private information, image (likeness) or name.

40 Resolution 428 (1970) of the Parliamentary Assembly of the Council of Europe, point C, para 2.

41 See Petrik, in: Petrik, Polgári Jog, pp 202/1-202/2 (28. pótlás).

42 See Wurmnest, in: Basedow *et al.*, Max Planck Encyclopedia, p 1204.

43 See *Shevill*, 23; Wurmnest, in: Basedow *et al.*, Max Planck Encyclopedia, p 1204.

and the state of mind of the aggrieved person, is indivisible.[44] In addition, the aggrieved or threatened person may apply for other preventive and remedial measures, such as an (interim) injunction or the right of reply. While the latter offers a possibility of having a rectification published in the newspaper or on the website where the injurious information was displayed, the former orders a person to refrain from commencing or continuing the violation of one's personality rights. The importance of these selected measures differs depending on the aspect of personality at stake. While reputation can largely be restored by the right of reply and by monetary compensation, privacy issues can only effectively be protected by injunctions, since, as David Eady points out:

> «Once the intimate details or the photograph or the records of medical problems have been exposed to millions of readers, the privacy has been lost effectively for ever.»[45]

B. Four national perspectives

I. Hungarian law

Hungarian civil law affords a comprehensive protection of every aspect of the personality in *Act No V of 2013 of the new civil code (2013. évi V. törvény a Polgári Törvénykönyvről, új Ptk.)*,[46] which is similar to the system established under the provisions of the former civil code, namely, *Act No IV of 1959 (1959. évi IV. törvény a Polgári Törvénykönyvről, Ptk.)*.[47] It explicitly recognises a general clause of the protection of personality

---

44 In this regard, see Thiede, GPR 2011, 259, 260-261 and Thiede, ecolex 2012, 131, 133 (concerning non-material harm). Cf. Pichler, MR 2011, 365, 367, point 4.1.

45 Eady, C.J.Q. 2010, 411, 413.

46 For details, see e.g. Székely/Vékás, in: Vékás, A Polgári Törvénykönyv magyarázatokkal, pp 55-74; Petrik, in: Petrik, Kommentár a gyakorlat számára, pp 77-105. Since the *új Ptk.* consists of books, the article numbers with the book number (colon) refer to this code in this subsection.

47 Repealed by the *új Ptk.* on 15.3.2014. However, as Art 8(2) of Act No CLXXVII of 2013 states, the provisions of the *Ptk.* apply to violations performed before that date and to situations where the violation commenced before that date and finished after it. Therefore, certain provisions of both codes are outlined. For details of the previous rules on personality rights, see e.g. Petrik, in: Petrik, Polgári Jog, pp 160/35 (26. pótlás) ff. Simple article numbers refer to these previous provisions.

rights, stipulating that «[h]uman dignity and the related personality rights must be respected by all.»[48] As is clear from this provision, personality rights stem from a mother right, namely, from the right to human dignity,[49] and everyone is obliged to respect them.[50] In addition, Hungarian civil law illustratively describes the most typical violations. Accordingly, the right to a good reputation is violated in particular by stating or rumouring an injurious and degrading false fact in relation to another person or by placing a true fact in a false light.[51] In addition, the *új Ptk.* stipulates in Art 2:45(1) that the right to honour can be violated through an expression of opinion, which is unduly offensive, abasing, and capable of having a detrimental impact on the social evaluation of another person. Personal attributions that are independent from the external evaluation of the society are protected in a fragmented manner within both codes. Their different aspects are safeguarded either by the framework clause of the general personality right or by specified rights, such as the right to private life or the right to one's own image. While the former right incorporated within Art 2:43(b) is not explicitly referred to in the rules of the *Ptk.*,[52] the latter went through a considerable change, since the drafters of the *új Ptk.* recast its wording. In particular, Art 2:48(1) codified the judicial practices developed on the basis of the expression 'misuse of the likeness' of a person under Art 80(1) by unequivocally rendering wrongful the alleged tortfeasor's act, namely, the production of a person's likeness as well as its utilization without the consent of the person concerned.[53]

---

48 2:42(2), first sentence as translated in Gócza, Civil Code, p 60. Cf. Art 75.

49 See Székely/Vékás, in: Vékás, A Polgári Törvénykönyv magyarázatokkal, p 56, point 1. Cf. decision 8/1990 (IV.23.), *AB*, para III; Petrik, in: Petrik, Kommentár a gyakorlat számára, p 82.

50 See Art 2:42(1) and Art 75(1).

51 Arts 78(2) and 2:45(2). By referring to the case BH2002.261, Fézer, A nem vagyoni (erkölcsi) sérelmek megítélése, p 307 notes that besides these situations, defamation also occurs when a person's image or recorded voice, or his personal way of salutation is used for advertising purposes without his consent. However, cf. decision of the Budapest-Capital Regional Court of Appeal [case 2 Pf. 21 008/2013/6, *Fővárosi Ítélőtábla* (BDT 2014.6.92, p 10)] in which it was held that defamation arises in respect of untrue statements.

52 See also Petrik, in: Petrik, Kommentár a gyakorlat számára, p 85; Székely/Vékás, in: Vékás, A Polgári Törvénykönyv magyarázatokkal, p 57, point 4.

53 Boronkay, In Medias Res, 2013, 111, 132. For the protection of the victim's image against unauthorised publication, see e.g. case 2 Pf. 21 008/2013/6, *Fővárosi Ítélőtábla* (BDT 2014.6.92, p 7ff). See also on the protection of the right to one's own image, especially in relation to the freedom of the press, Decision 28/2014

The Hungarian legal system provides various preventive and remedial measures for violations of personality rights. In addition to the objective sanctions listed in Arts 84(1)(a)-(d) and 2:51(1)(a)-(e),[54] which can be ordered independently from the blameworthiness ('felróhatóság') of the alleged tortfeasor,[55] monetary compensation for the non-material harm suffered (so-called subjective sanction) is also awardable. This subjective sanction, incorporated into Art 84(1)(e) by Act No IV of 1977, is the non-pecuniary damages ('nem vagyoni kártérítés') equipped with tortious liability elements.[56] By contrast, the *új Ptk.*, by replacing this concept through the «grievance award»[57] ('sérelemdíj'), removes its newly introduced subjective sanction from the tort liability system and regards it as an independent remedy within Art 2:52.[58] Irrespective of the divergent origins of these subjective sanctions, the victim is entitled to one of them on the grounds of a few identical conditions. First, both require the existence of an unlawful conduct on the part of the tortfeasor that has a causal link with the non-pecuniary harm caused therewith. Such an unlawful conduct

---

(IX.29.) *AB* (concerning the online publication of photographs of policemen taken at a demonstration).

54 Such as an order for refraining from further intrusion, imposing a fine that shall be used for public purposes (*Ptk.*) and unjust enrichment (*új Ptk.*). While claims for such orders are not subject to the period of limitation in the *Ptk.* [see case 2 Pf. 20.658/2012/5, *Fővárosi Ítélőtábla* (ÍH2013.60)], the *új Ptk.* imposes on them such a period (prescribed in Arts 6:21-6:25) by Art 2:51(1), which is generally 5 years.

55 Blameworthiness, as specified in PEL/von Bar, Liab. Dam., Chapter 3, Introduction, B, 6 (p 559, para 6), is generally used within the basic rule on tort liability [i.e., Arts 339(1), 6:519] «as a generic term for intention and negligence» and as «an individualised social standard». In addition, Petrik, in: Petrik, Polgári Jog, p 200/5 (29. pótlás) states that it comprises two elements: an objective element (a requirement that is generally expected in a given situation) and a subjective one (the ability of the alleged tortfeasor to understand that his act violates that requirement).

56 It is awardable due to Arts 339(1) and 355(1) and (4) [see case 2 Pf. 21 008/2013/6, *Fővárosi Ítélőtábla* (BDT 2014.6.92, p 11)]. Since the claim for non-pecuniary damages is subject to the period of limitation (Arts 324-327) being generally 5 years [Arts 360(4), 324(1)], the rules on this subjective sanction will be applicable at least until 14.3.2019 (cf. *supra* fn 54), unless Art 360(4) does not stipulate a longer period.

57 Harmathy, Annales Univ. Sci. Budapest., Sec. Iur. 2005, 5, 23. Note that the term 'non-pecuniary damages' employed in the entire book shall be viewed as covering this newly introduced Hungarian legal concept as well.

58 For details on its characteristics, see e.g. Székely/Vékás, in: Vékás, A Polgári Törvénykönyv magyarázatokkal, pp 70-73, point 3.

is established by virtue of the violation of a personality right. Secondly, both depend on the blameworthiness of the tortfeasor pursuant to the general rule of tort liability. The existence of this *terminus technicus* is presumed, and the defendant must exculpate himself by proving that he did not act in a blameworthy manner.[59] Besides these identical conditions, a significant difference between the two subjective sanctions lies in the necessity to prove the non-pecuniary harm. As the concept of non-pecuniary damages is based on the general rule of tort liability, the proof of serious non-pecuniary harm forms its essential element.[60] By contrast, the aggrieved person is entitled to the «grievance award» without having to prove any such harm. As a corollary, the new subjective sanction significantly eases the requirements for monetary vindication. According to László Székely, to date, 6.5 million HUF (approx. 21.320 EUR) has been the highest amount awarded as compensation for the victim's non-pecuniary harm caused by defamation.[61] Beyond these sanctions, (interim) injunctions can be ordered due to Arts 85(4), 341(1) supplemented with Art 156 of *Act No III of 1952 on the Code of Civil Procedure (1952. évi III. törvény a polgári perrendtartásról, Pp.)*. The right of reply ('sajtóhelyreigazítás') also constitutes a possible measure against any defamatory statement of facts. Its governing rules were moved on 1.1.2011 from Art 79 of the *Ptk.* to Art 12 of *Act No CIV of 2010 on the freedom of the press and the fundamental rules on media content (A sajtószabadságról és a médiatartalmak alapvető szabályairól)*, and they are supplemented by Chapter XXI of the *Pp.*

II. German law

German law employs a hybrid system of protection containing general and specific rules without explicitly guaranteeing a general protection of the

---

59 Arts 339(1), 2:52(2) and 6:519. The *Ptk.* specifies that the defendant must prove that «he has acted in a manner that can generally be expected in the given situation» (translation: Complex Jogtár Plusz express, Hatály 2009.VII.1.-), while Art 6:519 of the *új Ptk.* does not refer to this formulation expressly.

60 See e.g. case Pfv. III. 24313/1998, *LB* (BH 2001.1.12); case Gfv. VII. 30.112/2012, *Kúria* (BH 2013.4.98). However, as Székely/Vékás, in: Vékás, A Polgári Törvénykönyv magyarázatokkal, pp 70-72, point 3/b explain, proof is not always a decisive requirement.

61 Forgács, Interjú Székely László miniszteri biztossal, 2012.

personality. The lack of an express provision on a general right of personality is rooted in the drafting history of the *Civil Code of 1900 (Bürgerliches Gesetzbuch, BGB)*[62] since, as Huw Beverley-Smith, Ansgar Ohly, and Agnès Lucas-Schloetter explain, the majority of scholars rejected a theory of personality rights at the time the *BGB* was drafted.[63] Various attributions of the person are explicitly protected within Art 823(1). However, it remains silent on several non-physical aspects of the personality by solely stating that «[a] person who, intentionally or negligently, unlawfully injures the life, body, health, freedom, property or another right of another person is liable to make compensation to the other party for the damage arising from this.» In 1954, the *BGH* filled this obvious gap in the *Leserbrief* (letter to the editor) case[64] in accordance with Arts 1(1) (right to human dignity) and 2(1) (right to free development of one's personality) of the *Basic Law for the Federal Republic of Germany, 1949 (Grundgesetz für die Bundesrepublik Deutschland, GG)*. It pointed out that these constitutional rights require the recognition of a general personality right within the realm of private law. As a corollary of this decision, the general right of personality ('allgemeines Persönlichkeitsrecht') has been acknowledged as a constitutionally guaranteed subjective framework right ('Rahmenrecht') under Art 823(1). It protects a wide range of different aspects of the personality, such as privacy, self-determination, reputation and honour, and personal information, as well as one's own image.[65] Besides this framework right, specific rules also afford piecemeal protection of certain personality rights, which should be applied principally with priority *vis-à-vis* the general right of personality.[66] The *BGB* explicitly acknowledges the right to one's own name under Art 12 and lays down various provisions on tort liability for protecting the different attributions of

---

62 In this subsection, references to articles mean the provisions of the *BGB* in English as available at <http://www.gesetze-im-internet.de/englisch_bgb/>.

63 Beverley-Smith/Ohly/Lucas-Schloetter, Privacy, Property and Personality, pp 96-97.

64 Case *Leserbrief* I ZR 211/53 (25.5.1954), *BGH* (BGHZ 13, 334).

65 See Sprau, in: Palandt, BGB, pp 1384, paras 113 ff.; Beverley-Smith/Ohly/Lucas-Schloetter, Privacy, Property and Personality, pp 114-119; Fechner, Medienrecht, pp 67, paras 17 ff. For injury to reputation and public image, see e.g. case VI ZR 211/12 (17.12.2013), *BGH* (BGHZ 199, 237), 16.

66 Beverley-Smith/Ohly/Lucas-Schloetter, Privacy, Property and Personality, p 114; Fechner, Medienrecht, p 67, para 17. As Beverley-Smith/Ohly/Lucas-Schloetter, Privacy, Property and Personality, p 114 notice, in practice, the decision on which rule is applicable is determined on a case-by-case basis.

the personality. In this way, for example, Art 823(2) protects the right to reputation and honour by transferring the crimes of insult and defamation regulated under Arts 185-187 of the German *Criminal Code (Strafgesetzbuch, StGB)* into a civil law context.[67] Accordingly, in the case of defamation under Art 186 of the *StGB*, the defendant may prove that the statement complained of is true.[68] On the other hand, certain aspects of the personality are enshrined under separate acts. A seminal example of this legislative solution is perceived in the protection of the right to one's own image and likeness. This is granted subject to certain exceptions laid down in Arts 22 and 23 of the *Art Copyright Act of 1907 (Gesetz betreffend das Urheberrecht an Werken der bildenden Künste und der Photographie, KUG)* within Art 22 of the *KUG* against the unauthorized publication and/or dissemination of photos or likenesses.

As far as the remedies of violations of personality rights are concerned, the following summary can be offered. Besides restitutionary claims, such as that of unjust enrichment within Art 812(1),[69] the victim who considers that his general right of personality has been violated intentionally or negligently is entitled to claim compensation for his non-pecuniary harm ('Geldentschädigung') causally linked to the unlawful act of the wrongdoer.[70] This practice is a jurisprudential product established first by the way of analogy in the *Herrenreiter* (gentleman rider) case[71] and currently guaranteed in accordance with the *Ginsengwurzel* (ginseng root) judgment directly based on the above-mentioned provisions of the *GG*.[72] In this latter case, however, the *BGH* put forward two conditions that have to be fulfilled in order for non-material damages to be awarded: no other measures would wholly redress the victim's harm, and the injury must be sufficiently serious and grave.[73] Thus, *LG Regensburg* (Germany) awarded non-pecuniary damages for the plaintiff in the *de Visser* case concerning

---

67 See also other provisions, such as Art 824 (endangering credit) or Art 826 (intentional damage contrary to public policy).

68 On this, see case VI ZR 211/12 (17.12.2013), *BGH* (BGHZ 199, 237), 24.

69 For details on possible measures, see Fechner, Medienrecht, pp 98, paras 98 ff.; Sprau, in: Palandt, BGB, p 1388, para 129.

70 For the conditions of tort liability under Art 823(1), see van Dam, European Tort Law, p 79; Sprau, in: Palandt, BGB, p 1388, para 129.

71 Case *Herrenreiter* I ZR 151/56 (14.2.1958), *BGH* (BGHZ 26, 349) (it was held by analogy with Art 847).

72 Case *Ginsengwurzel* VI ZR 259/60 (19.9.1961), *BGH* (BGHZ 35, 363).

73 See Wagner, in: Koziol/Warzilek, Persönlichkeitsschutz, para 100; Sprau, in: Palandt, BGB, p 1388, para 130.

the placing online of photographs in which the plaintiff appears partly naked by holding:

> «Der Anspruch der Klägerin auf immaterielle Entschädigung in Geld beruht auf § 823 Abs. 1 BGB in Verbindung mit Art. 1 und 2 GG. Angesichts der Massivität des Eingriffs und der weltweiten Verbreitung erscheinen EUR 20.000 als gerechter Geldausgleich angemessen.»[74]

By requiring this, the *BGH* rendered the monetary compensation a subsidiary remedy, which is taken over by other measures, such as injunctions and the right of reply. The former measures can be granted due to the explicit provisions of the *BGB* or by way of analogy. Explicit reference to injunctions in relation to the violation of one's own name is provided in Art 12. Injunctions may also be ordered pursuant to the second sentence of Art 1004(1), which is supplemented with the procedural rules specified in Arts 935 and 940 of the *ZPO*.[75] The right of reply ('Gegendarstellung') is also available under certain conditions for the aggrieved person as a possible measure regarding violations of his personality rights. This is regulated in the German interstate treaties ('Staatsverträge'), such as Art 56 of the *Interstate Treaty on Broadcasting (Rundfunkstaatsvertrag)*, and under the press law of each federal state, like Art 10 of the *Saarland Media Law (Saarländisches Mediengesetz)*.

III. French law

French civil law demonstrates the third path to achieve civil law protection for the various aspects of the personality, such as privacy, image, voice, and reputation.[76] One of the main characteristics of this protection is that it is not afforded under a framework right, such as the general right of personality under Art 823(1) of the *BGB*. Instead, the abovementioned personality rights are categorised into two groups. «Real subjective rights», as Huw Beverley-Smith, Ansgar Ohly, and Agnès Lucas-Schloetter call

---

74 Case *de Visser* 1 O 1205/09 (2) (24.4.2012), *LG Regensburg*, 4. As the PCMLP, Costs in Defamation Proceedings, p 82 (italics in square brackets added) indicates, «[a] typical value *[of the litigation]* in a typical defamatory claim for one false statement is deemed to be about EUR 20,000.00.»

75 See e.g. Beverley-Smith/Ohly/Lucas-Schloetter, Privacy, Property and Personality, pp 138-139.

76 For other rights, see e.g. Art 16 (respect for human dignity and life) or Art 9-1 (presumption of innocence) of the *CC*.

them, safeguard those aspects of the personality, which are equipped with a certain materiality.[77] This concept encompasses, among others, the right to respect for one's private life ('droit au respect de la vie privée') incorporated into Art 9 of the French *Civil Code of 1804 (Code civil, CC)*[78] in 1970[79] and two judicially developed rights, namely, the right to one's own name and the right to one's own image.[80] The protection of all other aspects of personality rights, such as the right to reputation, is guaranteed under the general system of tort liability.[81] Consequently, Art 1382 provides for protection, saying that «[a]ny act whatever of man, which causes damage to another, obliges the one by whose fault it occurred, to compensate it.»[82] Two comments, however, need to be added in this respect. First, if the defamation also violates the privacy rights protected under Art 9, then this provision is to be applied.[83] Secondly, defamation is principally viewed in France as an offence and is regulated under the *Law on the Freedom of the Press of 29.7.1881 (Loi du 29 juillet 1881 sur la liberté de la presse, 1881 Press Act).*[84] According to Art 29(1) of the *1881 Press*

---

77 Beverley-Smith/Ohly/Lucas-Schloetter, Privacy, Property and Personality, p 154.

78 In this subsection, references to articles mean the provisions of the *CC* in English as available at <www.legifrance.gouv.fr/content/download/1950/13681/version/3/file/Code_22.pdf>.

79 Art 22 of Law No 70-643 of 17.7.1970 (*Loi n° 70-643 du 17 juillet 1970 tendant à renforcer la garantie des droits individuals des citoyens*). For the application of Art 9 (private life) in the judicial practice, see e.g. *TGI Nanterre* (Regional Court Nanterre), 1ère ch. du 27/03/2014 (14/02736) - *Julie Gayet c/ Société Mondadori Magazines France* as referred to in Bedat, Case Law, France, 2014.

80 Beverley-Smith/Ohly/Lucas-Schloetter, Privacy, Property and Personality, p 167. Although the right to one's own image is treated separate from privacy (see also van Dam, European Tort Law, pp 187-188), it is clear from the judicial practice that actions for its violation are brought under Art 9. Cf. the claim for unauthorised use of one's image in *Martinez and Martinez* (see *infra* Ch. VII.A.I.2); *TGI Nanterre*, 1ère ch. du 27/03/2014 (14/02736) - *Julie Gayet c/ Société Mondadori Magazines France* as referred to in Bedat, Case Law, France, 2014.

81 Beverley-Smith/Ohly/Lucas-Schloetter, Privacy, Property and Personality, p 154.

82 *Supra* fn 78. Cf. Art 1383, which determines liability for damage caused by negligent conduct or imprudence.

83 See Murad/Sonnenberger, Das Französische Zivilrecht, p 359, 1 D 253.

84 See also IPI, Defamation Law in the European Union, 2015, p 73, point II/a (Overview of Civil Law). Other countries also afford criminal law protection of personality rights (e.g. for Germany, see *supra* Ch. I.B.II and for Hungary, see *infra* Ch. III.D.III). Contra: House of Commons, Press standards, privacy and libel, p 36, para 119 noted that «in November 2009 criminal libel was removed from the statute books» in England and Wales. For a comparative overview of

Act, defamation is described as «any allegation or imputation of a fact which causes injury to the honour or reputation of the person or body to which the fact is imputed.»[85]

The importance of the two main categories of the personality rights is reflected not only in the different legal bases but also in the measures that can be claimed for. Besides various remedial measures guaranteed under the *CC*, such as the order of publication of the judgment,[86] the victim is entitled to monetary compensation for his non-pecuniary harm on the basis of two distinct groups of requirements depending on the legal nature of the violated right at stake. In the case of injuries to rights other than the real subjective rights, the requirements of the general tort liability, i.e., fault on the part of the defendant ('faute'), damage ('dommage') and causation ('lien de causalité') between the act and the damage, have to be satisfied.[87] By contrast, the necessary conditions for awarding pecuniary compensation for violations of real subjective rights are considerably different. Although scholars' opinions differ regarding the identification of the legal basis for such a remedial measure,[88] they agree that the mere violations of the real subjective rights imply the existence of 'faute' and non-pecuniary harm.[89] In Cees van Dam's words:

---

civil and criminal law provisions on defamation, see McMahon, Comm. Law. 2001-2002, 24-37; IPI, Defamation Law in the European Union, 2015.

85 Brüggemeier/Colombi Ciacchi/O'Callaghan, Personality Rights, p 92 (inverted commas omitted). Among others, this provision was also referred to in the criminal procedure in the *Ministére Public c/ Weiler* case [*TGI Paris*, 17ème ch., No d'affaire: 0718523043 (3.3.2011)] as is clear from the unofficial English translation of the judgment, available in Weiler, The Judgment, 2011. Cf. Art 29(2) of the *1881 Press Act* regulates insult ('injure').

86 Cf. as Bedat, Case Law, France, 2014 notes, this measure was also ordered in the decision of *TGI Nanterre*, 1ère ch. du 27/03/2014 (14/02736) in *Julie Gayet c/ Société Mondadori Magazines France*.

87 See Brüggemeier/Colombi Ciacchi/O'Callaghan, Personality Rights, pp 94-95. For the elements of liability under Art 1382, see also van Dam, European Tort Law, pp 57, 187.

88 In the opinion of Beverley-Smith/Ohly/Lucas-Schloetter, Privacy, Property and Personality, p 167 (italics in the original): «As for legal redress, the action is theoretically governed by the rules of tort law, that is of Article 1382 *Code civil*». Acc. to Anterion/Moréteau, in: Koziol/Warzilek, Persönlichkeitsschutz, para 16, however, «Art. 9 gives sufficient support to a claim in damages and it is no longer necessary to refer to the general provision of art. 1382 CC.»

89 Beverley-Smith/Ohly/Lucas-Schloetter, Privacy, Property and Personality, p 167 by referring to van Gerven; Anterion/Moréteau, in: Koziol/Warzilek, Persönlichkeitsschutz, para 16.

> «It could be argued that this implies a strict liability for infringing another person's right to privacy but one can also state that the *faute* test is incorporated in the infringement test.»[90]

Similar to this distinction, the legal bases for ordering injunctions also differ by virtue of the nature of the right concerned. Arts 809 and 849 of the *New Code of Civil Procedure (Nouveau Code de Procédure Civile, NCPC)* allow the plaintiff to bring a claim in summary procedure in cases of urgency ('juge des référés') to prevent actual or threatened harm. However, as Gert Brüggemeier, Aurelia Colombi Ciacchi, and Patrick O'Callaghan point out, instead of the summary judge's *a priori* intervention in accordance with Art 809 of the *NCPC*, «legal scholars remain as hesitant as the judiciary to grant measures intended to prevent an injury to personal honour when freedom of expression is at stake».[91] On the other hand, injunctions, including interim injunctive reliefs, can be ordered in accordance with Art 9(2).[92] In other words, Art 9(2) is applicable to the real subjective rights whose violations «are particularly serious and where damages will not be an appropriate answer.»[93] It stipulates that «[w]ithout prejudice to compensation for injury suffered, the court may prescribe any measures, such as sequestration, seizure and others, appropriate to prevent or put an end to an invasion of personal privacy; in case of emergency those measures may be provided for by interim order.»[94] Additionally, the right of reply is prescribed in different legislative acts depending on the channel through which the statement complained of is distributed.[95]

---

90 Van Dam, European Tort Law, p 187 (italics in the original).

91 Brüggemeier/Colombi Ciacchi/O'Callaghan, Personality Rights, pp 95-96.

92 Cf. *TGI Nanterre,* (jugement de référé) 18/09/2012 - *Catherine Elisabeth Middleton et a. c/ Sas Mondadori Magazine France et a.*

93 Anterion/Moréteau, in: Koziol/Warzilek, Persönlichkeitsschutz, para 35.

94 *Supra* fn 78. Note that this para employs the term 'personal privacy'. For the definition of this term and the concept of private life in Art 9(1), see Delany/Carolan, The Right to Privacy, pp 177-178.

95 Such as Art 6(IV) of Law No 2004-575 of 21 June 2004 for communications over the Internet *[Loi n° 2004-575 du 21 juin 2004 pour la confiance dans l'économie numérique (1)]*. See also Mondoloni, in: Glasser, International Libel & Privacy, p 296, fn 5.

IV. English law

Similar to French law, English law does not recognise a general right of personality. Rather, it grants a piecemeal protection to the various aspects of the personality by virtue of different legal bases from which the tort of defamation and the action for misuse of private information is outlined in the present subsection.

The tort of defamation (i.e., violation of reputation)[96] in English law is governed by the judicial practice of common law courts and statutory provisions, such as the rules of the *Defamation Act 1952*, *1996* and *2013*. A cause of action in libel is principally established if the plaintiff proves «that the defendant published in writing or other permanent form a statement about the claimant which bore a meaning defamatory of the claimant. ... If a statement is defamatory by this criterion, damage is presumed.»[97] The defamatory nature of the words is determined in two steps: first, the meaning of the words complained of has to be settled, and secondly, it must be decided whether that meaning is defamatory.[98] Although the falsity of the statement is presumed, and therefore, the proof of the truth of the statement constitutes a defence on the part of the defendant,[99] not every untrue statement is actionable.[100] As becomes clear from s.1(1) of the *Defamation Act 2013* applicable from 1.1.2014, «[a] statement is not defamatory unless its publication has caused or is likely to cause serious harm to the reputation of the claimant.»[101] This provision implies two

96 Based on the form of communication, English law distinguishes between two types of defamation: libel and slander, i.e., defamation in permanent and spoken form. As Svantesson, IRLCT 2009, 169, 172 notes, an audio file available for downloading on a website is in a permanent form and must be regarded as libel. Note that the term 'defamation' used in this book describes solely libel. For the values covered by the concept of reputation, such as dignity or honour, see Milo, Defamation and Freedom of Speech, pp 1-38.

97 *Ames & Anor v The Spamhaus Project Ltd & Anor* [2015] EWHC 127 (QB), 39 [sentence omitted; regarding common law definition, but see paras 48 ff. on s.1(1) of the *Defamation Act 2013*].

98 Parkers *et al.*, Gatley on Libel and Slander, p 31, para 2.1. Cf. Morse, CLP 2005, 133, 135 (regarding the features of English libel law).

99 S.2 of the *Defamation Act 2013*.

100 As Parkers *et al.*, Gatley on Libel and Slander, p 34, para 2.1 note, under certain circumstances «[a] true imputation may still be defamatory».

101 On the common law meaning of the term 'defamatory', see Parkers *et al.*, Gatley on Libel and Slander, p 32, para 2.1; *Ames & Anor v The Spamhaus Project Ltd & Anor* [2015] EWHC 127 (QB), 39 ff. Note that the main portion of the provi-

distinct questions, which were considered by Mr Justice Bean in *Cooke & Anor v MGN Ltd & Anor*, a case that is «the first case in which the interpretation of the Act has come before the courts.»[102] The first question is regarding the meaning of the term 'serious harm', and the second is how it can be proved that the plaintiff's harm reached that threshold. Considering the first issue, as Mr Justice Bean pointed out in *Cooke & Anor v MGN Ltd & Anor,* this provision requires a plaintiff «to show that serious harm has been caused or is likely to be caused to his reputation. It is not enough to show that the publication has caused or is likely to cause serious distress or injury to feelings.»[103] Regarding the 'threshold of seriousness' requirement, although built on common law considerations,[104] it «raises the bar for bringing a claim».[105] As far as the question of how it can be proved that the plaintiff's harm reached the threshold is concerned, Mr Justice Bean was of the opinion that evidence would not always be needed to fulfil the 'serious harm' test:

> «Some statements are so obviously likely to cause serious harm to a person's reputation that this likelihood can be inferred. If a national newspaper with a large circulation wrongly accuses someone of being a terrorist or a paedophile, then in either case (putting to one side for the moment the question of a prompt and prominent apology) the likelihood of serious harm to reputation is plain, even if the individual's family and friends knew the allegation to be untrue.»[106]

If the court finds that the contested statement is defamatory, and no defence is offered, it may award damages, which is viewed as a primary vindication in defamation. As the report from 2010 of the House of Com-

---

sions of the *Defamation Act 2013*, like s.1, extends only to England and Wales, but not to Scotland (see its s.17).

102 *Cooke & Anor v MGN Ltd & Anor* [2014] EWHC 2831 (QB), 28 (stated by the representatives of the parties). For the interpretation of s.1(1) of the *Defamation Act 2013*, see also *Ames & Anor v The Spamhaus Project Ltd & Anor* [2015] EWHC 127 (QB).

103 *Cooke & Anor v MGN Ltd & Anor* [2014] EWHC 2831 (QB), 30.

104 See *Thornton v Telegraph Media Group Ltd* [2010] EWHC 1414 (QB) and *Jameel v Dow Jones & Co* [2005] EWCA Civ 75 as identified in the Explanatory Notes to the Defamation Act 2013, para 11. See also Parkers *et al.*, Gatley on Libel and Slander, pp 38-40, para 2.4.

105 Explanatory Notes to the Defamation Act 2013, para 11. See also *Cooke & Anor v MGN Ltd & Anor* [2014] EWHC 2831 (QB), 37.

106 *Cooke & Anor v MGN Ltd & Anor* [2014] EWHC 2831 (QB), 43. For the assessment of serious harm within s.1(1) of the *Defamation Act 2013*, see also *Ames & Anor v The Spamhaus Project Ltd & Anor* [2015] EWHC 127 (QB), 48 ff.

mons, Culture, Media and Sport Committee indicates, «[t]he highest award in recent years is £200,000 .... The judgment noted that the award was "now generally recognised to be the maximum amount for compensatory damages in libel proceedings".»[107] In addition, under certain circumstances laid down in *Bonnard v. Perryman,*[108] an injunction may also be granted. However, as Normann Witzleb points out, it is difficult to obtain, and «it will be denied unless it is clear to the court that the defendant's action cannot be defended.»[109] Furthermore, there are various statutory provisions, under which certain measures, such as the request for a publication of correction or apology in the form of the offer to make amends prescribed in ss.2-4 of the *Defamation Act 1996*, could be granted.[110]

As far as the protection of privacy is concerned, the following summary can be offered. Although enacting a general law of privacy was considered on several occasions, until 2000,[111] English law guaranteed only piecemeal protection of the various aspects of privacy on the basis of statutory provisions and causes of action.[112] After the *Human Rights Act 1998 (HRA)* entered into force in 2000, and transported the provisions of the ECHR, such as Arts 8 and 10, into English law,[113] the equitable action for breach of confidence was chosen as a vehicle on which the protection against the wrongful use of private information would be afforded. Originally, this equitable action granted protection for certain information, such as personal, artistic, and literary confidences, or trade and state secrets, acquired in a confidential relationship.[114] By redefining this action, as Lord Nicholls stated in *Campbell v MGN Ltd,* it «has now firmly shaken

---

107 House of Commons, Press standards, privacy and libel, p 37, para 122 [emphases and fn omitted; judgment referred to: Lillie v Newcastle City Council, i.e., *Lillie & Reed v Newcastle City Council & Others* [2002] EWHC 1600 (QB)].

108 [1891] 2 Ch 269.

109 Witzleb, in: Witzleb *et al.*, Emerging Challenges in Privacy Law, p 409.

110 For details on remedies, see e.g. Rogers, in: Koziol/Warzilek, Persönlichkeitsschutz, paras 47-56.

111 House of Commons, Press standards, privacy and libel, p 12, para 10.

112 E.g. trespass, malicious falsehood, *Protection from Harassment Act 1997*. For details, see Jones *et al.*, Clerk & Lindsell on Torts, paras 27-01–27-48; Giliker, The Europeanisation of English Tort Law, pp 171-195; House of Commons, Press standards, privacy and libel, pp 12, paras 9 ff. English common law differs from its US counterpart, since in the US the recognition of the existence of a privacy tort began in 1890 with an article written by Warren/Brandeis, Harv. L. Rev. 1890-1891, 193-220.

113 House of Commons, Press standards, privacy and libel, p 12, para 10.

114 Jones *et al.*, Clerk & Lindsell on Torts, paras 27-05 – 27-06.

off the limiting constraint of the need for an initial confidential relationship.»[115] Accordingly, as his Lordship noted in another decision, the courts created a distinct action from it, namely, the action for misuse of private information:

> «As the law has developed breach of confidence, or misuse of confidential information, now covers two distinct causes of action, protecting two different interests: privacy, and secret ("confidential") information.»[116]

The result is a form of privacy law, which is framed by the rights guaranteed in the ECHR and developed by the English common law courts.[117] Considering remedies that can be ordered, it is to be noted that due to s.12(3) of the *HRA*, an interim injunction can be granted to order the defendant to restrain publication before trial if «the court is satisfied that the applicant is likely to establish that publication should not be allowed.»[118] When deciding on the need for an injunction, the court balances «the competing interests in private life (protected in Article 8 of the ECHR) and freedom of expression (protected in Article 10 of the ECHR) in each case.»[119] Additionally, under certain circumstances, damages may also be awarded, as Mr Justice Eady pointed out in *Mosley v News Group Newspapers Ltd*, «to afford an adequate financial remedy for the purpose of acknowledging the infringement and compensating, to some extent, for the injury to feelings, the embarrassment and distress caused.»[120] Since the action for misuse of private information is still evolving, it is worth mentioning a disagreement in respect of its classification. Namely, it is uncertain whether it is regarded as an equitable action or as a tort.[121] The importance

115 *Campbell v MGN Ltd* [2004] UKHL 22, [2004] 2 AC 457, 14 as cited in *Vidal-Hall & Ors v Google Inc* [2014] EWHC 13 (QB), 59.

116 Lord Nicholls in para 255 of *OBG Ltd v Allan and Douglas v Hello!* [2008] 1 AC 1 as cited in *Vidal-Hall & Ors v Google Inc* [2014] EWHC 13 (QB), 67.

117 Giliker, The Europeanisation of English Tort Law, p 195. See also *ibid.*, p 194.

118 For details on this, see Witzleb, in: Witzleb *et al.*, Emerging Challenges in Privacy Law, pp 407-440; Eady, C.J.Q. 2010, 411 ff. Cf. Official Statistics on privacy injunctions dealt with at hearings at the High Court or Court of Appeal at the Royal Courts of Justice in London, available at <https://www.gov.uk/government/collections/statistics-on-privacy-injunctions>.

119 Witzleb, in: Witzleb *et al.*, Emerging Challenges in Privacy Law, p 439.

120 *Mosley v News Group Newspapers Ltd* [2008] EWHC 1777 (QB), 235. Cf. Jones *et al.*, Clerk & Lindsell on Torts, paras 27-48.

121 *Vidal-Hall & Ors v Google Inc* [2014] EWHC 13 (QB), 50-69; *Google Inc v Vidal-Hall & Ors* [2015] EWCA Civ 311, 17 ff.; Jones *et al.*, Clerk & Lindsell on Torts, para 27-04.

of this classification lies, for example, in the awardable remedies, such as exemplary damages, or in the application of the choice of law rules in tort under s.9(1) of the *Private International Law (Miscellaneous Provisions) Act 1995*.[122] This uncertainty seems partly to be resolved in *Google Inc v Vidal-Hall & Ors*, in which the *Court of Appeal* held that the misuse of private information should be regarded as a tort in view of «service out the jurisdiction».[123]

V. Differences in the national legal landscape

The four national perspectives show a colourful legal landscape on the protection against invasion of privacy and defamatory statements. The main differences can be highlighted in respect of the categorisation and the legal protection of the different aspects of the personality, the use of presumption for awarding non-pecuniary damages, the amount of such damages and other possible measures, which prevent or vindicate violations of personality rights.

First, as a rule, Hungarian and German law recognises a framework right covering all manifestations of the personality, while French law and, even more evidently, English law grant fragmented protection. Particularly, the continental legal systems have developed long-standing practices for the protection of privacy. By contrast, invasion of privacy in the form of the misuse of private information became a judicially developed cause of action essentially after the *HRA* entered into force in English law.

Secondly, considering the right to reputation, it becomes clear that French law primarily grants protection under criminal law, while criminal libel was removed from the English statute books.

Thirdly, as far as monetary compensation for non-pecuniary harm caused by violations of personality rights is concerned, the examined national laws differ in the use of presumption in respect of the proof of the non-pecuniary harm. The *Ptk.*, the *BGB* and, for violations of rights other than real subjective rights, the *CC*, principally require the plaintiff to dem-

122 See Mr White in *Douglas v Hello! (No 3)* [2006] QB 125, 96 as cited in *Vidal-Hall & Ors v Google Inc* [2014] EWHC 13 (QB), 61; Giliker, The Europeanisation of English Tort Law, pp 185-189. See also *Google Inc v Vidal-Hall & Ors* [2015] EWCA Civ 311, 51.

123 *Google Inc v Vidal-Hall & Ors* [2015] EWCA Civ 311, 51. See also *Vidal-Hall & Ors v Google Inc* [2014] EWHC 13 (QB), 70.

onstrate his non-pecuniary harm. By contrast, the *új Ptk.*, regarding violations of real subjective rights, the *CC*, and, after determining that the words complained of are defamatory, s.1(1) of the *Defamation Act 2013*, display a more liberalised picture, since as a general rule, they presume the existence of such harm.

Fourthly, the amount of monetary compensation for non-pecuniary damage caused by defamation differs considerably. While it can reach £200.000 (roughly 239.000 EUR) in England, it can reach approximately only 21.300 EUR in Hungary.

Fifthly, besides the monetary compensation, the plaintiff is allowed to avail himself of the right of reply or (interim) injunctions in most of the surveyed legal systems. However, in France, there is hesitancy as regards preventing the publication of the allegedly defamatory material, as Gert Brüggemeier, Aurelia Colombi Ciacchi, and Patrick O'Callaghan explain.

These illustrative differences turn the legal systems into legal environments that are more generous with the victims, putting the alleged wrongdoers at a disadvantage. The presumption of the non-pecuniary harm clearly favours the victims. On the other hand, several differences in the national practices create for the alleged wrongdoers a high risk that they could be held criminally liable or that they could be ordered to pay large amount of non-pecuniary damages. Why, how, and to what extent these exemplarily national characteristics might influence the localisation of disputes concerning online violations of personality rights will be seen in the chapters below after a background note has been given on the characteristics of the Internet.

Chapter II: Background: characteristics of the Internet

The Internet (also known as cyberspace[124]) is a unique architecture of a worldwide network of computers that cooperate and communicate with each other on the basis of common software standards.[125] It is also referred to as «a network of networks»,[126] which began as APRANET, a US Department of Defense project in the 1960s to establish a nationwide grid of computers that would continue to operate even if a large part of the grid was destroyed or blocked. Since the 1990s, it has penetrated into persons' everyday life[127] and has revolutionised their ways of communicating.[128] The present background note aims to demonstrate this revolutionary nature of the Internet by taking a snapshot of its constantly changing and evolving characteristics in at least three respects: its geographical independence, its geolocation tools, and its actors. Finally, it compares these characteristics to the nature of traditional media, especially the press. In turn, and as the previous chapter, it aims to contribute to the localisation of online violations of personality rights.[129]

---

124 As it is pointed out in *Dow Jones and Company Inc v Gutnick* [2002] HCA 56; 210 CLR 575; 194 ALR 433; 77 ALJR 255 (10 December 2002), fn 100 (italics in the original): «The term was coined by Gibson, *Neuromancer*, (1984) at 51».

125 As Bigos, ICLQ 2005, 585, fn 33 observes, there are two basic common software standards, that is, protocols: (1) Transmission Control Protocol (TCP) consists of rules on establishing and breaking connections, while (2) Internet Protocol (IP) includes rules for assigning a unique numeric address (IP address) to connected computers.

126 David Post as referred to by Lessig, Stan. L. Rev. 1995-1996, 1403, 1406.

127 Cf. 65% of the individuals aged 16 to 74 used the Internet frequently in the EU in 2014 (see <http://epp.eurostat.ec.europa.eu/tgm/table.do?tab=table&init=1&language=en&pcode=tin00092&plugin=1>); more than 3 billion people worldwide did so (data from 30.6.2014, available at Internet World Stats, Usage and Population Statistics <http://www.internetworldstats.com/stats.htm>).

128 On the history of the Internet, see e.g. Bigos, ICLQ 2005, 585, 589-592; Encyclopaedia Britannica – Internet – Origin and development <http://www.britannica.com/EBchecked/topic/291494/Internet>.

129 If necessary, the present cursory note will be extended in the chapters below.

A. Geographical independence

The Internet and online information are geographically independent: they avoid physical borders and, by their nature, operate on a cross-border basis. This characteristic can clearly be perceived from two aspects: cross-border flow of information and worldwide accessibility.

Information uploaded by a person (publisher) to his own or a third party's website (website operator) is stored on his own or the third party's (host provider) computer (web server) as digital data in the form of '1's and '0's. When an online visitor connects to the Internet and requests online information, these digital data are transferred from router to router (known as the 'traceroute'[130]) until they reach the requesting computer, which translates and re-assembles these data into humanly understandable information and displays them on the online visitor's screen.[131] Transmission of data is performed on the most appropriate traceroute in order to ensure fast information exchange. To illustrate this speedy and, for the Internet users, unperceived transmission, the author requested the website of the Faculty of Law and Political Science of Eötvös Loránd University, Budapest (Hungary) (<www.ajk.elte.hu>) from Saarbrücken (Germany), as Appendix 1 shows. For the requested information saved on that website to get to the author's computer, 15 stations (routers) were required, crossing four different national networks, and thus countries in milliseconds. As is indicated, the requested information was transmitted through the Hungarian network operator to Switzerland. From Switzerland, it was sent to Spain, and then from Spain, it reached Germany and the author's requesting computer.

In addition to this cross-border flow of information, the worldwide accessibility of the Internet and online information become clear from the territorial and language independence as well as from the publication coverage. Once information is uploaded to the Internet, it is accessible irrespective of the physical location of the requested web server(s) and the requesting device(s). The requested information may be stored on a web server located thousands of kilometres away from the Internet user. Alternatively, based on different considerations, such as efficiency or fast data transmission, automated computer software may duplicate or move information between web servers even without the knowledge of the Internet

130 For details, see Dodge, Mapping How The Data Flows.

131 See also Bigos, ICLQ 2005, 585, 591-592.

users.[132] Thus, information may (simultaneously) be stored on web servers placed at many different places, countries, and even continents.[133] Like the requested web servers' locations, the Internet users' requesting devices are also made independent from physical borders by means of an unproblematic connection to the digital world in places where an Internet network is available. Accordingly, as well as cable-based computers, divergent devices without a physical wired Internet connection (known as wireless devices), such as laptops, tablets, smartphones, e-readers, and e-papers, along with smart watches, smart televisions, and other (forthcoming) devices (e.g. Google Glass or Facebook's Oculus), establish a smooth and fast Internet connection for their users.

By virtue of the existence of several services, the Internet users' limited language skills do not stop the consumption of the instantly distributed and globally accessible online information. First, various digital contents (e.g. emotions, like and dislike buttons, graphics, such as selfies and gifs) are non-verbal means of communication promoting self-expression without requiring any further explanations or language skills. In addition, a wide range of online translation services provides in many languages humanly understandable translations of machine typed, printed,[134] or spoken words[135] even though these services principally do not apply grammatical rules during translation.

The worldwide accessibility of the Internet and online information is also perceived from the publication coverage, which is principally 100%, since, as AG Cruz Villalón noted, «it is common knowledge that a website may be accessed anywhere in the world where there is internet access.»[136]

132 See DLA Piper, New Rules for a new age?, 2009, pp 11-12. See also Giannakaki, in: Akrivopoulou/Garipidis, Human Rights and Risks, p 13 (regarding cloud computing and data flow).

133 See also Giannakaki, in: Akrivopoulou/Garipidis, Human Rights and Risks, p 13 (regarding cloud computing and data flow); Down on the server farm, The Economist, 2008.

134 Such as online language dictionaries, online machine-based translation services (e.g. Google Translate <http://translate.google.de/>), integrated automated translation tools (e.g. in Facebook), add-ons (e.g. Quick Translator 1.0) or Word Lens <http://questvisual.com> for printed texts.

135 Such as Jibbigo Translator.

136 AG in *eDate and Martinez*, 44. Theoretically, the publisher can decrease the publication coverage [see geolocation tools (*infra* Intr. to Ch. II.B), privacy settings (*infra* fn 187)]. For their effectiveness, see the accompanying texts to these references.

This feature is, however, conditional. First, the global reach of online content does not mean that all the material is displayed on the Internet user's screen as soon as he connects to the Internet. As the ECJ aptly pointed out in paragraph 60 of *Lindqvist,* in order to access the information appearing on the Internet page, «an internet user would not only have to connect to the internet but also personally carry out the necessary actions to consult those pages.» Thus, the Internet is a kind of pull medium where the Internet users have to purposefully and actively request and pull the passively available information from a web server.[137] Currently, however, finding and pulling the information is made simple by the help of various Internet search engines[138] and other online applications, such as news aggregators. Additionally, it might be supposed that only online content is accessible, and thus, the 100% publication coverage exists only if the content is not deleted. Although this phenomenon is admittedly probable, numerous activities and services revitalise information, and thus they render the disappearance of online contents in cyberspace extremely difficult. Indeed, the uploaded online material may be disseminated, copied, and in other ways reproduced by Internet users;[139] thus, it may remain in the memory of search engines[140] and it may be preserved in Internet archives[141] for an indefinite period.

---

137 See Bigos, ICLQ 2005, 585, 605. On this, see also Svantesson, PIL and the Internet, pp 46-49.

138 Internet search engines (e.g. Bing <https://www.bing.com/> or Google <https://www.google.com/>) have their own searching methods, and they principally display different results on the same subject. [See e.g. Dogpile.com, Different Engines, Different Results, 2007. Note also that acc. to the concept of filter bubble (see Talk of Eli Praiser at <http://www.thefilterbubble.com/ted-talk>), the search results of different search engines might differ, since many Internet services (e.g. Facebook or Google) personalise search results and, in turn, isolate Internet users from others by closing them in their own information bubble.] To overtake these differences, search engines equipped with metasearch technology (e.g. MetaGer <https://metager.de/>; Dogpile <http://www.dogpile.com/>) combine the search results of many different Internet search engines.

139 See also AG in *eDate and Martinez*, 47; Case VI ZR 211/12 (17.12.2013), *BGH* (BGHZ 199, 237), 43; *infra* Ch. VII.B.II.1.a)cc).

140 Such as cache memory. See also Giannakaki, in: Akrivopoulou/Garipidis, Human Rights and Risks, p 12.

141 E.g. Internet Archive <http://archive.org/>. See also Internet Memory Foundation <http://internetmemory.org/en/>. Regarding emphasising the importance of archives, see e.g. the decisions of the ECtHR: *Węgrzynowski and Smolczewski v. Poland* (no 33846/07), 59 and *Times Newspapers Ltd (nos 1 and 2) v. United*

B. Geolocation tools

Geolocation tools (also known as 'geolocation technologies') serve to identify and localise Internet users for several reasons, such as content localisation to a specific geography or to a group of users, content personalisation for advertisement purposes, traffic analysis, authentication, or compliance with particular local legal rules.[142] Dan Jerker B. Svantesson categorises them into technical and non-technical tools and divides the former into two sub-groups, namely, sophisticated and unsophisticated tools. Finally, he distinguishes between client-side and server-side sophisticated geolocation technologies.[143]

The Internet user's wireless device, such as a smartphone, might be equipped with one or more client-side sophisticated geolocation tools. Such tools provide highly accurate information about the physical location of the Internet user via a satellite-based Global Positioning System (GPS) chip or triangulation of close wireless network towers.[144] The so-called server-side sophisticated geolocation technologies are operated on third parties' or content providers' own platforms.[145] These technologies principally employ the IP address of the Internet user's device[146] and translate it into a physical location by employing their own IP geolocation databases.[147] In addition, the Internet user's web browser can be regarded as

---

Kingdom (nos 3002/03 and 23676/03), 45. In this respect, see also AG in *Google Spain*, 123.

142 See Svantesson, PIL and the Internet, p 399. For details on these tools, see e.g. Svantesson, PIL and the Internet, pp 395-443; King, Alb. L.J. Sci. & Tech. 2011, 61-124; Edelman, Shortcomings and Challenges, 1-11; Trimble, Fordham Intell. Prop. Media & Ent. L.J. 2012, 567-657. These works have been highly valuable for the present section.

143 Svantesson, PIL and the Internet, pp 398-435, 441.

144 See King, Alb. L.J. Sci. & Tech. 2011, 61, 66; Svantesson, PIL and the Internet, pp 400-401.

145 E.g. Google Analytics <https://www.google.com/intl/en/analytics/>; MaxMind, GeoIP <http://www.maxmind.com/en/geolocation_landing?pkit_lang=en>.

146 An IP address is a numerical identifier that is assigned to a device when it connects to the Internet. The present section generally deals with the the fourth version of IP addresses (see *infra* fn 150). For details in this regard, see e.g. Trimble, Fordham Intell. Prop. Media & Ent. L.J. 2012, 567, 595-596; Edelman, Running Out of Numbers, 1.

147 For details, see Svantesson, PIL and the Internet, pp 401-414. IP geolocation databases are collections of IP addresses mainly maintained by the IP geolocation service providers on the basis of which they localise the Internet users' IP ad-

an unsophisticated geolocation tool that provides the visited website or server hosting the website with different ranges of information, such as its language and time zone settings or the version of the operating system.[148] Finally, non-technical geolocation tools, such as disclaimers, a dropdown menu, or the delivery address, rely on the Internet users' intention and self-reporting by asking them for different information, registration, or self-identification.[149]

I. Shortcomings of geolocation tools

The accuracy of the results produced by geolocation tools is disputed among academics on the bases of different considerations, which can be categorised into three groups: weaknesses in technology, evasion of such tools, and additional considerations.

1. Weaknesses in technology

As has been seen above, server-side sophisticated geolocation tools localise the Internet users' devices by virtue of their IP address. However, different types of IP addresses can be assigned to devices at the time when they connect to the Internet. While a few so-called static IP addresses are assigned to single devices over an extended period, the so-called dynamic IP addresses can be allocated to more than one device.[150] In particular, the same IP address is assigned to a device as long as it is connected to the Internet, and when it is disconnected, the dynamic IP address goes back into the pool of the Internet access provider for reassignment, and thus, it can be allocated to another device logging on to the Internet.[151] To put it another way, «a particular address could be utilized by several different

dresses.

148 See Svantesson, PIL and the Internet, pp 418-419.

149 See Svantesson, PIL and the Internet, pp 426-435.

150 Regarding static and dynamic IP addresses, see also Trimble, Fordham Intell. Prop. Media & Ent. L.J. 2012, 567, 594-595. Note that a new numbering system of IP addresses (IPv6) was developed because the fourth version of IP addresses (IPv4) had been exhausted. This ensures that more, if not all, devices logged onto the Internet will have a unique IP address permanently. For details, see Edelman, Running Out of Numbers, 1-13.

151 See Trimble, Fordham Intell. Prop. Media & Ent. L.J. 2012, 567, 595.

users over just a few days time–thus making matches between an individual and a specific IP address virtually impossible.»[152] The inherent nature of the IP addresses casts the first doubt on the accuracy of server-side sophisticated geolocation tools. The second doubt concerning the accuracy of the location results of such tools is associated with IP geolocation databases. Such databases are subject to criticism, emphasising that if providers of geolocation tools publish data on their effectiveness, it is not easy to verify the data because most providers «do not appear to publish their determinations of locations, nor make their determinations available on the web for free testing by interested Internet users.»[153] On the other hand, client-side sophisticated geolocation tools do not exist without drawbacks, and their nature may overshadow their efficiency. In particular, even while several devices are equipped with these tools, such as a GPS, they have an optional feature, i.e., the user may decide to switch them on or off.[154] Moreover, devices armed with such tools are principally used outdoors, and they need substantial energy, which may quickly make the battery of the device empty.[155]

2. Evasion of geolocation tools

A wide range of different kinds of evasion techniques exists, which enables Internet users to circumvent the geolocation tools utilised by the content or service provider.[156] For example, proxy servers[157] mask the Internet users' location and online activity by anonymising their Internet

152 King, Alb. L.J. Sci. & Tech. 2011, 61, 119 (fn omitted). For a potential solution to this problem, see *supra* fn 150.

153 Edelman, Shortcomings and Challenges, 1, 6. Cf. Svantesson, PIL and the Internet, pp 406-407; Google Developers – Google Maps API (<https://developers.google.com/maps/articles/geolocation>) state: «Some browsers use IP addresses to detect a user's location. However, as a user's IP address can only provide a rough estimate of a user's location, we don't recommend using this approach for geolocation.»

154 On this, see King, Alb. L.J. Sci. & Tech. 2011, 61, 73, 118.

155 Svantesson, PIL and the Internet, p 401.

156 Trimble, Fordham Intell. Prop. Media & Ent. L.J. 2012, 567, 569. For details, see e.g. *ibid.*, 599-605; Edelman, Shortcomings and Challenges, 1, 7-10. The author assumes that in line with the increased concern about privacy issues, more evasive techniques will come into play.

157 Such as Anonymizer <https://www.anonymizer.com/> or Anonymouse <http://anonymouse.org/>.

presence. In the opinion of Marketa Trimble, these techniques enable Internet users to travel freely in the digital world:

> «Traveling in cyberspace, or "cybertravel," allows Internet users to view the Internet as if they were in a location other than where they are physically present. ... Through cybertravel, Internet users are able to view or use content on the Internet that they would otherwise not be permitted to access because of geolocation tools that block access to content based on the geographical location of a user.»[158]

In addition, Internet users are able to employ «pseudonymous identities»[159] availing themselves of the fact that several data, such as age or sex, are not self-authenticating in cyberspace. Therefore, Internet users are able to submit false or incorrect information.

Besides masking identities, other tools may also render geolocation technologies ineffective.[160] Ghostery, for example, claims to detect «the "invisible" web, detecting trackers, web bugs, pixels, and beacons placed on web pages by Facebook, Google, and thousands of other companies interested in your activity.»[161]

As a final point in this context, it ought to be noted that the efficiency of server-side sophisticated geolocation technologies ends at the point when Internet users reproduce the information available at the website equipped with such geolocation tools. To put it another way, geolocators are attached to the website but are not linked to the online content. As a corollary, they do not monitor every website or platform on which the information has been reproduced. Similarly, AG Cruz Villalón asserted:

> «When information content is uploaded to the internet, individuals immediately become – voluntarily or involuntarily – distributors of the information, by means of social networks, electronic communications, links, blogs or any other methods which the internet provides. Even the restriction of content by means of paid access, which is occasionally subject to territorial limitations, faces serious difficulties when it comes to preventing the mass distribution of information. Accordingly, monitoring and measuring the impact of information, or entering it in the accounts becomes a task which is impossible to complete when the information concerned circulates on the internet.»[162]

---

158 Trimble, Fordham Intell. Prop. Media & Ent. L.J. 2012, 567, 569 (sentences omitted).

159 Chitsa, Name Calling On The Internet, 2011, p 2.

160 E.g. Disconnect <https://disconnect.me/>; Ghostery <https://addons.mozilla.org/de/firefox/addon/ghostery/>.

161 Ghostery <https://addons.mozilla.org/de/firefox/addon/ghostery/>.

162 AG in *eDate and Martinez*, 47 (fns omitted).

3. Additional considerations

Three additional considerations ought to be mentioned; these question the (accurate) identification of the location of Internet users or of the online information. First, as has been noted above, various providers usually collect different kinds of data about Internet users and website operators and about the number of clicks on the monitored website(s).[163] Thus, it follows, first, that the person whose personality right is allegedly infringed does not have any information about these data.[164] Secondly, much, if not all, of this information might be regarded as private data in most states and so are protected by states' data protection laws.[165] Accordingly, in case of necessity, the aggrieved person has to comply with the conditions laid down in the substantive law to obtain data from the above-mentioned provider(s). This is exacerbated by the fact that several providers are situated outside the EU. In these cases, a request for information about, for example, an Internet user's IP address involves legal systems other than those of the Member States, which are coordinated and, on a certain level, harmonised.[166] Secondly, the most modern enterprise-level, and thus the most reliable server-side sophisticated geolocation tools, are not cheap, and therefore, they are supposedly not affordable for many persons who lack financial resources. On this, Kevin F. King notes:

> «While these prices fall well within the budget of most large online retailers and major content providers, they are also clearly cost prohibitive from the standpoint of small businesses, non-profits, and individual bloggers.»[167]

Finally, the role of domain names in content localisation should be taken into account. In particular, one could argue that domain names,[168] as sub-

---

163 See also King, Alb. L.J. Sci. & Tech. 2011, 61, 115; Trimble, Fordham Intell. Prop. Media & Ent. L.J. 2012, 567, 595.

164 See also Hess, JZ 2012, 189, 191 (regarding the number of page views).

165 Cf. the *BGH* in its order VI ZR 135/13 (28.10.2014), *BGH* (GRUR 2015, 192) referred questions to the ECJ for a preliminary ruling by asking *inter alia* whether IP addresses under certain circumstances qualify as personal data as defined in Dir. 95/46/EC (OJ 1995 L 281/31).

166 For locations of Google in the EU, see Google – About – Company – Facts – Locations <http://www.google.com/about/company/facts/locations/>. It is argued that the presence of social media operators in the EU could lead to the application of EU data protection law. On this, see e.g. McDonald, The Guardian 2013.

167 King, Alb. L.J. Sci. & Tech. 2011, 61, 72 (fn omitted).

stitutes for the IP addresses of web servers, play a significant role in identifying the geographical location of websites and thus, their content. In reality, however, this is not the case. Although country-code top-level domain names (ccTLDs), such as '.hu', may indicate the origin of the websites (e.g. <www.ajk.elte.hu> is a Hungarian site), it is possible for a website to use the country-code of another state.[169] In addition, in an appreciable number of cases, such domain names do not coincide with the place and thus, the state where the web server is physically located.[170] Moreover, generic top-level domain names, such as '.org', '.net' or '.com', also lead to confusion because they do not point at an exact state.[171] These localisation problems are exacerbated by the expansion of generic top-level domain names (known as new generic top-level domains, new gTLDs), which enable, for example, companies to use their brand name as a domain name (e.g. '.adidas' or '.google').[172] It follows that, in general, domain names cannot be seen as reliable geographical identifiers.[173]

C. Actors in the digital world

The rise of the Internet has given rise to novel changes in information distribution and consumption patterns: it has modified the commercial policies and business plans of the media industries, and it has massively encouraged ordinary people to express themselves online.

Considering media outlets, it is commonplace that most of them have appeared in addition to their printed form in the digital world (so-called

168 The term refers to a human-friendly and easily memorable name that identifies one or more IP addresses. On this, see Webopedia – Domain name <http://www.webopedia.com/TERM/D/domain_name.html>.

169 See Svantesson, PIL and the Internet, p 45; Edelman, Shortcomings and Challenges, 1, 4.

170 See also Rüßmann, JurPC Web-Dok. 1998, Abs. 32; Rüßmann, K&R 1998, 422, 423.

171 See also Rüßmann, JurPC Web-Dok. 1998, Abs. 32; Rüßmann, K&R 1998, 422, 423. See e.g. the website of the Frankfurter Allgemeine <http://www.faz.net/>, which employs the domain name '.net'.

172 For details, see Overview: Get Ready for the Next Big.Thing <http://newgtlds.icann.org/en/announcements-and-media/video/overview-en>.

173 See also Svantesson, PIL and the Internet, pp 44-45.

'hybrid newspapers')[174] and that new media outlets have been established for publishing exclusively online-only content.[175] Much of the online media content is free of charge, offering free full-text articles, while others are subscription- and/or fee-based or can be read on the basis of a pay-per-view policy. On top of launching websites, most of the media outlets operate blogs, offer RSS feeds; and participate in other social media sites (also called social networking sites), such as Facebook or Twitter.[176]

In line with the online presence of the media industries, as Corinne Barnes asserts, «[i]t is becoming increasingly clear that, armed with easy-to-use new tools and mobile devices that make publishing so much easier, the online audience has the means to become an active participant in the creation and dissemination of news and information.»[177] As a corollary, the dynamic, interactive, and user-driven approach of the Internet has attracted an increasing number of individuals to create, search, post, blog, communicate, share, or consume online information easily and at a low cost at the push of a button. To put it another way, in cyberspace, people have «become commenters, editors, content creators, producers, and distributors.»[178] Reflecting individuals' need to actively participate, share, and thus reshape information in cyberspace, an enormous number of divergent social media platforms have been developed.[179] This trend has two consequences in relation to the point the present author is seeking to illustrate: the rise of user-generated content and the change in social interactions. The former can perfectly be demonstrated through the statistics of social media traffic (see Appendix 2). To take an example, 1.39 billion monthly active Facebook users were counted as of 31 December 2014, and the number of mobile monthly active users was found to be 1.19 bil-

---

174 Such as Frankfurter Allgemeine <http://www.faz.net/>; Heti Világgazdaság <http://hvg.hu/>. The online and offline content may be identical to or different from each other.

175 Only in electronic form: e.g. EuropeanDaily <http://europeandaily.com/> or Journal of Intellectual Property, Information Technology and E-Commerce Law <http://www.jipitec.eu/>.

176 E.g. Frankfurter Allgemeine on Twitter <@FAZ_Topnews>; The Economist on Facebook <https://www.facebook.com/TheEconomist>.

177 Barnes, Caribbean Quarterly 2012, 16, 25.

178 Giannakaki, in: Akrivopoulou/Garipidis, Human Rights and Risks, p 12 (regarding individuals and groups). Cf. *Lindqvist*, 58.

179 See Global Social Media Prism by ethority, German Edition V6.0 <http://www.ethority.de/weblog/social-media-prisma/>.

lion as of 31 December 2014.[180] These users have generated huge amounts of online information, as the whitepaper from Facebook, Ericsson and Qualcomm indicates:

> «Every day, there are more than 4.75 billion content items shared on Facebook (including status updates, wall posts, photos, videos and comments), more than 4.5 billion "Likes," and more than 10 billion messages sent. More than 250 billion photos have been uploaded to Facebook, and more than 350 million photos are uploaded every day on average.»[181]

Focusing on the EU, it should be recalled that according to statistics published by the Eurostat, 46% of individuals aged 16 to 74 used the Internet for participating in social media sites in 2014.[182] The second consequence of the rise of social media platforms is that novel social interactions between Internet users have emerged, and these differ considerably from the traditional social relationships in the physical world. In particular, they expand all kinds of contacts between people of different nationalities with different social and economic backgrounds or coming from the private or public sector.[183] Although users of social media sites are generally able to decide with whom they make friends, the nature of friendship is different in the physical and the virtual worlds. In the latter, the user has a dichotomous choice: either accept the friend request or not.[184] Consequently, many users accept the online friendship of those people who would not be regarded as friends in the physical world.[185] This leads to an enormous number of friend connections[186] and to a broad distribution of private information, except in cases where users change their privacy settings and determine to what extent their personal information should be viewable by

180 Facebook Company Info <http://newsroom.fb.com/company-info/>.

181 A Focus on Efficiency, A whitepaper, 2013, p 6. Cf. *CG v Facebook & Anor* [2015] NIQB 11, 19.

182 <http://epp.eurostat.ec.europa.eu/tgm/table.do?tab=table&plugin=1&language=en&pcode=tin00127>.

183 Cf. AG in *eDate and Martinez*, 43; V. Mayer-Schönberger and T.E. Foster as quoted in Svantesson, PIL and the Internet, p 3; Lipton, NWULR 2010, 477, 494 ff.

184 See also Lipton, NWULR 2010, 477, 487.

185 See also DLA Piper, New Rules for a new age?, 2009, p 9, para 2.2.1.

186 Cf. Facebook Newsroom states (<http://newsroom.fb.com/download-media/4227> via <https://archive.org>, saved on 26.7.2013) that there are 140.3 billion friend connections since it was launched.

others.[187] Apart from confirmed friendships on social networking sites, other participatory platforms, such as blogs, also tend to bring together Internet users in the digital world even when they have never met in the physical world. Hence, like-minded Internet users from different jurisdictions are able to follow the blog entries of (a) person(s) and, under certain circumstances, to leave comments on (a) certain subject(s).[188] As a corollary, Internet users may also gain and/or lose their online reputation.[189] As Dan Jerker B. Svantesson points out:

> «A person living in a small village, say 50 years ago, would typically have one single reputation – that held in the village. Today, however, many people have a reputation in the town they live and a completely different reputation online. Indeed, many people have a range of reputations online.»[190]

As has become clear, the term 'actors' in the digital world covers a wide range of different persons. However, these actors are generally clothed with different characteristics. First, in an appreciable number of cases, individuals do not check the facts of their content according to the same standards to which professional journalists are required to adhere, and their messages do not go through any editorial process before they press the 'send' button.[191] Secondly, the principal motivation of these online actors for placing information online can vary. In general, media outlets are profit-oriented legal persons, while the profit making activity is not decisive for most of the individual bloggers and other social media users.[192] In addition, it is assumed that because of the lack of financial resources and/or time, individuals and small media companies do not obtain reliable

---

187 Principally three kinds of privacy levels are offered: open content, limited access granted to groups or certain people and custom (private). For references to other solutions that limit the audience of the online content, see *supra* fn 136. For online privacy questions, see e.g. Lipton, NWULR 2010, 477-515.

188 Cf. Conflict of Laws.net <http://conflictoflaws.net/>.

189 See also Azar, The Dartmouth Law Journal 2008, 161, 177; Svantesson, IRLCT 2009, 169-177. For its importance, see online reputation management services, e.g. Reputation.com <http://www.reputation.com/> or Reputations Verteidiger <http://www.reputationsverteidiger.de/>.

190 Svantesson, IRLCT 2009, 169, 170.

191 Cf. Korieh Doudu as referred to in Jump in defamation cases, 2010. For defamation suits because of social media posts (mainly via Twitter), see Rolph, Teacher defamation highlights, 2014; Robertson/Double, Ten Years of Facebook, 2014.

192 As Leurdijk/Slot/Nieuwenhuis, The Newspaper Publishing Industry, 2012, pp 9, 24 and, in general, pp 53 ff. note, newspapers gain revenue from e.g. digital advertising or subscription fees. However, note that individuals can also gain profit through their online activities. On this, see e.g. Barnett, How to make money.

and accurate information about legal questions (e.g. protection of personality rights) in different states and do not have the ability to protect themselves in legal proceedings in other states. As Aron Mefford acknowledges:

> «[U]nlike multinational corporations that have access to vast legal resources, Net users are unlikely to be sophisticated enough to be able to modify behavior or draft around problems related to different jurisdictions even if they are aware of the transborder effects of their activities.»[193]

D. The Internet vis-à-vis the traditional media, especially the press

The present section aims to compare the nature of the Internet *vis-à-vis* the traditional media and especially the press in the light of the above-outlined characteristics.[194, 195]

As has been seen above, the publication coverage of online information is generally universal, and given its easy-to-reproduce nature and the shortcomings of geolocation tools, it is difficult to monitor and assess with accuracy the number of hits such information receives as well as its reach and audience. In contrast, the publication coverage of the traditional media starts, as Dan Jerker B. Svantesson points out, from 0%, and it is increased by determining (targeting) the places in which the publication is intended to be distributed.[196] The determination of the territorially fragmented places of distribution reflects the business strategy and commercial policy of the media outlet. Accordingly, the number of copies distributed in certain countries can be verified easily and with high accuracy, since it is the

193 Mefford, Ind. J. Global Legal Stud. 1997-1998, 211, 217 (fn omitted).

194 For comparison of these media, see also AG in *eDate and Martinez*, 42-48, 50; Svantesson, PIL and the Internet, pp 29-51; von Hinden, Persönlichkeitsverletzungen, pp 5-14.

195 The present section disregards the fact that offline publications can also be reproduced and disseminated on the Internet. Thus, it treats the physical and digital worlds separately. Cf. *infra* fn 1207.

196 Svantesson, PIL and the Internet, p 437. Cf. *eDate and Martinez*, 45; *Pammer and Hotel Alpenhof*, 68; *Dataco*, 35. However, it could be argued that the broad reach of the Internet and WWW is not a unique characteristic, since satellite broadcasting or internationally distributed newspapers also widely disseminate information. On this, see also *Dow Jones and Company Inc v Gutnick* [2002] HCA 56; 210 CLR 575; 194 ALR 433; 77 ALJR 255 (10 December 2002), 38-39 (Gleeson CJ, McHugh, Gummow and Hayne JJ.). For jurisdictional issues in relation to satellite broadcasting, see Fisher, Defamation via Satellite.

result of a prior voluntary business decision.[197] In turn, the audience of the traditional publication is predictable. Considering the fact that the circumvention of targeted places, although probable, is both unusual and costly in the physical world,[198] the accuracy of the distribution of paper-based copies is basically not challenged by evasive techniques.

Secondly, the accessibility of publications also differs in many aspects. While a reader wishing to access an offline publication should either order it as a whole unit by mail or go and buy it from a newsagent, online information is principally accessible at the click of a button, and it is available for reading in parts. In addition, online mass information is constantly searchable, and (relevant) information can easily be found in different languages even if the Internet user does not know about its existence. In contrast to this, either the reader has to be aware of the offline information in advance and purposefully search for it, or he has to take a considerable length of time to find the information. In this respect, it is also worth noting that because of the existence of archives and other technical features, in general, the online publication stays on the Internet forever and remains accessible at any time. An old paper-based publication, however, does not stay in the market: it is generally sent back to its publisher, and it is usually archived only by certain libraries and institutions. Thus, to access an old offline publication, the interested person must make considerable efforts, i.e., travel to the place where the publication can be read, or, where possible, order it by mail.

Thirdly, unlike the online publication, whose content is created by different actors and is not necessarily checked prior to uploading, the content of offline publication is in general decided, drafted, and controlled by the editorial board of the media outlets. Hence, ordinary people do not participate in the creation of its content, and letters to the editor are published only occasionally.[199]

Thus, it is clear that the Internet differs in many points *vis-à-vis* the traditional media, especially the press. Irrespective of these differences, however, one should not lose sight of one common characteristic of online and offline publications, that is, that they are strongly connected to the pa-

197 See also AG in *eDate and Martinez*, 44, 49, 50. Cf. *eDate and Martinez*, 46; AG 1994 in *Shevill*, 75.

198 Person 'A' supposedly will not fly to another state to acquire a newspaper distributed there but not in his home state.

199 See also von Hinden, Persönlichkeitsverletzungen, p 12.

per-based world: their creation, publication/uploading, comprehension, and possible injurious effects are linked to (a) physical place(s) and person(s).

The following chapters will examine the extent to which the above-outlined characteristics of the Internet and the similarities and differences between that information medium and other media, such as the traditional press, (should) play a role in the localisation of online violations of personality rights.

Chapter III: Mapping the legal landscape: the Brussels-Lugano Regime

A. Background of the Brussels-Lugano Regime

Judicial cooperation in civil matters between the European states has been evolving since the Treaty of Rome was signed in 1957. As a corollary, various instruments have been concluded or enacted that establish common rules on jurisdiction as well as on the recognition and enforcement of judicial and extra-judicial decisions (judgments) in civil and commercial matters. These instruments form part of two interconnected regimes, namely, the Brussels and the Lugano Regimes.[200] Based on their compulsory nature, these regimes have placed international legal relations between their participating states on a completely new basis. As Christian Kohler acknowledges:

> «Jurisdiction rules in cases with a foreign element, and rules on the recognition of foreign judgments, which took centuries to develop, no longer had any validity. Jurisdictional privileges and other expressions of national interest had to be foregone. Labyrinths of dogmas which had assumed awe-inspiring proportions in continental jurisprudence in connection with international procedural law were overturned—only, however, to be replaced by new ones.»[201]

The principal aim of the first two subsections of this section is to give a general overview of the main characteristics of the Brussels and Lugano instruments by focusing on their legal bases and nature, the territorial and temporal scope of their application, their relations with each other, and the competence of the ECJ for interpreting their provisions. In addition, subsection III focuses on the application of the Brussels-Lugano Regime in Hungary, while subsection IV takes a wider view and refers to other inter-

---

200 These regimes have prompted a substantial body of academic commentary, such as Layton/Mercer, European Civil Practice; Kropholler/von Hein, EuZPR; Magnus/Mankowski, Brussels I Regulation. For comprehensive details on the evolution of the Brussels-Lugano Regime, see Erik Jayme and Christian Kohler's annual publication in IPRax, Heft 1 in 1985 and Heft 6 from 1988 until 2007; Heinz-Peter Mansel, Karsten Thorn and Rolf Wagner's annual publication in IPRax, Heft 1 from 2008 until present.

201 Kohler, ICLQ 1985, 563, 563 (in relation to the BC; fn omitted).

national developments in the field of judicial cooperation in civil and commercial matters.

I. The Brussels Regime

By the operation of the Treaty of Rome, the six original Member States of the European Union[202] entered «into negotiations with each other with a view to securing for the benefit of their nationals: ... the simplification of formalities governing the reciprocal recognition and enforcement of judgements of courts or tribunals».[203] With the conclusion of the Convention of 27 September 1968 on jurisdiction and the enforcement of judgments in civil and commercial matters,[204] they went far beyond the objective of that provision because they agreed upon rules concerning not only the recognition and enforcement of judgments but also the allocation of direct international jurisdiction between their courts (known as 'double convention').[205] The convention entered into force in 1973; afterwards it was amended through four separate accession conventions in order to accommodate its text to the observations of the new Member States, which joined the EU, then the EEC and the EC.[206] The BC enjoys a special legal status. Although it is a public international law convention, it is embedded in the EU legal order not only through its legal basis, namely, the provi-

202 Belgium, the Federal Republic of Germany, France, Italy, Luxembourg and the Netherlands.

203 Chapeau and the fourth indent of Art 220 of the Treaty of Rome (emphases omitted).

204 OJ 1972 L 299/32.

205 Jenard Report, pp 7-8.

206 For Denmark, Ireland, the UK, and Northern Ireland, see OJ 1978 L 304/1; for Greece, see OJ 1982 L 388/1; for Spain and Portugal, see OJ 1989 L 285/1; for Austria, Finland, and Sweden, see OJ 1997 C 15/1. On this, see Kropholler/von Hein, EuZPR, pp 18-21, paras 13-21. For the consolidated text of the BC as amended by these accession conventions, see OJ 1998 C 27/1. For the application of the BC in the reunified Germany, see Jayme/Kohler, IPRax 1990, 353, 356-357; Jayme/Kohler, IPRax 1993, 357, 361-362 and for Berlin, see Kohler, IPRax 1989, 75 ff. Note that, as Layton/Mercer, European Civil Practice, paras 11.066, 11.068, 11.070 explain, the BC also applies to the French overseas territories (territorial collectivities), and Aruba [see also Almeida Cruz/Desantes Real/Jenard Report, para 33 (a) and (c)] as well as to Gibraltar. For Mayotte, see, however, *infra* fn 218.

sions of Art 220 of the Treaty of Rome[207] and its aim to eliminate obstacles to the functioning of the internal market,[208] but also because of its interpretation in two respects.[209] Firstly, because the Contracting States were «[a]nxious to prevent differences of interpretation of the Convention from impairing its unifying effect»,[210] they empowered the ECJ by the 1971 Protocol to give preliminary rulings on the interpretation of the provisions of the BC, the protocol annexed to the BC and of the 1971 Protocol,[211] and secondly, because, as the ECJ pointed out, the BC shall be interpreted «having regard ... to ... its relationship with the Treaty».[212]

In order to simplify and accelerate the procedure of the recognition and enforcement of judgments and to mould it more to the needs of the citizens and firms, the revision of the BC was commenced in 1998 at an intergovernmental level (the so-called third pillar) created by the Maastricht Treaty.[213, 214] After that, the Amsterdam Treaty[215] conferred competence on the EU, then the EC, to enact secondary legislative acts in the field of judicial cooperation in civil matters within Arts 61(c) and 67(1) of Title IV (Visas, Asylum, Immigration and other Policies related to Free Movement of Persons) of Part III (Community Policies) of the EC Treaty,[216] and

---

207 Art 293 of the EC Treaty. By referring to this article, Layton/Mercer, European Civil Practice, para 11.042 state that the BC and its accession conventions (see *supra* fn 206) «therefore form part of the Community legal order but are not instruments of the Community» (fn omitted).

208 See e.g. Jenard Report, p 13; *Owusu*, 33.

209 See also Kohler, FS Reinhold Geimer, pp 462-463.

210 Joint Declaration annexed to the BC (OJ 1998 C 27/26).

211 Art 1 of the 1971 Protocol. Official reports accompanying the BC, the 1971 Protocol and the accession conventions, except for the 1996 Accession Convention (i.e., Jenard Report, Schlosser Report; Evrigenis/Kerameus Report; Almeida Cruz/Desantes Real/Jenard Report) lend a helping hand to the interpretation of those instruments. For the courts enabled to request a preliminary ruling, see Arts 2 ff. of the 1971 Protocol and on this, see Kohler, E.L.Rev. 1982, Part I, 3, 4-7.

212 *Tessili*, 9 (emphases omitted). Cf. *Krombach*, 24; Kohler, E.L.Rev. 1982, Part I, 3, 14.

213 OJ 1992 C 191/1 (consolidated version: OJ 1997 C 340/145; entered into force: 1.11.1993).

214 See Commission Document COM(97) 609 final, p 2, point 1. See also Jayme/Kohler, IPRax 1998, 417, 421.

215 Consolidated version: OJ 1997 C 340/173 (entered into force: 1.5.1999).

216 Note that e.g. Magnus, Intr., in: Magnus/Mankowski, Brussels I Regulation, pp 21-22, para 35 and Jayme/Kohler, IPRax 1999, 401 402 emphasise doubts about the appropriateness of those legislative bases. Cf. Kohler, IPRax 2003, 401, 403-406.

thus, the revised Brussels rules were converted into Brussels I, which came into force on 1.3.2002.[217] Due to its legal nature as specified in Art 288 of the TFEU, it had a general application, and it was directly applicable to and binding in its entirety in all Member States,[218] except for Denmark. By the operation of Art 69 of the EC Treaty and Protocol No 5 on the position of Denmark (1997) annexed to the Treaty on European Union and the Treaty establishing the European Community,[219] Denmark was treated as an «unechte Drittstaat»[220] in which the provisions of Brussels I, with small modifications, were applicable through an agreement concluded between the EU, then the EC, and Denmark[221] under international law[222] from 1.7.2007.[223] By its entry into force, as Art 68 of Brussels I stated, the regulation superseded the BC between the Member States, and thus any reference to the BC was understood as a reference to this regulation.[224] This replacement was, however, only partial and relative, since the BC and 1971 Protocol *per se* remain directly applicable in two situations, and indirectly applicable in one case. The first is with regard to certain territories, which fall within its territorial scope and which were excluded from Brussels I due to Art 355 of the TFEU.[225] The second is concerning

217 Art 76 of Brussels I. As far as jurisdictional issues are concerned, acc. to Art 66(1) of Brussels I, it applies only to legal proceedings instituted after its entry into force, i.e., for the pre-2004 Member States, except for Denmark, on 1.3.2002 (for the UK and Ireland, see also Art 69 of the EC Treaty; Recital 20 of Brussels I); for Gibraltar, see Layton/Mercer, European Civil Practice, para 11.070; for the 10 Member States of 2004 on 1.5.2004 (OJ 2003 L 236), for Romania and Bulgaria on 1.1.2007 (OJ 2005 L 157); for Croatia on 1.7.2013 (OJ 2012 L 112).

218 Recital 6 of Brussels I. See also *supra* fn 217, Art 52 of the TEU, Art 355 of the TFEU, *Weber*, 36. For Cyprus, see also Protocol No 10 on Cyprus to the act of accession (OJ 2003 L 236/955); Art 355(5)(b) of the TFEU; *Apostolides*. For Mayotte, see Dec. 2012/419/EU (OJ 2012 L 204/131); for Saint-Barthélemy, see Dec. 2010/718/EU (OJ 2010 L 325/4). On this, see also Hartley, Choice-of-court Agreements, pp 44-47, paras 2.32-2.37.

219 OJ 2006 C 321E/201.

220 Jayme/Kohler, IPRax 2005, 481, 483.

221 OJ 2005 L 299/62. For details, see e.g. Nielsen, IPRax 2007, 506-509.

222 Art 2(1) of the EC/Denmark Agreement (OJ 2005 L 299/62); Jayme/Kohler, IPRax 2005, 481, 486.

223 See Information of the Council (OJ 2007 L 94/70).

224 As Layton/Mercer, European Civil Practice, para 32.011 promptly observe, although this provision cannot amend *per se* the 1988 LC, the courts of the Member States are constrained to read the reference to the BC in that convention as reference to Brussels I (now Brussels Ia).

225 Recital 23 and Art 68(1) of Brussels I. Accordingly, and having in mind the terri-

legal proceedings instituted before the entry into force of Brussels I in conjunction with Art 66(1) of Brussels I. In addition, the BC, indirectly through the application of the Brussels I rules, also affected jurisdictional issues and the recognition and enforcement of judgments in the EU. This was because Brussels I essentially retained the BC's structure and basic principles and ensured continuity between their provisions.[226] It follows that the interpretation of the rules of the BC was also valid for Brussels I whenever the provisions of these instruments were regarded as equivalent.[227] As AG Jääskinen pointed out, equivalence still exists even if there is a difference in the wording of a provision between the newer and older instruments, providing that this difference in wording «serves only to provide clarification, without introducing any substantial distortion between those instruments».[228] The effectivity of such continuity becomes evident from the case law of the ECJ on the interpretation of the rules of Brussels I. These cases are delivered by virtue of Art 19(3)(b) of the TEU and Art 267 of the TFEU[229] in the course of a preliminary ruling requested by any national courts or tribunals of the Member States.[230]

The third comprehensive review of the Brussels rules was commenced on the basis of Art 73 of Brussels I a few years after its entry into force. The COM re-evaluated its operation in practice and considered the amendments necessary to improve its application.[231] The revised version of those rules was adopted under Art 67(4) and points (a), (c) and (e) of Art 81(2) of Chapter 3 under Title V (Area of Freedom, Security and Justice) of Part Three (Union Policies and Internal Actions) of the TFEU. By

---

torial scope of application of the BC (see *supra* fn 206), the BC still applies: (1) between the 14 pre-2004 Member States other than France and the French overseas territories and territorial collectivities, except for Mayotte (see *supra* fn 218); (2) between the UK and Gibraltar (see Hartley, Choice-of-court Agreements, p 46, para 2.34); (3) the pre-2004 Member States and Aruba.

226 See e.g. Recital 19 of Brussels I; *Zuid-Chemie*, 18-19; *Falco*, 50.

227 E.g. *Hypoteční banka*, 29; *Zuid-Chemie*, 18; *eDate and Martinez*, 39.

228 AG in *Folien Fischer*, 33 [fn omitted, regarding the words 'may occur' within Art 5(3) of Brussels I].

229 Due to these rules, e.g. Art 155/A of the *Pp.* enables the Hungarian courts to refer questions for a preliminary ruling to the ECJ.

230 For details on preliminary ruling procedures, see e.g. Kropholler/von Hein, EuZPR, pp 43-52, paras 54-67. For the interpretation of the EC/Denmark Agreement (OJ 2005 L 299/62) by the ECJ, see Art 6 of that agreement. For preliminary references under the EC Treaty, see Kohler, FS Reinhold Geimer, pp 467-468. See also Commission Document COM(2006) 346 final.

231 See Recital 1.

operation of its Art 80, this regulation repealed the provisions of Brussels I. References to that latter act are constructed as references to Brussels Ia from the date of its application, that is, from 10.1.2015.[232] Equivalent to Brussels I, this legislative act is also binding and directly applicable in all Member States.[233] As a corollary of its status, its provisions are interpreted by the ECJ under the same legal bases as the rules of Brussels I. In addition, pursuant to Art 68, its relation to the BC corresponds to the relation that was maintained between Brussels I and the BC. Accordingly, first, the scope of application of the BC remains unchanged. Secondly, pursuant to Recital 34, Brussels Ia shall maintain the continuity between its provisions and the provisions of the previous Brussels instruments being identical in terms, just as Brussels I did in respect of the BC.

II. The Lugano Regime

Motivated by the success of the BC and with the aim of strengthening the judicial and economic cooperation between the European states and the creation of a dynamic, homogeneous European economic (and judicial) area embracing the Member States of the then EEC and the EFTA,[234] those states concluded the 1988 LC.[235] It entered into force between the fifteen pre-2004 Member States of the EU, Switzerland, Norway, Iceland, and Poland[236] and became known as a parallel public international law convention to the BC, given that it corresponds very closely to the 1989 BC, taking over not only its structure but also most of its provisions.[237] It

232 Art 81. Due to this article, Arts 75 and 76 shall, however, apply from 10.1.2014. As far as jurisdictional issues are concerned, acc. to Art 66(1), it applies only to legal proceedings instituted after its entry into force.

233 See also Recital 6. For the UK and Ireland, see Recital 40. For Denmark, see Recital 41 and the notification of Denmark to implement the contents of Brussels Ia [EC/Denmark Agreement (OJ 2013 L 79/4)].

234 See Jenard/Möller Report, paras 8, 10. For the position of Liechtenstein, which is not a Contracting State of the 1988 LC, see Kohler, IPRax 1997, 309-311; Jayme/Kohler, IPRax 2002, 461, 469.

235 It is accompanied by the Jenard/Möller Report.

236 Due to Arts 60(c) and 62(1)(b) of the 1988 LC, states can be invited to join. Accordingly, as Kengyel, FS Athanassios Kaissis, pp 471-473 observes, Poland acceded before joining the EU, then the EC, and the Czech Republic, Estonia, and Hungary aimed to join the 1988 LC. On this, see also Kengyel, in: FS Rolf A. Schütze, pp 348-349; *infra* Ch. III.A.III.

237 See Jenard/Möller Report, paras 1, 14.

preserves homogeneity in the European judicial area because, as Christian Kohler notices, «the national courts of the EU *and* the EFTA States when interpreting the LC followed the ECJ's case law on the parallel rules of the BC.»[238] In line with the revision of the BC mentioned above, work was also initiated to revise the provisions of this convention in order to retain the parallelism between the Brussels and Lugano instruments.[239] The 2007 LC[240] was agreed upon between the EU, then the EC, (except Denmark) on the one hand and Switzerland, Denmark, Norway, and Iceland on the other hand in 2007 after the advisory opinion of the ECJ on the exclusive competence of the EC to conclude this convention was delivered.[241] Although after becoming effective, the 2007 LC has remained open for other states who wish to join, it entered into force for the EU along with Denmark, and Norway, on 1.1.2010 and subsequently for Switzerland on 1.1.2011 and for Iceland on 1.5.2011.[242] By its entry into force and the operation of its Art 69(6), it replaces the 1988 LC and, therefore, any reference to the 1988 LC in other instruments shall be understood as a reference to this new convention.[243] This replacement is, however, only partial.

---

238 Kohler, in: EFTA Court, Judicial Protection, p 219 (italics in the original, fn omitted). On the maintenance of parallelism between the BC and 1988 LC, see also Protocol 2, Declaration No 2 and No 3 annexed to the 1988 LC. See also Kohler, in: EFTA Court, Decentred Integration, p 239; *infra* fn 248.

239 For its revision, see Council, 7700/99, LIMITE JUSTCIV 60 (30.4.1999). On this, see e.g. Jayme/Kohler, IPRax 1999, 401, 404-406.

240 It is accompanied by the Pocar Report.

241 ECJ Opinion 1/03 of 7.2.2006, 173. The exclusive competence of the EU to regulate issues on jurisdiction and the recognition and enforcement of judgments might also be underlined by the wording of the Brussels regulations; specifically, while Art 57(1) of the BC referred to conventions to which «the Contracting States are or will be parties», Art 71(1) of Brussels I and Brussels Ia omits the term 'will' and refers only to conventions «to which the Member States are parties». On this, see Layton/Mercer, European Civil Practice, para 11.060. However, for the special position of Denmark, see *supra* Ch. III.A.I. On the exclusive competence of the EU, see also *infra* fn 277.

242 See also Kohler, FS Alegría Borrás, p 566; Recital 8. For details on its drafting, its main differences from the 1988 LC and on its protocols see Wagner/Janzen, IPRax 2010, 298-310. As Hartley, Choice-of-court Agreements, p 51, para 2.47 notes, in accordance with Art 216(2) of the TFEU, the 2007 LC «must cover all the territories covered by the Brussels Regulation». Accordingly, it does not cover certain territories to which the BC and the 1988 LC apply (see *supra* fns 206, 225 and *infra* fn 244).

243 Note that it intends to replace the BC by providing in Art 69(7) an opportunity to those non-European territories that fall within the territorial scope of the BC to

Like the replacement of the BC, the 1988 LC also remains directly applicable in three situations, and indirectly applicable in one case. First, it is applicable to certain territories, which fall within its territorial scope and to which the 2007 LC does not apply.[244] Secondly, it applies to legal proceedings instituted before the entry into force of the rules of the 2007 LC in the state of origin.[245] Thirdly, it still applies through the working of the system of exchange of information established by Protocol 2 attached to the 1988 LC.[246] Finally, it is applicable indirectly, as through the required continuity and coherency between the Brussels-Lugano instruments, the interpretation of its provisions supposedly also affects the rules laid down in those instruments.

Of the three protocols attached to this convention, Protocol 2 reformulates the obligation undertaken in the second protocol to the 1988 LC regarding the uniformity of interpretation of those Brussels rules, which are substantially reproduced in the 2007 LC.[247] As a result, any court applying and interpreting the 2007 LC is obliged to «pay due account» to the principles determined in any relevant rulings regarding the provision(s) of that convention or any similar provision(s) of the other Brussels-Lugano instruments by the courts of the states bound by those instruments and by the ECJ.[248] The ECJ's power to interpret this convention stems directly

---

accede to the 2007 LC due to the accession procedure specified therein. See also Pocar Report, para 186. As Hartley, Choice-of-court Agreements, p 50, para 2.46 notes, no declarations for accession «appear to have been made.»

244 Namely, it applies to the Contracting States, the French overseas territories, territorial collectivities (except for Mayotte, see Jenard/Möller Report, para 94; *supra* fn 218), Gibraltar (see Layton/Mercer, European Civil Practice, para 11.070), and Aruba (see Hartley, Choice-of-court Agreements, p 49, para 2.42). Cf. *supra* fn 242.

245 See Art 63(1) of the 2007 LC, which determines the temporal scope of application of the 2007 LC.

246 Cf. Art 69(6) of the 2007 LC; Pocar Report, para 185(2). However note that work on setting up a system of exchange of information in accordance with Art 3 of Protocol 2 annexed to the 2007 LC is ongoing (see JURE collection <http://eur-lex.europa.eu/collection/n-law/jure.html>). Thus, this aspect of the application of the 1988 LC is to be replaced by this new system according to Art 3(3) of Protocol 2 annexed to the 2007 LC.

247 See Preamble of Protocol 2 annexed to the 2007 LC.

248 Art 1 of Protocol 2 annexed to the 2007 LC. Note that this provision refers only to certain Brussels-Lugano instruments [i.e., 1988 LC; Brussels I and its amendments; the 1968 BC (see *supra* fn 204) and the 1971 Protocol as amended by the four accession conventions; the EC/Denmark Agreement (OJ 2005 L 299/62)]. However, in the present author's opinion, its wording is a constraint to read the

from the primary law of the EU, since from the perspective of the Union, the convention forms part of EU law.[249] «[T]herefore the Court of Justice of the European Communities has jurisdiction to give rulings on the interpretation of the provisions of this Convention as regards the application by the courts of the Member States of the European Community».[250] Art 64 of the 2007 LC aims to prevent conflicts between the closely operated Brussels and Lugano Regimes (the so-called 'disconnection clause'[251]). Paragraph 1 states that the Brussels Regime continues to apply between the Member States; consequently, it takes priority over the 2007 LC. However, paragraph 2 outlines exceptions to this general rule according to which the jurisdictional rules of the 2007 LC prevail over the equivalent Brussels rules if the defendant has its domicile in one of the Lugano States, or if Art 22 or 23 of the 2007 LC allocates jurisdiction to the courts of such a state or for the purposes of *lis pendens* or of related actions as provided for in its Arts 27 and 28, when proceedings are instituted both in a Lugano State and in a Brussels State.

III. The Brussels-Lugano Regime in Hungary

According to the present author's knowledge at the time of writing this book, neither the BC nor the 1988 LC has entered into force in those Cen-

---

reference to the EC/Denmark Agreement (OJ 2005 L 299/62) as to the EC/Denmark Agreement (OJ 2013 L 79/4), while Brussels Ia could be regarded as an amendment of Brussels I (cf. *supra* fn 224). For a detailed and critical analysis of Protocol 2 annexed to the 2007 LC and for the meaning of the term 'any court', see Kohler, FS Alegría Borrás, pp 565-574; Kohler, in: EFTA Court, Judicial Protection, pp 218-227. Regarding the application of the expression 'pay due account' under Art 1 of Protocol 2 attached to the 1988 LC, see Kohler, in: Brand/Walter, Private Law, pp 231 ff. As Kohler (*ibid.*, p 232) notes, the Swiss *Bundesgericht* (Federal Supreme Court) made a reservation in 1998 acc. to which if the interpretation of the BC was strongly influenced by the law of the EC, such interpretation would not be followed [see *Tribunal fédéral* (Bundesgericht), Banque Bruxelles Lambert (Suisse)/République du Paraguay e.a., ATF 124 III 382 (ECJ Website No 1999/35)]. For further Swiss rulings on this and for the Norwegian view, see Kohler, in: EFTA Court, Decentred Integration, pp 242-243.

249 Preamble of Protocol 2 annexed to the 2007 LC. Cf. Jayme/Kohler, IPRax 2006, 537, 549. From the perspective of the EFTA States, it is a public international law convention. See also Kohler, in: EFTA Court, Judicial Protection, p 220.

250 Preamble of Protocol 2 annexed to the 2007 LC.

251 See ECJ Opinion 1/03 of 7.2.2006, para 154.

tral and Eastern European countries that have joined the EU since 2004, except for Poland, as was noted previously. This is principally because most of these countries formed part of the Soviet sphere of interest. After the Soviet Union collapsed, many of them aimed to accede to the 1988 LC.[252] To take an example, Hungary undertook steps to accede to the 1988 LC in accordance with Art 62(1)(b) of that convention. As a result, the Hungarian government, besides stating its intention to accede, communicated the information and furnished the details required by Art 63 of the 1988 LC in the Government Decision No 2392/1997 (XII.3.).[253] However, the above-mentioned revision of the BC and 1988 LC slowed down the accession process, which became obsolete on 1.5.2004 when Hungary joined the EU, then the EC, and accordingly, the rules of Brussels I entered into force therein. In addition, the EC/Denmark Agreement (OJ 2005 L 299/62) entered into force *vis-à-vis* Hungary on 1.7.2007; the 2007 LC has applied in Hungary since 1.1.2010, while Brussels Ia is principally applicable from 10.1.2015. It follows that proceedings instituted before those dates in Hungary were decided by virtue of the bilateral and multilateral agreements concluded between the respective Member or Contracting States and Hungary[254] or according to the Hungarian national rules on private international law. These latter rules are regulated in the *Law-Decree No 13 of 1979 on International Private Law (A nemzetközi magánjogról szóló 1979. évi 13. törvényerejű rendelet, Nmj.)*[255] and supplemented, for instance, by the *Pp.* or by *Act No LIII of 1994 on Court Litigation (1994. évi LIII. törvény a bírósági végrehajtásról, Vht.).*[256]

---

252 See *supra* fn 236. See also Harsági/Kengyel, IPRax 2009, 533 ff.

253 See Kengyel, in: FS Rolf A. Schütze, pp 353-356; Vékás, IPRax 2002, 142-143; Vékás, Eur. J.L. Reform 2002, 135-145.

254 For such agreements, see Vékás, Eur. J.L. Reform 2002, 135, 135; Vékás, IPRax 2002, 142, 142.

255 This law-decree covers all three aspects of PIL issues, namely, jurisdiction, applicable law, and the recognition and enforcement of judgments, in ten chapters. For details, see e.g. Mádl/Vékás, Nemzetközi magánjog; Mádl/Vékás, The Law of Conflicts, 1987.

256 It ought to be noted that Hungary, along with the other 2004-Member States, undertook an obligation within Art 5(2) of Act of Accession (OJ 2003 L 236/34) to accede to the conventions provided for in Art 293 of the EC Treaty (ex Art 220 of the Treaty of Rome) «and to those that are inseparable from the attainment of the objectives of the EC Treaty, and also to the protocols on the interpretation of those conventions by the Court of Justice». See also Jayme/Kohler, IPRax 2004, 481, 482. However, at the time of writing this book, the present author was not aware that these states had joined the BC. Therefore, it is supposed that a *lacuna*

Irrespective of the *de iure* inapplicability of the above-mentioned instruments, their effects on the Hungarian legal system, and in particular on the *Nmj., Pp.* and *Vht.*, are twofold. First, by preparing for the accession to the 1988 LC and to the EU, Hungary undertook several steps towards accommodating the provisions of those acts to that convention and to Brussels I.[257] Secondly, the explanatory reports and the settled case law of the ECJ held in relation to the *de iure* inapplicable Brussels-Lugano instruments are *de facto* also applicable to Hungary, since in conjunction with the aim of continuity mentioned above, those documents and judgments serve as significant interpretative sources of other Brussels-Lugano instruments. Hence, through the working of Brussels Ia, the EC/Denmark Agreement (OJ 2013 L 79/4), and the 2007 LC, they are indirectly applicable when Hungarian courts have recourse to their provisions.

IV. Other developments

Besides the Brussels-Lugano Regime, there have been other significant developments between countries around the world at a regional or a multilateral level to promote and strengthen integration and judicial cooperation in civil and commercial matters, and particularly in the area of cross-border litigation.[258] Two of those developments link directly to the Brus-

---

legis occurred from 1.5.2004 until 1.7.2007 between those states and Denmark, irrespective of the fact that Poland is a Contracting State of the 1988 LC. In addition, the present author is unaware that any post-2004 Member States have joined either the BC or the 1988 LC (except for Poland). Therefore, there is presumably another *lacuna legis* between those states and the Contracting States of the BC (see *supra* fns 206, 225) and the 1988 LC (see *supra* fn 244).

257 Act No CX of 2000 adjusted the rules of the *Nmj.* to the European rules. On this, see e.g. Vékás, IPRax 2002, 142, 143 ff.; Vékás, Eur. J.L. Reform 2002, 135, 140 ff.

258 E.g. Agreement between the Government of Australia and the Government of New Zealand on Trans-Tasman Court Proceedings and Regulatory Enforcement (on this, see Mortensen, J. Priv. Int. L. 2009, 213-242; Mortensen, J. Priv. Int. L. 2013, 1-38); Las Leñas Protocol of 27.6.1992 on Jurisdictional Co-operation and Assistance in Civil, Commercial, Labour and Administrative Matters; Inter-American Convention on Jurisdiction in the International Sphere for the Extraterritorial Validity of Foreign Judgments (1984); Riyadh Arab Agreement for Judicial Co-operation (1983); draft text of the OHADAC Principles on International Commercial Contracts. For further details on recent developments, see Background note drawn up by the Permanent Bureau of the HCCH (March 2012), Part

sels-Lugano Regime: (1) the Regional Convention between the Western Balkan countries is agreed in line with the provisions of the Brussels-Lugano Regime, while (2) the Brussels-Lugano Regime and the Judgments Project may reciprocally affect each other. Based on these close connections, these two developments are discussed succinctly below.

1. The Draft Regional Convention between the Western Balkan countries

Since 2011, Albania, Bosnia and Herzegovina, Macedonia, Montenegro, and Serbia[259] have aimed to strengthen their judicial cooperation in civil matters by drafting a Regional Convention on Jurisdiction and the Recognition and Enforcement of Foreign Judgments in Civil and Commercial Matters.[260] Several conferences and meetings were organised in order to comprehensively analyse the national legal systems of the participating states and to discuss the proposed provisions.[261] On 11-12 April 2013 in Belgrade (Serbia), the representatives of those countries agreed with the text of the draft convention and signed a declaration of intent for the signature and ratification of the convention.[262] The draft takes substantially into consideration the text of Brussels I and of the 2007 LC, and it is accompanied by an explanatory report.[263] «The instrument aims to

II, pp 7-13, available at <www.hcch.net/upload/hidden/2012/jdgm-backgr.pdf>; concerning Latin-America, see also Fernández Arroyo, YbPIL 2005, 85 ff.

259 News from 24.4.2013 – Christa Jessel-Holst coordinates preparation of parallel agreement to the Lugano Convention, available at <http://www.mpipriv.de/en/pub/news/institute_snapshots.cfm>.

260 See Doc. on Support of the Republic of Serbia to the initiative of the Republic of Slovenia related to accession of West Balkan Countries to Lugano Convention and other regional initiatives, 2011 (on file with author).

261 See Open Regional Fund for South-East Europe: Cross-Border Jurisdiction, January 2011, available at <http://www.giz.de/expertise/downloads/giz2012-en-orf-cross-border-juristiction-southeasteurope.pdf>.

262 See News – Christa Jessel-Holst (*supra* fn 259); Doc. on the Regional Conference of the Ministers of Interior and Ministers of Justice, Belgrade, 11-12.4.2013, point 6 (on file with author).

263 News – Christa Jessel-Holst (*supra* fn 259); Doc. on the Regional Conference of the Ministers of Interior and Ministers of Justice, Belgrade, 11-12.4.2013, point 6 (on file with author). Cf. EP Resolution, P7-TA(2010)0304 (7.9.2010), point 15 in which the EP raised the possibility that the 2007 LC could serve as a model and inspiration for an international judgments convention.

strengthen regional cooperation among the participating countries and further their gradual movement toward the European Union.»[264]

2. The Judgments Project

The Judgments Project refers to the comprehensive work undertaken by the HCCH, a global inter-governmental organisation, on two essential and interrelated subjects of private international law, namely, the international jurisdiction of courts and the recognition and enforcement of foreign judgments. The work on drafting a worldwide convention concerning these two matters started in 1992. In the course of the preparation of the preliminary draft convention, numerous meetings were organised, negotiations were conducted, and detailed studies were presented.[265] These efforts resulted in a preliminary draft Convention on Jurisdiction and Foreign Judgments in Civil and Commercial Matters (hereinafter draft Hague Judgments Convention) accompanied by a report drawn up by Peter Nygh and Fausto Pocar. Since a number of unresolved issues, such as Internet and e-commerce or consumer and employment contracts, failed consensus,[266] the HCCH decided in 2003 that the negotiations should concentrate only on jurisdictional issues relating to choice of court agreements and the recognition and enforcement of judgments delivered by the chosen courts. Those negotiations were successful and resulted in the conclusion of the Hague Convention on Choice of Court Agreements (2005).[267] In 2010, «[i]n the light of growing global interdependence,»[268] the continuation of the Judgments Project reappeared on the agenda of the Conference.[269]

264 News – Christa Jessel-Holst (*supra* fn 259).

265 A chronological overview of the Judgments Project with related documents is available at <http://www.hcch.net/index_en.php?act=text.display&tid=149>.

266 See e.g. Prel. Doc. No 16 of February 2002, para 5; Prel. Doc. No 17 of February 2002, especially paras 7 ff.; Brand, FS Hans van Loon, pp 89 ff., who focuses on the principle differences in jurisdictional approaches in the legal system of the US and of the EU, which created difficulties in negotiation.

267 For all relevant documents on this convention, see the Choice of Court Section of the HCCH <http://www.hcch.net/index_en.php?act=text.display&tid=134>. It is signed by the EU, then the EC [see Dec. 2009/397/EC (OJ 2009 L 133/1)].

268 Prel. Doc. No 14 of February 2010, para 18.

269 See Prel. Doc. No 14 of February 2010. See also e.g. Conclusions and Recommendations adopted by the Council on General Affairs and Policy of the Conference (5-7.4.2011), para 15.

Subsequently, an Experts' Group was set up in order to explore the background of the Judgments Project and recent developments as well as «to consider the desirability and feasibility of making provisions in relation to matters of jurisdiction (including parallel proceedings) in a future instrument».[270] Although the Experts' Group put forward a provisional view on possible issues regarding an instrument on jurisdiction,[271] the Permanent Bureau proposed that its discussion be resumed at a later stage.[272] As the work is still ongoing at the time of writing this book, it remains to be seen whether jurisdictional provisions will be included in this future instrument.[273] The project, as it currently stands, focuses on rules on the recognition and enforcement of judgments.[274]

Since the EU, as a Regional Economic Integration Organisation, is a member of the HCCH,[275] and due to the above-mentioned legal basis of the TFEU gaining internal competence in the area of international jurisdiction of courts and enforcement of foreign judgments,[276] the Judgments Project has considerable importance from two perspectives. First, the EU's view on jurisdictional matters, such as jurisdictional issues applicable to violations of personality rights, as matters relating to the exclusive exter-

270 Prel. Doc. No 3 of March 2013, Annex 2.

271 According to Annex 2 of Prel. Doc. No 3 of March 2013, it is expected to address some or all aspects of the following issues: required, additional, and prohibited grounds of jurisdiction as well as proceedings in more than one Contracting State.

272 Process Paper on the Continuation of the Judgments Project drawn up by the Permanent Bureau, August 2013, para 17.

273 See Process Paper on the Continuation of the Judgments Project drawn up by the Permanent Bureau, August 2013, para 18; Conclusions and Recommendations adopted by the Council on General Affairs and Policy of the Conference (24-26.3.2015), para 4.

274 See Prel. Doc. No 7B of February 2015. Note that Art 2(2)(k) of the preliminary draft text of the Working Party on the Judgments Project (Prel. Doc. No 7B of February 2015, pp 3 ff.) appears to exclude defamation from its scope.

275 The EU became a participant of the HCCH on 3.4.2007. See also Dec. 2006/719/EC (OJ 2006 L 297/1). Before this date, the EU authorised its Member States to sign the convention in the interest of the Union under the conditions set out in a decision, such as Dec. 2003/93/EC (OJ 2003 L 48/1) authorising the Member States to sign the 1996 Hague Convention on Jurisdiction, Applicable Law, Recognition, Enforcement and Cooperation in respect of Parental Responsibility and Measures for the Protection of Children. On this, see also Jayme/Kohler, IPRax 2001, 501, 505-506.

276 See *supra* Ch. III.A.I. See also Dec. 2006/719/EC (OJ 2006 L 297/1), Annex II, especially para 2 (b), para 5, third indent.

nal competence of the EU[277] might affect the further work on the project. Secondly, the Judgments Project might also influence the rules established by the Brussels-Lugano Regime.[278]

B. Governing objectives and underlying principles: focus on the persons

The coherent and uniform application of the systematised rules of jurisdiction laid down within the Brussels-Lugano Regime is safeguarded through their interpretation based on their governing objectives and underlying principles.[279] As Jannet A. Pontier and Edwige Burg point out:

> «An examination of the Court's case law clearly shows that the Court does not only have recourse to the model of principles after it has established that the words of the Convention are not able to provide a clear answer. Also in cases in which the words of the Convention, considered by themselves, clearly point to a solution, the Court still feels obliged to consider what the Convention's principles have to say.»[280]

The governing objectives and underlying principles are laid down in the preamble, recitals, and expert notes of the Brussels-Lugano instruments, and they are also developed by the judicial practice of the ECJ. Although they aim to promote a universal principle, namely, the principle of strengthening the legal protection of persons established in the Brussels-

---

277 ECJ Opinion 1/03 of 7.2.2006; Dec. 2006/719/EC (OJ 2006 L 297/1), Annex II, point 6. For external competence, see also Art 216 together with Art 3(2) of the TFEU (cf. Mansel/Thorn/Wagner, IPRax 2010, 1, 26); and the ERTA-doctrine established in *ERTA*, 16-19 and explained in Struycken, Recueil des Cours 311, pp 131-134. Exception to the EU exclusive external power is possible in situations concerning individual and exceptional cases between Member States and third countries. On this, see e.g. Recital 37 of Rome II; Declaration No 36 annexed to the Final Act of the Intergovernmental Conference which adopted the Treaty of Lisbon (OJ 2012 C 326/351). See also *supra* fn 241.

278 For the relation between the Judgments Project and other instruments incl. the EU, then EC, law, see Prel. Doc. No 19 of December 2003. As Prel. Doc. No 16 of February 2002, para 5/E indicates, a lack of consensus appeared on the relation between the Judgments Project and certain Brussels-Lugano instruments.

279 By analogy, see *Tessili*, 9. See also Pontier/Burg, EU Principles, p 5. As Pontier and Burg (*ibid.*, p 8) specify in this regard, the term 'objective' is synonym to the term 'principle'. Note that this section is principally based on, adopts, follows and expands the principles analysed and the title of the sections used in Pontier/Burg, EU Principles.

280 Pontier/Burg, EU Principles, p 10 (regarding the BC).

Lugano States,[281] they fulfil this aim through different directions. Two comments are called for on this feature of the governing objectives and underlying principles. First, they can be categorised into various groups and sub-groups according to the directions they represent. Secondly, it follows that they often compete with and contradict each other. Therefore, their application is relative.[282] For weighing and balancing the different principles to resolve the conflict between them, three expectations might provide guidelines. It is expected, first, that the ECJ keeps the universal principle in view; second, that it treats cases, which are similar in the perspectives of principles, alike; and third, that a preference for one principle over another does not lead to an unreasonable and disproportional solution.[283]

I. The principle of legal certainty

The principle of legal certainty, which aims to strengthen the legal protection of persons established in the EU,[284] was one of the main aims to be achieved by laying down common rules of jurisdiction in a genuine and legally systematised manner in 1968.[285] In addition, this principle is also a driving force of each of the jurisdictional rules of the Brussels-Lugano Regime; it is referred to in Recital 15, which states that «[t]he rules of jurisdiction should be highly predictable».[286] The maintenance of the legal certainty and predictability of jurisdictional rules has considerable importance for the different procedural actors. It is necessary for the national courts to decide easily on their competence. In addition, it is essential for the plaintiff «to identify easily the court in which he may sue and the de-

281 See Pontier/Burg, EU Principles, p 13; *Duijnstee*, 10-12 as referred to in Pontier/ Burg, EU Principles, p 19. For this principle, see also *de Visser*, 39; *Hypoteční banka*, 33 (mentioning solely the defendant), 44.

282 See also Pontier/Burg, EU Principles, p 12 and in detail *ibid.*, pp 12-15.

283 For the last two expectations, see Pontier/Burg, EU Principles, pp 13-15. They conclude (*ibid.*, p 13), however, that the general principle «does not have the capacity to provide guidance when the Court is faced with conflicting mid-level principles.»

284 See e.g. *Hypoteční banka*, 44; *de Visser*, 39.

285 See e.g. Jenard Report, pp 7, 15; Pontier/Burg, EU Principles, p 92.

286 Note that this requirement is weakened in Brussels Ia, since Recital 11 of Brussels I required that «[t]he rules of jurisdiction must be highly predictable».

fendant reasonably to foresee in which court he may be sued».[287] Besides facilitating the predictable identification of the competent forum, Georg Philipp Krog acknowledges an additional result of legally certain jurisdictional rules, namely, that they also facilitate the «predictability of the applicable law in international matters enabling the parties to clarify their respective rights, obligations and responsibilities.»[288]

1. The principle of equality and uniformity of rights and obligations

The principle of equality and uniformity of the rights and obligations arising out of the Brussels-Lugano Regime for its Member and Contracting States and the persons concerned is a sub-principle of the doctrine of legal certainty.[289] It is guaranteed by the autonomous and independent interpretation of most of the concepts and provisions employed therein.[290] Its importance and close connection with the other sub-principles of this section was pointed out by the ECJ in *Mulox*, which stated:

> «That autonomous interpretation alone is capable of ensuring uniform application of the Convention, the objectives of which include unification of the rules on jurisdiction of the Contracting States, so as to avoid as far as possible the multiplication of the bases of jurisdiction in relation to one and the same legal relationship and to reinforce the legal protection available to persons established in the Community by, at the same time, allowing the plaintiff easily to identify the court before which he may bring an action and the defendant reasonably to foresee the court before which he may be sued.»[291]

The autonomous and independent interpretation of most of the concepts is ensured «primarily by reference to the scheme and purpose»[292] of the

---

287 See e.g. *DFDS Torline*, 36; *Kronhofer*, 20.

288 Krog, IPRax 2004, 154, 154. See also Kohler, E.L.Rev. 1982, Part II, 103, 112 who observes that «the choice of jurisdiction … may also entail a concealed "choice" of the *lex causae*» (emphases omitted; italics in the original).

289 For details, see Pontier/Burg, EU Principles, pp 71-82.

290 Such as 'civil and commercial matters' (e.g. *Eurocontrol*, 3; on this, see also Kohler, IPRax 2015, 52, 52), 'tort, delict or quasi-delict' (e.g. *Kalfelis*, 16). For details on the interpretation of the terms used in the BC, see e.g. Kohler, E.L.Rev. 1982, Part I, 3, 7-13; Kohler, ICLQ 1985, 563, 565-569.

291 *Mulox*, 11.

292 *B and Others*, 50 (regarding Brussels I). See also similarly, *Zuid-Chemie*, 17; *Wintersteiger*, 31.

Brussels-Lugano Regime.[293] In addition, it is also safeguarded by the impact of fundamental rights. In particular, as the ECJ held in *B and Others*, «the provisions of EU law, such as those of Regulation No 44/2001, must be interpreted in the light of fundamental rights which, according to settled case-law, form an integral part of the general principles of law whose observance the Court ensures and which are now set out in the Charter».[294] By virtue of Art 51(1) of the Charter, not only is the ECJ addressed by its provisions, but so are the national courts of the Member States when they apply or implement a regulation,[295] such as Brussels Ia.[296] Fundamental rights might affect the interpretation of the Brussels-Lugano Regime from two aspects.[297] First, fundamental rights that have a substantive legal nature give guidance in case of necessity to the common understanding of the definitions of the rights and values employed under the scope of jurisdictional rules.[298] Secondly, those that have a procedural character, such as access to justice, the rights of the defence, or the plaintiff's right to bring an action before a court to rule on the merits of his claim under Art 47 of

---

293 For additional methods of interpretation, see Kropholler/von Hein, EuZPR, pp 52-63, paras 68-81; Magnus, Intr., in: Magnus/Mankowski, Brussels I Regulation, pp 31-39, paras 91-110.

294 *B and Others*, 51. See also AG in *eDate and Martinez*, 52. Regarding the general principles of EU law, see Art 6(3) of the TEU. Note that due to Art 6(1) of the TEU, the Charter «shall have the same legal value as the Treaties.» For references in regulations to respect the fundamental rights guaranteed in the Charter, see e.g. Recital 38; Recital 38 of Reg. (EU) No 606/2013 (OJ 2013 L 181/4). Cf. by analogy, AG in *CDC*, fn 23 (see also *ibid.*, 32) in which AG Jääskinen pointed out that secondary legislation (such as Brussels I) must be interpreted and applied in a manner conforming with primary legislation of the EU.

295 See von Danwitz/Paraschas, Fordham Int'l L.J. 2011-2012, 1396, 1406.

296 For details on the application of the Charter, see e.g. *McB*; *GREP*; *Åkerberg Fransson*; *Melloni*; Blanco, J. Priv. Int. L. 2012, 135-157; Rosas, Jurisprudence 2012, 1269-1288; von Danwitz/Paraschas, Fordham Int'l L.J. 2011-2012, 1396-1425; van Bockel/Wattel, ECL 2014, 273-289. Regarding the application of the Charter to the UK and Poland, see Dougan, CML Rev. 2008, 617, 665-671.

297 Art 52(3) of the Charter (see also *Åkerberg Fransson*, 44) requires rights within the Charter that correspond to rights guaranteed by the ECHR be given the same meaning and scope as those laid down by the ECHR. However, acc. to that provision, the EU could also provide protection that is more extensive. Note that although the EU shall accede to the ECHR (in this regard, see ECJ Opinion 2/13 of 18.12.2014), at the time of writing the present book, this convention has not been formally incorporated into the EU law (cf. *Åkerberg Fransson*, 44). See also *infra* fn 770.

298 On this, see *infra* Ch. V.C.II.6 and *infra* Ch. VII.B.II.1.b).

the Charter, ensure a fair trial over Member and Contracting States by laying down common procedural safeguards.[299]

The method of autonomous and independent interpretation is supplemented by an additional requirement regarding special jurisdictional rules, such as Art 7(1) or (2), which are alternative[300] to and which derogate from[301] the general jurisdictional rule of Art 4(1) by virtue of Art 5(1).[302] According to the case law of the ECJ, these rules «must be restrictively interpreted and cannot give rise to an interpretation going beyond the cases expressly envisaged by the Convention».[303] Nonetheless, as AG Geelhoed observed, the nature of this restrictive method of interpretation has a threshold limitation, that is, it excludes application by analogy, since its interpretation «cannot go so far as to deprive Art 5 of its practical effect.»[304]

The creation of autonomously interpreted concepts and uniform rules of jurisdiction, however, does not mean that the Brussels-Lugano instruments aim to unify the rules of substantive law and of procedure in the Member and Contracting States.[305] Thus, they leave three narrow paths for the application of national law within their system. First, they expressly call the internal law of the Member and Contracting States to interpret limited number of concepts, such as the determination of domicile of natural persons under Art 62 outlined in *infra* Ch. III.C.I.1. In addition, they demand that the court seised of the matter «shall apply its rules of private international law» to determine whether, for example, a legal person or a trust is domiciled,[306] or the seat of a legal person in certain circumstances specified within Art 24(2) is located in such a state. Finally, the Brussels-Lugano Regime does not regulate every aspect of procedure, and conse-

---

299 On this, see *infra* Ch. V.C.II.6 and *infra* Conclusion and summary to Ch. VII.C.I.

300 See e.g. Recital 16.

301 See e.g. *Shevill*, 18; *Kronhofer*, 13; *Zuid-Chemie*, 21; *eDate and Martinez*, 40.

302 Regarding special rules of jurisdiction, see also *infra* Ch. III.C.II.

303 *Kronhofer*, 14 (regarding the BC). See also *Melzer*, 24. Cf. Kohler, E.L.Rev. 1982, Part I, 3, 17-18.

304 AG in *Tacconi*, 35 (regarding the BC).

305 See e.g. *Shevill*, 35. Except for two cases: (1) rules of territorial jurisdiction (so-called venue) essentially listed in Chapter II replace the national procedural rules on venue (see also Pocar Report, para 34); (2) Art 64 as outlined in *infra* Ch. III.D.III.

306 For legal persons (i.e., company, other legal person or association of natural or legal persons, unless otherwise indicated), see Art 53(1) of the BC and of the 1988 LC. On trusts, see e.g. Art 63(3). See also *infra* Ch. III.C.I.1.

quently, it leaves several gaps, such as the method of enforcing the foreign judgment or the kinds of provisional orders recognised, which shall be filled by the national procedural rules of the Member State in which the court is seised.[307] The application of national rules must, however, fulfil an overarching condition. They are applicable in so far as they do not impair the effectiveness of the Brussels-Lugano Regime[308] and do not «infringe European Union law».[309]

2. Legal certainty as to the scope of the Brussels-Lugano Regime

The principle of legal certainty also implies clarity as to the substantive scope of the Brussels-Lugano Regime in order to enable the parties and the court to decide whether the dispute falls within the scope of the regime. The substantive scope requires that the subject matter of the action or the legal relationship between the parties to the action[310] shall concern civil and commercial matters and involve a foreign element.

Concerning the first requirement expressly stated in Recital 10 and Art 1(1), it becomes clear that the independently interpreted concept of civil and commercial matters covers all the main subjects except for certain issues, which are defined in the second sentence of Art 1(1) and in Art 1(2). Matters are classified as such by virtue of their nature and regardless of the character of the court or tribunal that is seised of the proceedings.[311] Although an in-depth consideration of the concept of civil and commercial matters is beyond the scope of this subsection,[312] it is nevertheless worthwhile reinforcing that this concept covers various types of torts, such as

---

307 See e.g. Layton/Mercer, European Civil Practice, para 11.024; *Kongress Agentur*, 19; *Shevill*, 36.

308 See e.g. *Shevill*, 36; *Kongress Agentur*, 20, 22; Layton/Mercer, European Civil Practice, para 11.024. For the principle of effectiveness, see Layton/Mercer, European Civil Practice, paras 11.053-11.056.

309 *De Visser*, 45. Cf. regarding *Åkerberg Fransson*, van Bockel/Wattel, ECL 2014, 273, 284 note that «any national measure that jeopardises the effectiveness of EU law, in whatever manner, falls within the scope of EU law and is therefore susceptible to scrutiny under the Charter.»

310 See e.g. Evrigenis/Kerameus Report, para 26; *Eurocontrol*, 4.

311 See Jenard Report, p 9. For the meaning of the term 'court', see e.g. Art 62 of the 2007 LC; Art 3; Recital 11.

312 For details, see Jenard Report, pp 9-10; Kohler, E.L.Rev. 1982, Part II, 103-107; Pontier/Burg, EU Principles, pp 87-91. Cf. *Austro-Mechana* (request).

violations of personality rights.[313] However, it does not include public law issues, such as revenue, customs, administrative matters, or «the liability of the State for acts and omissions in the exercise of State authority (*acta iure imperii*)».[314] Accordingly, actions between a public authority and a private person fall within the scope of the Brussels-Lugano Regime in so far as the public authority is not acting in the exercise of its public law powers.[315] In addition, due to Art 7(3) the defendant may be sued «as regards civil claim for damages or restitution which is based on an act giving rise to criminal proceedings, in the court seised of those proceedings, to the extent that that court has jurisdiction under its own law to entertain civil proceedings». To put it another way, the fact «that criminal proceedings and criminal judgments of all kinds are excluded»[316] from the scope of the Brussels-Lugano Regime, as being public law issues, does not prevent the possibility of a civil claim ancillary to criminal proceedings falling under the scope of the regime.[317]

The second requirement, namely, the existence of a foreign element in the dispute, stems from the nature of the jurisdictional rules, since they consider international jurisdictional questions. As a corollary, it does not apply to cases purely internal to a particular Brussels-Lugano State.[318]

313 On this, see *infra* Ch. IV.A.

314 Italics in the original. This formulation is added first into Brussels Ia. The previous Brussels-Lugano instruments do not include this reference.

315 See e.g. *Land Berlin*, 33; *Eurocontrol*, 4; *Lechouritou*, 31. On this, see also Kohler, IPRax 2015, 52 ff. It is, however, questionable whether the public authority or official using social networking sites acts in the course of its power, and therefore, it is excluded from the application of the Brussels-Lugano Regime or not.

316 Schlosser Report, para 29 (regarding the BC).

317 See e.g. *De Cavel (2)*, 8-9; Layton/Mercer, European Civil Practice, para 15.100. See also *infra* Ch. III.D.III; *Aannemingsbedrijf Aertssen and Aertssen Terrassements* (request).

318 See Layton/Mercer, European Civil Practice, para 11.017. However, Layton and Mercer (*ibid.*, para 11.017, fn 83) also note that «[a]s a matter of the law of the UK, the question whether a case falls within the scope of the Brussels-Lugano regime is relevant even for cases purely internal to the UK s.16(1)(a) of the 1982 Act». Cf. albeit in the context of the pre-2001 text of the *Nmj.*, the *Supreme Court of Hungary* pointed out in case Gfv. X. 31.666/2002. sz., *Legf. Bír.* (BH 2004.9.376) that this law-decree does not apply solely to disputes internal to another state. The purpose of that law-decree due to its Art 1 is, in the interest of the development of peaceful international relations, to determine *inter alia* the jurisdiction and procedural rules applicable in a dispute containing a foreign component (person, object of property or right). However, the dispute at stake had no such connection to Hungary at all. Instead, it is held to be linked to Russia.

However, this requirement is not defined because it «may depend on the particular facts of the proceedings of which the court is seised.»[319] For the existence of such a foreign element, and thus, for the application of the rules of jurisdiction, it is required, as the ECJ held in *Hypoteční banka*, «that the situation at issue in the proceedings of which the court of a Member State is seised is such as to raise questions relating to determination of the international jurisdiction of that court.»[320] Then it went on to hold that «[s]uch a situation arises in a case ... in which an action is brought before a court of a Member State against a national of another Member State whose domicile is unknown to that court.»[321] As Alexander Layton and Hugh Mercer observe, the most obvious examples of the existence of an international element are demonstrated by the special heads of jurisdiction. It follows that even if both parties have their domicile in the same Brussels-Lugano State, if the controversy concerns a tort committed in another Brussels-Lugano State, the controversy has an international character.[322]

3. Avoiding multiplication of courts and fragmentation of proceedings

It becomes clear from the settled case law of the ECJ that the principle of legal certainty aims to avoid, among the special heads of jurisdiction, the multiplicity of courts having jurisdiction in respect of one and the same type of legal relationship.[323] In other words, the interpretation of those rules should not aim to establish any additional jurisdictional grounds beyond those laid down therein, since otherwise, the rules on jurisdiction would become unforeseeable and unpredictable for the different procedural actors. In particular, this proposition covers two divergent aspects. The first is that the interpretation of jurisdictional rules, especially connecting factors, should avoid situations in which alternative courts have

319 Jenard Report, p 8. For details, see e.g. Jenard Report, p 8; Layton/Mercer, European Civil Practice, paras 11.017-11.018.

320 *Hypoteční banka*, 35.

321 *Hypoteční banka*, 35 (emphases omitted).

322 See Layton/Mercer, European Civil Practice, para 11.018. Cf. *Maletic*, 22 ff. for determining the foreign element regarding an online travel agency and its contracting partner, which has its registered office in the Member State in which the consumer is domiciled.

323 See e.g. Pontier/Burg, EU Principles, p 98. See also *Besix*, 27; *Dumez*, 18.

jurisdiction.[324] In this regard, the ECJ pointed out in the context of contracts in *Besix*:

> «Where parties have agreed a contractual obligation not to do something, applicable without any geographical limit, that approach does not avoid a multiplicity of competent courts, since it leads to the result that the places of performance of the obligation in question are in all the Contracting States. ...
>
> Consequently, that interpretation ... is likely to reduce the predictability of the competent court, so that it is incompatible with the principle of legal certainty.»[325]

The second aspect requires the avoidance of such an interpretation of jurisdictional rules, which create situations in which different courts have jurisdiction regarding various aspects of one and the same legal relationship (i.e., avoidance of the fragmentation of proceedings).[326] The disregard of this requirement is, however, evident from the case law of the ECJ. In *Pinckney*, for instance, the ECJ fragmented the dispute concerning infringement of the plaintiff's copyright. In particular, the ECJ opted for an interpretation of the concept of harmful event laid down in Art 5(3) of Brussels I, which restricted the extent of the jurisdiction of the competent court to rule on the damage caused solely in the territory where it is seised.[327]

4. The extent of national courts' duties to examine jurisdiction

The rules regarding the extent of a national court's duties to examine its own or other courts' jurisdiction is laid down in the Brussels-Lugano Regime and developed through the case law of the ECJ. They facilitate legal certainty from different perspectives.

First, national courts of the Member and Contracting States are obliged to apply the unified jurisdictional provisions of the Brussels-Lugano Regime «whether or not they are pleaded by the parties.»[328] As a corollary, they have no discretion in applying those jurisdictional rules, except in exclusively specified situations.[329] Hence, the principle of *forum non con-*

---

324 For details, see Pontier/Burg, EU Principles, pp 100-103.

325 *Besix*, 34-35 (regarding the BC; sentence and emphases omitted).

326 For details, see Pontier/Burg, EU Principles, pp 103-107.

327 For details on this practice, see *infra* Ch. V.C and *infra* Ch. VII.C.I.

328 Jenard Report, p 8. On the legal nature and binding character of the Brussels-Lugano instruments, see *supra* Ch. III.A.I-II.

329 Such as Arts 30, 33 and 34, except for Art 33(3) (see *infra* Ch. III.B.II.2). How-

veniens, which is a legal institution deeply rooted in the traditional English law, is, in general, exiled from the regime. In Christian Kohler's words, «the courts seised in State A cannot decline jurisdiction on the ground that, having regard to the interests of the parties and to the applicable law, the case may more conveniently be heard by the courts of State B, which also have jurisdiction.»[330]

Secondly, this sub-principle requires that the court seised should be able to decide whether it has international jurisdiction due solely to the provisions of the Brussels-Lugano Regime and without having to consider the substance of the case.[331] The ECJ followed this line of reasoning in the *Folien Fischer* decision in which it held in relation to Art 5(3) of Brussels I:

> «During the stage at which jurisdiction is verified, the court seised does not examine either the admissibility or the substance of the application ... in the light of national law, but identifies only the points of connection with the State in which that court is sitting, which support its claim to jurisdiction».[332]

Three comments are called for on this finding.

First, the courts examine only the existence of those points of connection. Moreover, they do it of their own motion. This duty is generally acknowledged in the Jenard Report,[333] expressly imposed on the courts by certain provisions of the Brussels-Lugano Regime,[334] and continually approved by the ECJ.[335] The examination of jurisdiction is done exclusively

---

ever, note that these rules do not confer jurisdiction *per se*. Note also that as the Schlosser Report, para 81 observes, transfer of local jurisdiction is also possible within the same state, providing that the connecting factor of the Brussels-Lugano Regime confers only international, and not local (on this, see *supra* fn 305), jurisdiction.

330 Kohler, ICLQ 1985, 563, 571. On the compatibility of the *forum non conveniens* doctrine with the Brussels-Lugano instruments, see e.g. *Owusu*, 37-46; Hartley, Recueil des Cours 319, pp 169-174.

331 See e.g. *Peters*, 17. Cf. AG in *Folien Fischer*, 27-31; Pontier/Burg, EU Principles, pp 108-109.

332 *Folien Fischer*, 50 (emphases omitted). See also *Kolassa*, 62. Cf. e.g. *Shevill*, 37.

333 Jenard Report, pp 38-39.

334 Queirolo, in: Magnus/Mankowski, Brussels I Regulation, p 542, para 5 points out that Arts 25 and 26 of Brussels I (see Arts 27 and 28 of Brussels Ia) indicate that the court must of its own motion examine its jurisdiction under Art 22 of Brussels I (see Art 24 of Brussels Ia) and in the case when the defendant fails to appear. In addition, it also examines its own jurisdiction if one of the parties expressly requests it.

335 See e.g. *Effer*, 7. See also Layton/Mercer, European Civil Practice, para 21.015.

by the court seised itself. This exclusivity stems from the uniform and compulsory jurisdictional regime that does not authorise a court of another Brussels-Lugano State, apart from the limited exceptions noted in *infra* Ch. III.B.III, to review the jurisdiction of the court seised.[336] Hence, in accordance with the *lis pendens* rules, as outlined in *infra* Ch. III.B.II.2, if «the jurisdiction of the court first seised is contested, the court second seised may, if it does not decline jurisdiction, only stay the proceedings and may not itself examine the jurisdiction of the court first seised.»[337] This finding was approved in *Turner* in which the ECJ *inter alia* pointed out that a prohibition imposed by a court of a Contracting State of the BC restraining a party from commencing or continuing proceedings before the court of another Contracting State undermines the latter court's jurisdiction to determine the dispute (known as anti-suit injunction). Any such injunction interferes with the jurisdiction of the court, and it is incompatible with the system of the BC.[338]

Secondly, the extent of the verification duties to which national courts are subject when they determine their own jurisdiction under the regime is principally governed by the national law of the Member and Contracting States,[339] providing that it does not impair the effectiveness of the regime.[340] The Brussels-Lugano Regime offers only limited guidance on this aspect. Relying on its ruling in *Hi Hotel*, the ECJ noted in *Kolassa* in respect of Art 5(3) of Brussels I that «the court seised may regard as established, solely for the purpose of ascertaining whether it has jurisdiction under that provision, the applicant's assertions as regards the conditions for liability in tort, delict or quasi-delict».[341] Therefore, in the course of

---

336 See e.g. *Overseas*, 24.

337 *Overseas*, 26. This is so because of the high degree of trust accorded to the administration of justice of each of the Brussels-Lugano States (also known as mutual trust). For details on *lis pendens* rules and mutual trust, see e.g. Crespi Reghizzi, YbPIL 2009, 427, 436-442. See also *infra* Ch. III.B.III.

338 See *Turner*, 24 ff., especially 27 and 31. For comments on this case, see Rauscher, IPRax 2004, 405-409; Hartley, Recueil des Cours 319, pp 174 ff. See also *West Tankers*. However, for an anti-suit injunction issued by an arbitral tribunal situated in a Member State, see AG in *Gazprom*. Regarding the recognition and enforcement of judgments (a restriction of the power of the court of the Member State in which recognition is sought to determine its own jurisdiction since it is bound by the decision of the court of origin), see *Gothaer*, 39.

339 As the Heidelberg Report, para 402, second indent notes, the national practice of the Member States varies.

340 On this, see *supra* Ch. III.B.I.1. See also *Kolassa*, 60.

341 *Kolassa*, 62. See also *Hi Hotel*, 20. Cf. Jenard Report, p 39.

the determination of the jurisdiction under Brussels I, the court is not required to conduct a comprehensive taking of evidence regarding the disputed facts that are relevant both to the question of jurisdiction and to the existence of the claim.[342] Such comprehensive taking of evidence would risk prejudicing the assessment of the substance.[343] However, as the ECJ went on to rule, «[i]t is ... permissible for the court seised to examine its international jurisdiction in the light of all the information available to it, including, where appropriate, the allegations made by the defendant.»[344]

Finally, and closely related to the second comment, it ought to be noted that although the above recommended assessment of facts as to the determination of jurisdiction is closely linked to the consideration of the merits of the case, as AG Jääskinen noted in *Folien Fischer,* those two spheres differ from each other, and they must thus not be confused. At the jurisdictional level, in particular under Art 7(2), the assessment of facts disregards the violation which has been committed and instead considers the violation potential of a particular conduct.[345] Closely related to this, the ECJ held in respect of the damage in *Hejduk*:

> «The issue of the extent of the damage alleged by Ms Hejduk is part of the examination of the substance of the claim and is not relevant to the stage in which jurisdiction is verified.»[346]

II. The principle that disputes should be decided in an appropriate forum

The principle that disputes should be decided in an appropriate forum plays a significant role in the jurisdictional rules codified in Chapter II, as those rules aim to determine which courts of a particular Brussels-Lugano State are most appropriate for establishing jurisdiction.[347]

342 *Kolassa*, 65.

343 *Kolassa*, 63.

344 *Kolassa*, 65 (emphasis omitted). Cf. Schlosser Report, para 22; Kohler, ICLQ 1985, 563, 573-574; *Universal Music International Holding* (request).

345 AG in *Wintersteiger*, 31. Cf. *Wintersteiger*, 26; AG in *DFDS Torline*, 52. Cf. also Vlas, NILR 1995, 413, 417 who asserts in relation to torts (case references omitted): «Whether or not injury has been suffered, is only relevant for the outcome of the proceedings, but not for the jurisdiction of the court».

346 *Hejduk*, 35.

347 See e.g. Jenard Report, p 15; Pontier/Burg, EU Principles, p 115, and for details, *ibid.*, pp 115-233.

1. The principles of sound administration of justice and proximity

The principles of sound administration of justice and proximity are the driving forces of several jurisdictional rules, such as Art 7(1) or (2). They imply the existence of a close connection between the dispute and the courts other than that of the defendant's domicile. In turn, this close connection justifies the allocation of jurisdiction for reasons relating to the sound administration of justice and the efficacious conduct of proceedings.[348] It follows that the designated courts are territorially the best qualified to decide on the controversy[349] because they have the practical advantage of ease of taking of evidence, first-hand knowledge of the facts, and knowledge of the law applicable to the dispute.[350]

As becomes evident from the case law of the ECJ, which is considered in greater detail in the following chapters, this principle has provided fruitful ground for (over)stretching the interpretation of the connecting factors employed within Chapter II, such as the concept of the place where the damage occurred under Art 7(2). In particular, based on this principle, the ECJ justified not only the multiplication of courts, but, as was noted in *supra* Ch. III.B.I.3, also the fragmentation of proceedings into multiple territories and thus, the establishment of numerous miniaturised jurisdictions, which is obviously contrary to the principle of legal certainty outlined above. However, the supplemented wording of Recital 12 of Brussels I, which treats the principles of sound administration of justice, proximity and legal certainty on an equal footing, might put an end to this extensive judicial practice and restore the fine balance between these principles. Specifically, Recital 16 introduces an additional requirement regarding these principles by stating:

> «The existence of a close connection should ensure legal certainty and avoid the possibility of the defendant being sued in a court of a Member State which he could not reasonably have foreseen. This is important, particularly in disputes

---

348 See e.g. Recital 16; *Bier*, 11; *Dumez*, 17; *Marinari*, 10; *Pinckney*, 27. For details on these sub-principles, see Pontier/Burg, EU Principles, pp 162-205. Note that two different terms are used under certain circumstances for the term 'close link': (1) a particularly close connection (e.g. *Bier*, 11; *Henkel*, 46; *Dumez*, 17; *Kronhofer*, 15); (2) the closest connection [e.g. Bataller Opinion and Report (5.5.2011), point 2.2; *Color Drack*, 40; AG in *Melzer*, 61].

349 See e.g. *Effer*, 6; *Pinckney*, 28.

350 See Pontier/Burg, EU Principles, p 160. See also *Bier*, 17; *Henkel*, 46; *Melzer*, 27.

concerning non-contractual obligations arising out of violations of privacy and rights relating to personality, including defamation.»[351]

2. The principle that parallel proceedings should be avoided

As has become clear from the provisions of the Brussels-Lugano Regime and from the settled case law of the ECJ, the principle that disputes should be decided in an appropriate forum also requires that an entire case should be decided before a single court. In other words, this sub-principle in the interests of the proper administration of justice aims to avoid parallel proceedings before the courts of different states by requiring the concentration of proceedings, which is regarded as «one of the primary objectives»[352] of the regime. In particular, this principle implies that related disputes should be brought before a single court and that same or related actions that have already been brought before different courts should be decided by a single forum.[353]

The former aspect is grounded on the presumption that where certain facts of the case are directly linked to a court, that court is the best qualified to decide the case due to the practical advantages of evidences and the efficacious conduct of proceedings.[354] This is the case within Art 8(1). As outlined in *infra* Ch. III.D.V, it designates the appropriate court in disputes in which a number of defendants are involved.

The latter aspects regulated in Section 9 of Chapter II emphasise that if a case is already connected to a court «because this court has jurisdiction with regard to a case that is part of that dispute, that court may be the best qualified to hear *all* the different aspects of the dispute because of the disadvantages of separate proceedings.»[355] In particular, they principally aim to resolve the possible conflicts of jurisdiction based on a chronological order of the courts seised by obliging or enabling the court other than the first seised to stay or decline its proceedings.[356] It follows that, contrary to

351 Dissenting opinion: Zwiefka Draft Report (28.6.2011), Amendment 2 to Recital 13, under the point «Justification», stated that «[t]his reference to a particular species of dispute is gratuitous and unnecessary.»

352 Bourel as referred to in AG 1995 in *Shevill*, 20 (regarding the BC).

353 For details, see Pontier/Burg, EU Principles, pp 161-162 and pp 205-223.

354 Pontier/Burg, EU Principles, p 206. See also text to *supra* fn 350.

355 Pontier/Burg, EU Principles, p 206 (italics in the original).

356 It follows that the time of seising, i.e., when the proceedings are instituted in the court of a Member (or third) State, is crucial. It is regulated in Art 32, which sup-

Art 8(1), they do not allocate jurisdiction in relation to the substantive issues of the dispute. Rather, they confer so-called 'procedural jurisdiction', i.e., jurisdiction to define jurisdiction, upon the first court, providing that their conditions for application are satisfied.[357] These aspects can be divided into two distinct scenarios depending on the location of the court first seised: Arts 29 and 30 deal with intra-Brussels-Lugano States conflicts of jurisdiction, while Arts 33 and 34 regulate cases that involve parallel proceedings pending before a court of a third state.[358]

As far as the first category of conflicts is concerned, it is notable that Art 29 governs those proceedings that meet three cumulative and independently defined conditions.[359] Specifically, they must involve the same subject matter, and the same cause of action between the same parties must be brought in the courts of different Brussels-Lugano States.[360] This provision orders any courts other than the first seised to stay their proceedings of their own motion and that when the jurisdiction of the first seised court is established, they shall decline jurisdiction in favour of the first seised court.[361] To ease the decision on the priority of the courts, Art 29(2)

---

plements the uniform determination introduced in Art 30 of Brussels I and incorporated also into Art 30 of the 2007 LC with two provisions. On this, see Recital 21; Nielsen, CML Rev. 2013, 503, 517-518. Before the uniform determination of the time of seising, see *Zelger*, 10-15; *Gantner*, 27 (regarding this case, see Jayme/Kohler, IPRax 2003, 485, 490). Cf. *Aannemingsbedrijf Aertssen and Aertssen Terrassements* (request; regarding proceedings under the Belgian Code of Criminal Procedure).

357 See Fentiman, in: Magnus/Mankowski, Brussels I Regulation, p 560, para 6. See also *supra* fn 329.

358 Cf. Recitals 23, 24. The previous Brussels-Lugano instruments do not consist of any rule regarding third states' proceedings. In this regards, see Fentiman, in: Magnus/Mankowski, Brussels I Regulation, pp 580-581, paras 62-65 (Arts 27-28 of Brussels I); Layton/Mercer, European Civil Practice, para 22.021 (Art 27 of Brussels I).

359 See e.g. AG in *I. Weber*, 64 («cumulative»); *Gubisch*, 11 and *Tatry*, 46 («independent»).

360 Note that the criterion of same subject matter is not expressly referred to in each language version of the regulation. However, it is indicated in e.g. the French language version of Art 29(1) («le même objet»), and it is continuously required in the settled case law of the ECJ (e.g. *Gubisch*, 14; *Tatry*, 37) as being crucial for the determination of *lis pendens*. For details on this requirement, see Fentiman, in: Magnus/Mankowski, Brussels I Regulation, pp 586-588, paras 12-18.

361 Art 29(3). For the circumstances under which the jurisdiction of the court first seised must be regarded as established, see *Cartier*, especially paras 44-45 [regarding Art 27(2) of Brussels I].

introduces a supplementary rule on the dialogue of courts according to which «upon request by a court seised of the dispute, any other court seised shall without delay inform the former court of the date when it was seised in accordance with Article 32». In addition, if related actions are pending in the courts of different Brussels-Lugano States, Art 30(1)-(2) gives discretionary power to any court other than the court first seised to stay its proceedings or, under certain circumstances to decline jurisdiction to allow the actions to be consolidated with the related action.[362]

On the other hand, Arts 33 and 34 give the discretionary power to the court of the Member State seised to decide whether it stays, continues, or dismisses its proceedings under two conditions.[363] First, its jurisdiction is established on Art 4, 7, 8, or 9, and secondly, proceedings shall be pending before a court of a third state at the time when a court in a Member State is seised of an action. The court of the Member State is, however, obliged to dismiss its proceedings under Art 33(3) regarding same actions «if the proceedings in the court of the third State are concluded and have resulted in a judgment capable of recognition and, where applicable, of enforcement in that Member State.»

Finally, Art 31 establishes a rule that does not deal with same or related aspects of the actions. Instead, it regulates cases when actions come under the exclusive jurisdiction of several courts. Priority also plays a significant role in these cases, except for certain scenarios regulated within Art 31(2)-(4) and arising between courts of Member States in which one of them is designated by an exclusive choice of court agreement as laid down in Art 25 and outlined in *infra* Ch. III.D.VI. In this latter scenario, Brussels Ia gives priority to the chosen court regardless of whether it is first or second seised to decide on its jurisdiction. Accordingly, any other court has to stay proceedings until the chosen court declares either that it has jurisdiction or that it declines it.[364]

---

362 The court second seised must weigh up all relevant factors in assessing whether it is appropriate to stay its proceedings. For possible factors under Art 30(1), see AG in *I. Weber*, 102-111.

363 For factors to be assessed, see Recitals 23-24 and Arts 33-34.

364 See Commission Document COM(2010) 748 final, p 8, para 3.1.3; Recital 22. These rules added to Brussels Ia are unknown in the previous Brussels-Lugano instruments and until their introduction, the ruling laid down in *Gasser*, 54 was accepted, acc. to which Art 21 of the BC «must be interpreted as meaning that a court second seised whose jurisdiction has been claimed under an agreement conferring jurisdiction must nevertheless stay proceedings until the court first seised has declared that it has no jurisdiction.»

3. The principle of party autonomy

The principle of party autonomy, as the third sub-principle of the requirement that disputes should be decided in an appropriate forum, implies that the parties have the right to confer jurisdiction on a court upon which they have agreed of their own free will. As a corollary, that court should be competent to decide the dispute.[365] The existence of the principle of party autonomy is evident from several articles of the Brussels-Lugano Regime, such as Arts 25 and 26 as briefly outlined in *infra* Ch. III.D.VI and VII.

4. The principle of protection of the weaker party

The principle of protection of the weaker party requires that jurisdiction be allocated between the courts of the Member and Contracting States in such a manner that the weaker party in a dispute «is given jurisdictional advantage over the stronger party so as to counterbalance his relative weakness.»[366] Besides Art 4(1), which aims to shield the defendant due to his procedural position,[367] such protective jurisdictional rules are enumerated in Sections 3 to 5 of Chapter II.[368] They lay down special protective provisions in matters relating to insurance and consumer contracts as well as individual contracts of employment,[369] which aim to protect the weaker parties of those contracts, namely, the policyholder, the insured, and the beneficiary of the insurance, the consumer as well as the employee.[370] The more favourable treatment regarding these persons' interests is afforded

---

365 For details, see Kohler, Recueil des Cours 359, pp 367-397; Pontier/Burg, EU Principles, pp 142-159.

366 Pontier/Burg, EU Principles, p 117 and for details, see *ibid.*, pp 117-141.

367 See *infra* Ch. III.C.I.

368 It is worth noting that Art 5(2) of the BC, the 1988 LC and the 2007 LC protect the maintenance creditor as a weaker party. This provision was, however, excluded from Brussels I on 18.6.2011, when Reg. (EC) No 4/2009 (OJ 2009 L 7/1) on maintenance obligations became applicable [see its Arts 68(1) and 76]. Equally, Brussels Ia does not contain any rule on matters relating to maintenance obligations (see Recital 10). For details on the relation between Reg. (EC) No 4/2009 (OJ 2009 L 7/1) and the Brussels-Lugano Regime, see Kropholler/von Hein, EuZPR, pp 75-76, para 103 and pp 189, paras 55a ff.

369 The BC and 1988 LC regulate this kind of contract under Art 5(1).

370 Brussels Ia treats the injured party under the rules of jurisdiction in matters relating to insurance with these weaker parties on an equal footing in Arts 26(2), 31(4), and 45(1)(e).

because they are deemed economically weaker and less experienced in legal matters than their professional co-contractors are.[371] One of the most characteristic protections guaranteed by these rules is that they allow the weaker party to bring proceedings against the stronger party in the court where he is domiciled or habitually resident.[372]

III. Jurisdictional principles as bases for the liberal recognition and enforcement of judgments

As is clear from the previous discussion, the ECJ has applied and developed various principles to ensure the uniform application of the jurisdictional provisions of the Brussels-Lugano Regime. At the same time, those principles operate as bases for the liberal recognition and enforcement judgments. By doing so, they strongly interconnect the rules on jurisdiction, as well as on recognition and enforcement, and guarantee that these two systems of rules complement each other harmoniously to promote the universal principle of strengthening the legal protection of persons established in the Brussels-Lugano States.

Because of the systematised and uniformly interpreted jurisdictional rules, national courts rely on a high degree of 'trust' in each other's administration of justice (i.e., legal system and judicial institutions) by principally accepting the legitimacy and correctness of each other's internal decision-making process.[373] This fosters and simplifies the mechanism of recognition and enforcement of judgments. Accordingly, Art 52, in conjunction with Arts 58(1) first subparagraph and Art 59, requires that the court of the Member State in which the recognition of the judgment is in-

371 Cf. Recital 18; AG in *Kronhofer*, 25 (regarding the holder of an insurance policy or a consumer); *Pammer and Hotel Alpenhof*, 58 (regarding the consumer); *Ivenel*, 9 ff. (employment contract).

372 See Arts 11(1)(b), 13(2), 18(1) as well as Art 5(2) of the BC, the 1988 LC and the 2007 LC. Cf. *infra* fn 396.

373 See Recital 26; *Gasser*, 72; *Turner*, 24; *Trade Agency*, 40; *Eurofood*, 40-42 (in relation to insolvency proceedings); *supra* fn 337. In this regard Kühn Baca, The Principle of Mutual Recognition, p 12 describes the principle of mutual recognition as being «a *"journey into the unknown"* ... where national authorities are in principle obliged to recognize standards emanating from the national system of any Member State on the basis of mutual trust, with a minimum of formality.» (Emphases and fn omitted; italics in the original). Cf. Kohler, in: Mansel, Vergemeinschaftung, pp 44-45.

voked, or in which the enforcement of the judgment, court settlement, or authentic instrument is sought, is not allowed to review the substance of the judgment given in the Member or Contracting State of origin. In addition, by virtue of Art 45(4), jurisdictional reviews are of importance only in relation to special rules exhaustively outlined in detail in Art 45(1)(e).[374] The court examining the grounds of those special rules shall be bound by the findings of fact on which the court of origin established its jurisdiction in accordance with Art 45(2). Finally, the second sentence of Art 45(3) prohibits the application of the test of public policy as referred to in Art 45(1)(a) to the jurisdictional rules. Apart from these prohibitory clauses, the sound and proper application of the above-mentioned principles also reduces the appearance of situations, which leads to the reasons enumerated within points (a)-(e) of Art 45(1) and within Art 46 for refusing the recognition or enforcement of judgments in other Member or Contracting States.[375] Particularly, the principles of legal certainty, and that disputes should be decided in an appropriate forum minimise the delivery of judgments in default of appearance and judgments that are (manifestly) contrary to the public policy or irreconcilable with other judgments.

By simplifying the mechanism of recognition and enforcement of judgments, the principles and the uniform rules of jurisdiction, in turn, strengthen the principle of mutual recognition. This principle, which was originally developed in the context of the internal market freedom, namely, the fundamental freedom of free movement of goods, in the

---

374 The exceptions referred to in Art 45(1)(e) are limited to cases when a weaker party, including the injured party and employee, is the defendant, while the previous Brussels-Lugano instruments, such as Art 35(1) of the 2007 LC, do not expressly specify weaker parties and do not refer to the rules on individual contracts of employment. In addition, Brussels Ia omits a reference to Art 72 contrary to the previous Brussels-Lugano instruments. Furthermore, Jayme/Kohler, IPRax 1989, 337, 341 observe that the interpretation of Art 54B(3) of the 1988 LC [for similar wording, see Art 64(3) of the 2007 LC] might also allow the review of jurisdiction.

375 Briefly, the grounds of refusal as laid down in Art 45 are as follows: the judgment is manifestly (this term is omitted in BC and 1988 LC, however, for the case law of the ECJ, see AG in *Diageo Brands*, 41-42) contrary to the public policy of the Member or Contracting State addressed; it was given in default appearance; under certain circumstances it is irreconcilable with another judgment and it conflicts with Section 6 of Chapter II or Sections 3-5 of Chapter II as noted in *supra* fn 374. For a comprehensive list of possible grounds of refusal, see e.g. Hartley, Recueil des Cours 319, pp 300-312; Layton/Mercer, European Civil Practice, paras 24.011-24.014.

landmark *Cassis de Dijon* judgment,[376] has become a cornerstone principle of the Brussels-Lugano Regime.[377] It underlies and fosters the free movement of judgments,[378] and reinforces the construction of the European Judicial Area.[379] This principle can easily be identified in the recitals and in the preamble of the Brussels-Lugano instruments,[380] in various EU documents,[381] as well as in the primary law of the Union concerning measures adopted in the area of judicial cooperation in civil matters.[382] The central element of this principle is that the judgment given in a Member State should be recognised and enforced in all other Member States without the need for any special procedure or declaration of enforceability prior to the enforcement in the Member State addressed (also known as *exequatur* procedure).[383] Under this system, recognition «must have the result of conferring on judgments the authority and effectiveness accorded to them in the State in which they were given.»[384] This covers, for instance, the *res judicata* effect of the foreign judgment.[385] As Jürgen Basedow notes, this effect «precludes the parties to the foreign litigation from contesting both the facts established in and the legal consequences drawn from a foreign decision – to the extent that such aspects are covered by *res*

376 E.g. Hess, ZVglRWiss 2012, 21, 22-23.

377 For details on this principle, see Kohler, ZSR 2005, 263-299; Jayme/Kohler, IPRax 2001, 501 ff.; Hess, ZVglRWiss 2012, 21-37; Kühn Baca, The Principle of Mutual Recognition, pp 1-34; Weller, Mutual Trust, 2014, 1 ff.

378 See Heidelberg Report, para 543. On free movement of judgments, see also e.g. Pontier/Burg, EU Principles, pp 27-44.

379 On this, see Kohler, IPRax 2003, 401 ff.; Kohler, ZSR 2005, 263 ff.

380 Such as Recital 3 or 26.

381 Such as Tampere Programme (1999); Hague Programme (OJ 2005 C 53/1); Stockholm Programme (OJ 2010 C 115/1); Assises de la Justice: Shaping Justice policies in Europe for the years to come at <http://ec.europa.eu/justice/events/assises-justice-2013/index_en.htm>; Commission Document COM(2014) 144 final.

382 Arts 67(4), 81(1) and 81(2)(a) of the TFEU. Cf. Mansel/Thorn/Wagner, IPRax 2010, 1, 25.

383 See Recitals 26, 27. Note that the previous Brussels-Lugano instruments do not abolish the *exequatur* procedure. For details on this issue, see e.g. Cuniberti/Rueda, RabelsZ 2011, 286 ff.; Nielsen, CML Rev. 2013, 503, 524-528.

384 Jenard Report, p 43. See also *Hoffmann*, 10; *Gothaer*, 34.

385 On this effect, see e.g. BIICL, Recognition, Res Judicata and Abuse of Process; Hobér, Recueil des Cours 366, pp 126 ff.

judicata under the foreign law.»[386] Consequently, a foreign judgment that is recognised pursuant to Art 35 must principally have the same effect in the state in which recognition is sought as it does in the state of origin (the so-called 'principle of extended effect').[387] One of the significant features of the extended effect lies in the fact that national laws attach *res judicata* effect to different parts of the judgment.[388] However, judgments are not treated equally. In other words, under these different national legal practices, there is one exception, which was pointed out by the ECJ in *Gothaer*. The case concerned a judgment of the Belgian court in which it declined jurisdiction over a dispute on the basis that the parties concluded a valid jurisdiction clause in favour of the Icelandic courts. Irrespective of this judgment, one of the parties brought proceedings in the *LG Bremen* (Germany). The third question referred for a preliminary ruling was essentially concerned with the effect of the Belgian judgment on the jurisdiction of the German courts. To answer this question, the ECJ held that the recognition of judgments delivered by courts of the Member States, declining jurisdiction under Brussels I, which are handed down by virtue of the common rules of jurisdiction provided for by EU law, is governed by its own *sui generis* system, as described in paragraphs 39 to 41 of the judgment.[389] According to this *sui generis* system, the concept of *res judicata* under Union law «does not attach only to the operative part of the judgment in question, but also attaches to the *ratio decidendi* of that judgment, which provides the necessary underpinning for the operative part and is inseparable from it».[390] Finally, the ECJ concluded in paragraph 43 of *Gothaer* that «Articles 32 and 33 of Regulation No 44/2001 must be interpreted as meaning that the court before which recognition is sought of a judgment by which a court of another Member State has declined jurisdiction on the basis of a jurisdiction clause is bound by the finding – made in

---

386 Basedow, Recueil des Cours 360, pp 258-259, para 322 (italics in the original). For the effects of the judgment in an enforcement procedure, see *Apostolides*, 66; Bach, EuZW 2013, 56, 57.

387 See *Gothaer*, 34; *Hoffmann*, 11.

388 As is clear from the discussion in Hobér, Recueil des Cours 366, pp 126 ff., the *res judicata* effect varies in national law: some attach such an effect principally to the operative part of the judgment (e.g. Germany; see *ibid.*, p 132), while others attach the effect to the operative part and to certain elements of the reasoning of the decision (e.g. UK; see *ibid.*, p 126). See also Bach, EuZW 2013, 56.

389 *Gothaer*, 42.

390 *Gothaer*, 40 (italics in the original). For comments on this case, see Bach, EuZW 2013, 56 ff.

the grounds of a judgment, which has since become final, declaring the action inadmissible – regarding the validity of that clause.»

C. General jurisdictional provisions

I. Article 4: Actor sequitur forum rei

Art 4(1) lays down the general jurisdictional rule, stating that subject to the Brussels-Lugano Regime, persons domiciled in a Brussels-Lugano State shall be sued in the courts of that state irrespective of their nationality.[391] Art 4(2) reinforces this latter formulation by stating that persons who are not nationals of the Brussels-Lugano State «in which they are domiciled shall be governed by the rules of jurisdiction applicable to nationals of that» Brussels-Lugano State.[392] This so-called *actor sequitur forum rei* doctrine (i.e., the plaintiff follows the court of the defendant) puts great emphasis on the defendant's domicile[393] with the purpose of protecting that person by allowing him to defend himself more easily.[394, 395] As a

391 Note that Act No CX of 2000 (see *supra* fn 257) adjusted the Hungarian general rule of jurisdiction laid down in Art 54 of the *Nmj.* to this rule. This amendment was of great importance, since, as is clear from Mádl/Vékás, The Law of Conflicts, pp 333-334, prior to that act, Art 54 of the *Nmj.* said: «Hungarian courts or other authorities may take jurisdiction over any case in which their jurisdiction is not excluded by this Law-Decree».

392 On this, see also Jenard Report, pp 14-15 (emphases omitted; regarding the BC): «By ruling out the criterion of nationality, the Committee is anxious ... to allow foreign nationals domiciled in the Community, who are established there and who thereby contribute to its economic activity and prosperity, to benefit from the provisions of the Convention.»

393 See also Recital 15. However, this factor is weakened in Recital 15 by its use of the verb «should», since Brussels I employs the verb «must» in its Recital 11.

394 See e.g. *Handte*, 14. Cf. Jenard Report, p 18. In addition, Halpern, Yale J. World Pub. Ord. 1982-1983, 369, 380, by referring to M. McDougal and W. Reisman, adds that behind the concept of the defendant's domicile stands «an amalgam of the reasonable interest of a state in a person habitually within its territory and the assumption that persons in the territory may be assumed to have adopted by implication the norms and values expressed in the local law.» On the other hand, Verheul, FS Judge Erades, p 201 takes a critical view by questioning the rationale behind the defendant's domicile rule: «the forum rei rule cannot be justified by its intrinsic value. In proceedings between parties domiciled in different countries, there is no reason whatsoever to favour the defendant. The plaintiff may be in the right; in roughly 50% of the cases he is. Why should he, rather than the de-

corollary, the location of the plaintiff does not constitute an essential link on which the jurisdictional rules under the Brussels-Lugano Regime stand, irrespective of the fact that it is not uncommon in certain provisions.[396] By establishing a link between the dispute and the forum, the connecting factor of domicile confers international jurisdiction only on the courts of a Brussels-Lugano State. Consequently, it leaves the determination of the venue for the national law of that state.[397]

1. Determination of domicile

The Brussels-Lugano Regime provides rules to determine the concept of domicile for individuals and legal persons irrespective of their procedural position.[398]

The court seised determines an individual's place of domicile in a two-step analysis under Art 62. First, it applies its internal law to determine whether a party is domiciled in the Brussels-Lugano State whose courts

---

fendant, be required to travel abroad?»

395 Note that the concept of the defendant's domicile allocates jurisdiction not only under Art 4(1) but also in other provisions, such as Arts 8(1), 11(1)(a) and 21(1)(a). The jurisdiction of the court could also be established at the defendant's place of domicile implicitly under Arts 25 and 26 (on these articles, see *infra* Ch. III.D.VII and VI).

396 See *Group Josi* in which the claimant incorporated in a non-Contracting State of the BC, namely, in Canada, availed itself of the rules of the BC and sued the defendant domiciled in Belgium. For comments on this case, see Jayme/Kohler, IPRax 2000, 454, 459. See also Switzerland: *Bundesgericht* 18.12.2008, BGE 135 III 185 as referred to in Kohler, in: EFTA Court, Decentred Integration, p 246. Contra: decision of the *Supreme Court of Norway* [Norges Høyesterett, 20.12.2012, HR-2012-2393-A – Rt-2012 – 1951 *(Trico Subsea AS v Raffles Shipping Projects Pte Ltd)*] as commented in Kohler, in: EFTA Court, Decentred Integration, pp 237-249; Fötschl, IPRax 2014, 187-194 (acc. to the majority's opinion, Art 2 of the 2007 LC did not apply in the case in which the plaintiff was domiciled in a non-Contracting State, and the dispute did not link to Norway, except that the defendant was domiciled there). Note that the plaintiff's place of domicile is of jurisdictional importance e.g. in Arts 11(1)(b), 13(2) and 18(1). In addition, the jurisdiction of the court could also be established at the plaintiff's place of domicile implicitly under Arts 7(2), 25, 26 and Art 5(2) of the BC, the 1988 LC and the 2007 LC. Cf. *supra* fn 372.

397 Cf. Recital 13; Pocar Report, para 23; Evrigenis/Kerameus Report, para 40.

398 See Jenard Report, p 16.

are seised of a dispute.[399, 400] If he is not domiciled in the forum state, paragraph 2 calls that court to prove whether the person in question is domiciled in another Brussels-Lugano State in accordance with the internal law of that state. By examining the internal law of the other Brussels-Lugano States, Alexander Layton and Hugh Mercer explain that it is principally not necessary to determine whether the individual has a domicile in each Brussels-Lugano State, and it will normally be sufficient if the individual is domiciled in any one of them.[401] It is worth noting that the Brussels-Lugano Regime remains silent on the moment at which the individual's domicile is to be judged. According to the predominant academic opinion, the crucial time is the time of the initiation of proceedings.[402] A subsequent transfer of domicile to a third state does not affect the jurisdiction of the court seised because the principle of *perpetuatio fori* applies.[403]

Contrary to the determination of the concept of an individual's domicile, the Brussels-Lugano instruments, except for the BC and the 1988 LC, provide for an autonomous interpretation of the term 'domicile' regarding legal persons «so as to make the common rules more transparent and avoid conflicts of jurisdiction.»[404] Thus, Art 63(1) determines three alter-

399 As the Jenard Report, p 17 specifies, the concept of domicile might be defined under the internal law in the civil and civil procedural law. For the present purpose, as it goes on to state, «the latter should obviously be used since the problem is one of jurisdiction.» Note that EP Resolution, P7-TA(2010)0304 (7.9.2010), point 19 proposed an autonomous European definition of domicile of individuals.

400 Note that the UK departed from the concept of domicile as it is traditionally understood there and adopted new definitions for the purposes of the Brussels-Lugano Regime. On this, see Schlosser Report, paras 71-75; Layton/Mercer, European Civil Practice, para 14.003.

401 Layton/Mercer, European Civil Practice, para 30.014.

402 See Vlas, in: Magnus/Mankowski, Brussels I Regulation, p 808, para 4 («moment of instituting the proceedings»); Kropholler/von Hein, EuZPR, p 126, para 15 [action was brought («Einreichung der Klage») within the meaning of Art 30 of Brussels I]. See also *Canada Trust Company v. Stolzenberg and Gamba* [2000] UKHL 51; [2000] 4 All ER 481; [2000] 3 WLR 1376 (12.10.2000) [issue of the writ, regarding Arts 2 and 6(1) of the 1988 LC] and on this decision, see Jayme/Kohler, IPRax 2001, 501, 510; Layton/Mercer, European Civil Practice, para 30.004. For details on this time, see Löser, Zuständigkeitsbestimmender Zeitpunkt, pp 108-121; Gampp, Perpetuatio fori internationalis, pp 132-135.

403 For details on the principle of *perpetuatio fori*, see e.g. Löser, Zuständigkeitsbestimmender Zeitpunkt; Gampp, Perpetuatio fori internationalis.

404 Recital 15. Note that the BC and the 1988 LC refer to the rules of PIL of the court seised (on this, see *supra* Ch. III.B.I.1).

native concepts, which correspond to the criteria laid down in Art 54 of the TFEU.[405] In particular, it localises the legal person's domicile at the place where it has its statutory seat, central administration, or principal place of business.[406] As Trevor C. Hartley points out, the first place refers to the place that is stated in the legal document that established the company (*statut* of the company), namely, where the company's seat is located.[407] In addition, he identifies the place of central administration with the place where the most essential decisions are taken and the last place with the centre of the company's economic activities.[408]

The concept of individuals' domicile must not, however, be confused with the concept of habitual residence.[409] The main differences between these terms can be summed up as follows.[410] The concept of domicile is a legal concept,[411] and it does not form part of the Brussels-Lugano Regime, since as previously mentioned, it is determined under the internal law of the Brussels-Lugano States. Consequently, a request for its interpretation could normally not be referred to the ECJ for a preliminary ruling.[412] By

405 See Commission Document COM(1999) 348 final, p 24. See also Pocar Report, para 31. Cf. Kaye, Law of the European Judgments Convention, pp 1442-1443 (italics in the original) points out that «the French concept itself of domicile being defined as the '*principal* establishment' of a party.»

406 An exception under this rule is laid down in Art 24(2), which refers to the rules of PIL of the state in which the court seised is located in order to determine the seat of the legal person. For the determination of the domicile of trusts, see Art 63(3) and in this regard, see also *supra* Ch. III.B.I.1.

407 For the special meaning of the term 'statutory seat' in Ireland, Cyprus and the UK, see Art 63(2).

408 Hartley, Recueil des Cours 319, pp 77-78.

409 Note that depending on the activity in which individuals may be involved, two main categories of the concept of habitual residence can be determined: where the business [see e.g. Art 23(2) of Rome II] or private-professional activities [see also the distinction in e.g. Recitals 23, 24 of Reg. (EU) No 650/2012 (OJ 2012 L 201/107); Baetge, in: Calliess, Rome Regulations, pp 610-612, paras 18-30] are performed. As is clear from the foregoing discussion, the second aspect constitutes the principal focus of this book.

410 For the comparison of the two concepts, see also Jenard Report, pp 15-18, 25; Mankowski, in: Magnus/Mankowski, Brussels I Regulation, pp 224-225, paras 180-181; Vlas, in: Magnus/Mankowski, Brussels I Regulation, p 808, para 3; Layton/Mercer, European Civil Practice, paras 30.005 ff.

411 See Jenard Report, p 25; AG in *A*, 31.

412 For this latter aspect, see Layton/Mercer, European Civil Practice, para 30.009. However, note that the definition of the term 'domicile' may not impair the effectiveness of EU law (see *supra* Ch. III.B.I.1).

contrast, habitual residence is a factual concept, which encompasses all relevant factual circumstances, such as the length and continuity of the residence, the individual's family and social relationships, the availability of accommodation, employment, and property interests.[413] Furthermore, a common understanding of the widely used concept of habitual residence can be drawn from the *acquis communautaire*.[414] The Borrás Report determines it as «the place where the person had established, on a fixed basis, his permanent or habitual centre of interests, with all the relevant facts being taken into account for the purpose of determining such residence».[415] Viewed in this light, a plausible and conscious definition of the concept is to localise it at the place or in the state with which the person has his closest ties.[416] Therefore, it is understood in the present book as the place where the person's professional and/or personal-familial centre of interests is situated.[417] In Dietmar Baetge's words:

> «So wird der Begriff, in Übereinstimmung mit der Rechtsprechung des Europäischen Gerichtshofs, überall als Mittelpunkt der Lebensinteressen verstanden und anhand tatsächlicher Kriterien persönlicher, familiärer und beruflicher Art bestimmt.»[418]

---

413 See Baetge, in: Basedow *et al.*, Max Planck Encyclopedia, p 814; Baetge, in: Calliess, Rome Regulations, p 611, para 26; Altenkirch, in: Huber, Rome II Regulation, pp 416-417, para 11. For details on this concept, see e.g. Baetge, FS Jan Kropholler, pp 77 ff.; Baetge, in: Basedow *et al.*, Max Planck Encyclopedia, pp 813-815; Baetge, in: Calliess, Rome Regulations, pp 610-612, paras 17-31; Hilbig-Lugani, GPR 2014, 8-16. For children's habitual residence, see also *A*, 30-44; *Barbara Mercredi*, 41 ff. and on this, see Mankowski, GPR 2011, 209-213; Mansel/Thorn/Wagner, IPRax 2012, 1, 20-21.

414 See also similarly Spindler, AfP 2012, 114, 117; Hess, JZ 2012, 189, 192; Baetge, in: Calliess, Rome Regulations, pp 610-611, para 23.

415 Borrás Report, para 32.

416 See also e.g. Vlas, in: Magnus/Mankowski, Brussels I Regulation, p 808, para 3.

417 For reference to the concept as the 'centre of interests' or the 'centre of life', see e.g. case references, such as *di Paolo*, 17 and *Swaddling*, 29 in Altenkirch, in: Huber, Rome II Regulation, p 416, para 11; Baetge, in: Basedow *et al.*, Max Planck Encyclopedia, p 814, point 3; Baetge, in: Calliess, Rome Regulations, p 611, para 25 («factual centre of living»).

418 Baetge, FS Jan Kropholler, p 88. Cf. Hilbig-Lugani, GPR 2014, 8, 15-16 (proposing a transparent and uniform interpretation of the concept of habitual residence).

2. A supplement to domicile: the last known domicile

As has become evident, the concept of domicile is a predominant connecting factor within the Brussels-Lugano Regime, which confers jurisdiction not only under Art 4(1), but also within several special jurisdictional provisions. This automatically raises the question of whether the unified jurisdictional rules, which generally hinge on the defendant's domicile, lose their effectiveness in cases where the domicile of the defendant is unknown, i.e., it is not localisable under Art 62. The ECJ was faced with this question in *Hypoteční banka* in relation to the localisation of the concept of the consumer's domicile under Art 16(2) of Brussels I. The dispute arose between Hypoteční banka, a company governed by Czech law, and Mr Lindner, a German national whose current address was unknown. The Czech company sought to secure payment of a sum of approximately 4.4 million Czech crowns (CZK), corresponding to the arrears on a mortgage loan that it had granted to Mr Lindner.[419] By stretching the determination of the concept of a natural person's domicile, the ECJ ruled that pursuant to Art 16(2) of Brussels I, the courts of the Member State where the consumer had his last known domicile have jurisdiction to hear the dispute, providing that two conditions are fulfilled. The first is that the national court before which proceedings against a consumer are brought, which in the present case was *Okresní soud v Chebu* (district court, Czech Republic), is unable to determine, in accordance with Art 59 of Brussels I, the defendant's domicile. Secondly, the national court has no firm evidence enabling it to conclude that the defendant is, in fact, domiciled outside the EU.[420] Such an approach appeared to the ECJ to be based on the logic of Brussels I and be in keeping with the system established by it.[421] In particular, it held that it is consistent with the principles of legal certainty and foreseeability, strengthens the legal protection of persons established in the EU, promotes the application of uniform rules of the Brussels-Lugano Regime, and ensures a fair balance between the rights of the litigants.[422]

This ruling raises two sensitive issues. First, it remains unclear whether the concept of last known domicile is also applicable to legal persons as consumers. Secondly, it is questionable whether the concept of the defen-

419 *Hypoteční banka*, 2, 20.
420 *Hypoteční banka*, 40-42, 47, 55 first indent.
421 *Hypoteční banka*, 43.
422 *Hypoteční banka*, 44-46.

dant's last known domicile introduced under a protective jurisdictional provision also supplements the concept of domicile employed in rules of jurisdiction other than protective ones. Two objections to the generalisation of this concept could be raised. First, it could be argued that the concept of last known domicile is introduced under the interpretation of Art 16(2) of Brussels I and not under Art 4(1) of Brussels I regarding the general rule of jurisdiction. Secondly, the ECJ was at pains to stress that its introduction was also justified on the basis of the special circumstances of the dispute, namely, that «the defendant was under an obligation to inform the other party to the contract of any change of address occurring after the long-term mortgage loan contract had been signed.»[423] These possible objections, however, do not appeal greatly to the present author. First, the concept of domicile is a universal concept within the Brussels-Lugano Regime, whose meaning, as is clear from the previous section, does not differ on the basis of the legal relationship or on the role of the parties involved. Secondly, as noted above, the ECJ principally justified this newly introduced concept by referring to the logic of Brussels I and to the system established by it.

II. Article 5: Alternative grounds of jurisdiction

Art 5 differs from Art 4 in that, in conjunction with Art 6, it treats the uniformly determined concept of domicile as a condition under which jurisdictional provisions of the Brussels-Lugano Regime in principle apply, rather than as a connecting factor that allocates jurisdiction to a court to hear the dispute.[424] It follows that paragraph 1 exhaustively identifies those jurisdictional rules under which the defendant domiciled in a Brussels-Lugano State may be sued in the courts of another Brussels-Lugano State. These rules encompass a wide-range of jurisdictional provisions. Arts 7-9 within Section 2 cover special jurisdictional grounds, which differ from each other considerably, since they regulate various kinds of subject matter and situations. Arts 10-23 of Sections 3-5 lay down provisions to protect the weaker party of insurance and consumer contracts as well as of individual contracts of employment. Section 6, which consists of only one single article, namely, Art 24, provides rules on exclusive jurisdiction.

---

423 *Hypoteční banka*, 46, 47, 55 first indent.
424 Cf. Recital 8.

Finally, Arts 25-26 within Section 7 regulate rules on the choice of court agreements and the uncontested voluntary submission of the defendant.[425]

Art 5(2) refers to the national, so-called exorbitant,[426] jurisdictional rules,[427] which shall not be applicable to persons domiciled in the Brussels-Lugano Regime.[428] Such an exorbitant rule is found in Hungary in Art 57 of the *Nmj.*[429] This national provision confers jurisdiction on the Hungarian courts if the defendant's assets are located in Hungary. In particular, it states that even if the defendant has no domicile or habitual residence in Hungary, the Hungarian courts have jurisdiction in proceedings concerning property law, providing that the defendant has assets in Hungary that can be declared enforceable. Any claim against the defendant shall be regarded as the defendant's asset situated in Hungary, if the domicile of the person, who owes the claim, is in Hungary or if the claim is secured by a thing located in Hungary.[430]

III. Article 6: (Inter)nationalism v eurocentrism

Art 6 considers situations in which the defendant is not domiciled in a Brussels-Lugano State. In these situations, in accordance with paragraph 1, the jurisdiction of the court of each Brussels-Lugano State shall be de-

---

425 Cf. Layton/Mercer, European Civil Practice, para 14.013. For an outline of certain rules of jurisdiction, see *infra* Ch. III.D.

426 Acc. to Prel. Doc. No 7 of April 1997, para 138 «jurisdiction is exorbitant when the court seised does not possess a sufficient connection with the parties to the case, the circumstances of the case, the cause or subject of the action, or fails to take account of the principle of the proper administration of justice. An exorbitant form of jurisdiction is one which is solely intended to promote political interests, without taking into consideration the interests of the parties to the dispute.» On exorbitant rules of jurisdiction, see also Nuyts Report, paras 74 ff.; de Winter, ICLQ 1968, 706 ff.; Struyven, Jura Falconis 1998-1999, 521-548; Halpern, Yale J. World Pub. Ord. 1982-1983, 369 ff.; Verheul, FS Judge Erades, pp 196-209.

427 For the list of exorbitant rules of jurisdiction, see Notice from Member States (OJ 2015 C 4/2). Cf. Art 3(2) of the BC and the 1988 LC; Annex I of the 2007 LC.

428 Except for Arts 7(3), 25, 26 and 35 (see Layton/Mercer, European Civil Practice, para 14.014) under which the applicant may rely on the exorbitant bases of jurisdiction.

429 Note that the list published to Brussels Ia [Notice from Member States (OJ 2015 C 4/2)] refers to Art 57(a) of the *Nmj.* However, that provision has no point (a).

430 See also Csehi, Residual Jurisdiction in Hungary, p 19.

termined by the law of that state.[431] When claiming against such defendants, Art 6(2) enables the plaintiffs to invoke the jurisdictional rules, including the above-mentioned exorbitant bases of jurisdiction, in the same way as nationals of that state can. However, plaintiffs, whatever their nationality, may invoke only the national rules of the state in which they are domiciled.[432]

Certain bases of jurisdiction are also applicable irrespective of the defendant's domicile.[433] Such rules, which are expressly provided under paragraph 1, are the exclusive rules of jurisdiction (Art 24), the rule on choice of court agreements (Art 25),[434] the rules on disputes relating to consumer contracts in which the consumers are the plaintiffs [Art 18(1)], and the rule on individual contracts of employment in which the employees are the plaintiffs [Art 21(2)].[435, 436] Moreover, several provisions are

---

431 For residual jurisdictional rules of the Member States, see Nuyts Report and national reports, available at <http://ec.europa.eu/justice/civil/document/index_en.htm>.

432 See also Layton/Mercer, European Civil Practice, para 14.022.

433 See Recital 14. Note that there was a wide academic discourse on the extension of the scope of application of many or all of the provisions of Brussels I into the international legal order, such as (1) GEDIP, in particular the proposal prepared at their session in Bergen in September 2008, see GEDIP Document available at <http://www.gedip-egpil.eu/gedip_documents.html> and in Fallon/Kinsch/Kohler, Le droit international privé, pp 701 ff.; on this, see also Kohler, IPRax 2009, 285-287; (2) Heidelberg Report, para 875; (3) Commission Document COM(2009) 174 final, pp 4-5, point 3.2 and Commission Document COM_SEC(2010) 1547, pp 19-27, point 2.2. Note that the EP regarded the proposal of the COM premature [Zwiefka Draft Report (28.6.2011), p 47, point 2]. However, see e.g. Recital 7 and Art 71b(2)-(3) of Reg. (EU) No 542/2014 (OJ 2014 L 163/1) regarding the rules to be applied with respect to the Unified Patent Court and the Benelux Court of Justice.

434 This provision is novel since the previous Brussels-Lugano instruments require that one or more of the parties shall be domiciled in a Brussels-Lugano State [e.g. Art 23(1) of the 2007 LC]. However, those previous instruments regulate, for instance within Art 23(3) of the 2007 LC, situations in which the parties not domiciled in any Brussels-Lugano States agree upon the jurisdiction of such a state (so-called 'prorogation from outside', see Magnus, Art 23, in: Magnus/Mankowski, Brussels I Regulation, p 464, para 53). For details on Art 23(3) of Brussels I, see Magnus, Art 23, in: Magnus/Mankowski, Brussels I Regulation, pp 463, paras 53 ff.; Kohler, IPRax 1986, 340-345 [regarding Art 17(3) of the BC].

435 The last two provisions are introduced in Brussels Ia (see also Recital 14), while the previous Brussels-Lugano instruments do not refer to them expressly.

436 Others, which are not expressly listed therein but which are supposedly also ap-

applicable in cases when the legal person defendant, namely, the insurer, or the stronger party of the consumer contract or the employer, is not domiciled in a Brussels-Lugano State but has a branch, agency, or other establishment in one of those states and the dispute arises out of the operations of the branch, agency, or establishment.[437] In these cases, Arts 11(2), 17(2) and 20(2) establish that the defendant shall be deemed to be domiciled in that state. In addition, the operation of the Brussels-Lugano Regime on the international legal order has been the subject of various judgments of the ECJ. In *Owusu*, for instance, the ECJ stressed that the general jurisdictional rule under Art 2 of the BC is (also) applicable in disputes even if «the proceedings have no connecting factors to any other Contracting State».[438]

Admittedly, it is clear that the determination of the expression «the defendant is not domiciled» within Art 6(1) is a matter of great importance. The interpretation of that expression was dealt with in *de Visser*. The dispute forming the subject matter of the request for a preliminary ruling in this case found its origin in a violation of the plaintiff's personality rights by means of content placed online. Particularly, Ms G brought an action against Mr de Visser, who was probably an EU citizen[439] and whose whereabouts were unknown, for liability arising from the uploading to a website of photographs in which she appeared partly naked.[440] By its fourth question referred to the ECJ for a preliminary ruling, *LG Regensburg* (Germany) essentially asked whether Art 4(1) of Brussels I «is to be interpreted as precluding the application of Article 5(3) of that regulation to an action for liability arising from the operation of an internet site brought against a defendant who is probably a European Union citizen but whose whereabouts are unknown.»[441] The ECJ ruled that in circumstances such as those in this dispute, Art 4(1) of Brussels I, and thus, the expres-

---

plicable irrespective of the defendant's domicile, encompass the rules on *lis pendens* (Art 27 of Brussels I) and uncontested voluntary submission (Art 24 of Brussels I). On this, see Commission Document COM(2003) 427 final, p 10. However, for views expressed on this in legal writing, see *supra* fn 358 and *infra* fn 507. Contra: Jenard Report, p 38, which stresses that under Art 18 of the BC (now Art 26) the defendant must be domiciled in a Contracting State.

437 On the meaning of these entities, see *infra* Ch. III.D.IV.

438 *Owusu*, summary of the judgment. Cf. decisions of the ECJ and various national courts in *supra* fn 396.

439 *De Visser*, 37, 39, 40 and 42.

440 *De Visser*, 2.

441 *De Visser*, 37.

sion 'the defendant is not domiciled', «does not preclude the application of Article 5(3) of that regulation to an action for liability arising from the operation of an internet site against a defendant who is probably a European Union citizen but whose whereabouts are unknown if the court seised of the case does not have firm evidence to support the conclusion that the defendant is in fact domiciled outside the European Union.»[442] It follows from this finding that the expression 'the defendant is not domiciled' within Art 6(1) thus became a grey zone, which is conditional upon the interpretation of the term 'firm evidence'.[443]

D. The arsenal of jurisdictional bases for violations of personality rights

The present section aims to describe, without going too much into detail, the arsenal of the most important jurisdictional bases of the Brussels-Lugano Regime, which enable the person who claims that his personality rights are (threatened to be) violated online to bring an action for establishing the non-contractual liability of the alleged publisher. The description is given in a reverse hierarchical order; it starts with the general head of jurisdiction, continues through the special jurisdictional grounds, and ends with the rules on the prorogation of jurisdiction.

I. Article 4(1): Defendant's domicile

As becomes evident from *supra* Ch. III.C.I, the victim can always avail himself of Art 4(1) and, accordingly, bring his entire claim in the court of the Brussels-Lugano State where the defendant is domiciled.

---

442 *De Visser*, 42. The present author is undecided whether the continuous reference to the finding that the defendant 'is probably a EU citizen' (for mentioning the growing importance of EU citizenship, see e.g. Kohler, FS Europa-Institut, p 312) is accidental or bears considerable importance for the interpretation of the expression 'the defendant is not domiciled' within Art 6(1).

443 Contra: Jenard Report, p 13 notes that «a very clear distinction can be drawn between litigants who are domiciled within the Community and those who are not».

II. Article 7(2): Jurisdiction in tort

Various attributions of the personality can be protected through different rights, such as trade mark and copyright, and their violations can be committed by more than one person. This automatically poses the question of how these violations could be localised. The Brussels-Lugano Regime lays down a special rule of jurisdiction in tort under Art 7(2). Since this provision is considered at greater length in *infra* Ch. IV, it is sufficient to note here that it confers jurisdiction on a particular court of the Brussels-Lugano State(s)[444] in which the harmful event, namely, either the event giving rise to the damage or the damage, occurred or may occur. The present subsection aims to outline how these two approaches are applied in the settled case law of the ECJ to violations of trade marks and copyright as well as to infringements allegedly performed by more than one person.[445]

1. Violation of trade marks

If a person's name or likeness is protected as a trade mark,[446] and he is the proprietor of that trade mark, he could sue the perpetrator who places online and uses the registered name or likeness without the proprietor's consent by analogy with *Wintersteiger*.[447] The dispute in this case concerned the application of Wintersteiger, a company established in Austria, to prevent Products 4U, a company established in Germany, from using

---

444 See chapeau of Art 7; AG in *Melzer*, 34; AG in *Pinckney*, 67; Pocar Report, para 34. See also Jenard Report, p 22. However, the local court has to have subject matter jurisdiction under the national procedural law (see also AG in *Melzer*, 34). Cf. *supra* fn 305.

445 Note that business reputation, which does not fall within the scope of the present book, could also be protected through competition law rules. Thus, jurisdiction over unfair competition could be determined in accordance with Art 7(2). On the application of these approaches to competition law issues, see *Coty Germany*; AG in *CDC*. Cf. *infra* fn 753.

446 See e.g. Beverley-Smith/Ohly/Lucas-Schloetter, Privacy, Property and Personality, pp 121 ff. (regarding German law).

447 However, it must be added that violations of trade marks are principally associated with material damage, while the present book focuses on the non-commercial violation of the personality and on non-material damage (see note on the usage and style guidelines of this book).

the Austrian trade mark 'Wintersteiger' as a keyword on the website of a paid referencing service provider.[448] The ECJ held in respect of the interpretation of Art 5(3) of Brussels I that the trade mark proprietor can bring proceedings before the courts of the Member State in which the trade mark is registered. «Those courts have the power to determine all the damage allegedly caused to the proprietor of the protected right because of an infringement of it and to hear an application seeking cessation of all infringements of that right.»[449] Alternatively, the place of the causal event that gives rise to an alleged violation of a national trade mark was localised at the place of establishment of the tortfeasor, since that is the place where the activation of the display process of the allegedly injurious advertisement was decided.[450]

2. Violation of copyright

In certain situations, violations of personality rights and copyrights may arise from the alleged perpetrator's same act or omission. To take an example, suppose that person 'A' took photographs of himself (so-called selfies). Admittedly, those records consist of his image and/or personal environment, and therefore, they can be protected by his personality rights, such as the right to use that image. In addition, since the holder of the personality rights took the photographs, he is also the copyright owner of those materials. Yet suppose that he uploads them onto an online platform, such as Facebook or Flickr, and allows only a limited number of people to view them.[451] However, a hacker, or even one of his acquaintances who has justified access to those contents, then reproduces those records and makes them available to the public or to a limited number of other people either in a printed form or on a digital platform without the consent of the personality rights and copyright holder.[452] Since the ECJ has repeatedly

448 *Wintersteiger*, 2.

449 *Wintersteiger*, 28.

450 *Wintersteiger*, 34, 37.

451 Cf. privacy settings in *supra* fn 187.

452 Cf. Case 158 C 28716/11 (15.6.2012), *AG München* (ZUM 2013, 159). In this case, the court was confronted with a dispute in which the plaintiff posted among her Facebook-friends certain photographs of her and her husband – at that time he was her partner. Allegedly, one of her acquaintances who had access to these photographs passed them to a daily newspaper, which published them. For com-

upheld the difference between the features of intellectual property rights, including copyright, and personality rights in the sense that the former rights are subject to the principle of territoriality,[453] a violation of copyright claim might be another basis for suing the alleged tortfeasor who supposedly misused one's images or other personal records.[454]

The localisation of violations of copyright under Art 5(3) of Brussels I was dealt with in *Hejduk* in which the dispute arose between Ms Hejduk, domiciled in Vienna (Austria), and EnergieAgentur.NRW GmbH (hereinafter EnergieAgentur), which had its seat in Düsseldorf (Germany).[455] The plaintiff, Ms Hejduk, claimed that EnergieAgentur made her photographs available on its website for viewing and downloading without her consent and without providing a statement of authorship. Consequently, she brought an action before the *Handelsgericht Wien* (Austria) for damages and for authorisation to publish the judgment at the expense of the defendant.[456] The ECJ localised the causal event, by the analogous application of the above-outlined *Wintersteiger* case, at the place where EnergieAgentur had its seat, «since that is where the company took and carried out the decision to place photographs online on a particular website.»[457] For the determination of the jurisdictionally relevant place of where damage occurred, the ECJ referred to the territorially limited protection afforded by

ments on this case, see Geuer, jurisPR-ITR 2013.

453 See e.g. *Hejduk*, 22, 36; *Pinckney*, 31 ff.

454 However, note that copyright encompasses the author's economic and moral rights. While the violation of the first kind of rights results in material damage, the infringement of the latter category (also known as the author's personality rights, Urheberpersönlichkeitsrechte), which is reminiscent of personality rights (in this regard, see also Bogdan, Masaryk U. J.L. & Tech. 2013, 193, 200), causes non-material harm to the author. As is clear from the foregoing discussion, the present book focuses on the second kind of harm.

455 See also similar cases, such as *Pinckney* [regarding an online violation of the author's economic rights (note that the English language version of para 39 of the judgment refers solely to copyrights, while the German and the French versions refer to the author's economic rights: 'droits patrimoniaux d'un auteur', 'Urhebervermögensrechte')]; *Hi Hotel* (regarding paper-based publication of photographs).

456 *Hejduk*, 2, 10-12.

457 *Hejduk*, 25. See also *ibid.*, 24. It appears from the wording of the judgment that it broadened the scope of jurisdictionally relevant events by referring not only to the place where the decision is taken (cf. *Wintersteiger* and on this, see *supra* Ch. III.D.II.1) but also where the decision is carried out.

each Member State of copyright and rights related to copyright,[458] and to the jurisdictional principle of sound administration of justice. Then, it essentially concluded that the court in the forum state can rule on the damage that has occurred in the territory where it sits, providing that the rights are protected and the content is accessible in that state.[459]

3. Co-perpetrators

Several recent judgments of the ECJ[460] have dealt with the question of whether Art 5(3) of Brussels I is to be interpreted as meaning that where there are several alleged perpetrators of damage supposedly caused to certain rights protected in the Member State of the court seised, that special rule of jurisdiction allows jurisdiction to be established in respect of one of those perpetrators. In short, it is questionable whether jurisdiction can be established on the basis of a harmful event attributed to one of the alleged perpetrators over another alleged perpetrator. Mindful of the fact that the concept of harmful event encompasses two elements, namely, the event giving rise to damage and the damage, it is convenient to consider the question of attribution of these elements separately.

Regarding the attribution of the causal event, the ECJ held that «in circumstances in which one only of several supposed perpetrators of alleged damage is sued in a court within whose jurisdiction he has not acted, it cannot be considered that the causal event occurred within the jurisdiction of that court for the purposes of Article 5(3) of Regulation No 44/2001».[461] Accordingly, Art 5(3) of Brussels I does not allow jurisdiction to be established on the basis of the location of the causal event re-

458 Note that the question referred for a preliminary ruling [see *Hejduk*, 14; Order *Hejduk* 10 Cg 180/11t (3.7.2013), *Handelsgericht Wien* (Vienna Commercial Court, Austria) (GRUR Int. 2013, 1171-1172)] concerned «infringement of rights related to copyright» («Verletzung urheberrechtlicher Leistungsschutzrechte»), while due to e.g. AG in *Hejduk*, 1, 3, 21 (in German) the dispute concerned solely violation of the author's economic rights and not her moral rights. The third view on the substance of the case is held by the ECJ, since it dealt with copyright and rights related to copyright (see e.g. *Hejduk*, 38).

459 *Hejduk*, 34, 38. See also *Pinckney*, especially 43 ff.; *Hi Hotel*, 34 ff.

460 See *Melzer*, 19 (damages regarding trading in stock market futures); *Pinckney*, 22; *Hi Hotel*, 23; *Coty Germany*, 39 (Community trade mark, unfair competition). Cf. *DFDS Torline* as noted in *infra* Ch. IV.B.I.1.e).

461 *Hi Hotel*, 31. See also *Melzer*, 40; *Coty Germany*, 50.

garding one of the alleged perpetrators of the damage who has not acted within the jurisdiction where the court is seised.[462]

As far as the second element of the concept of harmful event, namely, the damage, is concerned, it appears from the settled case law that the ECJ has continuously upheld the possibility of attributing the effect of the act subsequently performed by one of the supposed perpetrators with regard to another supposed perpetrator.[463] In particular, in accordance with *Pinckney*,[464] as Martin Husovec explains, «an Austrian company that neither acts nor causes any effect through its own acts in France can be still sued in France, only because some unrelated (?) second company from the UK furthered its infringement by making the e-commerce website with infringing goods accessible there.»[465] Thus, in his opinion, the ruling suggests that a court could decide upon a territorially restricted claim against a defendant that is not domiciled and that did not act or directly cause an effect by its act in the forum state by virtue of the effect, which was subsequently caused by someone else, whose website was merely accessible in the forum state.[466]

Two conclusions *vis-à-vis* violations of personality rights allegedly committed by several perpetrators can be summed up based on the preceding discussion. First, the holder of the personality rights is not allowed to bring proceedings against one of the supposed perpetrators in accordance with the concept of causal event before a court of the Brussels-Lugano State where the perpetrator did not act. Secondly, and by contrast, the holder of the personality rights who considers that his rights have been violated is entitled to sue one of the supposed perpetrators at the place where the damage occurred even if (1) the alleged perpetrator is established and acted in another Brussels-Lugano State and (2) his act caused damage within the jurisdiction of the court seised only through the subsequent act of another perpetrator.[467]

---

462 *Hi Hotel*, 32. See also *Melzer*, 41; *Coty Germany*, 51.

463 Regarding the attribution of effect test, see e.g. Husovec, IIC 2014, 370-374 (comments on *Pinckney*); von Hein, EuZW 2014, 664, 667-668 (comments on *Coty Germany*).

464 For similar cases, see *Hi Hotel* and *Coty Germany*.

465 Husovec, IIC 2014, 370, 371.

466 Husovec, IIC 2014, 370, 371.

467 Mindful of *Pinckney*, connection between the defendant's act and the subsequent act(s) of the other alleged perpetrator(s) is not necessarily required. The ECJ, specifically, in *Pinckney*, 16 noted (italics in square brackets added): «It does not appear from the summary of the facts in the main proceedings that Mediatech

III. Article 7(3): Criminal offence

As becomes evident from *supra* Ch. III.B.I.2, Art 7(3) enables the holder of the personality rights, who considers that his personality rights have been infringed, to bring «a civil claim for damages or restitution which is based on an act giving rise to criminal proceedings, in the court seised of those proceedings, to the extent that that court has jurisdiction under its own law to entertain civil proceedings».[468] Irrespective of the full effect given to those national rules and without prejudice to any more favourable national provisions, Art 64 sets forth a minimum procedural standard for the protection of the rights of the defence of the defendant domiciled in a Member State and being prosecuted in another Member State of which he is not a national. This minimum standard is guaranteed in cases when the defendant is accused in criminal proceedings of an offence that was not intentionally committed.[469] In addition, as the Pocar Report explains, the ECJ extended the application of this provision to intentional offences.[470]

In Hungary, Chapter XXI of *Act No C of 2012 on the Criminal Code (2012. évi C. törvény a Büntető Törvénykönyvről, Btk.)* is dedicated to crimes against human dignity and several fundamental rights. Thus, it lays down *inter alia* rules on crimes against personal secrets (Art 223) and against letters of correspondence (Art 224) as well as on defamation (Art 226).[471] The rules on entertainment of the civil claim ('polgári jogi igény') based on one such crime are laid down in *Act No XIX of 1998 on the Code*

[the defendant who first acted] organised the distribution of the CDs by those companies *[alleged co-perpetrators who subsequently acted and presumably directly caused the damage]* or that it had any connection with them whatsoever.» See also AG in *Pinckney*, 19, 36.

468 See also Jenard Report, pp 9, 26. On this provision, see also Kohler, in: Will, Schadensersatz, pp 74 ff. For a comparative overview of such civil claims in the Member States, see European Judicial Network in civil and commercial matters <http://ec.europa.eu/civiljustice/comp_crime_victim/comp_crime_victim_ec_en.htm>.

469 See also Jenard Report, pp 9, 63. On the interpretation of the expression 'offence which is not intentionally committed', see *Rinkau*, 15-16; Layton/Mercer, European Civil Practice, para 15.100.

470 Pocar Report, para 66 by referring to *Krombach*, 44, 45.

471 Cf. Mainstrat Study, pp 42-44, which outlines the criminal protection of personality rights in the Member States. Cf. *supra* fn 84.

of Criminal Procedure (1998. évi XIX. törvény a büntetőeljárásról, Be.)[472] supplemented by the *Pp.*[473]

IV. Article 7(5): Operation of a secondary establishment

If the media outlet domiciled in a Brussels-Lugano State has a branch, agency, or other establishment (hereinafter secondary establishment) in another such state, the person who considers that his personality rights have been violated could bring proceedings in the courts of the place in which this branch is situated under Art 7(5).[474] However, the ECJ has identified conditions that must be met.[475] The first condition concerns the definition of the term 'secondary establishment', which must imply «a centre of operations which has the appearance of permanency, such as the extension of a parent body. It must have a management and be materially equipped to negotiate business with third parties, so that they do not have to deal directly with the parent body».[476] Secondly, the dispute must arise out of the operation of this secondary establishment. This concept comprises *inter alia* actions concerning torts arising from the activities in which the secondary establishment has engaged on behalf of the parent body, if those activities are performed in the state in which the secondary establishment is established.[477] As regards the first condition, the foreign

472 Such as Art 54, 335 or 379 of the *Be*.

473 For further details, see Csehi, Residual Jurisdiction in Hungary, pp 13-14; Kengyel/Harsági, Európai Polgári Eljárásjog, pp 84-85, paras 114-117.

474 See also Kubis, Internationale Zuständigkeit, pp 178-180.

475 For details on this special rule of jurisdiction, see e.g. Mankowski, in: Magnus/Mankowski, Brussels I Regulation, pp 277-287, paras 270-301; Layton/Mercer, European Civil Practice, paras 15.101-15.113.

476 *Mahamdia*, 48. See also *Somafer*, 12 and for comment on this case, see Jayme/Kohler, IPRax 1995, 343, 348-349. Regarding the position of virtual branch, see e.g. Mankowski, in: Magnus/Mankowski, Brussels I Regulation, p 279, para 275.

477 *Somafer*, 13; *Mahamdia*, 48. Note that in 1995 in *Lloyd's Register*, 22, in a contractual context, the ECJ held that if the contract was concluded by the secondary establishment in the name of its parent body, it did not have to be performed in the Contracting State of the BC in which the secondary establishment is established {cf. UK/England: *Anton Durbeck v. Den Norske Bank* [2003] 2 WLR 1296 (CA) and for comment on this case, see Pulkowski, IPRax 2004, 543-546}. However, as *Mahamdia* delivered in 2012 shows, the ECJ returned to the position held in *Somafer* and required that the obligation in question be performed in the state in which the secondary establishment is established.

correspondent office of the media outlet may be equipped with a centre of operations, which has the appearance of permanency and contributes to the identification and representation of the state in which its parent company is established.[478] In short, it can be regarded as a secondary establishment in accordance with the meaning of Art 7(5).[479] As regards the second condition, it should be recalled that the purpose of establishing a foreign correspondent office is to represent its parent company and to collect information to be published. Accordingly, it normally collects information and sends it to the parent company, which decides on the relevance, newsworthiness, sensational nature, and publication of the information. However, it could also be possible that the foreign correspondent office takes the decision on those matters in the name of the media outlet.[480] In these latter situations, the second condition might also be met and thus Art 7(5) might be applied.

V. Article 8(1): More than one defendant

While *supra* Ch. III.D.II.3 concerned the interpretation of Art 7(2) and the attribution of the elements of liability to one of the supposed co-perpetrators, Art 8(1) facilitates the principle that the entire dispute should be decided before a single forum.[481] In particular, by the operation of this provision, a person domiciled in a Brussels-Lugano State may also be sued where «he is one of a number of defendants, in the courts for the place where any one of them is domiciled».[482] Its application is, however, subject to the condition that «the claims are so closely connected that it is expedient to hear and determine them together to avoid the risk of irreconcilable judgments resulting from separate proceedings».[483] As is clear

478 See, by analogy, *Mahamdia*, 50.

479 On this, see also Kubis, Internationale Zuständigkeit, p 179.

480 See also Kubis, Internationale Zuständigkeit, p 180.

481 On this, see also *supra* Ch. III.B.II.2.

482 Cf. *Land Berlin*, 56 in which the ECJ rejected the application of Art 6(1) of Brussels I to persons not domiciled in another Member State «in the case where they are sued in proceedings brought against several defendants, some of whom are also persons domiciled in the European Union.»

483 Art 8(1), second subsentence. Note that although the wording of the BC and the 1988 LC does not include this requirement (on this, see also *Roche*, 21), the Jenard Report, p 26 and the settled case law of the ECJ (*Kalfelis*, 12; *Réunion européenne*, 48; *Roche*, 20-21) referred to this requirement. This requirement has

from the settled case law of the ECJ, the risk of irreconcilable decisions generally exists if there is a divergence in the outcome of the dispute and if that divergence occurs in connection with the same situation of fact and law.[484] As a result, the condition of close connection covers two requirements, namely that the anchor and the other claim arise in the context of a single factual and legal situation, which must be present at the time «when the proceedings are instituted».[485, 486]

The first requirement regarding the same factual situation requires that the defendants can foresee that they may be sued in the Brussels-Lugano State where at least one of them is domiciled.[487] As AG Trstenjak pointed out in *Painer*, this requirement is not met in the case of unconcerted parallel conduct, specifically, «where the facts on which the applicant bases its anchor claim and the other claim are such that the conduct of the anchor defendant and of the other defendant concerns the same or similar legal interests of the applicant and is similar in nature, but occurs independently and without knowledge of one another.»[488] Similarly, the ECJ appeared in *Painer* to attribute importance to the connectedness of conducts, since it held that the fact that the defendants «did or did not act independently may be relevant».[489]

The second requirement is the existence of the same legal situation that has been interpreted in several decisions. *Painer* is perhaps the most relevant case in relation to disputes concerning violations of personality rights. In this case, the dispute arose between a freelance photographer,

---

its origin in Art 30(3) (see also *Kalfelis*, 11; *Roche*, 22; Pocar Report, para 69). However, Arts 8(1) and 30(3) differ from each other in several aspects, as is noted in *infra* Ch. V.C.II.7.b).

484 See *Painer*, 79; *Land Berlin*, 43.

485 *Kalfelis*, 12.

486 For an analysis of the decisions of the ECJ delivered on the interpretation of these conditions, see Torremans, I.P.Q. 2014, 1-12.

487 See AG in *Painer*, 91. See also *Painer*, 81 (in relation to the requirement on the legal basis).

488 AG in *Painer*, 92.

489 *Painer*, 83. Cf. likely same factual situation, e.g. *Solvay*, 27, 30, 29 (29: the defendants, Honeywell companies, are each separately accused of committing the same violations regarding the same products and such violations were committed in the same Member States, so that they have an adverse impact on the same national parts of the European patent); *Land Berlin*, 45. There is no same factual situation, for example, as described in *Solvay*, 25, when «the defendants are different and the infringements they are accused of, committed in different Contracting States, are not the same».

Ms Painer, and one Austrian and four German publishers. The Austrian and one of the German publishers published their materials only in the home market, while the materials of the other three German publishers were also published in both German and Austrian territory. In addition, one of those latter German publishers operated a website. The dispute concerned *inter alia* payment of appropriate remuneration and damages for the plaintiff's loss, which arose because of an alleged infringement of her copyright under the Austrian and German law.[490] One of the questions referred by the *Handelsgericht Wien* was, in essence, whether Art 6(1) of Brussels I «must be interpreted as precluding its application if actions against several defendants for substantially identical copyright infringements are brought on national legal grounds which vary according to the Member States concerned.»[491] The ECJ held that the identical legal basis of the actions is not an indispensable condition for the application of Art 8(1).[492] Accordingly, it went on to say that a difference in the legal basis between the actions brought against the different defendants does not, in itself, preclude the application of this rule, «provided however that it was foreseeable by the defendants that they might be sued in the Member State where at least one of them is domiciled».[493] This finding is even stronger in cases, like the present case, in which the national laws on which the claims are based are substantially identical.[494] Accordingly, the ECJ concluded that the provision in question

> «must be interpreted as not precluding its application solely because actions against several defendants for substantially identical copyright infringements are brought on national legal grounds which vary according to the Member States concerned. It is for the referring court to assess, in the light of all the elements of

---

490 On the factual background, see *Painer*, 27 ff.

491 *Painer*, 72.

492 *Painer*, 80. See also *Land Berlin*, 44.

493 *Painer*, 81. See also AG in *Painer*, 80 stating that «even in a field which is not fully harmonised, certain minimum requirements may nevertheless have been harmonised. Even with actions to which different national laws are applicable, such a case may ultimately be governed by the same law in substance, the common requirements of Union law.» See also *Land Berlin*, 45 ff. and especially 47, which says (emphases omitted): «identical nature exists even though the legal basis relied on in support of the claim against the eleventh defendant ... is different from that on which the action brought against the first 10 defendants is based. As the Advocate General stated, in point 99 of her Opinion, all of the claims relied on in the various actions ... are directed at the same interest, namely the repayment of the erroneously transferred surplus amount.»

494 See *Painer*, 82. See also AG in *Land Berlin*, 96.

the case, whether there is a risk of irreconcilable judgments if those actions were determined separately.»[495]

By analogy, it means that Art 8(1) does not preclude its application solely because claims against several defendants for substantially identical violations of personality rights are brought on national legal grounds, which vary according to the Member and EFTA States concerned but which are harmonised to a certain extent on the basis of the ECHR.[496] It is for the referring court to assess, in the light of all the elements of the case, whether there would be a risk of irreconcilable judgments if those claims were determined separately.

VI. Article 25: Choice of court agreements

In disputes which have arisen or which may arise in relation to a particular legal relationship, choice of court agreements, in general, have two simultaneous effects. By determining the jurisdiction of the chosen courts («prorogation effect»), the jurisdiction of the otherwise competent courts is removed («derogation effect»).[497] Accordingly, pursuant to Art 25, the personality right holder and the person who has allegedly infringed or might infringe in the future the right holder's personality right may conclude a choice of court agreement to designate the court or the courts of a particular Brussels-Lugano State to hear their dispute on the infringement of personality rights. The parties of the contract may concur upon such an agreement irrespective of their domicile.[498] Such an agreement, which might be rare but which is theoretically possible in respect of violations of

---

495 *Painer*, 84.

496 See *supra* Intr. to Ch. I.

497 See Magnus, Art 23, in: Magnus/Mankowski, Brussels I Regulation, p 455, para 28. See also Kohler, IPRax 1983, 265, 266 who treats these effects as negative and positive impacts of the choice of court agreements. For details on choice of court agreements, see Kohler, Recueil des Cours 359, pp 367-397; Magnus, Art 23, in: Magnus/Mankowski, Brussels I Regulation, pp 436-514, paras 1-175; Layton/Mercer, European Civil Practice, paras 20.001-20.115. Note that Art 25 introduces some new provisions that, although unknown in the previous Brussels-Lugano instruments, are largely in accordance with the provisions of the Hague Convention on Choice of Court Agreements (2005) (on this, see *supra* Ch. III.A.IV.2), such as the rule on substantive validity (on this, see Nielsen, CML Rev. 2013, 503, 522).

498 Art 25(1). On this, see also *supra* fn 434.

personality rights,[499] «is based on a recognition of the independent will of the parties to a contract in deciding which courts are to have jurisdiction to settle the disputes».[500] The jurisdiction of the court conferred by the agreement shall be exclusive, unless the parties have agreed otherwise.[501] If there is a contract (main contract) between the parties, the forum-selection clause can be concluded separately from that main contract or it may also form part of that contract. In the latter case, the doctrine of separability applies according to which, as Peter Arnt Nielsen notes, the forum-selection clause shall be treated as an agreement independent of the other terms of the contract whose validity cannot be contested except on the basis that the contract is not valid according to the first indent of Art 25(5).[502] Art 25(1) itself imposes uniform requirements for the formal validity of the agreement in order to guarantee, according to the ECJ, the «legal certainty and that the parties have given their consent.»[503] On the other hand, its substantive validity, that is, whether it is null and void, should be determined under the law of the Member State of the court or courts designated by the agreement, including the conflict of law rules of that state.[504] In this way, Brussels Ia «introduces a harmonised conflict of law rule on the substantive validity of choice of court agreements, thus ensuring a similar outcome on this matter whatever the court seised.»[505]

---

499 To take an example, suppose that a photographer took photographs of person 'A' and for this purpose, he concludes a contract with that person, which also consists of a choice of court agreement in cases when those photographs are published by the photographer without the consent of person 'A'.

500 *Coreck Maritime*, 14 (regarding Art 17 of the BC). Cf. *supra* Ch. III.B.II.3 (party autonomy).

501 Art 25(1). Acc. to the wording of Art 17(1) of the BC and the 1988 LC, choice of court agreement confers solely exclusive jurisdiction.

502 See Nielsen, CML Rev. 2013, 503, 523. This provision is unknown in the wording of the previous Brussels-Lugano instruments.

503 *Elefanten Schuh*, 25. Cf. Request for a preliminary ruling in *El Majdoub* regarding Art 23(2) of Brussels I (communication by electronic means – click wrapping).

504 See Recital 20. The previous Brussels-Lugano instruments do not express this condition but as Layton/Mercer, European Civil Practice, para 20.038 notice, it is deemed as a preferable solution among academics. As the Heidelberg Report, para 377 observes, the legal practice of the Member States under Brussels I differs from each other, since they either refer to the *lex fori* or to the *lex cause*. See also Nielsen, CML Rev. 2013, 503, 523.

505 Commission Document COM(2010) 748 final, p 9, point 3.1.3. This might be so because, as Nielsen, CML Rev. 2013, 503, 523 observes, neither Rome I nor the Rome Convention on the law applicable to contractual obligations, 1980 (OJ

VII. Article 26: Uncontested voluntary submission

Art 26 governs situations when the publisher voluntarily and without a contest submits himself to the jurisdiction of the court in which the victim has brought an action.[506, 507] In particular, the first sentence of Art 26(1) allocates jurisdiction to the court of a Member State before which the publisher enters an appearance. The allocation of jurisdiction is valid irrespective of the jurisdiction derived from other provisions of the Brussels-Lugano Regime. It follows that this provision applies even if the court is seised in breach of the jurisdictional rules.[508] Two exceptions to this general rule are determined within the second sentence of Art 26. The first is where the defendant enters an appearance to contest the jurisdiction, «thereby expressing his intention not to accept that court's jurisdiction».[509] The second is where the jurisdiction of the court is not established because another court has exclusive jurisdiction in accordance with Art 24.[510]

1998 C 27/34) regulates this matter.

506 For details, see Layton/Mercer, European Civil Practice, paras 20.117-20.132; Calvo Caravaca/Carrascosa González, in: Magnus/Mankowski, Brussels I Regulation, pp 514-527, paras 1-31; Jenard Report, p 38. Cf. *B and Others*, 47 ff. (regarding the appearance of the representative *in absentia* for a defendant).

507 Since the provision itself does not regulate whether this provision is applicable irrespective of the defendant's place of domicile, it is worth to mention three theses expressed in legal writing as outlined in Calvo Caravaca/Carrascosa González, in: Magnus/Mankowski, Brussels I Regulation, pp 525-527, paras 28-31 (regarding Brussels I). Acc. to the 'parallel thesis', at least one of the parties domiciled in a Brussels-Lugano State is required, while the second thesis requires that the defendant be domiciled in a Brussels-Lugano State. Finally, pursuant to the third thesis, namely, the 'expansive thesis', the parties' domicile is irrelevant. Calvo Caravaca and Carrascosa González note (*ibid.*, p 526, para 31) that the third one is shared among most of the legal academics. Cf. *supra* fn 436.

508 See *Cartier*, 34. It also means, as Jenard Report, p 18 notes, that Art 26 applies even if the jurisdiction of the court is established on an exorbitant jurisdictional basis (on exorbitant rules of jurisdiction, see *supra* Ch. III.C.II).

509 *Cartier*, 35. For the nature of defence put forward by the defendant on the substance of the dispute, see *Cartier*, 36-37.

510 Note that Art 26(2) introduces a new rule that requires that the court, before assuming its jurisdiction, ensures that the defendant weaker party under Sections 3-5 (on this, see *supra* Ch. III.B.II.4) is informed of the consequences of entering or not entering an appearance and of his right to contest the jurisdiction of the court.

Chapter IV: Jurisdiction in tort: a general note on Art 7(2) with particular regard to violations of personality rights

The person who claims that his personality rights are (threatened to be) violated can bring an action against the alleged perpetrator under numerous provisions outlined in *supra* Ch. III.D from which Art 7(2) establishes a direct and particularly close link between this action and the competent court. Drawing upon solutions presented in several legal systems of the original Contracting States to the BC and in the majority of the bilateral conventions, the inclusion in the BC of this special rule of jurisdiction was overwhelmingly justified by the «high number of road accidents.»[511] This optional rule that derogates from Art 4 says:

> «A person domiciled in a Member State may be sued in another Member State:»
>
> «(2) in matters relating to tort, delict or quasi-delict, in the courts for the place where the harmful event occurred or may occur».

As is clear from its wording, the subject matter of Art 7(2) is «tort, delict or quasi-delict», while its connecting factor attributes international and local jurisdiction to a particular court for the place within the Brussels-Lugano State where «the harmful event occurred or may occur».[512] Mindful of the fact that these terms are interpreted autonomously,[513] the present chapter aims to give a brief general note on their meaning and applicability with particular regard to violations of personality rights.

A. Matters relating to tort, delict, or quasi-delict

The ECJ characterises the concept of matters relating to tort, delict, or quasi-delict[514] as an autonomous concept encompassing a wide range of

---

511 Jenard Report, p 26. Except for the term 'may occur', which was added later (see *supra* Ch. III.A.I).

512 On this, see also *supra* Intr. to Ch. III.D.II.

513 On this, see *supra* Ch. III.B.I.1.

514 As Mankowski, in: Magnus/Mankowski, Brussels I Regulation, p 234, para 196 notices, the inclusion of the terms 'delict' and 'quasi-delict' is an acknowledgement of the different solutions employed in national substantive laws, e.g. in Scotland and France. He also pointed out (*ibid.*, fn omitted): «The only conclu-

actions that seek to establish the liability of the defendant and that are not related to matters relating to a contract within the meaning of Art 7(1)(a).[515] These two elements of the concept are classified as «a positive condition relating to the object of the action and … a negative condition relating to the cause of action.»[516] The latter requires an examination to determine whether actions, irrespective of their classification under national law, are contractual in nature. The concept of matters relating to a contract within Art 7(1)(a), as the ECJ pointed out in the *ÖFAB* case, «is not to be understood as covering a situation in which there is no obligation freely assumed by one party towards another. Therefore, the application of the rule of special jurisdiction provided for matters relating to a contract … presupposes the establishment of a legal obligation freely consented to by one person towards another and on which the claimant's action is based».[517] Consequently, tortious matters cover issues where there is no obligation freely assumed by one party towards another.[518] Besides numerous torts, this negative condition is present in disputes concerning violations of personality rights, since, in these cases, principally no contractual relationship exists between the perpetrator and the aggrieved person.[519] In this regard, Michael Bogdan notices:

> «[T]he person sustaining real or potential damage (usually the plaintiff) has not voluntarily entered into the legal relationship with the person claimed to be responsible for the damage (usually the defendant). The situation has rather been imposed upon the plaintiff by a unilateral act or omission of the defendant.»[520]

---

sion gained should be that (3) covers torts regardless whether they establish strict or fault-based liability.»

515 See e.g. *Kalfelis*, 17; *Brogsitter*, 20; *ÖFAB*, 32; *Kolassa*, 44. As AG Darmon noted in *Kalfelis*, 17, it may be considered that tort constitutes the counterpart of contract.

516 AG in *Folien Fischer*, 45.

517 *ÖFAB*, 33 (emphases omitted). See also *Handte*, 15; *Réunion européenne*, 17; *Kolassa*, 39.

518 See also e.g. *Tacconi*, 27; Nagy, J. Priv. Int. L. 2012, 251, 253-254.

519 For torts covered, incl. violations of personality rights, see e.g. Kropholler/von Hein, EuZPR, pp 202-207, paras 74-74a; Mankowski, in: Magnus/Mankowski, Brussels I Regulation, pp 236-239, paras 200-202. For violations of personality rights, see also Nagy, J. Priv. Int. L. 2012, 251, 254; AG 1994 in *Shevill*, 4 ff.

520 Bogdan, Masaryk U. J.L. & Tech. 2011, 1, 4 (in general). Cf. AG 1995 in *Shevill*, 43. However, if such a relationship exists between the perpetrator and the victim, it is necessary to determine how the tort is related to the contract in accordance with *Kalfelis*, 17. This relatedness acc. to *Brogsitter*, 29 «may be established by taking into account the purpose of the contract.» For comments on this case, see

In addition, the positive condition relates to the object of the action established in *Kalfelis* and repeatedly upheld in the subsequent decisions of the ECJ. It requires that the claim brought by the plaintiff shall seek to establish the liability of the alleged perpetrator. Liability arises when «a causal connexion can be established between the damage and the event in which that damage originates.»[521] It follows that Art 7(2) covers a wide range of diverse actions, such as those briefly considered in *supra* Ch. I, namely, actions to make good the damage that has already occurred (i.e., compensation), to compel the defendant to desist from committing an act liable to cause damage, or to obtain a declaration that an act is unlawful (i.e., positive declaratory actions).[522]

B. *The place where the harmful event occurred or may occur*

More than 45 years ago, the drafters of the BC selected the harmful event as an element that forms one of the facts of torts to allocate them to a legal system. Mindful of the fact that the court seised identifies only whether this point of connection occurred in the Brussels-Lugano State in which it sits,[523] the interpretation and application of this connecting factor carries considerable importance.

Wendenburg/Schneider, NJW 2014, 1633-1636. Cf. AG in *Kalfelis*, 16-30.

521 *Bier*, 16. See also *ÖFAB*, 34. Event means act or omission, i.e., inactivity (see also *Kolassa*, 52-53; Mankowski, in: Magnus/Mankowski, Brussels I Regulation, pp 243-244, para 214).

522 Cf. AG in *Folien Fischer*, 46; *DFDS Torline*, 19-28; AG in *DFDS Torline*, 28-42. For preventive actions, see *infra* Ch. IV.B.II. Note that the ECJ has not set the legal nature of the right of reply yet. The prevailing opinion of academics regards it as an action falling within the concept of tortious matters. See e.g. Roth, Die internationale Zuständigkeit, pp 143-146; Art 6(1) of Commission Document COM(2003) 427 final (applicable law). Contra: Kropholler/von Hein, EuZPR, p 205, para 74 ('Gegendarstellungsanspruch'). For pro and contra arguments, see Kubis, Internationale Zuständigkeit, pp 114-118. In addition, it is also worth noting that negative declaratory actions also fall within the scope of application of Art 7(2) (see *Folien Fischer*, 54).

523 On this, see *supra* Ch. III.B.I.4.

I. The place where the harmful event occurred

The meaning of the concept of harmful event is not defined within the Brussels-Lugano Regime. It was left intentionally open by the drafters of the BC, who stated:

> «The Committee did not think it should specify whether that place is the place where the event which resulted in damage or injury occurred or whether it is the place where the damage or injury was sustained. The Committee preferred to keep to a formula which has already been adopted by number of legal systems (Germany, France).»[524]

Apparently, the drafters charged the ECJ with the interpretation of this concept, which has given clarification in a long-standing line of judgments dating back to 1976 when it was first dealt with in *Bier*. This case concerned pollution matters. Specifically, Mines de potasse d'Alsace SA, a mining company established in France, discharged chloride into the inland waterway of the Rhine. Although the discharges were authorised by the officers of the French prefecture,[525] they caused damage to the plantations of Handelskwekerij G. J. Bier BV (Bier), the first plaintiff, an undertaking engaged in horticulture in the Netherlands, obliging Bier to take expensive measures in order to limit that damage. Accordingly, Bier and the Reinwater Foundation, a Dutch organisation, brought an action for compensation for the damage caused in a court of the Netherlands in accordance with Art 5(3) of the BC. Due to the questions of the *Gerechtshof's-Gravenhage* (Hague Court of Appeal) being referred for a preliminary ruling, the ECJ was faced with a typical distance tort, since the elements of tort (i.e., causal event and damage) occurred in two different Member States.[526] First, AG Capotorti delivered his opinion in which, after examining several potential interpretations of the concept of harmful event, he noted in relation to the cumulative solution embracing both elements of tort that it does not fit with the letter and spirit of the BC since:

> «[I]t is at odds with the letter of the Convention because Article 5 (3) refers to the *court of the place* where the harmful event occurred, that is, to a single court and a single place, and thus seems to rule out the possibility that more than one place could be taken into consideration or more than one court declare itself to have ju-

---

524 Jenard Report, p 26. Cf. AG in *Bier*, 3 (p 1751) with slightly different wording; Art 5(3) of Commission Document COM(97) 609 final, and in this latter respect, see Pocar Report, paras 58-59.

525 AG in *Bier*, 8 (pp 1756-1757).

526 See also AG 1994 in *Shevill*, 51.

> risdiction, under the provisions of the Convention, with regard to the same harmful event. What is certainly more important, it is at odds with its spirit, in that the objective pursued by the Convention, namely to divide international jurisdiction amongst the different States in accordance with a distributive criterion in such a way as to reduce instead of increasing the scope of the jurisdiction of each State precisely where there already exists an objective basis for conferring jurisdiction upon another.»[527]

Regardless of this opinion, and similar to the Jenard Report, the ECJ established twin criteria in paragraphs 24-25 of its judgment according to which:

> «[W]here the place of the happening of the event which may give rise to liability in tort, delict or quasidelict and the place where that event results in damage are not identical, the expression 'place where the harmful event occurred', in Article 5(3) of the Convention, must be understood as being intended to cover both the place where the damage occurred and the place of the event giving rise to it.
>
> The result is that the defendant may be sued, at the option of the plaintiff, either in the courts for the place where the damage occurred or in the courts for the place of the event which gives rise to and is at the origin of that damage.»

As a corollary, this ruling enables the victim to choose between those criteria in cases when the place of origin of the damage and the place of its outcome are not identical. Therefore, in an appreciable number of cases, «it is for the claimant to choose the court which best suits his interests. That approach guarantees the practical effect of the rule laid down in Article 5(3) *[of Brussels I]* while at the same time allowing the victim of the damage a certain amount of decision-making discretion which, in addition, ensures the proximity of the court seised to the relevant facts of the dispute.»[528] Based on this optional character of the concept, numerous scholars and Advocates General have observed that the optional character favours the plaintiff because, as Trevor C. Hartley points out, «it allows him to choose whichever forum is most advantageous to him.»[529] In addition, the preferential treatment of the plaintiff (i.e., victim) is not only stressed on the basis of the optional character of the concept of harmful event, but

527 AG in *Bier*, 7 (pp 1755-1756) (italics in the original).

528 AG in *Wintersteiger*, 17 (italics in square brackets added).

529 Hartley, E.L.Rev. 1977, 143, 145. Cf. AG in *Folien Fischer*, 48; AG in *Dumez*, fn 55; Kohler, in: Schwind, Europarecht, p 146; Kuipers, GLJ 2011, 1681, 1683; Roth, Die internationale Zuständigkeit, pp 198-199. Contra [Art 7(2) is not aimed to favour or protect the victim]: *Folien Fischer*, 45-47; *Kainz*, 31; AG 1994 in *Shevill*, 18; AG 1995 in *Shevill*, 41; AG in *Melzer*, 60; Nagy, J. Priv. Int. L. 2012, 251, 262.

also on the basis of the drafting history of the BC. Hence, Peter Huber observes that Art 59 of the French *Ancien Code de Procédure Civile* was the model rule of Art 5(3) of the BC, which recognised the protection of the victim.[530] Irrespective of these observations, the ECJ «was, however, careful to avoid policy arguments of this kind in its reasoning.»[531] While giving both criteria the same weight (i.e., «both are in principle equivalent and on equal footing»[532]), it justified their optional character on the principles of sound administration of justice and proximity by stipulating:

> «Taking into account the close connexion between the component parts of every sort of liability, it does not appear appropriate to opt for one of the two connecting factors mentioned to the exclusion of the other, since each of them can, depending on the circumstances, be particularly helpful from the point of view of the evidence and of the conduct of the proceedings.»[533]

These open-textured limbs founded on the physical damage in *Bier* have served as starting points for interpreting the concept of harmful event in other distance and scattered torts[534] involving either pecuniary or non-pecuniary damage. In relation to the latter type of damage, the ECJ clearly ruled in *Shevill*, which is analysed in detail in the following chapter, that:

> «Those observations, made in relation to physical or pecuniary loss or damage, must equally apply, for the same reasons, in the case of loss or damage other than physical or pecuniary, in particular injury to the reputation and good name of a natural or legal person due to a defamatory publication.»[535]

The application of these twin criteria to disputes concerning violations of personality rights encounters some difficulties. This is because the ECJ in

530 Huber, ZEuP 1996, 295, 305.

531 Hartley, E.L.Rev. 1977, 143, 145. See also AG in *Folien Fischer*, 48.

532 Mankowski, in: Magnus/Mankowski, Brussels I Regulation, p 239, para 203 (fn omitted). See also Kosmehl, FS Thomas Rauscher, p 91; Thiede, GPR 2011, 259, 260.

533 *Bier*, 17. In addition, the ECJ held (*Bier*, 20) that in the absence of the place of the damage, Art 5(3) of the BC would lose its effectiveness, since the place of the causal event often coincides with the general rule of jurisdiction. Finally, note that it is possible that the place of the causal event cannot be determined, and thus, solely the place of the damage locates the dispute (see *Réunion européenne*, 33, and on this, see also *infra* Ch. VII.D.II.1).

534 Torts in which the causal event (threatens to) give(s) rise to damage in more than one state. Cf. AG 1994 in *Shevill*, 52 (regarding violations of personality rights).

535 *Shevill*, 23. Note that Fawcett/Torremans, Intellectual Property and Private International Law, para 5.43 criticise this ruling, saying that it might have been better if the ECJ had differentiated between types of damage and applied *Bier* only regarding financial or material loss.

Bier introduced a certain amount of flexibility in its interpretation by remaining silent regarding which event and which and whose damage is to be deemed as jurisdictionally relevant. However, violations often involve a series of activities and consequences possibly taking place at different places and times. Accordingly, it is not entirely clear which one of the acts leading to the violation and which of the losses caused by that violation shall be regarded as the jurisdictionally relevant event and damage. To take an example, consider the following simplified factual scenario. After buying a computer, researching materials, and creating injurious content, person 'A' makes such content available to the public. Thus, everyone in the public arena, including the victim, is able to possess and comprehend that content, which causes pain and suffering to the victim and to his close relatives. Is it the first act in the chain, or should it be the final one, which directly causes damage? Alternatively, does it cover all activities? Does damage mean the direct or indirect harm caused to the direct and/or indirect victim? The following subsections outline selected methods presented in legal writing and in the judicial practice of the ECJ[536] to determine how these approaches should be interpreted in order to avoid opting for extensive criteria, which might lead to a complete reversal of the central mechanism, spirit, and letters of Art 7(2). In this way, they contribute to the analysis undertaken in the following chapters of connecting factors in disputes concerning offline and online violations of personality rights.

1. The place of the event, which gives rise to and is at the origin of the damage, occurred

Scholars principally determine the concept of a jurisdictionally relevant event negatively by excluding from its scope mere acts of preparation (i.e., jurisdictionally irrelevant acts).[537] Their methods, however, differ in defining such acts and thus, in cutting the series of activities resulting in damage, as the following cursory abstracts demonstrate.

536 Note that these cases did not concern issues of personality rights.

537 E.g. Kropholler/von Hein, EuZPR, pp 216-217, para 83a; Schack, MMR 2000, 135, 137. Cf. Roth, Die internationale Zuständigkeit, pp 193 ff.

a) Peter Mankowski: *lex cause*

Peter Mankowski proposes defining the scope of mere acts of preparation by having «recourse to the law of the state where the activity in question can be located, and to ask it whether it regards such activity already to be a tortious activity.»[538] As a result, the law at the place where the activity is performed determines whether, to what extent, and under which conditions it protects which values and by doing so whether the act in question is an act of preparation.[539]

b) Sebastian Kubis: imputation and procedural valuations

Although the physical activity of the perpetrator is also of importance in his theory,[540] Sebastian Kubis essentially delimitates the preparatory from the jurisdictionally relevant acts based on imputation («Zurechnung»).[541] In this way, he ascribes crucial importance to the will and conception («Vorstellung») of the perpetrator: It depends on the perpetrator's conception whether his act left the stage of preparation and can thus be regarded as a jurisdictionally relevant act. If, in the perpetrator's opinion, other subsequent activities are not necessary, the imputation is justified. Put in a different way, the stage of preparation is left when the perpetrator has done everything he could do, in his opinion, which is necessary, for instance, for the distribution of a statement:

> «Von einer Vorbereitungshandlung kann also nicht mehr die Rede sein, sobald der Täter aus seiner Sicht alles zur Verbreitung der Äußerung Erforderliche getan hat.»[542]

Finally, Sebastian Kubis asserts that the delimitation of those acts does not depend on substantive law valuations («Wertungen des materiellen

---

538 Mankowski, in: Magnus/Mankowski, Brussels I Regulation, p 244, para 215. Cf. Schack, MMR 2000, 135, 137; *Shevill*, 34-41 and the submission of the German government in *Marinari*, 16, 17, and on this, see Jayme/Kohler, IPRax 1995, 343, 348. See also *infra* fns 561, 583.

539 Mankowski, in: Magnus/Mankowski, Brussels I Regulation, p 244, para 215.

540 Kubis, Internationale Zuständigkeit, pp 143-145, 178.

541 Kubis, Internationale Zuständigkeit, pp 148-149 (in general). Cf. Roth, Die internationale Zuständigkeit, p 189; Mankowski, in: Magnus/Mankowski, Brussels I Regulation, pp 244-245, para 215.

542 Kubis, Internationale Zuständigkeit, p 148.

Rechts») but on procedural ones,[543] especially on the interests of the parties and on the connection of the act with the forum. In the light of these considerations, in his opinion, violations of personality rights can be localised solely at the place of the causal event and, in particular, at the place where the defendant physically acted and where the content was distributed, if it was imputable to him.[544]

c) Isabel Roth: procedural valuations

Isabel Roth differentiates between jurisdictionally relevant and irrelevant parts of the act («Teilakte», hereinafter act, activity) on the grounds of four procedural valuations, i.e., jurisdictional interests ('prozessuale Wertungen', «Zuständigkeitsinteressen»).[545] First, she notes that if the competent court is located at the place of tort, then there is a particularly close relationship to the dispute, which accelerates and eases the clarification of the disputed facts. Thus, the concept of causal event for the purpose of jurisdiction is essentially determined by its evidence-related meaning for the dispute.[546] It follows that a jurisdictionally relevant act is not restricted to the act, which gives rise to liability under the substantive law ('haftungsbegründender Teilakt').[547] Instead, it is limited to the act that forms a significant part ('wesentlicher Teilakt') of the subject matter of the dispute,[548] and thus of the tort, and that is a physical one («körperliches Tätigwer-

543 Kubis, Internationale Zuständigkeit, p 149. Note that Roth, Die internationale Zuständigkeit, pp 189-191 criticises Kubis by noting that these valuations are not essential for his method, since he treats imputation as being equal to the concept of attempt that is known in the field of criminal law. As she states, criminal and liability laws have a behaviour guiding function. The potential perpetrator orientates himself towards the standardised righteous behaviour prescribed by the substantive law. The rules of PIL have also a kind of behavioural guiding function by designating the applicable law to which the perpetrator might adjust his behaviour. However, rules of jurisdiction do not serve substantive legal and behavioural guiding functions.

544 Note that Kubis, Internationale Zuständigkeit, pp 122, 178 is of the opinion that since personality rights are everywhere and nowhere, there is no place of the damage for violations of these rights. See also *infra* Ch. VI.B.I.

545 Roth, Die internationale Zuständigkeit, p 193. The present cursory abstract is provided by the author's free translation from *ibid.*, pp 193-206.

546 Roth, Die internationale Zuständigkeit, p 193.

547 Roth, Die internationale Zuständigkeit, p 194.

548 Roth, Die internationale Zuständigkeit, pp 193-194.

den»), i.e., actively taken by the perpetrator and manifested to the external world. In the context of distance and scattered torts, this means that those subsequent acts, which take place between the physical activity and the occurrence of the result, must be excluded from the scope of jurisdictionally relevant acts.[549] Isabel Roth treats the criterion of privileging the plaintiff as the second procedural valuation, which shapes the scope of jurisdictionally relevant acts. She states that the place of harmful event is aimed to privilege the plaintiff, since it establishes a ground of jurisdiction in addition to the defendant's domicile. Accordingly, the jurisdictionally relevant act should ensure such an additional place of jurisdiction.[550] The third procedural valuation is the right of the defendant to a fair procedure under the rule of law, which consequently requires courts with the appropriate jurisdiction ('zumutbare Gerichtsstände'). Isabel Roth notices that since the law of jurisdiction does not have a kind of behavioural guiding function («verhaltenssteuernde Funktion»),[551] the jurisdiction of the courts is appropriate at those places where the perpetrator was able to influence the injurious activity and where a sufficient domestic connection can be established between the court and the dispute ('hinreichender Inlandsbezug der Streitigkeit').[552] She also adds that not every activity justifies the establishment of jurisdiction. When the injurious content was prepared at different places and times, the sufficient connection is given at the place where the defendant predominantly acted (centre of gravity of the act).[553] The fourth procedural valuation, namely, the interest of the state in restoring legal peace and providing procedural satisfaction for the litigants, is fulfilled at the place where a significant component of the tortious act was committed.[554]

549 Roth, Die internationale Zuständigkeit, p 195.

550 Roth, Die internationale Zuständigkeit, pp 198-199.

551 On this, see *supra* fn 543.

552 Roth, Die internationale Zuständigkeit, p 205. For details, see also *ibid.*, pp 200-205.

553 Roth, Die internationale Zuständigkeit, p 204.

554 Roth, Die internationale Zuständigkeit, p 206. For details, see *ibid.*, pp 205-206.

d) Peter Kaye: the original act

Based on *Bier*, Peter Kaye[555] advocates that the place where the event giving rise to the damage occurred is the place in which the original activity, which appears factually to have initiated the chain of events culminating in damage and which may give rise to tortious liability, took place.[556] He explains that in the absence of the original act, such as uttering, writing, broadcasting, or posting the defamatory statement, the damage would not have occurred.[557] This is true irrespective of the fact that the original act leads only to the occurrence of the damage through a sequence of activities taking place in states other than the state of the original act. Peter Kaye bases this view on the particularly close link that the place of the original act has with the subject matter of the dispute. While activities occurring thereafter may be necessary to the occurrence of the damage, their existence and location are not the necessary consequences of the defendant's original act, and they are to that extent matters of chance and not completely appropriate as jurisdictional connecting factors. In addition, he notices that their location of occurrence is principally beyond the defendant's control. Furthermore, he also argues that, for jurisdictional purposes, it is not a matter of great import that

> «the court applied to might not know whether a particular event can be taken to have resulted in damage so as to place tortious liability upon the actor or whether instead the chain of causation was broken by a *novus actus interveniens* (or whether the original act is supplemented by a further allegedly negligent action on the part of the defendant or another)».[558]

This position was justified based on *Bier*, since the ECJ referred to the place of the causal event that «may» give rise to liability in tort. As a result, for jurisdictional purposes, it is important that the relevant act establishes a factual link with the territory, irrespective of whether liability is founded on the substance as stemming from that act. Thus, the absence of liability does not change the existence of the factual link in tortious matters created by the act.[559]

---

555 Kaye, Civil Jurisdiction, pp 578-581.

556 Kaye, Civil Jurisdiction, p 580.

557 However, cf. the original event in relation to *Shevill* proposed by Kaye, Law of the European Judgments Convention, pp 1462-1464 and mentioned in *infra* Ch. V.B.I.1.

558 Kaye, Civil Jurisdiction, p 579 (italics in the original).

559 Kaye, Civil Jurisdiction, p 579.

e) The present author's view: the original act with particular regard to procedural principles

The essential difference in the above outlined methods to determine the scope of jurisdictionally relevant and irrelevant acts is rooted in their legal basis. While Peter Mankowski's and, indirectly and partially, Sebastian Kubis' methods[560] give a predominant role to substantive legal considerations, Isabel Roth's and Peter Kaye's methods justify the differentiation objectively on the grounds of procedural principles. The present author prefers the latter methods, since they seem to be more harmonious with the intention of the Brussels-Lugano Regime, which, as the ECJ underscored in *Marinari*, «did not intend to link the rules of territorial jurisdiction with the national provisions concerning the conditions under which non-contractual civil liability is incurred.»[561] In addition, the latter methods are also in line with the *DFDS Torline* decision of the ECJ in which the dispute arose from the campaign of economic sabotage organised by two Swedish trade unions against DFDS, a shipowner whose ship served the route between Göteborg (Sweden) and Harwich (UK) and which was subject to Danish law. SEKO, a Swedish trade union, served a notice of industrial action that in itself could not have caused harm to DFDS. However, this industrial action called upon another Swedish union to give notice of a sympathy action; accordingly, notice of taking such an action was given. DFDS brought proceedings in the *Arbejdsret* (Danish labour court) against the Swedish unions to prevent those actions and determine their lawfulness. Although SEKO suspended its action and the other action was withdrawn, DFDS removed its ship from the planned route, which was served by another ship leased for that purpose. Thus, it also brought another action before the *Sø- og Handelsret* (Danish Maritime- and Commercial Court) against SEKO for damages allegedly suffered as a result of the notice of industrial action. This latter court decided to stay its decision on the action for damages pending the decision of the *Arbejdsret*.[562] Ques-

---

560 Regarding Kubis' method, see *supra* fn 543.

561 *Marinari*, 18. See also *supra* Ch. III.B.I.4. Note that there is an academic discourse generated by *Shevill* and *Marinari* regarding whether the concept of harmful event is interpreted independently or by referring to the *lex cause*. *Shevill*, 41 gives the impression of the latter method, while the former is clear from *Marinari*. For details, see Kohler, ZEuP 1996, 452, 465-467. Cf. *infra* fn 583.

562 For the principal fact pattern, see *DFDS Torline*, 6-12. Cf. Jayme/Kohler, IPRax 2004, 481, 487; Hergenröder, GPR 2005, 33-36.

tion 1(b), which was referred to the ECJ by the *Arbejdsret* for a preliminary ruling, essentially asked if it was necessary for the application of Art 5(3) of the BC «that the harm incurred must be a certain or probable consequence of the industrial action in itself, or whether it is sufficient that that industrial action is a necessary condition of sympathy action which may result in harm.»[563] This raised the question of how far the court must go into the merits of the case to determine whether it has jurisdiction.[564] To answer the question, the ECJ first pointed out that a causal connection could be established between the damage allegedly suffered by DFDS and SEKO's notice of industrial action even if it could not in itself have caused the damage. Then, it went on to rule that for the application of Art 5(3) of the BC «it is sufficient that the industrial action is a necessary precondition of sympathy action which may result in harm.»[565] As a result, the damage allegedly occurred does not have to be a certain and probable consequence of the industrial action; it suffices that the industrial action, which was held in paragraph 41 of *DFDS Torline* to be the causal event, is a necessary precondition of the subsequent activity that may result in damage.[566]

The recourse to the original act is even more obvious in *Kainz*. The dispute arose between Mr Kainz, who had his residence in Salzburg (Austria), and Pantherwerke AG, which was registered in Germany, concerning a claim for damages on the ground of liability for a defective product brought by Mr Kainz following an accident that he suffered in Germany while riding a bicycle manufactured in that Member State by Pantherwerke AG but bought from a retailer in Austria.[567] The elements of the causal chain were the following: manufacture of the bicycle – putting it into circulation, meaning distribution of the bicycle to the retailer – putting it into circulation, meaning commercial distribution of the bicycle by the retailer to the end consumer – riding the bicycle by the end consumer – accident and occurrence of the damage. By its first question, the *Oberster Gerichtshof* (Austrian Supreme Court) essentially requested the identifica-

563 *DFDS Torline*, 29.

564 See also AG in *DFDS Torline*, 50.

565 *DFDS Torline*, 34. See also *Kolassa*, 52.

566 Cf. attribution of effect test as noted in *supra* Ch. III.D.II.3. In the opinion of the present author, however, it can be argued that the wording of the ruling (i.e., «it is sufficient») does not exclude the possibility that other events could also be regarded as jurisdictionally relevant.

567 *Kainz*, 2.

tion of the place of the causal event by pointing out three possible places, namely, the place where the manufacturer was established, the place where the product was put into circulation, and the place where it was acquired by the user.[568] The ECJ held that the place of the causal event is the place where the product was manufactured. It underscored this decision by stating that it establishes proximity and facilitates the efficacious conduct of proceedings and the sound administration of justice. This is because it enables *inter alia* the possibility of gathering evidence to establish the defect of the bicycle. In addition, it reasoned that the manufacturer and the victim can reasonably foresee that place.[569]

Furthermore, the recourse to the place where the original act attributable to the perpetrator was physically performed is also important in cases concerning the liability of co-perpetrators, in which the ECJ consistently put significant emphasis on the defendant's act and on the place where that act was performed.[570]

However, note that, as Arnaud Nuyts points out, the recourse to the defendant's act is only one of the methods available to identify the jurisdictionally relevant place of the causal event in the settled case law of the ECJ. The second method, with which the first one principally coincides, is the reference to the place where the perpetrator has its establishment. In particular, it is evident from the case law, as he goes on to stress, that the ECJ was «careful, in *each instance*, to point out the existence of that coincidence before concluding that this was the place where the harmful event occurred.»[571]

---

568 *Kainz*, 17-18. Note that the second question asked for the interpretation of the expression 'put into circulation' (*Kainz*, 17). This question was not considered by the ECJ.

569 *Kainz*, 27-28. For comments on this case, see e.g. Dietze, EuZW 2014, 234-235. Cf. *Zuid-Chemie*, 13, 25 in which it was a common ground between the parties that the place of the causal event was the place where the contaminated product was manufactured that coincided with the place of the defendant's establishment. Kropholler/von Hein (EuZPR, p 218, para 83c) identify the place of the causal event in this latter case with the seat of the manufacturer («Herstellersitz»).

570 *Melzer*, 19 ff.; *Hi Hotel*, 30-32; *Coty Germany*, 49-51. Cf. *Pinckney*, 29. See also *supra* Ch. III.D.II.3.

571 Nuyts, in: Nuyts, International Litigation, pp 118-119 (italics in the original). He mentions three examples: *Bier* (on this, see *supra* Ch. IV.B.I), *DFDS Torline* (on this, see this subsection) and *Shevill* (on this, see *infra* Ch. V). In addition to these cases, see also the following cases, in which the ECJ located the causal act at the place of the defendant's establishment in the form of the place where the decision on performing the causal event is taken: *Wintersteiger*, 37, 38; AG in

2. The place where the damage occurred

It has been seen above that difficult questions can present themselves concerning the determination of the concept of causal event. Similarly, it is not always entirely clear what is understood under the criterion of the place where the damage occurred that was introduced in *Bier* as the second subdivision of the concept of harmful event, which must be in a causal connection with the jurisdictionally relevant act. This is so because this place, as the ECJ held, «may vary according to the nature of the right allegedly infringed».[572] Guidelines may, however, be inferred from the case law of the ECJ in respect of the interpretation of the expression 'the damage occurred'. The ECJ specified this criterion in *Dumez* and *Marinari*.

In the former case, the plaintiffs, successors to the rights of French companies, brought proceedings against certain German banks in France for financial loss suffered by them because the German banks cancelled the loans granted to the prime contractor for a property-development project in Germany, which, in turn, suspended the project, and the German subsidiaries of the French companies became insolvent.[573] The French *Cour de cassation* essentially asked whether the concept of damage under Art 5(3) of the BC covered «the consequence of the harm suffered by persons who were the immediate victims of damage occurring at a different place, which would enable the indirect victim to bring proceedings before the court of the State in which he is domiciled».[574] The ECJ answered this question negatively by holding that the place where the damage occurred «can be understood only as indicating the place where the event giving

Pinckney, 57, 58; *Hejduk*, 23-26 (note that the ECJ also referred to the place where the decision is carried out, see *supra* fn 457); *Kolassa*, 53 (note that the ECJ also referred to other acts). See also cases in which the jurisdictionally relevant act of the defendant coincides with the place of its establishment: *Melzer*, 38; *Hi Hotel*, 40; *Kainz*, 33; *Coty Germany*, 49. Note that *Handelsgericht Wien* asked about the localisation of the causal event under Art 5(3) of Brussels I in *Hejduk*, 14 by directly referring to «the Member State in which the alleged infringer is established». It is remarkable because it did not refer to a particular act (on this case, see *supra* Ch. III.D.II.2).

572 *Hejduk*, 29.

573 *Dumez*, 2-3. See also Nagy, J. Priv. Int. L. 2012, 251, 255.

574 *Dumez*, 7.

rise to the damage ... directly produced its harmful effects upon the person who is the immediate victim of that event.»[575] Consequently, it held that:

> «[T]he rule on jurisdiction laid down in Article 5(3) of the Convention cannot be interpreted as permitting a plaintiff pleading damage which he claims to be the consequence of the harm suffered by other persons who were direct victims of the harmful act to bring proceedings against the perpetrator of that act in the courts of the place in which he himself ascertained the damage to his assets.»[576]

It follows, as Peter Kaye asserts, that «indirect/'ricochet'/knock-on/ consequential damage to an indirect victim *[is]* not jurisdiction-conferring under Article 5(3)».[577]

In *Marinari,* in which the direct and indirect damage happened to the same person, the ECJ further specified the nature of jurisdictionally significant damage. The facts can be summarised as follows. Mr Marinari, domiciled in Italy, lodged with the English bank a bundle of promissory notes. The bank considered them to be of dubious origin. Thus, it refused to return them and informed the police about its concerns, whereupon, the police arrested Mr Marinari. After his release, Mr Marinari sued the bank in Italy, seeking, on the one hand, payment of the face value of the promissory notes and, on the other hand, compensation for the damage he claimed to have suffered because of his arrest, the breach of several contracts, and damage to his reputation. The question referred by the *Corte Suprema di Cassazione* (Italian Court of Cassation) for a preliminary ruling was focused on the localisation of the physical and financial harm. It principally asked whether the place of the damage means «only the place in which physical harm was caused to persons or things, or also the place in which the damage to the plaintiff's assets occurred».[578] By rejecting the latter place,[579] the ECJ went on to state in respect of the place of the damage that:

> «[T]hat term cannot be construed so extensively as to encompass any place where the adverse consequences can be felt of an event which has already caused damage actually arising elsewhere.

---

575 *Dumez*, 20 (emphases omitted).

576 *Dumez*, 22. Cf. AG in *CDC*, 50.

577 Kaye, Law of the European Judgments Convention, p 1324 (italics in the original omitted; italics in square brackets added).

578 *Marinari*, 8.

579 See *Marinari*, 13.

> Consequently, that term cannot be construed as including the place where, as in the present case, the victim claims to have suffered financial damage following upon initial damage arising and suffered by him in another Contracting State.»[580]

As a result, *Dumez* and *Marinari* restrict the width of the second *Bier*-approach in two respects. First, the place of the indirect damage that was suffered by an indirect victim is regarded as irrelevant.[581] Secondly, the damage, which is consequential of the damage actually arising elsewhere, is disregarded even if, as AG Jääskinen observed, it is possible to compensate for the consequential damage under the *lex fori* or the *lex cause*.[582] This could be justified by the fact that, like the concept of causal event, the concept of damage is interpreted autonomously and regardless of the conditions laid down in the substantive law on tort, such as the existence and extent of the damage.[583]

Besides the distinction between direct and indirect damage, and irrespective of the fact that the ECJ in *Shevill* applied the findings held in relation to financial damage to non-material harm,[584] there are signs indicating a different trend. In other words, on the basis of AG Jääskinen's opinion delivered in paragraph 70 of *Pinckney*, it might be argued that the kind of damage – i.e., material or non-material – might have an impact on the interpretation of the concept of damage and, thus, on its localisation for jurisdictional purposes:

580 *Marinari*, 14-15. On this case, see Jayme/Kohler, IPRax 1995, 343, 348. Cf. *Universal Music International Holding* (request concerning *inter alia* the distinction between initial and consequential financial damage).

581 Interestingly, the indirect co-perpetrator can be sued for the harm caused by the subsequent act of the direct co-perpetrator (see *supra* fn 467). Thus, the scope of the causal event is broader than the scope of the damage.

582 AG in *Coty Germany*, fn 51.

583 See *supra* Ch. IV.B.I.1.e) (regarding causal event); *supra* Ch. III.B.I.1 and 4 (regarding autonomous interpretation and the relation between jurisdiction and substantive law). For the academic discourse on its interpretation (i.e., independently or acc. to the *lex cause*), cf. *supra* Ch. IV.B.I.1.a) and *supra* fns 538, 561. Note that *Coty Germany*, 57-58 might fear partly reopening that discourse, since the ECJ referred to the *lex fori* (in this regard, see also *Coty Germany*, 40) to determine whether the causal act caused damage in Germany and thus, the jurisdiction of the court at that territory can be established. However, it is also worth noting that (1) in *Shevill* the ECJ referred to the *lex cause*, and (2) this reference was repeated neither in the conclusion of that judgment (para 59) nor in its operative part.

584 On this, see *supra* Ch. IV.B.I.

> «In effect, the non-material damage that might result from an infringement of the reputation or the private life of an individual is, as a general rule, more intense in the place where he has the centre of his interests, a matter that naturally clashes with the jurisdiction rules. Conversely, 'that assessment ... does not apply also to the determination of jurisdiction in respect of infringements of intellectual property rights'. The material damage resulting from the infringement of one of the categories of exclusive copyright referred to above does not have the necessary link with the localisation of the centre of the author's interests, but rather with the localisation of his public.»[585]

Finally, it is worth dedicating some attention to the wording of the settled case law of the ECJ. Read literally, several decisions lack precision regarding how the damage arose. They refer to the place where the damage occurred or where it was suffered.[586] This distinction is of essential importance for determining jurisdiction according to AG Darmon in *Marinari*, since only the former refers to the place where the initial damage manifested itself, while the latter is a broader approach covering consequential damage at the *forum actoris* (i.e., the place where the plaintiff is habitually resident or domiciled).[587] However, as Peter Kaye observes, in paragraph 15 of *Marinari* and in the ruling itself (supposedly, he understood paragraph 21 of the judgment) the ECJ referred to the jurisdictionally relevant initial damage that was suffered by the victim in another Contracting State, while the term 'occurred' should have been used due to the opinion of AG Darmon.[588] Thus, he notes that «[c]ertainly in the reported English text of the judgment in *Marinari* the Court did not appear to comply with this definitional scheme of the Advocate General.»[589]

---

585 Fns omitted. Furthermore, note that AG Cruz Villalón in *Hejduk* distinguished between delocalised and localisable damage and proposed disregarding the concept of jurisdictionally relevant damage for the former kind (on this, see also *infra* Ch. VII.B.I). However, as is clear from *supra* Ch. III.D.II.2, the ECJ did not follow his opinion.

586 E.g. Jenard Report, p 26 ('sustained'); *eDate and Martinez*, 47-48 ('suffered', 'occurred'); AG in *Dumez*, 55(2) ('suffered').

587 See AG 1994 in *Marinari*, 28-49; AG 1995 in *Marinari*, 5. Cf. AG 1995 in *Shevill*, 38-48. For details on *forum actoris*, see *infra* Ch. VII.B.II.1.c)aa).

588 Kaye, Law of the European Judgments Convention, pp 1383-1384. In addition, he (*ibid.*, p 1395) also states another argument for discarding AG Darmon's distinction laid down in *Marinari*, namely, «[e]ffects take place as soon as they are suffered by the victim».

589 Kaye, Law of the European Judgments Convention, p 1383 (italics in the original). See also *ibid.*, p 1392.

II. The place where the harmful event may occur

In addition to torts that have already occurred, Art 7(2) also allocates jurisdiction in disputes concerning prospective tortious matters, as its wording clearly indicates by use of the expression 'may occur'. Although the Schlosser Report and several decisions of the ECJ delivered on Art 5(3) of the BC acknowledged jurisdiction at the place of prospective torts, the BC, together with the 1988 LC, does not expressly refer to future torts.[590] The term 'may occur' was first added to Art 5(3) of Brussels I. This difference in the wording of the Brussels-Lugano instruments, however, does not question the applicability of the case law delivered on Art 5(3) of the BC and the 1988 LC to the interpretation of the equal provision within the other Brussels-Lugano instruments, since this additional term provides only a clarification without introducing any considerable alteration.[591] It follows that the term 'may occur' in Art 7(2) refers to the fact that the court of the place where the damage or the causal event is threatened to occur has jurisdiction over a claim under the same conditions as those required for an action for tort that has already occurred. The occurrence of the potential damage and causal event, however, must be actual and real rather than a theoretical possibility.[592] Otherwise, as AG Jääskinen asserted, «the special ground of jurisdiction constituted by matters relating to tort or delict could be created on a discretionary basis.»[593] As a corollary, the plaintiff is enabled to bring actions, such as injunctions, to prevent the occurrence of prospective and identifiable torts.[594]

A tricky question may arise regarding how the concept of harmful event can be localised in prospective tortious matters.[595] Peter Mankowski an-

---

590 On this, see *Henkel*, 42, 46-50 (to *Henkel*, see Jayme/Kohler, IPRax 2003, 485, 490); *DFDS Torline*, 27, 33; Pocar Report, para 61; AG in *Folien Fischer*, 49.

591 See AG in *Folien Fischer*, 33; AG in *Melzer*, 28. Cf. *supra* Ch. III.A.I.

592 See also AG in *Folien Fischer*, 49; Pocar Report, para 62; Mankowski, in: Magnus/Mankowski, Brussels I Regulation, p 273, para 261.

593 AG in *Folien Fischer*, 49.

594 See also Nagy, J. Priv. Int. L. 2012, 251, 254. Cf. e.g. *eDate Advertising* (see *infra* Ch. VII.A.I.1) that concerned a preventive measure.

595 Another question could be the moment that separates the past and future damage. To put it differently, by analogy with *Cooke & Anor v MGN Ltd & Anor* [2014] EWHC 2831 (QB), 31, an English decision regarding s.1(1) of the *Defamation Act 2013*, it could be argued that the term 'caused' involves looking backwards in time, while the words 'may occur' involve looking forwards. However, the moment that marks the dividing line between past and future is not clear. It cannot

swers this question by differentiating between two scenarios: where the event has already occurred in the past and where this is not the case.[596] According to the first one, and under the assumption that the past and the future torts are similar, he lays down a presumption that the future tort will occur where the tort in the past took place. For the second scenario, when «the past does not provide a helping hand regularly or on a reliable basis with the possibility that the tort might be staged for the first time»,[597] he differentiates between two possibilities. First, when the tortfeasor announces the place of his act, he can be seised at that place. On the other hand, in the absence of any such announcement, one has to look at the facts of the particular case.

III. Subsequent disappearance of the harmful event: *perpetuatio fori* within Art 7(2)

It is questionable whether the principle of *perpetuatio fori* mentioned in *supra* Ch. III.C.I.1 is also applicable to tortious matters, i.e., the court originally seised retains its jurisdiction if the (danger of the) harmful event disappears or the causal event is suspended after the initiation of the proceedings at the place where it sits.[598] The ECJ was confronted with the latter part of this question in *DFDS Torline* outlined in *supra* Ch. IV.B.I.1.e), since as has been noted, SEKO suspended the implementation of its industrial action pending a ruling on its legality. To decide this question, the ECJ first reconfirmed the importance of foreseeability of the rules of jurisdiction.[599] Then it went on to rule that the subsequent suspension of the causal event after the initiation of the proceedings was irrelevant, and thus,

---

be the time of publication, since at that time, no harm has occurred yet. Possibly, the time of initiation of the proceedings would be an appropriate time. See also Mr Justice Bean in *Cooke & Anor v MGN Ltd & Anor* [2014] EWHC 2831 (QB), 32, who preferred «the date on which the claim is issued».

596 Mankowski, in: Magnus/Mankowski, Brussels I Regulation, pp 272-273, paras 259-261.

597 Mankowski, in: Magnus/Mankowski, Brussels I Regulation, p 272, para 260 (full stop, fn omitted).

598 For details, see Löser, Zuständigkeitsbestimmender Zeitpunkt, pp 87-97; Gampp, Perpetuatio fori internationalis, pp 113-136.

599 *DFDS Torline*, 36. On the requirement of foreseeability of jurisdictional rules, see *supra* Ch. III.B.I.

the principle of *perpetuatio fori* applied to Art 5(3) of the BC. In particular, it stated:

> «That objective *[foreseeability]* would not be achieved if, after an action falling within Article 5(3) of the Brussels Convention is brought before the court of a Contracting State having jurisdiction, the suspension by the defendant of the tortious conduct giving rise to that action could have the effect of depriving the court seised of its jurisdiction, and of jurisdiction being assigned to a court in another Contracting State.»[600]

In addition to this ruling, it is worth noting a so-called pseudo rule of *perpetuatio fori* ('unechte Regelung der internationalen Zuständigkeitsfortdauer'[601]), which can be derived from the special nature of Art 7(2). Practically speaking, this provision suggests an even earlier point of establishment of jurisdiction, since the jurisdiction-conferring concept of harmful event creates a particularly close connection between the dispute and the forum before the initiation of the proceedings, more precisely at the time of causation. This is so because, at that time, the causal connection is established between the damage and the event from which that damage originated.[602] Thus, the jurisdiction of the court is theoretically established already at the time of causation, and it continues to exist regardless of any

600 *DFDS Torline*, 37 (italics in square brackets added). Cf. AG in *DFDS Torline*, 59-66, especially 64; Löser, Zuständigkeitsbestimmender Zeitpunkt, p 88. For reference to this case, its evaluation, and the question of *perpetuatio fori* within the special rule of jurisdiction in tort, see Gampp, Perpetuatio fori internationalis, pp 114-115, 129, 132.

601 Gampp, Perpetuatio fori internationalis, p 121.

602 In the present author's view, the occurrence of damage bears considerable importance and determines the relevant time when the causal event and the damage establish a jurisdictionally relevant link between the dispute and the forum [see also *infra* Ch. VII.B.II.1.e)]. Cf. (1) Kubis, Internationale Zuständigkeit, p 132 regards the time when the tort is committed («Zeitpunkt der Begehung der unerlaubten Handlung»). (2) Baetge attaches importance to the causal event or the damage depending on the tort at stake under Rome II. Baetge, in: Calliess, Rome Regulations, p 612, para 31, regarding the concept of habitual residence, states that due to Art 4(2) of Rome II, «the relevant point in time is the time 'when the damage occurs'.» He also notes (*ibid.*) that the relevant point in time is the time when the event giving rise to the damage occurs, for example, under Art 10(2) of Rome II. (3) Art 7 of the Consultation on a preliminary draft proposal for a council regulation on the law applicable to non-contractual obligations, available at <http://ec.europa.eu/justice/news/consulting_public/rome_ii/news_hearing_rome2_en.htm> opts for «the time of the tort or delict» in relation to a «non-contractual obligation arising from a violation of private or personal rights or from defamation».

subsequent changes in the place of existence of the harmful event. However, these connections differ from the principle of *perpetratio fori* in the sense that the latter principle, as was noted above, governs situations when the jurisdictionally relevant factor disappears after the initiation of the proceedings. In Edda Gampp's words:

> «Dennoch handelt es sich nicht um Regelungen der Zuständigkeitsfortdauer im eigentlichen Sinn, da jene einen Fortbestand der Zuständigkeit gerade für den Fall bewirken sollen, daß die zuständigkeitsbegründenden Umstände während des Prozesses fortfallen.»[603]

C. Participation in the role of the plaintiff and the defendant

Generally, in proceedings concerning violations of personality rights under Art 7(2), the defendant will be the publisher who is allegedly responsible for the (prospective) publication of injurious content, and the plaintiff is the person who considers that his personality rights are (threatened to be) violated. This book is based on this pattern, as is evident from its aim to critically analyse and reform the *eDate and Martinez* judgment, whose factual background, as described in *infra* Ch. VII.A.I, centred on that pattern. However, this must not always be the case. The defendant can also be a person other than the publisher, as it would appear from the wording of *Shevill*:

> «[T]he plaintiff always has the option of bringing his entire claim before the courts either of the *defendant*'s domicile *or* of the place where the *publisher* of the defamatory publication is established.»[604]

By an analogous application of the settled case law of the ECJ, it is clear that the defendant can be another person, like an alleged co-perpetrator,[605] a director, a member of the board of directors, or a shareholder of the media outlet,[606] provided that certain circumstances are satisfied. On the other hand, the plaintiff can be another person, such as a person to whom

603 Gampp, Perpetuatio fori internationalis, p 122.
604 *Shevill*, 32 (author's italics). See also *eDate and Martinez*, 43.
605 For cases concerning the liability of co-perpetrators, see *supra* Ch. III.D.II.3.
606 See, by analogy, *Kronhofer*, *ÖFAB*. See also *Holterman Ferho Exploitatie u.a.* (request).

the claim was transferred.[607] This latter scenario is evident from *ÖFAB*, in which the claim for compensation for financial loss had been transferred from the original creditor to another. The seventh question of the *Hovrätten för Nedre Norrland* (Sweden), referred for a preliminary ruling, essentially asked whether this transfer had any impact on the determination of the court having jurisdiction under Art 5(3) of Brussels I.[608] In answer to this question, the ECJ first upheld that this provision is founded on the principles of proximity and predictability, and that it aims to establish a particularly close connection between the courts of the place where the harmful event occurred and the dispute.[609] Then, it pointed out:

> «A dispute concerning claims relating to 'tort, delict or quasi-delict' continues, in principle, to be closely connected to the place where the harmful event occurred, even though the claims at issue have been transferred.»[610]

As a result, the ECJ concluded that the transfer of the claim by the initial creditor to another has no impact on the determination of the jurisdiction of the court within Art 5(3) of Brussels I.[611]

---

607 For persons (like in person, legal representative, family member, or public prosecutor) who can enforce personality rights under certain conditions specified in national law, see e.g. Art 2:54 of the *új Ptk*.

608 See *ÖFAB*, 13 and 56 ff.

609 *ÖFAB*, 57, 58.

610 *ÖFAB*, 57.

611 *ÖFAB*, 59. For details on persons, as litigants, see also e.g. Kropholler/von Hein, EuZPR, p 233, para 93.

Chapter V: Jurisdiction in offline violations of personality rights: the *Shevill* judgment

As noted in *supra* Ch. IV.B.I, *Bier* established open-textured twin criteria under Art 7(2) for the interpretation of the concept of harmful event, and these can be easily adjusted to specific torts by balancing the governing objectives and underlying principles of the Brussels-Lugano Regime.[612] Such a balancing exercise is a delicate issue in disputes concerning cross-border defamation through the offline press, since these disputes involve a complex chain of successive acts that can be simplified as follows: production and printing of the newspaper – putting it into circulation, meaning distribution of the newspaper to regionalised non-reader retailers (retailers) – putting it into circulation, meaning distribution of the newspaper from the retailers to third party readers (readers) – comprehension of the newspaper by the readers – injury to reputation.[613] The policy-based selection of jurisdictionally relevant concepts amounting to causal event and damage for the purpose of Art 7(2) was undertaken by the ECJ in *Shevill* in 1995, which provided a sound basis for ruling on online violations of personality rights in *eDate and Martinez*. Thus, by analysing *Shevill*, the present chapter basically describes complex issues and possible problems relating to the localisation of the concept of harmful event in offline violations of personality rights, particularly defamation. By doing so, it paves the way for the scrutiny of *eDate and Martinez* undertaken in *infra* Ch. VII.

A. Shevill in a nutshell

The present section outlines the factual and procedural background of *Shevill* and the questions referred for a preliminary ruling by the *House of Lords* (UK) to the ECJ, and finally, it summarises the judgment of the ECJ.[614]

612 On the governing objectives and underlying principles, see *supra* Ch. III.B.
613 See Kaye, Law of the European Judgments Convention, pp 1456-1457.
614 If necessary, this outline will be extended in the sections below.

I. Factual and procedural background

Paragraphs 2-15 of *Shevill* show that the defendant was Presse Alliance SA, a company incorporated under French law with a registered office in Paris. It published a newspaper, France-Soir, in which an article in French[615] appeared in 1989. The article alleged that the first plaintiff, Ms Shevill, who resided in England, had worked three months at a bureau de change in Paris (France) in the summer of 1989 and had been involved in laundering drug money. In addition, it claimed that the bureau de change was also involved. The newspaper was mainly distributed in France and had a very small circulation in the UK, effected through independent distributors. It was estimated that more than 237.000 copies were sold in France and approximately 15.500 copies distributed in other European countries, of which 230 were sold in England and Wales (5 in Yorkshire where Ms Shevill resided).[616] Although the defendant published a retraction and an apology, Ms Shevill brought proceedings in England claiming that due to the publication in England and Wales, she had suffered damage including hurt feelings, great distress, and embarrassment, and accordingly, she asked for damages.[617] The defendant claimed that the court lacked jurisdiction because under Art 5(3) of the BC the place where the harmful event occurred was not England but France. On appeal from the *Court of Appeal* to the *House of Lords*, the latter authority referred a number of questions to the ECJ.[618]

II. The questions referred

The *House of Lords* referred seven questions to the ECJ for a preliminary ruling. Of these seven questions, as the ECJ pointed out, the first three and

615 *Shevill and Others v. Presse Alliance S.A.* [1992] 2 *W.L.R.* 1 (C.A.), p 13/H.

616 Note that slightly different numbers are indicated (200.000 – 15.000 - 250 - 10) in *Shevill and Others v. Presse Alliance S.A.* [1992] 2 *W.L.R.* 1 (C.A.), pp 1/F, 4/F.

617 See *Shevill and Others v. Presse Alliance S.A.* [1996] 3 *W.L.R.* 420 (H.L.(E.)), p 420/F. In addition, note that three French-registered companies {see *Shevill and Others v. Presse Alliance S.A.* [1992] 2 *W.L.R.* 1 (C.A.), p 4/G} related to the bureau de change were also plaintiffs in the dispute (see *Shevill*, 4, 6-7). Regarding legal persons as victims, see *infra* Ch. VII.D.II.2.

618 On the decision of the *Court of Appeal*, see Hartley, E.L.Rev. 1992, 274-276.

the sixth dealt with the localisation of the concept of harmful event within Art 5(3) of the BC. In other words:

> «*[These questions]* essentially seek guidance from the Court as to the interpretation of the concept "the place where the harmful event occurred" used in Article 5(3) of the Convention, with a view to establishing which courts have jurisdiction to hear an action for damages for harm caused to the victim following distribution of a defamatory newspaper article in several Contracting States.»[619]

III. The judgment of the ECJ

After reaffirming its findings in *Bier* and *Dumez*,[620] the ECJ went on to localise the concept of harmful event as follows:

> «[T]he answer to the first, second, third and sixth questions referred by the House of Lords must be that, on a proper construction of the expression "place where the harmful event occurred" in Article 5(3) of the Convention, the victim of a libel by a newspaper article distributed in several Contracting States may bring an action for damages against the publisher either before the courts of the Contracting State of the place where the publisher of the defamatory publication is established, which have jurisdiction to award damages for all the harm caused by the defamation, or before the courts of each Contracting State in which the publication was distributed and where the victim claims to have suffered injury to his reputation, which have jurisdiction to rule solely in respect of the harm caused in the State of the court seised.»[621]

B. The place where the harmful event occurred

As is clear from the foregoing, the ECJ adapted the concepts of causal event and damage to the special characteristics of disputes in which the victim seeks to establish the liability of the publisher for the non-pecuniary harm caused to her by the publishing of defamatory material. The present section elicits the meaning of these concepts and indicates possible troublesome features that stem from their interpretation and *de facto* application.

---

619 *Shevill*, 17 (italics in square brackets added). Question nos 4-5 and no 7 are dealt with in other parts of this book (e.g. *supra* fns 538, 561 and 583).

620 *Shevill*, 19-22. On these decisions, see *supra* Ch. IV.B.I; *supra* Ch. IV.B.I.2.

621 *Shevill*, 33.

I. The place of the event, which gives rise to and is at the origin of the damage, occurred

The place of the event that gives rise to and is at the origin of the damage was identified by the ECJ as the place where the publisher of the defamatory publication is established, i.e., where its establishment is situated.[622] In particular, it described that place as follows:

> «[T]he place of the event giving rise to the damage … can only be the place where the publisher of the newspaper in question is established, since that is the place where the harmful event originated and from which the libel was issued and put into circulation.
>
> However, that forum will generally coincide with the head of jurisdiction set out in the first paragraph of Article 2 of the Convention.»[623]

Accordingly, the ECJ developed a complex approach, which, in the absence of a clear reasoning, poses several questions, as outlined below. First, an attempt is made to determine its possible meaning in the aforementioned chain of successive acts, and secondly, the assumption of general coincidence with Art 4(1) is examined.

1. The publisher's establishment in the chain of successive acts

It is rather difficult to comprehend why the ECJ opted for the place of the publisher's establishment instead of simply designating the place of production of the newspaper directly as the place of the causal event. In this regard, Gerhard Wagner appears to be of the opinion that, according to a conceptually precise handling of the applicable law in tort, the place of the causal event should be located where the perpetrator or his people acted. This would mean that torts committed by the press could be located at the seat of the publisher or the editorial board as well as at the place of printing, publication, and distribution, in so far as these activities are controlled by the publisher. However, among other grounds, the proliferation of the

622 See also AG in *eDate and Martinez*, 37 referring to the «State of establishment of the publisher».

623 *Shevill*, 24, 26 (emphases omitted). It is not entirely clear what the ECJ intended to mean under the term 'put into circulation'. It might refer to the distribution of the newspaper to the retailers or to the readers. Since the latter act is supposedly understood as the place of the damage, it is argued that it refers to the place where the newspaper was dispatched to the retailers [cf. *infra* Ch. V.B.II.1.a)].

places of the causal event that would unjustifiable privilege the victim militates against such an approach. Gerhard Wagner goes on to notice that without expressly mentioning these findings the ECJ probably therefore decided in favour of the place of the publisher's establishment because it regarded the aims for an efficient settlement of disputes under Art 5(3) of the BC as being best served.[624] With respect, the present author remains unconvinced by Gerhard Wagner's opinion and instead shares the view expressed by Karl Kreuzer and Paul Klötgen. They appear to hold that the ECJ supposedly took it as a starting point that those places would coincide with each other, since they did in *Shevill*, and consequently, it did not consider situations in which those places would be at different locations.[625] Viewed in this light, it might be queried which exact point in the chain of successive acts was intended to be meant by the concept of publisher's establishment. Peter Kaye proposes understanding it as the place of putting the newspaper into circulation, i.e., «circulation of the defamatory statement to the reader or listener, directly or through despatch by the defendant publisher or third party intermediary.»[626] He explains that this point is the moment of release at which the publisher's act is complete and at which he relinquishes direct or indirect control or responsibility for execution of the statement. In addition, he adds that this point has the greatest policy significance also because, among other reasons, it is distinct from the defendant's place of domicile.[627] Therefore, he regrets that the ECJ chose effectively to approve the place of production and printing in the form of the place where the publisher is established:

> «As for stage 1 production, whilst, in a sense, this is the most active stage in the overall sequence of events leading to damage, it is also the most incomplete and distant from the latter regarding causation and is the most likely to correspond with Article 2 defendant's domicile.»[628]

Irrespective of this objection, the place of production and printing as the place of establishment could also be underscored by the opinions of Ad-

---

624 See Wagner, RabelsZ 1998, 243, 281.

625 See Kreuzer/Klötgen, IPRax 1997, 90, 93-94. Cf. Kubis, Internationale Zuständigkeit, p 131.

626 Kaye, Law of the European Judgments Convention, p 1462.

627 Kaye, Law of the European Judgments Convention, pp 1462-1463. Cf. his proposal on the originating act in *supra* Ch. IV.B.I.1.d); Schack, in: Hübner *et al.*, Das Persönlichkeitsrecht, p 127 who regards the place of distribution as the place of harmful event («Tatort»); Kubis in *supra* Ch. IV.B.I.1.b) and *infra* Ch. VI.B.I.

628 Kaye, Law of the European Judgments Convention, p 1464.

vocates General and the submissions put forward in the course of proceedings.[629] This understanding is also in conjunction with *Kainz.*[630] The place of production, similar to the place where the defective product was manufactured, facilitates the principles of sound administration of justice, efficacious conduct of proceedings, and predictability. In particular, it ensures the possibility of gathering evidence to establish the defamatory nature of the material and the motivation of the publisher, and it is foreseeable by the litigants. In addition, production is the original activity, which appears factually to have initiated the chain of successive acts that culminated in the injury to reputation, and which may give rise to establishing the publisher's liability.[631] On the other hand, the term 'production' or 'manufacture' of the defamatory material could not only be understood as the place of the creation of the publication but also as the place where the publisher decides upon the publication. This view is compatible with the settled case law of the ECJ delivered under Art 7(2) in disputes concerning violations of rights other than personality rights.[632] In legal writing, locating the concept of causal event in the place where the decision about the publication is taken is also accepted, which, in Karsten Thorn's opinion, is equivalent to the place of the seat of the publisher:

> «[E]s *[ist]* richtig, *[den Handlungsort]* auf den Verlagssitz als Ort der Verhaltenszentrale abzustellen, von dem aus nicht nur die Redaktion, sondern eben auch der Vertrieb des Mediums gesteuert wird.»[633]

---

629 On this, see Kaye, Law of the European Judgments Convention, pp 1461-1462, 1464; AG 1995 in *Shevill*, 5, 11 (printing). See also the written observations of the defendant and the French government in *Shevill and Others v. Presse Alliance S.A.* [1995] 2 W.L.R. 499 (E.C.J.), pp 505/D, 508/E that propose the place where the newspaper was printed and put into circulation. Cf. national practice as referred to in AG 1994 in *Shevill*, 29-41; question no 1(a) as referred for a preliminary ruling in *Shevill*, 16.

630 On this, see *supra* Ch. IV.B.I.1.e).

631 Cf. *supra* Ch. IV.B.I.1.c)-d).

632 See also *supra* fn 571.

633 Thorn, FS Bernd von Hoffmann, p 749 (fn omitted, italics in square brackets added). Giving a different view, Wagner, RabelsZ 1998, 243, 281-282 suggests that under the term 'place of the publisher's establishment' the «Sitz der über den Inhalt des Presseerzeugnisses entscheidenden Instanz» could be understood. In other words, Wagner, ERPL 2005, 21, 35 suggests that this place refers to «the seat of the particular editorial staff responsible for a particular edition of the product.»

2. The publisher's establishment as the place of domicile

The finding of the ECJ, according to which the publisher's establishment generally coincides with the concept of domicile under the general rule of jurisdiction, has its origin in *Bier*, and it is widely accepted in legal writing.[634] Consequently, the concept of causal event loses its effectiveness and it is rendered meaningless.[635] In this regard, Georg Philipp Krog states:

> «[A]rticle 5 is only applicable if the alternative forum decided by the term "in the courts for the place where the harmful event occurred or may occur" is in another state than the state where the defendant is domiciled. If the alternative forum is in the same state as the state where the defendant is domiciled, the matter will then regulated by article 2».[636]

Two comments are called for on these findings. First, the concept of the publisher's establishment does not always coincide with the concept of domicile.[637] A limited number of exceptions to this presumption exist.[638] The first is when, for example, in accordance with Art 53 of the BC, the rules of PIL of the forum determine a place as the seat of the legal person publisher (domicile) as being different from the place where the publisher's establishment is situated.[639] The second is when, after committing the violation of a personality right but before initiating proceedings, the publisher transfers his domicile into another Brussels-Lugano State. This is so because the place of the defendant's domicile is defined at the time of the initiation of the proceedings, while the place of the causal event is determined at the time of causation.[640] In addition, based on the concepts used in the TFEU, it could also be argued that the concept of the publisher's establishment covers not only the primary establishment of the

634 See *Bier*, 20 (see *supra* fn 533); Thorn, FS Bernd von Hoffmann, p 749; Kubis, Internationale Zuständigkeit, p 132. Cf. Jenard Report, p 16 notes that domicile introduces «the idea of a more fixed and stable place of establishment on the part of the defendant».

635 *Shevill*, 26-27. See also *Bier*, 20.

636 Krog, IPRax 2004, 154, 156 (regarding the 1988 LC).

637 Contra (stating that they coincide always, without exceptions): Kreuzer/Klötgen, IPRax 1997, 90, 94; Löffler, Mediendelikte, p 216. Cf. AG 1995 in *Shevill*, 13.

638 For the first two, see also Kubis, Internationale Zuständigkeit, p 132.

639 On this, see *supra* Ch. III.C.I.1.

640 On this, see *supra* Ch. III.C.I.1; *supra* Ch. IV.B.III. However, as a kind of rebut of this argument regarding the time of causation in online (potential) violations of personality rights, see *infra* Ch. VII.B.II.1.e).

publisher, i.e., domicile,[641] but also his secondary establishment, such as his agency, branch, or subsidiary.[642] Consequently, when the defendant is the secondary establishment of the publisher, there will be no coincidence with the primary establishment, namely, with its domicile.[643]

The second comment, which raises a possible objection to the previously mentioned assumption, is more complex and principally reflects the present author's view. In particular, although she agrees with the general coincidence of the concepts of domicile and establishment at the level of their meaning, she remains unconvinced about their *de facto* coincidence in their application. Viewing these concepts on the basis of their purpose and general scheme, the following possible objections against their *de facto* coincidence could be put forward.

First and foremost, Art 4(1) confers international jurisdiction on the courts of a Brussels-Lugano State in which the defendant is domiciled. Accordingly, it determines only which courts of a particular state are competent in general, and it leaves it to the rules of the civil procedure of that state to designate a particular court that has local jurisdiction, i.e., venue.[644] By contrast, Art 7(2) allocates international and local jurisdiction to a particular court of a Brussels-Lugano State (i.e., the Brussels-Lugano Regime overrides the national rules of civil procedure).[645] To take an example, suppose that the publisher is incorporated and it has its registered office in Saarbrücken (Germany), while the injury to reputation occurred in Hungary, Germany, and Lithuania. If the aggrieved person sues the publisher pursuant to Art 4(1), this rule allocates jurisdiction to the German courts, and so the German rules of civil procedure determine the local jurisdiction, i.e., the particular court that is competent to hear the dispute (i.e., a kind of nationalisation of the uniform rules of the Brussels-Lugano Regime). Accordingly, by virtue of Art 13 of the *ZPO*, the general jurisdiction is determined on the basis of domicile. Alternatively, in accordance with Art 35 of the *ZPO*, the plaintiff may select from among several rules of jurisdiction and bring proceedings under Art 32 of the *ZPO* in the court of the place of the damage or the causal event, i.e., «in the jurisdic-

641 On this, see *supra* Ch. III.C.I.1.

642 Art 49(1) of the TFEU.

643 See also Stone and Nuyts (in *infra* Ch. VI.A.I.1), who suppose that under certain circumstances, Arts 7(2) and Art 7(5) may coincide with each other. On secondary establishment, see also *supra* Ch. III.D.IV.

644 On this, see *supra* Ch. III.C.I.

645 On this, see *supra* Intr. to Ch. III.D.II; *supra* Intr. to Ch. VI.

tion of which the tortious act was committed».[646] Consequently, as a result of the joint application of Art 4(1) and the aforementioned German rules of civil procedure, the plaintiff is entitled to sue in the courts of three different places: (1) the place of the defendant's domicile, (2) the place of the causal event, and (3) the place of the damage. These places, depending on their national meaning, might be situated at different locations and, accordingly, might allocate local jurisdiction to courts of first instance sitting at different places in the same state.[647] By contrast, if the plaintiff sues the publisher in accordance with Art 7(2) at the place of his establishment, this place generally determines both the international and the local jurisdiction on the basis of the autonomous meaning of the concepts under the Brussels-Lugano Regime and without recourse to the national rules of civil procedure. It follows from all these considerations that although the meaning of the connecting factors employed under Arts 4(1) and 7(2) generally coincide, because of the different nature of jurisdiction (i.e., international and/or local), they might designate different courts in the same state.

Secondly, it could be argued that not only might different courts be designated by those rules, but that courts might perhaps also have a different extent of jurisdiction. In particular, as is noted in *infra* Ch. VII.C.II, while the general rule of jurisdiction confers an unlimited extent of jurisdiction on the competent court to decide upon the entire damage caused, the extent of the jurisdiction of the competent court for the place of the publisher's establishment under Art 7(2) could be understood as being restricted to the Brussels-Lugano States-wide damage.

Finally, while the concept of domicile under Art 4(1) must be established at the time of the initiation of the proceedings,[648] Art 7(2) principally establishes a particularly close connection between the dispute and

---

646 Art 32 of the *ZPO* as available in English at <http://www.gesetze-im-internet.de/englisch_zpo/englisch_zpo.html>. See also *supra* fn 26. Note that national law has recourse to its national methods and terminologies for localising domestically the dispute, irrespective of those developed within the Brussels-Lugano Regime. Hence, the concepts of damage and causal event may be determined differently from this regime for local jurisdictional purposes. See e.g. case 1 U 511/13 (7.11.2013), *OLG Jena* (AfP 2014, 75-76) in which the German court had recourse to the collision of conflicting interests criterion (cf. approach of the *BGH* in *supra* Intr.) in order to determine venue at the place of the damage. Cf. case 324 S 1/14 (19.9.2014), *LG Hamburg* (AfP 2015, 183-184).

647 This is true for states in which the first instance jurisdiction is territorially scattered throughout the state.

648 See *supra* Ch. III.C.I.1.

the place of the court that was seised at the time of causation. In this regard, Peter Kaye also asserts:

> «What is less appealing ... is the Court's decision to select publisher's establishment as place of causative event, ... as creating confusion concerning whether establishment at the date of proceedings or as at some earlier point in time is intended where change has occurred, presumably the latter in view of the special connection policy outlined in *Bier* as the objective of Article 5(3)».[649]

In the light of the foregoing, it can be concluded that the concept of the publisher's establishment theoretically coincides with, but in its application might be distinct from, the place of the defendant's domicile. Irrespective of this conclusion, strictly speaking, the defendant's interest is still favoured, since the concept of the publisher's establishment principally allocates jurisdiction to the court sitting in his home country where he is supposedly more familiar with the culture, language, and legal system than in that of the aggrieved person. In addition, the publisher could intentionally choose that state for legal considerations and/or on economic grounds. Viewed in this light, it can be upheld that the place of the causal event does not fulfil its function of providing an alternative forum to the defendant's domicile. Nevertheless, the ECJ was aware of this result, and it did not attempt to change or oppose it.[650] Moreover, it is also worth noting that the phenomenon of coincidence of the connecting factor under the special rule of jurisdiction with the concept of the defendant's domicile, irrespective of the requirement laid down in Art 5(1), is not uncommon within the Brussels-Lugano Regime.[651]

II. The place where the damage occurred

As noted previously, the ECJ localised the place of the damage in the state in which the defamatory publication was distributed and where the victim

---

649 Kaye, Law of the European Judgments Convention, p 1461 (emphases omitted, italics in the original). See also *supra* Ch. IV.B.III. However, see *supra* fn 640.

650 Strictly speaking, a possible objection could be based on *Kainz* [see *supra* Ch. IV.B.I.1.e)] in which, although the referring court proposed three interpretations regarding the concept of causal event, the ECJ opted for a fourth one, namely, the place of the manufacture of the defective product. Nevertheless, that place coincided with the place of the manufacturer's establishment.

651 See *supra* fn 395.

claims to have suffered injury to his reputation.[652] It arrived at this conclusion, first, by stipulating that the place of the damage is the place where the causal event «produced its harmful effects upon the victim.»[653] Then, it went on to state:

> «In the case of an international libel through the press, the injury caused by a defamatory publication to the honour, reputation and good name of a natural or legal person occurs in the places where the publication is distributed, when the victim is known in those places.
>
> It follows that the courts of each Contracting State in which the defamatory publication was distributed and in which the victim claims to have suffered injury to his reputation have jurisdiction to rule on the injury caused in that State to the victim's reputation.»[654]

This approach is far from evident in its application. It is first uncertain what the concepts of distribution and injury to reputation mean, and secondly, it remains unclear whether their application is cumulatively required or, alternatively, whether one incorporates the other by virtue of presumption.[655] The present subsection aims to approach these uncertainties one by one.

1. The concept of distribution

The concept of distribution, which was predominantly proposed as the connecting factor in legal theory,[656] may refer to different actions. Based

---

652 Cf. concepts crystallised in legal writing: (1) main emphasis on distribution: Nielsen, J. Priv. Int. L. 2013, 269, 276; Hartley, ICLQ 2010, 25, 28; *infra* fn 656; (2) main emphasis on being known: Thorn, FS Bernd von Hoffmann, pp 749-751; (3) the place of the main harm: Huet as referred to in AG 1994 in *Shevill*, 80-83; (4) the place of the victim's domicile: Gaudemet-Tallon and Bourel as referred to in AG 1994 in *Shevill*, 42-44.

653 *Shevill*, 28. Cf. *Dumez*, 20.

654 *Shevill*, 29-30. See also *Shevill*, 33 and its operative part. Cf. COM, and the Spanish and French governments in AG 1994 in *Shevill*, 50.

655 On this, see similarly Kaye, Law of the European Judgments Convention, pp 1460, 1465-1466.

656 See AG 1994 in *Shevill*, 52, 111; AG 1995 in *Shevill*, 37; *supra* fn 652. Essentially, this criterion was also identified in AG 1994 in *Shevill*, 41 as a common solution worked out in the national system of the Contracting States of the BC. By contrast, this place is regarded as the place of the harmful event in e.g. Löffler, Mediendelikte, pp 201, 211; the UK as referred to in AG 1994 in *Shevill*, 50 and AG 1995 in *Shevill*, 31 (it proposed the place of communication to third par-

on the aforementioned chain of successive acts, it can be understood as the distribution of the newspaper to the retailers. Alternatively, it can be regarded as the distribution of the newspaper from the retailers to the readers. Accordingly, when these two acts do not occur at the same place, they confer jurisdiction on the courts of different Brussels-Lugano States. Read in this light, on the basis of legal certainty, it is necessary to equip one of these acts, and thus one of these places, with a jurisdictionally relevant character for the purpose of the concept of damage.

a) Distribution to the retailers

The place of distribution of the newspaper from the publisher to the retailers cannot be regarded as a convincing place of the damage for two main reasons. First, by recalling the ECJ's aforementioned finding in relation to the concept of the publisher's establishment, it becomes evident that that place is presumed to coincide *inter alia* with the place from which the libel was put into circulation; thus, it determines the place of the causal event.[657] Secondly, it is self-evident that the sole act of distribution of the disputed newspaper to the retailers does not produce its harmful effects upon the victim, since at this point, the defamatory material has not yet been revealed to the readers.[658]

b) Distribution to the readers

The concept of distribution of the disputed newspaper from the retailers to the readers is presumably intended to be meant under the concept of distribution. The following arguments can be put forward in support of this interpretation. First, AG Darmon noticed in his opinion that the place of the damage is the place where the defamatory material is spread out and has become known:

---

ties; note that as Hartley, ICLQ 2010, 25, 26 notes, 'communication' is an English legal terminology and it is equivalent to the continental term of 'distribution'). Cf. *supra* fn 627.

657 See *supra* Ch. V.B.I.1. See also Kaye, Law of the European Judgments Convention, p 1460; *supra* fn 623.

658 On this, see the concept of injury to reputation in *infra* Ch. V.B.II.2.

> «The harm occurs in the place of the final element making up the tort, that is to say, in the case of torts committed in a newspaper ... in each State where the newspaper is distributed ... .
>
> Damage to a person's reputation and/or honour arises in the various places where a defamatory remark is revealed to third parties. Consequently, the damage becomes apparent when that "information" is brought into public knowledge».[659]

In addition, as *supra* Ch. II.D noted, distribution reflects the intentional business strategy and commercial policy of the publisher. Thus, the distribution coverage can be verified easily and with high accuracy in each state of distribution, as is also clear from *Shevill*, in which the ECJ calculated the number of copies of France-Soir sold in the different states, especially in England and Wales as well as in France.[660] This reflects the estimated number of readers reached in a particular state and, consequently, it contributes to the assessment of the extent of damage caused therein.[661] It follows that distribution occurs where the publisher intentionally and voluntary targets a state on a commercial basis or free of charge.[662] As Dagmar Coester-Waltjen notes:

> «Wer sich auf einen Markt begibt, muß damit rechnen, dort gerichtspflichtig zu werden!»[663]

This view *per se* excludes the place in which the publication is not intentionally distributed. To take an example, suppose that a person domiciled in Germany bought in Hungary a newspaper that was not distributed in Germany. He took a single copy of this Hungarian newspaper to his hometown where he comprehended defamatory material about the victim. In this case, the fact that the defamatory material was read in Germany does not confer jurisdiction on the German courts, because that country was not targeted by the publisher, and consequently, the comprehension in that state was only accidental.[664]

---

659 AG 1994 in *Shevill*, 52-53 (emphases omitted).

660 See *supra* Ch. V.A.I and *Shevill*, 9.

661 On this, cf. Hartley, ICLQ 2010, 25, 28-29; Hess, CML Rev. 2012, 1075, 1088.

662 See Commission Document COM(2003) 427 final, p 18 («commercial basis»); the COM, the Spanish and French governments as referred to in AG 1994 in *Shevill*, 50 («voluntary distribution»); Metro, a daily newspaper (free of charge in many states, such as Hungary). For references to intended distribution, see also Coester-Waltjen, FS Rolf A. Schütze, pp 183-184; Rüßmann, JurPC Web-Dok. 1998, Abs. 36.

663 Coester-Waltjen, FS Rolf A. Schütze, p 184.

664 On this, see Coester-Waltjen, FS Rolf A. Schütze, pp 183-184; Spindler, AfP 2012, 114, 115; Rüßmann, JurPC Web-Dok. 1998, Abs. 37-38. Contra: Thorn,

Finally, it is worth noting that the extent of distribution coverage of the intentionally distributed newspaper is irrelevant. In other words, the extent of publication in the forum state may be small as a proportion of the total. This is clear from *Shevill*, since, as just noted in *supra* Ch. V.A.I, France-Soir was mainly distributed in France, and it had a very small circulation, approx. 0,001%, in England and Wales.[665]

2. The concept of injury to reputation

The concept of injury to reputation is not defined in *Shevill.* In the absence of such an explanation, it is reasonable to have recourse to the predominant view expressed in legal writing. Accordingly, the right to reputation is injured where the defamatory publication «comes to the knowledge of third parties and a person' s reputation is liable to be harmed.»[666] In other words, it is injured at the place where third parties read and comprehend the contested publication.[667] That is the place where the defamatory material produces its harmful effects upon the victim and has an adverse impact on the attitude of people towards the victim.[668] Hence, those places to

---

FS Bernd von Hoffmann, p 749 and see also *ibid.*, pp 750-751; Buchner in *infra* Ch. VI.B.III. Cf. Case 29 U 2713/07 (6.12.2007), *OLG München*, ECJ Website No 2009/33 (concerning a «[n]ewspaper not regularly distributed in Germany or only sporadic cross-border distribution»).

665 Since the *forum non conveniens* doctrine is inapplicable within the Brussels-Lugano Regime (on this, see *supra* Ch. III.B.I.4), the court cannot decline jurisdiction on the basis of a modest circulation. A possible objection against the jurisdiction of such a peripheral court could perhaps be the argument of abuse of process. This argument was referred to in Garnett/Richardson, J. Priv. Int. L. 2009, 471, 482 (regarding libel tourism), and it was also invoked in *TGI Paris*, 17ème chamber, No d'affaire: 0718523043 (3.3.2011) - *Ministére Public c/ Weiler*, as the unofficial English translation available in Weiler, The Judgment, 2011 indicates.

666 Commission Document COM(2003) 427 final, p 18 (space in the original). Similarly, AG 1994 in *Shevill*, 53.

667 See Thorn, FS Bernd von Hoffmann, pp 749, 751; Mankowski, in: Magnus/ Mankowski, Brussels I Regulation, p 263, para 249b; Reymond, YbPIL 2011, 493, 499. See also question no 1(b) referred for a preliminary ruling in *Shevill,* 16; written observation of the French government in *Shevill and Others v. Presse Alliance S.A.* [1995] 2 W.L.R. 499 (E.C.J.), p 508/E that proposes the place «where the newspaper was read by particular individuals.»

668 Cf. *Thornton v Telegraph Media Group Ltd* [2010] EWHC 1414 (QB), 95 (regarding the meaning of 'defamatory' in English law).

which the reader, after comprehension, travels are irrelevant for jurisdictional purposes, since the injury is not regarded as ongoing until the reader's view has changed back to the same as it was before the defamatory material had been read.[669]

Viewing the concept of injury to reputation in this light, the next uncertainties with which this concept might be surrounded relate to certain questions referred by the *House of Lords* for a preliminary ruling. Specifically, it is uncertain whether the victim must have a significant reputation in the state where the court called for a decision on the dispute and whether the reader(s) had to know or know of the victim prior to reading and had to understand those words as referring to the victim.[670] This is so because the ECJ referred to the criterion 'to be known' only in paragraph 29 of *Shevill*, stating that the injury to reputation occurs where the defamatory publication is distributed only when the victim is known there.[671] It follows from the plain wording of the judgment that instead of answering those preliminary questions with precision, the ECJ held that the victim must simply be known. Consequently and supposedly, the other factors of the questions are of no importance for jurisdictional purposes. If they had been of importance, the ECJ would have decided them easily given the facts of the case. Although presumably Ms Shevill was known in France because of her temporary summer work there, she was probably better known in England, since she resided there. Secondly, as Douglas W. Vick and Linda Macpherson notice:

> «When the libel writs were issued, there was no direct evidence that anyone in the United Kingdom aware of Fiona Shevill's reputation had read and understood the contents of the French-language publication that was the subject of the lawsuit.»[672]

Accordingly, due to paragraph 29 of *Shevill*, it is supposed that the simple fact that the victim is known at the place of the damage is sufficient for jurisdictional purposes. It is not jurisdictionally relevant whether the victim has a significant or a poor reputation there, whether the reader knew or

---

669 On the ongoing nature of the injury, see Svantesson, PIL and the Internet, p 335.

670 See question no 1(c) and no 2 referred for a preliminary ruling in *Shevill*, 16. On question no 2, see also the written observation of the defendant in *Shevill and Others v. Presse Alliance S.A.* [1995] 2 *W.L.R.* 499 (E.C.J.), p 505/E.

671 See also Nagy, J. Priv. Int. L. 2012, 251, 258.

672 Vick/Macpherson, Va. J. Int'l L. 1995-1996, 933, 977. See also similarly, Hartley, ICLQ 2010, 25, 28; *Shevill and Others v. Presse Alliance S.A.* [1992] 2 *W.L.R.* 1 (C.A.), p 6/E.

knew of him prior to reading the defamatory publication, or whether he understood that article to refer to the victim. So far so good.[673] However, the existence and need for the criterion 'to be known' become disputable in the context of the whole judgment, since, as has been mentioned, it appears only in paragraph 29 but not in the other parts of it. Similarly, the opinions of Advocates General did not place any great emphasis on this criterion, since only AG Léger referred to the state «where that person is particularly well known».[674] The subsequent loss of this criterion in Csongor István Nagy's opinion might be justified due to the fact that «[i]n this case it seems to be needless to place too much weight on the question of reputation: if the victim was not known in England, she was not known anywhere.»[675] Based on a possible logic in the structure of the decision, another explanation, which would maintain the existence of the criterion 'to be known', could be put forward as follows. As cited above, paragraph 30 generally identifies the place of the damage by referring to «the courts of each Contracting State in which the defamatory publication was distributed and *in which the victim claims to have suffered injury to his reputation*».[676] These courts thus have jurisdiction to hear the dispute and decide upon the injury caused in that state to the victim's reputation. Paragraph 29 of *Shevill* could be regarded, however, as a special clause for localising injury caused to reputation. To put it differently, it could be read as a specification of the state «in which the victim claims to have suffered injury to his reputation» by stating that:

> «In the case of an international libel through the press, the *injury* caused by a defamatory publication *to the* honour, *reputation* and good name of a natural or legal person *occurs in the places where the publication is distributed, when the victim is known in those places.*»[677]

Viewed in this light, paragraph 30 might be read as conferring jurisdiction on the courts of each Contracting State in which the defamatory publication was distributed and in which the publication was distributed when the victim was known there.

---

673 A possible danger of the open-textured criterion is that it might give rise to discretion on the part of national courts to require, to a certain extent, that the victim be known.

674 AG 1995 in *Shevill*, 15.

675 Nagy, J. Priv. Int. L. 2012, 251, 258.

676 Author's italics.

677 Author's italics. Note that the language of the judgment subsequently lost the reference to injury to honour and good name.

Finally, it is worth noting that the wording of *Shevill* divides the views expressed in legal writing. Károly László Simon puts forward doubts in relation to the requirement 'to be known' by stating that it is strange for jurisdictional purposes, since the question of whether the plaintiff is known or unknown in a certain state is subject to proof, and it is rather a substantive legal than a procedural question:

> «Ez a feltétel önmagában meglehetősen furcsa egy joghatósági ok megállapítási feltételeként, hiszen az, hogy az adott tagállamban a felperest ismerik-e vagy sem, bizonyítás tárgyát fogja képezni, ráadásul inkább anyagi jogi, mintsem eljárásjogi kérdés».[678]

Another reason that could challenge this requirement is that it regards the state in which the victim is not known (i.e., he has a «nil» or «neutral» reputation[679]) as jurisdictionally irrelevant. It follows that this victim is deprived of the possibility of initiating proceedings against the publisher in the state where he is unknown. However, as is emphasised in legal writing and practice, even if the victim had not been known previously, defamation may still occur, since people in the state of distribution may start to dislike the victim, whose neutral situation as being unknown is arguably changed to a negative one. As Dan Jerker B. Svantesson states:

> «Indeed, the simple fact that a person was previously unknown, does not mean that that same person cannot be defamed (e.g., be exposed to hatred, contempt or ridicule, or shunned or avoided, or, lowered in the estimation of others) due to a defamatory publication.»[680]

---

678 Simon, in: Kengyel/Simon, Tanulmányok, pp 104-105. See also Simon, Európai Jog 2010, 15, 21. Similarly cf. Coester-Waltjen, FS Rolf A. Schütze, p 183.

679 See Svantesson, PIL and the Internet, p 346.

680 Svantesson, PIL and the Internet, p 346 (fns omitted). See also Kaye, Law of the European Judgments Convention, p 1465; von Hinden, Persönlichkeitsverletzungen, pp 90-91; UK/England: *Ames & Anor v The Spamhaus Project Ltd & Anor* [2015] EWHC 127 (QB), 40 ff. in which the judge *inter alia* considered whether persons who are unknown or little-known in England could also claim defamation under English law. In addition, note that the recent judicial practice of the ECtHR [e.g. *Ungváry and Irodalom Kft v. Hungary* (no 64520/10)] appears to approach defamation under Art 8 of the ECHR by using the so-called '*Axel Springer* criteria' established for balancing Arts 8 and 10 of the ECHR in the context of privacy complaints (on this, see Tomlinson, Privacy and Defamation, 2014). Thus, it assesses *inter alia* how well known the person defamed is. Regarding this assessment the ECtHR pointed out in *Axel Springer AG v. Germany* (no 39954/08), 91 that «whilst a private individual unknown to the public may claim particular protection of his or her right to private life, the same is not true of public figures». Due to this practice of the ECtHR, it is supposed that under

In contrast, several scholars claim that due to *Shevill*, the victim must enjoy a reputation, i.e., must be known.[681] It could be argued that the requirement 'to be known' facilitates the principle of legal certainty, since excluding those states in which the victim is unknown enables the publisher to foresee the possible jurisdictionally relevant forum, which for an average person, is mainly his domicile or habitual residence. Accordingly, while «Mister Weltberühmt» is known in numerous states, and so can bring an action before the courts of each of those states, 'Herr Nobody' may seek only to establish the liability of the publisher in the courts of the state where he is habitually resident.[682] In this regard, Karsten Thorn similarly notes:

> «Während dies bei den meisten Personen – wie wohl auch bei Frau Shevill – dazu führt, dass im Wesentlichen ein Staat, nämlich der ihres gewöhnlichen Aufenthalts, als Erfolgsort in Betracht zu ziehen ist, liegt bei absoluten Personen der Zeitgeschichte im Regelfall ein Streudelikt vor, bei dem der Verletzungserfolg parallel in mehreren Rechtsordnungen eintritt.»[683]

All in all, for the present purposes – in view of the absence therein of any specific discussion of the point in relation to offline violations of personality rights – probably not too much should be read into the actual wording of the judgment. Therefore, it should suffice to conclude that the criterion 'to be known' gives rise to several uncertainties and open questions; it also generates academic discourse on its existence and necessity. How the ECJ coped with these troublesome issues and different views is shown in *infra* Ch. VII.B.II in which the concept of place of the damage adapted to online violations of personality rights is analysed.

Art 8 of the ECHR unknown persons are enabled to claim protection of their reputation similarly to the protection of their right to private life. Contra: Thorn, FS Bernd von Hoffmann, p 749; Mankowski, in: Magnus/Mankowski, Brussels I Regulation, p 263, para 249b, who states: «If the victim is completely unknown by diligent standards in a certain country, his reputation will not be harmed there in a relevant manner for he did not have a discernible one which could have been diminished by the respective statement.»

681 See e.g. Wagner, ERPL 2005, 21, 26-27; Vick/Macpherson, Va. J. Int'l L. 1995-1996, 933, 980-981; Kuipers, CML Rev. 2012, 1211, 1213; Hohloch, JuS 1995, 928-929. See also reference to *Shevill*, 29 and to this criterion as a necessary element of the place of the damage, see AG in *eDate and Martinez*, 35-37, 50, 55-56; AG in *DFDS Torline*, 72.

682 Terms are used in Volken, SZIER 1996, 69, 133.

683 Thorn, FS Bernd von Hoffmann, p 749.

3. Connection between the concepts of distribution and injury to reputation

The third criterion on which the ECJ in *Shevill* remained silent is whether the two above-discussed concepts are to be applied cumulatively or whether one incorporates the other in the form of presumption.[684] The former understanding would mean that if the places of distribution and injury to reputation were to occur in different states, none of them would comply with the criteria, and so the concept of place of the damage would be rendered ineffective.[685] Thus, the present author sympathises with the latter understanding and regards the concept of distribution as a legal fiction. She presumes that the place of the damage in disputes concerning defamation through the press is the place of distribution, since that is the place where the readers supposedly comprehend the contested publication and, consequently, where the injury to reputation occurs.[686]

C. The extent of jurisdiction

The words 'extent of jurisdiction' determine the territorial scope of the jurisdiction of the competent court to decide upon the dispute brought before it. Normally, the uniform rules of jurisdiction laid down in the Brussels-Lugano Regime confer an unlimited extent of jurisdiction on the court to adjudicate the whole dispute. Nevertheless, the ECJ somewhat limited this in *Shevill*. In particular, it held that the place of the causal event could only be the place where the publisher is established, «since that is the place where the harmful event originated and from which the libel was issued and put into circulation. The court of the place where the publisher of the defamatory publication is established must *therefore* have jurisdiction

684 On this, see Kaye, Law of the European Judgments Convention, p 1460; *supra* Intr. to Ch. V.B.II.

685 On this, see Kaye, Law of the European Judgments Convention, p 1460.

686 Similarly see Nagy, J. Priv. Int. L. 2012, 251, 269. Cf. *Zuid-Chemie*, 32 in which regarding product liability, the ECJ held that Art 7(2) designates the place where the initial damage arises «as a result of the normal use of the product for the purpose for which it was intended.» By analogy with this finding, it could be argued that the normal use of the newspaper for the purpose for which it was intended is that it is read by readers in the state and at the place where it is distributed. However, see the counterarguments and the decision of the *OLG München* referred to in *supra* fn 664.

to hear the action for damages for all the harm caused by the unlawful act.»[687] It follows, as Jane C. Ginsburg notices, that «that forum is competent to award damages for the full harm caused by the defamatory statement, both in the forum and in other contracting States.»[688] By contrast, «the courts of each Contracting State in which the defamatory publication was distributed and in which the victim claims to have suffered injury to his reputation are territorially the best placed to assess the libel committed in that State and to determine the extent of the corresponding damage.»[689] As a result, different courts deal with the various aspects of the same dispute, since it is fragmented into multiple jurisdictions. Although this practice (known as the mosaic approach) is not uncommon in EU law[690] and different national laws,[691] such as in France for the rules of jurisdiction in tort that supposedly guided the ruling of the ECJ,[692] it raises different uncertainties. In particular, it is doubtful whether it is compatible with the specific nature of cross-border defamation as well as with the governing objectives and underlying principles of the Brussels-Lugano Regime. This approach also divides the views of academics in that they either welcome it or militate against it by favouring instead an unlimited extent of jurisdiction.[693] In support of the latter view, Christian Kohler points out:

---

687 *Shevill*, 24-25 (author's italics).

688 Ginsburg, Recueil des Cours 273, p 307.

689 *Shevill*, 31. The written observations of the Spanish and French governments as well as the COM in *Shevill and Others v. Presse Alliance S.A.* [1995] 2 *W.L.R.* 499 (E.C.J.), pp 507/D, 508/F, 511/B-D support this view.

690 For EU legislation, see *infra* fn 717. For the case law of the ECJ regarding Art 7(2), see *supra* Ch. III.B.I.3 and *supra* Ch. III.D.II.1-3.

691 E.g. (1) Germany: Roth, Die internationale Zuständigkeit, pp 298-299, 304-305; (2) US (regarding the former multiple publication rule): Roth, Die internationale Zuständigkeit, pp 306-307; Kubis, Internationale Zuständigkeit, p 135; (3) France: see *infra* fn 692 and its accompanying text; Roth, Die internationale Zuständigkeit, p 306. Cf. Art 10(4) of the draft Hague Judgments Convention (*infra* Ch. VI.A.II.4); Prel. Doc. No 7 of April 1997, paras 79-81.

692 On this, see Jayme/Kohler, IPRax 1995, 343, 348; Huber, ZEuP 1996, 295, 303. For French judicial practice under Art 5(3) of the BC, see Reinmüller, IPRax 1985, 233-235.

693 E.g. in favour of the (1) mosaic approach: Huber, ZEuP 1996, 295, 304 ff.; (2) unlimited extent of jurisdiction: Geimer/Shütze and Kropholler as referred to in AG 1994 in *Shevill*, 30-32, 61; Reinmüller, IPRax 1985, 233, 235. See also other academics as referred to in Roth, Die internationale Zuständigkeit, fn 1286 and fn 1287. For the meaning of the term 'unlimited extent of jurisdiction', see *infra* Ch. VII.C.II.

> «[D]ie Beurteilung tatsächlich und wirtschaftlich zusammenhängender Verletzungsvorgänge, die mit mehreren Mitgliedstaaten verknüpft sind, durch ein Gericht mit umfassender Zuständigkeit sachgerechter ist als isoliert-parallele Verfahren vor Gerichten mit nur lokaler Zuständigkeit ..., zumal die hierbei auftretenden Rechtshängigkeits- und Rechtskraftfragen die Rechtsverfolgung zusätzlich erschweren können.»[694]

The following section briefly addresses the problematic issues that might arise from the application of the mosaic approach in two respects: practicability at the level of substantive law and compatibility at the level of the Brussels-Lugano Regime.[695]

I. Practicability

The justification for introducing a limited extent of jurisdiction in *Shevill*, according to which the court at the place of the damage is «territorially the best placed to assess the libel committed in that State and to determine the extent of the corresponding damage»[696] is seriously disputable. In particular, it is highly questionable whether the assessment of the libel, that is, the defamation, committed and the determination of the extent of non-pecuniary harm caused can territorially be fragmented into independent mosaic pieces at the level of substantive law. This doubt becomes more evident based on the finding of the ECJ according to which the mosaic approach leads to situations in which different courts rule «on various aspects of *the same dispute*».[697]

---

694 Kohler, FS Ulrich Everling, p 662 [emphases omitted; regarding Art 94(2) of Reg. (EC) No 40/94 (OJ 1994 L 11/1)].

695 For similar analysis of the mosaic principle that serves considerable basis for the present examination, see Roth, Die internationale Zuständigkeit, pp 297-332; Kubis, Internationale Zuständigkeit, pp 134-141; Löffler, Mediendelikte, pp 201-216.

696 *Shevill*, 31 (full stop omitted). Cf. question no 3 referred for a preliminary ruling in *Shevill*, 16.

697 *Shevill*, 32 (author's italics). On this, see also question no 6 referred for a preliminary ruling in *Shevill*, 16.

1. Assessment of the defamation committed

In a simplified manner, in order to assess the defamation committed, the court must establish that a defamatory statement distributed to third parties violates the right to reputation of the person concerned.[698] National legal systems guarantee different measures to prevent or remedy such violations. As the action brought in *Shevill* concerned a remedial measure, namely, the monetary compensation for the non-pecuniary harm suffered,[699] it is the focus of the present discussion. To award such a measure, the court must establish that the publisher is liable for the distribution of the defamatory material. Thus, by introducing the mosaic approach, the ECJ appeared to hold that the cornerstone elements of the dispute, namely, distribution, liability, and the right to reputation, are dividable among states.

Concerning distribution, it might be supposed that the mosaic approach can be traced back to its nature, i.e., it is regionalised, and thus, strictly speaking, it is broken down into several domestic distribution systems. Viewing it in this light, Severin Löffler observes that distribution takes place completely independently without any spatial connection and possibly at different times in each state.[700] In addition, he also underlines that each regional distribution requires an own business decision on the part of the publisher. Distribution channels must also be established, and thus, it is necessary to deal with each national regulatory framework, above all to prove whether the statement is protected by the freedom of expression or, alternatively, whether it violates the concerned person's personality right in the state of distribution.[701] By contrast, Sebastian Kubis observes that fragmentation into domestic distributions is as arbitrary as the adoption of an independent distribution in each state or even more extremely in the territory of each kiosk where the copies of the newspaper were sold. He argues that a regional distribution is a dependent component («Teilakt») of the entire act of distribution. Deviation from this practice is, however, possible in situations when there are two different editions of a news magazine produced editorially completely independently from each other:

698 For details on the substantive legal rules on defamation, see *supra* Ch. I.

699 See *supra* Ch. V.A.I.

700 Löffler, Mediendelikte, p 210. He (*ibid.*, p 210) uses this description similarly to that which exists in criminal law for the determination of the unity of an offence.

701 Löffler, Mediendelikte, p 210. For the conflict between these rights, see *supra* fn 36.

one for the national and one for the foreign market. Nevertheless, in Sebastian Kubis' opinion, this is rare, since the different versions of news magazines and daily newspapers are normally coordinated and linked to each other. Consequently, he concludes that there are no different acts of distribution concerning their common parts but only a uniform act of distribution.[702] He also goes on to note:

> «Nichts spricht dafür, daß ausgerechnet im heutigen, integrationswilligen Europa Ländergrenzen an der Einheitlichkeit der Verbreitung etwas ändern sollten. Daher kommt bei der internationalen Verbreitung von Medien das Vorliegen mehrerer voneinander unabhängiger Handlungen nur selten in Betracht. Vielmehr ist die "inländische" Verbreitung regelmäßig ein unselbständiger Teilakt der gesamten Verbreitung.»[703]

Having in mind the close cooperation and connected integration of the Brussels-Lugano States,[704] the co-ordinated activities of regionalised distributors that reflect the same business strategy of the publisher, and the fact that principally, in the wake of *Shevill*, it is the publisher and not the regionalised distributor who is sued,[705] the present author has great sympathy with Sebastian Kubis' position. Therefore, she is of the opinion that the international distribution of a newspaper should be regarded as a uniform act of which each regionalised distribution is a dependent component.

Secondly, the present author remains unconvinced of the territorial split in situations when, in each set of mosaic proceedings, the same victim contests the same publication created under the publisher's same commercial policy and business strategy, and distributed by the same publisher. Eventually, the liability of the publisher for the same content lies at the heart of each mosaic action. Sebastian Kubis also notes:

> «Gestritten würde ja in allen Verfahren um dieselbe Äußerung des angeblichen Verletzers.»[706]

---

702 Kubis, Internationale Zuständigkeit, pp 136-137. He adds (*ibid.*, p 137) in the context of advertisement centrally broadcast that it is regarded as identical act even if the advertisement is translated into the language of the targeted state.

703 Kubis, Internationale Zuständigkeit, p 136 (fn omitted).

704 Cf. *supra* fn 34; *supra* Ch. III.A.II (aims for concluding the Lugano Conventions).

705 See e.g. national cases as referred to in *infra* fn 815, especially *Ewins v Carlton* [1997] 2 ILRM 223, Irish High Court, 3.3.1997.

706 Kubis, Internationale Zuständigkeit, p 138.

Similarly, Douglas W. Vick and Linda Macpherson also seem unconvinced about splitting the dispute:

> «[I]t is difficult to imagine a more inefficient result than allowing claimants to bring multiple actions in multiple forums for statements contained in a single newspaper or magazine article.»[707]

Finally, regarding the supposed distributable character of the right to reputation, the following challenges can be put forward. In this book, the right to reputation is regarded as an ideal right, which is enjoyed by and inseparably attached to the right holder.[708] It follows that it is a single right, which can neither be exploited commercially nor be divided between borders.[709] As Günther Beitzke states:

> «L'honneur est partout et indivisible.»[710]

Similarly, objecting to the finding of the ECJ in *Shevill*, Sebastian Kubis points out:

> «Es handelt sich um ein einheitliches Rechtsgut, das jedem Menschen "weltweit" zusteht. ... Jeder Mensch hat weltweit nur ein einziges Persönlichkeitsrecht, das keinen Halt vor Ländergrenzen macht. Die Territorialisierung des Persönlichkeitsschutzes durch den *EuGH* rückt jene hingegen in bedenklicher Weise in die Nähe der Registerrechte. Das wird dem verfassungs- und menschenrechtlich gewährten Schutz des allgemeinen Persönlichkeitsrechts nicht gerecht. Daher entwertet die zuständigkeitsrechtliche Mosaikbetrachtung die Persönlichkeitsrechte auch in ihrer materiellen Substanz.»[711]

The legal practice of the ECJ underscores these challenges, since it has constantly denied the territorial nature of personality rights and thus of the right to reputation. In *Wintersteiger*, for example, it upheld the opinion of AG Cruz Villalón, according to whom, personality and intellectual property rights differ considerably. AG Cruz Villalón based his opinion on the finding that the latter rights «are protected on a territorial basis and are concerned with the commercial exploitation of a product.»[712]

707 Vick/Macpherson, Va. J. Int'l L. 1995-1996, 933, 986.

708 See *supra* Ch. I.A.

709 See also von Hinden, Persönlichkeitsverletzungen, pp 33, 156.

710 Beitzke, G. as quoted by von Hinden, Persönlichkeitsverletzungen, p 156.

711 Kubis, Internationale Zuständigkeit, pp 140-141 (sentences and fn omitted; italics in the original).

712 AG in *Wintersteiger*, 20; *Wintersteiger*, 24 [regarding the infringements of these rights and the interpretation of Art 5(3) of Brussels I]. On this case, see *supra* Ch. III.D.II.1. Cf. von Hinden, Persönlichkeitsverletzungen, p 156 notes (regarding personality right as an ideal right) that violations of competition law or intellec-

2. Determination of the extent of non-pecuniary harm

Similar to the preceding observations, the split of the non-pecuniary harm and the determination of its extent are also seriously disputable. Non-pecuniary harm, such as injury to feelings, pain and suffering, social discredit, mental distress, worry, or physical discomfort, is attributable to the victim's bodily, spiritual, and/or social-environmental sphere. As a result, it cannot be defined on the basis of objective terms and irrespective of the feelings, subjective inclinations, views, and social environment of the victim. Its personal and mathematically undeterminable nature serves as the basis of the argument according to which the monetary compensation for such harm cannot be divided among borders.[713] Consequently, it is highly possible that when determining the mosaic extent of the non-pecuniary harm and of other factors (such as the intention, motivation, and behaviour of the publisher; the danger of repetition; and the form of deterrence), there will be many different weights and different legal standards in accordance with the number of proceedings initiated in different mosaic jurisdictions.[714] The multiple assessments of these factors are not only arbitrary, but such multiple assessments might also lead to the collection of a higher amount of total monetary compensation than in a centralised place where a single court would assess them only once. In this regard, Isabel Roth asserts:

> «Es ist den Gerichten nicht möglich, diese staatenübergreifenden Bemessungskriterien begrenzt auf ihr Hoheitsgebiet in die Schadensschätzung einzubeziehen. Aus diesem Grund besteht die Gefahr, dass Faktoren, wie die Wiederholungsgefahr und die Abschreckung, bei einer Betrachtung der addierten Ersatzansprüche übermäßig stark in die Gesamtschadensbemessung einfließen. Ein bedeutender Kritikpunkt an der territorialen Schadensbemessung ist damit die Gefahr eines unangemessen hohen Gesamtschadensanspruchs.»[715]

Finally, as is clear from the Heidelberg Report, the difficulty in assessing the non-pecuniary harm on a territorial basis was also stressed during the revision of Brussels I:

---

tual property right are violations of territorial rights or interests, while violation of personality means one violation of the same unitary right in several states.

713 See *supra* Ch. I.A (with references).

714 See also Roth, Die internationale Zuständigkeit, pp 321-328; Vick/Macpherson, Va. J. Int'l L. 1995-1996, 933, 986.

715 Roth, Die internationale Zuständigkeit, p 326.

> «Polish professionals underline that practical application of rules resulting from the *Shevill*-case are difficult, especially the rule that jurisdiction of Member State is limited to the value of this part of damage which were injured by the publication only in the territory of this member state.»[716]

II. Compatibility with the governing objectives and underlying principles

The present subsection sheds light on the compatibility of the mosaic approach with the numerous governing objectives and underlying principles of the Brussels-Lugano Regime outlined in *supra* Ch. III.B.

1. The wording of Art 7(2): is the limited extent of jurisdiction covered?

The wording of *Shevill* might be regarded as a very strained interpretation of Art 7(2), since, contrary to other secondary legislation of the EU,[717] this provision does not refer to the mosaic approach explicitly at all.[718] Explicit reference to it can be read into the wording of the proposal put forward by the COM in 1997 in the course of the revision of the BC where it states that the courts «for the place where the damage or part thereof was sustained»[719] have jurisdiction. Viewed in this light, this text promoted the legitimation of the mosaic approach. However, this formulation disappeared from the wording of Art 5(3) of the proposal for Brussels I in 1999.[720] Consequently, it may be supposed that the EU legislators did not intend to limit the extent of jurisdiction of the court designated by one of the criteria of the concept of harmful event. Therefore, the lack of any di-

---

716 Heidelberg Report, para 213 (italics in the original).

717 E.g. Art 83(2) of Reg. (EC) No 6/2002 (OJ 2002 L 3/1); Art 98(2) of Reg. (EC) No 207/2009 (OJ 2009 L 78/24); Art 94(2) of Reg. (EC) No 40/94 (OJ 1994 L 11/1) (on this, see Kohler, FS Ulrich Everling, pp 656 ff.); Art 101(3) of Reg. (EC) No 2100/94 (OJ 1994 L 227/1); Art 69(2) of the draft Community Patent Convention (1975) as referred to in AG 1994 in *Shevill*, 88; Art 17(2) of Protocol on the settlement of litigation concerning the infringement and validity of community patents (OJ 1989 L 401/34) and on this, see also Roth, Die internationale Zuständigkeit, pp 310-311.

718 See also Roth, Die internationale Zuständigkeit, p 310; Reinmüller, IPRax 1985, 233, 235.

719 Commission Document COM(97) 609 final, Art 5(3). See also *supra* Ch. IV.B.I.

720 See Commission Document COM(1999) 348 final, Art 5(3).

rect reference to such a limitation might cast a shadow over the legitimacy of the mosaic approach.

2. The wording of *Shevill*: is local jurisdiction covered?

The precise scope of the limited extent of jurisdiction under the mosaic principle is a matter of some uncertainty. Although the concept of harmful event allocates international and local jurisdiction to a specific court of a Brussels-Lugano State,[721] the ECJ appeared to confer a limited extent of jurisdiction on «the courts of each Contracting State».[722] In other words, instead of referring to a particular place of the state, similar to the place where the publisher is established, this formulation generally designates all the courts of a particular state and gives the impression that it confers only international jurisdiction. Bearing in mind, however, that the special rule of jurisdiction in tort under Art 7(2) also allocates venue, three understandings of this formulation would be possible.[723] According to the first one, the court for the place where some damage occurred would be equally competent in respect of the entire damage caused in the state, and the plaintiff would have the option to select one of them.[724] Alternatively, local jurisdiction could be conferred on the court for the place where the main harm is sustained in line with *Shenavai* and with the proposal of André Huet.[725] The third possible understanding would be that each court

---

721 In this regard, it is also noteworthy that in *Shevill*, the action was brought only for the damage that occurred in England and Wales although the Contracting State of the BC was the UK and France-Soir was also distributed in Northern Ireland, Scotland, and the Channel Islands as *Shevill and Others v. Presse Alliance S.A.* [1995] 2 *W.L.R.* 499 (E.C.J.), p 502/D and Kaye, Law of the European Judgments Convention, p 1404 note. On this, see also Kaye, Law of the European Judgments Convention, pp 1470-1471.

722 *Shevill*, 33. On local jurisdiction, see *supra* Intr. to Ch. III.D.II; *supra* Intr. to Ch. IV.

723 For this uncertainty and for the first two possible understandings, see Layton/Mercer, European Civil Practice, para 15.096.

724 See case 4 NC 3/08s (20.2.2008), *Oberster Gerichtshof* (Austria), ECJ Website No 2009/25 as referred to in Voinov/de Lapasse/Janzen, Twelfth Report, p 11. Cf., by analogy, AG in *Pinckney*, 67.

725 For Huet, see *supra* fn 652. *Shenavai* dealt with a number of obligations arising out of the same contract, and the ECJ held (para 19) that the principal obligation determines jurisdiction (also known as the '*maxim accessorium sequitur* principle') (see also e.g. *Color Drack*, 40).

of a particular state would be competent to decide upon the harm that occurred in the judicial district where it is situated.[726]

3. Depriving the twin criteria of their inherent natures

As was noted in *supra* Ch. IV.B.I, in *Bier*, the ECJ introduced the twin criteria under the concept of harmful event on an equal footing, «since each of them can, depending on the circumstances, be particularly helpful from the point of view of the evidence and of the conduct of the proceedings.»[727] It follows that the governing objectives and underlying principles of the Brussels-Lugano Regime[728] should also be equally applicable to them. In addition, as noted in the aforementioned subsection, numerous academics regard their optional character as a tool, which aims to favour the plaintiff by allowing him to select the place to initiate proceedings. These findings seem to be questioned in *Shevill* in no less than three respects.

a) Equal treatment

The underlying grounds for introducing the mosaic approach give rise to considerable doubts about the maintenance of the equal treatment of the concepts under Art 7(2) for the following reasons.[729] First, AG Darmon applied the principles of proximity, sound administration of justice, efficacious conduct of proceedings, and restrictive method of interpretation exclusively to the concept of the place of the damage.[730] By doing so, he treated the concept of causal event as being akin to the general ground of jurisdiction to which the aim for centralising proceedings rather than the principle of proximity and the method of restrictive interpretation apply:

---

726 This would be compatible with the sole wording of AG 1994 in *Shevill*, 65, 73, 74, 98, 103.

727 *Bier*, 17. On these principles, see *supra* Ch. III.B.II.1.

728 On this, see *supra* Ch. III.B.

729 On this, see also Kreuzer/Klötgen, IPRax 1997, 90, 94; Reinmüller, IPRax 1985, 233, 235.

730 AG 1994 in *Shevill*, 68, 70, 71, 76, 79. On these principles, see *supra* Ch. III.B.II.1 and *supra* Ch. III.B.I.1.

> «[I]t is already possible for proceedings to be centralized in the courts of the defendant's domicile or in those of the causal event. Such centralization should not be additionally obtainable by virtue of any special and, let me repeat, restrictive jurisdiction.»[731]

Secondly and similarly, although the ECJ upheld its findings laid down in *Bier*, it justified the limited extent of jurisdiction based on the principle of sound administration of justice.[732]

In the light of the foregoing, it is rather difficult to comprehend why the principles based on which the twin criteria were established and which underline special rules of jurisdiction within Art 7(2) in general could serve repeatedly as justifications for attaching a limited extent of jurisdiction to one of them. In addition, it is also considerably doubtful why the ECJ and AG Darmon attributed to the concept of causal event characteristics different from those with which the concept of the place of the damage is armed and akin to those with which the concept of the defendant's domicile within Art 4(1) is equipped.[733]

b) Optional character

The mosaic approach obliges the plaintiff to bring sets of proceedings before the courts of the Brussels-Lugano States where portions of his damage occurred in order to collect monetary compensation for his 'entire' damage, providing that he does not wish to initiate proceedings in the courts either of the defendant's domicile or of the place in which the publisher is established.[734] Therefore, it essentially renders the optional character of the twin criteria ineffective.

---

731 AG 1994 in *Shevill*, 79. See also AG 1994 in *Shevill*, 66, 70, 76; AG 1995 in *Shevill*, 11; AG in *eDate and Martinez*, 38.

732 *Shevill*, 31. For reference to this principle in relation to the mosaic approach, see also e.g. AG 1994 in *Shevill*, 70, 73; AG 1995 in *Shevill*, 54, 55.

733 See *Shevill*, 32; AG 1994 in *Shevill* as referred to in *supra* fn 732.

734 See *Shevill*, 32. On this, see also e.g. Roth, Die internationale Zuständigkeit, p 308; Kreuzer/Klötgen, IPRax 1997, 90, 94-95; Fawcett/Torremans, Intellectual Property and Private International Law, para 9.117. However, see *supra* Ch. V.C.I.2 (regarding the determination of the mosaic extent of non-pecuniary harm); *supra* Ch. V.B.II.2 and this subsection (regarding states that are supposedly excluded for jurisdictional purposes on the basis that the victim is unknown there; thus, the full compensation for the damage is doubtful). For the interconnection of domicile and establishment, see *supra* Ch. V.B.I.2.

The pressure on the plaintiff to initiate proceedings before one of the latter courts is exacerbated by the following reason. By supposing that the criterion 'to be known' is an inherent part of the concept of damage, this concept assumes that the substantive law designated by the rules of PIL of the forum also requires such a criterion be met for violation of the right to reputation. Thus, the mosaic approach excludes as jurisdictionally irrelevant those places where the victim is unknown, but due to the substantive law applicable to the dispute, he could possibly claim protection of his right to reputation and gain remedial measures accordingly.[735] Consequently, if he wants to obtain monetary compensation at those places, he has no option: he has to bring an action in the court for the place of the defendant's domicile or the publisher's establishment. This seems impractical and arbitrary, since, as *supra* Ch. V.B.I.2 indicated, the publisher can easily influence the location of those places. Consequently, the plaintiff is not only affected by the publisher's unilateral publication that caused him damage, but he also depends on the publisher's pleasure and is obliged to sue at a place that was possibly selected by the publisher for legal or other beneficial grounds.[736]

c) Causality and connectivity

The ECJ justified the unlimited extent of jurisdiction by a simple reference to the jurisdictionally relevant acts performed at the place of the causal event. Because that place is regarded as «the place where the harmful event originated and from which the libel was issued and put into circulation»,[737] that court «*must therefore have* jurisdiction to hear the action for damages for all the harm caused by the unlawful act.»[738] In absence of any additional reasoning, it might be useful to draw some support for the interpretation of this finding from AG Darmon's opinion. As is evident from that document, the unlimited extent of jurisdiction was underscored essentially by the predominant view expressed in the French legal writing and judicial practice: all damage caused by and therefore connected to the causal act.[739] As a corollary, Paul Lagarde points out:

735 On this, see also *supra* Ch. V.B.II.2.
736 On this, see also similarly Roth, Die internationale Zuständigkeit, pp 312-313.
737 *Shevill*, 24.
738 *Shevill*, 25 (author's italics). Cf. AG 1994 in *Shevill*, 60.
739 See AG 1994 in *Shevill*, 60, 62.

> «[A] court in one of the places where the damage arose can only be competent to hear and determine claims in respect of the harmful consequences of the act in the country in which it sits, since there exists no connection between the damage caused in another country and that court, by virtue of either the place where it arose or the place where the wrongful act was committed».[740]

The justification of the limited extent of jurisdiction at the place of the damage solely due to the lack of any causal connection between the damage that occurred at different places does not attract greatly. It is not evident why the extent of the jurisdiction of the competent court should be dependent on the existence of such causal connection. As Severin Löffler notes:

> «Auf die Kausalverbindung kann es daher allenfalls im Zusammenhang mit der Bejahung der Ubiquität ankommen, nicht aber hinsichtlich der Kognitionsbefugnis.»[741]

In addition, it is doubtful why the court for the place of the causal event is better placed to hear the claim for the damage as a whole than is the court of the place where the damage occurred.[742] Just as the court with an unlimited extent of jurisdiction at the place of the damage would do, this former court must deal with (legal) documents drafted in a language other than that of the forum. In addition, it must collect evidence possibly from faraway places in order to assess the defamation committed and determine the extent of the corresponding non-pecuniary harm that occurred in states with partly different cultural and social communities.[743] Moreover, even if no damage occurred at the place of the causal event, the court sitting there still possesses jurisdiction in respect of all the damage. It is then irrational that the court for the place where at least the main damage arose should not also enjoy jurisdiction over the entire harm caused.[744] Finally, it also seems contrary to AG Darmon's finding, according to which «the principle of proximity cannot justify preference being given either to the courts

740 Lagarde, as quoted in AG 1994 in *Shevill*, 62. Cf. AG 1994 in *Shevill*, 71. As Löffler, Mediendelikte, p 205 observes, this view has been overruled in France.

741 Löffler, Mediendelikte, p 205 (fn omitted).

742 Cf. Kubis, Internationale Zuständigkeit, p 135.

743 Similarly, Roth, Die internationale Zuständigkeit, p 315.

744 See also Kaye, Law of the European Judgments Convention, p 1447 (as a possible challenge to the limited extent of jurisdiction, he refers to the state where some damage arose). Regarding the concept of main damage, see *supra* fns 652 and 725.

for the place where the causal event occurred or to those for the place where the damage arose».[745]

4. Libel tourism

a) In general: libel tourism in the Brussels-Lugano States

The term 'libel tourism' is predominantly defined as referring to the plaintiff's stratagem by which he elects to bring his action for defamation in a court of a particular state where it is considered most likely he will receive a favourable judgment,[746] i.e., he searches for his own justice. This litigation practice is regarded in trans-national libel suits as essentially unethical in no less than two respects: first, it serves the plaintiff's legal tactics to circumvent undesired legal systems, and secondly, it leads to forums with insignificant ties to the dispute.[747] By contrast, this practice is legitimately allowed within the Brussels-Lugano Regime,[748] and it is recognised in *Bier* by the introduction of the twin criteria under the concept of harmful event.[749] By selecting the forum, the libel tourist shops not only for a forum but also for an entire legal system. This selection is driven by different considerations, which make one legal system more attractive than another by favouring the plaintiff more than the other does. In this respect, Arthur T. von Mehren notices:

745 AG 1994 in *Shevill*, 57.

746 See Nielsen, J. Priv. Int. L. 2013, 269, 269; Hartley, ICLQ 2010, 25, 25; EP Resolution, P7_TA(2012)0200 (10.5.2012), point C. There are two types of libel tourism, namely, forum and law shopping (see e.g. AG in *Tacconi*, 32).

747 For further (pro and contra) arguments, see Forum Shopping, Harv. L. Rev. 1989-1990, 1677-1696. For details on libel tourism, see e.g. Levi, Am. J. Comp. L. 2012, 507-553; Hartley, ICLQ 2010, 25-38; Garnett/Richardson, J. Priv. Int. L. 2009, 471-490; Nielsen, J. Priv. Int. L. 2013, 269-288; Kuipers, GLJ 2011, 1681, 1682-1687.

748 E.g. the concept of domicile of legal persons under Art 62 (on this, see *supra* Ch. III.C.I.1); rules of jurisdiction applicable to violations of personality rights (see *supra* Ch. III.D).

749 On this, see *supra* Ch. IV.B.I; Roth, Die internationale Zuständigkeit, p 312; Kubis, Internationale Zuständigkeit, p 135. Cf. Vick/Macpherson, Va. J. Int'l L. 1995-1996, 933, 973.

> «The party that a given forum advantages depends upon the interaction of the facts of the case with that forum's conflictual, procedural, and substantive law.»[750]

Accordingly, the nature of the rules of civil procedures, PIL, and the substantive law, largely contribute to the libel tourist's choice. This is so because these areas are not (fully) harmonised between the Brussels-Lugano States. In particular, the procedure law of each state in which the competent court is situated (i.e., *lex fori*) governs principally most of the procedural matters, such as the form, length, and instances of proceedings; litigation expenses; and the rules on the gathering, presentation, and evaluation of evidences.[751] Similarly, rules of PIL applicable to disputes concerning violations of personality rights are also regulated at a national level in each Brussels-Lugano State, with each state possibly designating different substantive laws.[752] It is, nevertheless, noteworthy that between the Member States, Rome II attempted to cover harmonised rules of PIL for «non-contractual obligations arising out of violations of privacy and rights relating to personality, including defamation». However, due to the different views taken on the matter, no compromise was reached and, consequently, it was excluded from the scope of this regulation.[753]

b) In particular: libel tourism in the wake of *Shevill*

In *Shevill*, the ECJ remained silent on the disadvantages linked to the mosaic approach.[754] Neither did it consider the possible problem of libel tourism. By contrast, Advocates General were concerned with this subject. AG

---

750 Von Mehren, Recueil des Cours 295, p 196.

751 For a comparative survey on matters of civil procedure, see European E-Justice portal <https://e-justice.europa.eu>; PCMLP, Costs in Defamation Proceedings. However, regarding a project on the drafting of Principles of Transnational Civil Procedure for Europe, see <http://www.unidroit.org/work-in-progress-studies/current-studies/transnational-civil-procedure>.

752 On the rules of PIL in the Member States, see Mainstrat Study. On selected substantive laws, see *supra* Ch. I.

753 See Art 1(2)(g) of Rome II. For legislative history and possible developments, see Mainstrat Study, pp 72-77; EP Resolution, P7_TA(2012)0200 (10.5.2012). However, note that if the defamation committed in a business context by the competitor of a business person, it could fall under the term 'unfair competition' and thus, under the scope of Art 6 of Rome II [on this, see Fawcett/Carruthers/North, PIL, pp 785, 809 and case I ZR 131/12 (12.12.2013), *BGH* (GRUR 2014, 601), 35 ff; regarding jurisdictional rules, see *supra* fn 445].

754 See *Shevill*, 32.

Darmon pointed out that the mosaic principle avoids the multiplication of competent courts, and thus, forum shopping, since «the competence of each of them is restricted to the damage arising within their respective judicial districts.»[755] AG Léger shared the opinion of his colleague and, acknowledging the plaintiff-friendly nature of the English defamation law, added that an unlimited extent of jurisdiction would pose a danger for English courts «of becoming the natural choice of forum in such matters.»[756] Finally, he underlined the need to prevent forum shopping and thus justified the mosaic approach on the basis of the differences existing in the law of defamation of the Contracting States.[757] In line with the opinions of Advocates General, numerous academics have considered the mosaic principle to be an approach that discourages forum shopping.[758]

These arguments are not very convincing. Possible objections can be put forward as follows. First, it could be argued that the limited extent of jurisdiction does not discourage the victim from availing himself of the English or other national law of defamation. Instead, it encourages libel tourism by eliminating obstacles, such as concentration of proceedings, which otherwise might have prevented plaintiffs from bringing claims in the UK or in any other Brussels-Lugano State.[759] As Christopher Forsyth asserts in relation to *Shevill:*

> «[T]he true reason for proceedings in England was, doubtless, that the English law of libel was more sympathetic towards plaintiffs than the French law. ... The effect of the ECJ's judgment is thus that the plaintiffs were able to sue in England: they were able to shop for a favourable forum.»[760]

Indeed, differences of the selected national substantive legal systems on the legal protection of the right to reputation and the adjudication of defamation outlined in *supra* Ch. I, contrary to AG Léger's finding, may in-

755 AG 1994 in *Shevill*, 74. See also AG 1995 in *Shevill*, 17.

756 AG 1995 in *Shevill*, 56.

757 AG 1995 in *Shevill*, 57.

758 See e.g. Mankowski, in: Magnus/Mankowski, Brussels I Regulation, p 242, para 211; Huber, ZEuP 1996, 295, 307. See also e.g. Kubis, Internationale Zuständigkeit, p 135; Hohloch, JuS 1995, 928, 929.

759 See also EP Resolution, P7_TA(2012)0200 (10.5.2012), point C. For the same conclusion (regarding forum shopping), see also Vick/Macpherson, Va. J. Int'l L. 1995-1996, 933, 987-988; Kreuzer/Klötgen, IPRax 1997, 90, 96. In addition, AG Léger's finding on the plaintiff-friendly nature of the English law of defamation could be disputed, since the provisions of the *Defamation Act 2013* (*supra* Ch. I.B.IV) might mitigate this nature.

760 Forsyth, C.L.J. 1995, 515, 516 (sentences omitted).

duce libel tourism irrespective of the limited extent of jurisdiction of the competent court. As was noted in *supra* Ch. I.B.V, the different legal practices turn states into legal environments that benefit, to a certain extent, the plaintiff, and in turn, put the publisher at a disadvantage. For example, the use of presumption or the high amount of awards together with the high cost of litigation might be sufficient grounds for intimidating the press and forcing it either to refrain from publishing or to settle even in situations when it would consider that it had a good chance of winning the dispute.[761] It follows that the mosaic principle encourages libel tourism by failing «to narrow the choice of forums available to claimants».[762]

5. Procedural economy

The mosaic approach fits uneasily with the doctrine of procedural economy.[763] It places a substantial burden on the plaintiff to bring a series of parallel claims in the courts of many Brussels-Lugano States, take legal advice, cope with language difficulties, and gather and provide evidence pursuant to the different conditions of national legal systems in order to recover the 'entire' extent of his damage caused by the publisher's act.[764] It follows that mosaic proceedings are principally too expensive and time consuming for the plaintiff.[765] Furthermore, the mosaic approach is also burdensome for the publisher. Because of the possibly high number of competent forums, it becomes difficult to predict before which court he

761 Cf. *infra* Ch. V.C.II.5 and 6. See also EP Resolution, P7_TA(2012)0200 (10.5.2012), point D. For settlements agreed essentially in libel proceedings brought in London (England), see Nielsen, J. Priv. Int. L. 2013, 269, 270 (e.g. settlement between a professor of radiology and a healthcare company).

762 Vick/Macpherson, Va. J. Int'l L. 1995-1996, 933, 988. Cf. Garnett/Richardson, J. Priv. Int. L. 2009, 471, 489 mention that *Olafsson v Gissurarson* [2008] EWCA Civ 152 concerned a libel suit in England between two Icelandic residents.

763 Cf. Vick/Macpherson, Va. J. Int'l L. 1995-1996, 933, 986; Roth, Die internationale Zuständigkeit, pp 317-318.

764 See also Kreuzer/Klötgen, IPRax 1997, 90, 95. Cf. de Winter, ICLQ 1968, 706, 716 (in general, regarding international litigation). On procedure law, see *supra* Ch. V.C.II.4.a). On the problem of exclusion of states where the victim is unknown, see *supra* Ch. V.B.II.2; *supra* Ch. V.C.II.3.b).

765 See also Mankowski, in: Magnus/Mankowski, Brussels I Regulation, p 242, para 209; Nygh/Pocar Report, p 62 («too expensive»); von Welser, GRUR-Prax 2011, 513 (costly).

could be sued[766] and what legal standards could be applied; consequently, he has little guidance in making his reporting practices compatible to minimise litigation.[767]

Besides the uneconomical fragmentation of proceedings, the mosaic approach is similarly unconvincing from the aspect of the recognition and enforcement of judgments. The plaintiff has to have each mosaic judgment recognised or enforced in the Brussels-Lugano State where such recognition or enforcement is desired.[768] This might be costly and time-consuming for the litigants and might place an extensive workload on the authorities addressed.

6. Interpretation in the light of the fundamental rights

The interpretation of Art 7(2), and especially the concept of damage that reads into the mosaic approach, could be regarded as inconsistent with the principle of equality and uniformity of rights and obligations, which principle is safeguarded by the application of fundamental rights. Put a different way, the mosaic approach, especially in the light of the findings put forward in relation to libel tourism and procedural economy, appears not to facilitate the right to access to justice, the victim's right to reputation, and the publisher's freedom of expression as guaranteed in Arts 7, 11, and 47 of the Charter.[769, 770]

---

766 See also AG in *eDate and Martinez*, 51. Contra: AG 1994 in *Shevill*, 75 who underscored that the mosaic approach ensures foreseeability.

767 See also Vick/Macpherson, Va. J. Int'l L. 1995-1996, 933, 986. On the role of the rules of PIL, see also *supra* Ch. V.C.II.4.a).

768 On this, see also Kubis, Internationale Zuständigkeit, p 137. On the recognition and enforcement of judgments, see *infra* Ch. V.C.II.8.

769 Cf. (1) PCMLP, Costs in Defamation Proceedings, pp 182 ff. (regarding access to justice and freedom of expression as set out in the ECHR *vis-à-vis* the litigation cost and the Conditional Fee Agreements in England and Wales); (2) Kessedjian, C.: Private International Law Aspects of Cyberspace: Global Communication, Universal Jurisdiction?, paper presented at ASIL/NVIL Fourth Hague Joint Conference on 5.7.1997 as referred to in Ginsburg, Recueil des Cours 273, p 310 [regarding Art 5(3) of the BC and the 1988 LC in Internet torts as well as the plaintiff's right to easy access to justice].

770 Note that the meaning and scope of these rights and the freedom of expression correspond to those afforded under Arts 8, 10 and 6(1) of the ECHR [see CONVENT 49, Explanations relating to the Charter of Fundamental Rights of the European Union (2010), available at <http://www.europarl.europa.eu/charter/

The miniaturised national procedures possibly associated with (high) litigation costs and lengthy processes do not facilitate access to justice for the litigants. It follows that the defendant's rights of the defence might be jeopardised and the plaintiff's right to bring proceedings before a court in order to determine the merits of the claim might seem to be disregarded.

Secondly, and consequently, the mosaic approach has an indirect side effect on the protection of the victim's right to respect for his private life and on the publisher's freedom of expression. The former is interfered with because it is possible that the plaintiff whose reputation is violated in different states will principally not take the time and effort to initiate proceedings in each mosaic jurisdiction. In addition, the possible requirement 'to be known' at the place of the damage deprives him of the protection of his reputation in states whose substantive law affords protection irrespective of the fact that he is unknown there.[771] However, the mosaic approach is more disadvantageous for the publisher. Even if the victim does not bring an action in each mosaic jurisdiction, the simple risk and potential costs of being sued in a foreign jurisdiction may already in itself have a negative effect on the publisher's working method and freedom of expression.[772] In order to avoid such a risk, the publisher may restrict its own freedom of expression by exercising self-censorship and refraining from the exercise of their role of «public watchdog»[773] in a democracy, and thus, from disseminating information on matters of public interest. The Heidelberg Report aptly summarises these negative impacts on the media as follows:

> «[I]t is sometimes submitted that, due to the multitude of legal systems, one has to comply with the standards of all legal systems so that eventually the most restrictive legal system decides about the admissibility of a certain conduct. Especially for media cases, it is argued that this framework may unduly liberties such as freedom of trade or transnational free speech.»[774]

---

convent49_en.htm>, pp 49-50; regarding Art 7 of the Charter, see also *McB*, 53; regarding Art 47 of the Charter, see also *Melloni*, 50]. Cf. *supra* fns 36 (on reputation falling under Art 8 of the ECHR) and 297 (on the relationship of the Charter and the ECHR).

771 On this, see *supra* Ch. V.B.II.2; *supra* Ch. V.C.II.3.b).

772 See also Kuipers, CML Rev. 2012, 1211, 1222; Reymond, YbPIL 2011, 493, 502-503. Cf. *supra* Ch. V.C.II.4.b); *supra* Ch. V.C.II.5.

773 Von Hannover v. Germany (No. 2) (nos 40660/08, 60641/08), 110.

774 Heidelberg Report, para 214 (fn omitted).

7. Rules of *lis pendens* and related actions

The mosaic approach raises some disputable points in relation to the principle outlined in *supra* Ch. III.B.II.2 according to which the entire dispute should be decided before a single forum in order to avoid parallel proceedings. In particular, the ECJ underscored that there are «disadvantages to having different courts ruling on various aspects of the same dispute»[775] but it remained silent as regards specifying those disadvantages. Supposedly, it drew its conclusion from the view of the Advocates General. In this regard, AG Darmon admitted that mosaic proceedings might result in conflicting but not irreconcilable judgments:

> «It cannot be denied that the main problem with such limitation of jurisdiction lies in the proliferation of competent forums and, consequently, in the danger of conflicting ° but not irreconcilable ° decisions delivered by the courts seised.»[776]

In this way, he clearly accepted that the mosaic approach may produce conflicting judgments, i.e., judgments handed down in parallel proceedings involving related actions that «can be separately enforced and their legal consequences are not mutually exclusive.»[777] On the other hand, he obviously denied that courts with mosaic competence deliver irreconcilable judgments, i.e., judgments held in parallel proceedings between the same parties involving the same cause and subject matter of the action, which cannot be separately enforced and whose legal consequences are mutually exclusive.[778] He justified his finding by recalling the inherent nature of the mosaic approach that enables a court only to decide upon the damage that occurred in the territory in which it sits:

> «[T]he jurisdiction of the courts of a Contracting State in which damage arises is limited to that part of the damage which occurred within their judicial district; consequently, where two courts are called upon, following the occurrence of the same causal event, to hear a claim for compensation for the damage, *they do not have concurrent jurisdiction.*»[779]

---

775 *Shevill*, 32.

776 AG 1994 in *Shevill*, 72. See also AG 1995 in *Shevill*, 23. Cf. AG in *Bier*, 8 (p 1756) stating that in circumstances «when damage is caused in several States by one and the same act» they might lead to conflicting decisions; Roth, Die internationale Zuständigkeit, p 318 (regarding conflicting judgments).

777 *Tatry*, 52. See also *Tatry*, 54.

778 See *Hoffmann*, 22. For the 'triple-identity test', see also *supra* Ch. III.B.II.2.

779 AG 1994 in *Shevill*, 98 (author's italics). See also, AG 1994 in *Shevill*, 72, 100-103; AG 1995 in *Shevill*, 21-23; Huber, ZEuP 1996, 295, 304.

His opinion is, however, not clear at this point. By referring generally to concurrent jurisdictions, his finding not only denies the relevance of the rules of *lis pendens*, but also ignores the provisions of related actions.[780] It is obviously contrary to his previous finding in which he accepted the possible relatedness of the actions by the reference to the conflicting judgments. Thus, it is open to question whether the rules of related actions are applicable to claims brought in relation to the various items of the same controversy. In addition, it is also disputable whether the rules of *lis pendens* are inapplicable.[781]

a) Do parallel mosaic procedures involve the same dispute?

As is clear from the foregoing discussion, for the application of the rules of *lis pendens*, the parallel procedures between the same parties must deal with actions involving the same cause of action and the same object. The satisfaction of the first condition cannot seriously be disputed, since, presumably, the holder of the personality rights seeks to establish in the court of each state where the jurisdictionally relevant damage occurred the liability of the same publisher, and they are the opposing parties in each parallel mosaic procedure.[782]

The second condition, namely, the same cause of action, can be approached from two perspectives: first, by recalling the independently defined concept of cause of action under Art 7(2), and secondly, by having recourse solely to the settled case law delivered on Art 29. Regarding the first perspective, as noted in *supra* Ch. IV.A, actions for violations of personality rights share the same cause, since the nature of each of them is non-contractual. Thus, an undisputable conclusion based on the equivalency of independent concepts established within the Brussels-Lugano Regime is that the causes of the actions brought in different sets of mosaic

780 See also AG 1994 in *Shevill*, 99 stating that actions are not related.

781 Cf. (1) Layton/Mercer, European Civil Practice, para 15.094 note that the mosaic parts of the damage are caused by the same cause of action and that the rules of *lis pendens* or related actions may be applicable to the mosaic actions. (2) Roth, Die internationale Zuständigkeit, p 319 stresses that the mosaic approach is contrary to the purpose of the rules on *lis pendens* and related actions (regarding Arts 27 and 28 of Brussels I).

782 Cf. by analogy, AG in *I. Weber*, 56. Generally on the concept of same parties, see *ibid.*, 50-61.

proceedings are identical. However, different logics underlying the provisions might facilitate discrepancy in the autonomous interpretation of this concept. Therefore, it is also worth examining the second perspective. Due to the case law delivered by the ECJ solely on the rules of *lis pendens*, the term 'cause of action' comprises the facts and the law relied on as the basis of the action.[783] While it can hardly be rebutted that the legal basis of the actions brought for establishing the liability of the publisher for the damage caused are identical,[784] doubts may occur about the identity of the facts. Although the ECJ presumably regarded the cross-border defamation as a bunch of territorially independent miniaturised violations, it is possible to draw some considerable support for the opposite view. First, as was argued above, the fragmentation of defamation and of the extent of the harm into separate pieces is seriously disputable.[785] Secondly, the ECJ itself regarded the dispute in *Shevill* as a single controversy by admitting the existence of disadvantages stemming from the fact that different courts rule «on various aspects of *the same dispute*».[786] Viewed in this light, it can also be supposed that the cause of the actions brought separately in different sets of mosaic proceedings is the same.

The third condition of *lis pendens* refers to the same subject matter of the actions, which «means the end the action has in view».[787] The nature of the subject matter of the actions can be approached in a similar way as the previous condition was. First, actions falling under Art 7(2) deal the same subject matter, since they all seek to establish the liability of the defendant.[788] Secondly, by recourse to the settled case law of the ECJ, in particular to *Tatry*, the following can be ascertained. In that case, the dispute concerned a procedure commenced by the owner of a vessel in a Dutch court against certain owners of goods asking for a declaration that he was not responsible for any damage to, or loss of, the goods. Afterwards, the owners of the goods started a procedure in an English court

783 *Tatry*, 38.

784 Actions for monetary compensation for non-pecuniary harm principally have their origin in tort law, irrespective of the fact that, for example, the French and Hungarian rules are partly independent of the general rule on tortious liability (see *supra* Ch. I.B.I and III). On the legal bases of the actions, see e.g., by analogy, *Mærsk*, 38.

785 See *supra* Ch. V.C.I.

786 *Shevill*, 32 (author's italics).

787 *Tatry*, 40.

788 On this, see *supra* Ch. IV.A.

asking for compensation. The ECJ found that the second action concerned the same subject matter as the first one, since the issue of liability was the focal point of both actions.[789] As a result, both approaches arrived at the same conclusion: if the issue of liability is «at the heart of the actions»,[790] they deal with the same subject matter. Moreover, the ECJ pointed out in *Tatry* that the pleas for ordering the defendant to pay damages «are the natural consequence of those relating to the finding of liability and thus do not alter the principal object of the action.»[791] By applying these findings to *Shevill*, it could be argued that the actions brought in different mosaic jurisdictions share the same subject matter, since all of them seek to establish the liability of the publisher for the identical newspaper article. In addition, the territorially fragmented extent of damage and thus damages are only the legal consequences of liability and so do not play any role in establishing the identity of the subject matter of the actions.[792] Nevertheless, possible objections to these findings might appear. First, as just noted in *supra* Ch. V.C.I.1, the ECJ presumably territorially split the publisher's liability. Thus, it could be said, although perversely, that the mosaic actions seek to establish the national aspects of the publisher's liability. The second possible objection essentially aims to promote procedural fairness. It could be argued that since the competent court, irrespective of the outcome of another mosaic procedure, decides only upon the damage that arose in the territory of the state where it is situated, the plaintiff still has something to gain in other parallel mosaic proceedings.[793] If the subject matter of the actions were viewed as being identical, the plaintiff would be deprived of the possibility of being compensated for the different mosaic aspects of the injury to his reputation.

In the light of the foregoing, the application of the rule of *lis pendens* to parallel mosaic proceedings is far from clear. Specifically, it is subject to the balance of the aforementioned complex issues, which might create a discretionary power for each court to apply or ignore these rules. If the court concluded that mosaic actions were not the same, and thus these

---

789 *Tatry*, 42. For the facts of the case, see *Tatry*, 1 ff.

790 *Gubisch*, 16.

791 *Tatry*, 43.

792 Note that, by analogy with *Gantner*, 26 and AG in *Mærsk*, 43, the determination of the identical nature of actions is not affected by the fact that the defendant disputes the existence and the amount of the claim. Account should be taken only of the plaintiff's claim, regardless of the defence raised by the defendant.

793 Regarding this train of thought, see, by analogy, AG in *I. Weber*, 67.

rules were not applicable, they could, however, still be regarded as related actions, since this question arises only if the conditions for the application of Art 29 are not met.[794]

b) Are the mosaic actions related?

Although the wording of the concept of relatedness under Art 30(3) and of the concept of connectedness within Art 8(1) is identical, given the fundamental differences in their logic, the former concept is interpreted more restrictively than the latter.[795] As a result, if, in the wake of *Painer*, it was argued within *supra* Ch. III.D.V that actions brought for violations of personality rights could be regarded as connected actions, the more widely interpreted concept of relatedness under Art 30(3) covers the mosaic actions without any doubts being raised.

c) An adjunct problem: courts with different extents of jurisdiction

An adjunct problem of the preceding issues is the application of the rules of *lis pendens* and related actions in circumstances when parallel proceedings are brought in courts, which are equipped with different extents of jurisdiction. In particular, when the aggrieved person brings separate actions before the court of a mosaic jurisdiction and before a court with an unlimited extent of jurisdiction, i.e., the court for the place of the causal event or the courts of the state where the defendant is domiciled.[796] This problem is exacerbated if the damage occurred not solely in the territories of the

794 See *Tatry*, 49.

795 On the relation between the two provisions, see also *supra* fn 483. On differences, see: (1) the former derogates from Art 4(1) and allocates adjudicatory authority, while the latter is applicable irrespective of Art 4(1); (2) the former is applied by the plaintiff, while the latter is employed by the court. On this, see also AG in *Painer*, 69-71; AG in *Roche*, 81 ff.

796 See also, Kubis, Internationale Zuständigkeit, p 139. The present author would propose applying *Tatry*, 35 in which the ECJ dealt with the concept of same parties in circumstances when two proceedings involve not only the same parties but, in addition, different ones. Therefore, by analogy, the overlapping parts of the actions could be regarded as identical. However, because of the above-mentioned reasons, this proposal is also provided with serious pitfalls, especially regarding the separability of the same dispute.

Brussels-Lugano States but also outside of those territories, and the aggrieved person sues not only in a mosaic jurisdiction but also in a third state in which, generally, the extent of the jurisdiction of the court is not limited.[797]

8. Rules on the recognition and enforcement of judgments

As a corollary of the strong interconnection of the rules on jurisdiction, as well as on the recognition and enforcement of judgments, the problematic and uncertain issues indicated in the preceding subsections largely return to, and thus are reflected on, the recognition and enforcement of the judgments delivered in each mosaic jurisdiction.[798] By arguing that these judgments are delivered in respect of the same disputes, they could be regarded as irreconcilable and, accordingly, their recognition or enforcement could be refused under certain circumstances specified in Art 45(1)(c) or (d). In addition, as a consequence of the phenomenon of (legitimate) libel tourism, if the plaintiff avails himself of a legal regime in which the applicable law provides extensive protection of the right to reputation by eliminating the guarantees of the freedom of expression, the Brussels-Lugano State addressed could refuse the judgment given that it is manifestly contrary to its public policy.[799]

Besides grounds for refusal, another serious issue, as Christian Kohler notices, concerns the *res judicata* effect of the mosaic judgment.[800] In particular, it is questionable whether this effect is confined to the territory of

797 See similarly Roth, Die internationale Zuständigkeit, p 319. Regarding rules in respect of third states, see also *supra* Ch. III.B.II.2.

798 For the outline of the rules on the recognition and enforcement of judgments, see *supra* Ch. III.B.III.

799 See also Nielsen, J. Priv. Int. L. 2013, 269, 284-287. For this ground of refusal and the meaning and interpretation of the term 'public policy', see e.g. AG in *Diageo Brands*, 35 ff. Cf. US: as Nielsen, J. Priv. Int. L. 2013, 269, 270-271, fns 10, 11 points out, in accordance with certain statutes (e.g. the SPEECH Act or in New York the Libel Terrorism Protection Act), the recognition and enforcement of foreign defamation judgments are denied, unless the foreign court applied defamation law that affords at least as much protection for the freedom of expression as would have been granted by the Constitutions of the US and the state addressed, together with the relevant law of that state.

800 Regarding Kohler's notice, see *supra* Intr. to Ch. V.C; regarding the effect of *res judicata*, see *supra* Ch. III.B.III.

the state where the competent court, which delivered the judgment, has its seat. Alternatively, does it produce its effect among all Brussels-Lugano States without limiting this effect to the territory of the state of origin? To draw some serious support for the latter view, first, the principles underlying the Brussels-Lugano Regime shall be recalled. In particular, the principles of strengthening the legal protection of people established in the Brussels-Lugano States, legal certainty, and mutual recognition of judgments[801] militate in favour of such understanding.[802] Secondly and more fundamentally, the opinion of AG Jääskinen delivered in *Folien Fischer*, in which he answered a proposal put forward by the French government, justifies such a view. In particular, the French government proposed a territorial restriction of the authority of *res judicata* of the judgment given on the basis of an action for a negative declaration, providing that actions of that type are not admissible as such in French law on tort.[803] In this regard, AG Jääskinen first pointed out that the purpose and very *raison d'être* of Brussels I is to lay down rules of jurisdiction which apply to the courts of all Member States simultaneously and which ensure that for one and the same dispute, a single decision is given that has international effects.[804] Then, he went on to state:

> «There is no contradiction between this point and the case-law arising from the judgments in *Shevilland Others* and *eDate Advertisingand Others*, in which the Court restricted the territorial jurisdiction of the courts in certain situations but not the authority of *res judicata* of the decisions given by those courts.»[805]

---

801 However, note that Commission Document COM(2010) 748 final, pp 6-7 [see also its Art 37(3)(a)] proposed retaining temporarily the *exequatur* procedure for judgments in cases in which an individual claims that rights relating to his personality or privacy have been violated by the media [solely by the media, without reference to individual bloggers (*supra* Ch. II.C)!]. It stated in *ibid.*, p 7 that the divergences in the protection of personality rights under national substantive laws and the absence of any harmonised rules of PIL in this field [see *supra* Ch. V.C.II.4.a)] «make it premature to presume the required level of trust yet exists between legal systems in order move beyond the *status quo* on this matter» (italics in the original, full stop omitted). However, Zwiefka Draft Report (28.6.2011), p 47 replied to this proposal as follows: «for reasons of legal certainty it would be better to have no exemptions.» Finally, the EU legislators ignored the proposal of the COM in the final text of Brussels Ia.

802 See also, by analogy, *Gubisch*, 18.

803 AG in *Folien Fischer*, 67.

804 AG in *Folien Fischer*, 68-69.

805 AG in *Folien Fischer*, fn 41 (italics and compound spelling of words in the original).

It follows that a peripheral court in a place with modest distribution coverage would render a binding judgment, providing that the substantive matter of the dispute is regarded as a single one and, particularly, the liability of the publisher for distributing the same newspaper article is regarded as uniform und undividable.[806]

In addition, an adjunct and tricky question concerns the EU concept of *res judicata*. As outlined in *supra* Ch. III.B.III, this *sui generis* concept applies to judgments in which the court rules on the merits of the case regarded as intermediate findings on the basis of which it assesses its own jurisdiction under the Brussels-Lugano Regime. Its speciality lies in its nature, since it provides a binding nature not only for the operative part of the judgment, but also to its *ratio decidendi*. Therefore, it could be supposed that if the court in a mosaic jurisdiction declined jurisdiction based on the merits of the case that reasoning would be binding on the other courts. To take an example, assume that the aggrieved person brings proceedings in the courts of Aruba, since he claims that this Contracting State to the BC[807] is the place where the damage occurred. However, the Aruban court declines jurisdiction in accordance with Art 53 of the BC, since it finds that the publisher is not domiciled pursuant to the law designated by its rules of PIL in the territory of any Brussels-Lugano State.[808] Does this intermediate finding on the merits of the dispute, which was necessary for the Aruban court to assess its own jurisdiction, bind the court of another Contracting State of the BC, such as Germany, where the victim brings proceedings due to the mosaic approach as being the territory where another part of his damage occurred?[809] This leads to a point of some subtlety, which lies at the heart of the fact that several Member States are Contracting States neither of the BC nor of the 1988 LC.[810] By slightly changing this factual scenario, what would be the result if, after the delivery of the judgment, the plaintiff brings a claim in a Hungarian court where the rules of the BC are not applicable. Does the possible EU

806 Similarly Nagy, J. Priv. Int. L. 2012, 251, 272-273. However, to avoid this result, Nagy (*ibid.*, 273) prefers to understand the question of illegality of the publisher's conduct as having a distributive (and thus, territorial) nature.

807 For the Contracting States of the BC, see *supra* fns 206 and 225.

808 On this provision, see *supra* Ch. III.B.I.1.

809 Cf. Bach, EuZW 2013, 56, 58 (a theoretical scenario regarding choice of court agreements).

810 See *supra* fn 256.

res judicata effect of the judgment restrict the power of the Hungarian court to ascertain its own jurisdiction?

Conclusion and summary

In sum, the restriction of the extent of the jurisdiction of the competent court for the place where the damage occurred leads to numerous problematic, even tricky issues and open questions, which run counter to the inherent nature of cross-border defamation and, to a certain extent, reverse the central mechanism, spirit, and letters of the Brussels-Lugano Regime. In particular, it risks the appropriate application and fine balance of the cornerstone principles underlying Art 7(2) and disregards all aspects of the principle of legal certainty[811] at the expense of the litigants and the courts. Moreover, it also suggests a kind of distrust of each other's administration of justice and decision-making capacity to protect the right to reputation and to redress defamation.[812] Finally, it fragments the unified system of rules of jurisdiction and decentralises the same dispute by conferring decision-making power on the courts of each Brussels-Lugano State where the jurisdictionally relevant damage under the second *Shevill*-test occurred.[813]

D. Shevill and its impacts

Shevill specified the open-textured twin criteria of *Bier* for disputes concerning cross-border defamation through the offline press by establishing concepts that are fictitious and rigid in their wording, and flexible, complex, and disputable in their interpretation. In particular, the concept of the publisher's establishment is open to several different understandings, since it is treated as being the place where the harmful event originated and from which the libel was issued and put into circulation as well as being the place that generally coincides with the defendant's domicile. In addition, the concept of the place of the damage, by conferring jurisdiction on the courts of those Brussels-Lugano States in which the defamatory publication was distributed, and in which the victim claims to have suf-

811 See *supra* Ch. III.B.I.
812 On this, see also Roth, Die internationale Zuständigkeit, pp 330-331.
813 Similarly, Kreuzer/Klötgen, IPRax 1997, 90, 95.

fered injury to his reputation, is even more troublesome, since the exact meaning of this connecting factor is far from clear. Finally, the limitation of the extent of jurisdiction of these latter courts disregards the inherent nature of cross-border defamation, and it is principally incompatible with most of the governing objectives and underlying principles of the Brussels-Lugano Regime. In other words, as noted above, the mosaic approach promotes ease of administration of justice and litigational justice at the expense of predictability and foreseeability.[814]

These special problems and greater-than-usual complications attached to the *Shevill*-approaches, however, have not deterred the national judicial practice from applying them to other means of communication, such as information broadcast via television.[815] In addition, it is accepted in legal writing that the *Shevill*-approaches are applicable not only to defamation but also to violations of divergent personality rights. As AG Cruz Villalón pointed out:

> «*Shevill* ... is not confined exclusively to the print media, since its scope also encompasses other means of communication such as information broadcast via television or radio. It also covers a wide range of infringements of personality rights, be they defamation in the sense usually attributed to this type of harm in continental legal systems, or the defamation typical of common law systems.»[816]

While the localisation of defamation through the broadcast of information has attracted the views of a considerable number of academics,[817] the localisation of violations through the Internet has been made the focus of legal writing over the last decades. In particular, this medium, with its spe-

814 Thus, it is contrary to Recital 16 as mentioned in *supra* Ch. III.B.II.1.

815 For the application of the concept of the place of the damage, see Ireland: *Ewins v Carlton* [1997] 2 ILRM 223, *Irish High Court*, 3.3.1997 as outlined in McGonagle, Jurisdiction in Television Libel, 1998 (concerning television documentary made by Carlton Television and mainly distributed by Ulster Television in mainland Britain and Northern Ireland. It was also received to a certain extent in Ireland); Norway: Case of the *Supreme Court of Norway* (*Norges Høyesterett*), 17.10.2001, HR-2000-00799 – Rt-2001 – 1322 (240-2001) as outlined in Krog, Determination of Jurisdiction, 2002 (concerning an allegedly defamatory documentary about Norwegian seal hunters produced by a journalist and broadcast by a Swedish broadcasting company on Swedish television, which could also be received in Norway) and commented in Krog, IPRax 2004, 154-157.

816 AG in *eDate and Martinez*, 39 (italics in the original, fn and emphases omitted). See also e.g. Vick/Macpherson, Va. J. Int'l L. 1995-1996, 933, 984 (regarding other mass media).

817 E.g. Fisher, Defamation via Satellite (regarding satellite).

cial and constantly evolving characteristics,[818] has generated lively scholarly discourse on localising online defamation and, even more widely, online violations of personality rights. Whether these proposals maintain or modify the *Shevill*-approaches or alternatively whether they suggest adopting connecting factors other than those which were introduced in *Shevill*, is discussed in the next chapter.

818 See *supra* Ch. II.

Chapter VI: Jurisdiction in online violations of personality rights: reviewing 16 years' proposals

As *supra* Ch. II demonstrated, the characteristics of the Internet and online publication differ considerably from the inherent nature of the traditional media and paper-based publications. Those differences are leaving their marks on online violations of personality rights. In particular, these violations are even more complex than their offline counterparts are and involve a chain of successive acts that can be simplified as follows: creation of the content – uploading it to a web server – request for it from the web server by the online visitor – transferring it through the traceroute[819] to the online visitor's Internet device – displaying it on the screen of the online visitor's Internet device – comprehension of the content by the online visitor. The point of this chain that is proposed as the jurisdictionally relevant concept of causal event or damage varies significantly in legal writing and judicial practice. In addition, it is also not unusual that legal fictions or other solutions are preferred for this purpose.[820] Accordingly, the present chapter categorises into three groups the proposals put forward for localising online (potential) violations of personality rights basically within Art 7(2) over a period of 16 years between *Shevill* and *eDate and Martinez* and reviews them briefly.[821]

A. Maintaining the twin criteria within Art 7(2)

An overwhelming number of proposals maintain the twin criteria within the concept of harmful event established in *Bier* and tailor them essentially

---

819 See *supra* Ch. II.A.

820 National cases referred to in this chapter deal with the special rule of jurisdiction in tort under the Brussels-Lugano Regime, unless otherwise indicated.

821 Note that a few proposals [e.g. the proposal of Nagy in *infra* Ch. VI.A.II.1.b), Reymond in *infra* Ch. VI.A.II.2.b)cc) or Dickinson in *infra* Ch. VI.B.IV] are expressed after the delivery of *eDate and Martinez*. Proposals consider either defamation or (potential) violations of personality rights. Roth, Die internationale Zuständigkeit, pp 180-186 and pp 231-272 have been highly valuable for the present chapter.

on the basis of *Shevill* to the characteristics of online violations of personality rights. This section, therefore, aims to outline solutions formulated for localising the concepts of causal event and damage.

I. The place of the event, which gives rise to and is at the origin of the damage, occurred or may occur

Proposals for localising the concept of causal event in online violations of personality rights either uphold *Shevill* or focus on different points of the aforementioned chain of successive acts. Alternatively, it is also possible that they propose rebuttable presumptions.

1. The place of the publisher's establishment *à la Shevill*

Several views support the approach to the place of the publisher's establishment introduced in *Shevill*. For instance, AG Cruz Villalón, in his opinion delivered in *eDate and Martinez*, proposed this criterion without any further reasoning.[822] In this regard, Peter Stone also notes:

> «The *Shevill* principles extend to a television broadcast and, no doubt, to a publication by means of a webpage on the internet. In the latter case the relevant establishment of the website operator under the first principle will be its domicile or secondary establishment from, and by the staff attached to, which the website is maintained, rather than the place at which its website is located, and jurisdiction based on the place of conduct will overlap with that conferred by Articles 2 or 5(5).»[823]

822 *eDate and Martinez*, 67. See also similarly Nielsen, J. Priv. Int. L. 2013, 269, 279. Cf. observation submitted by the Greek government in Minutes of Proceedings drawn up for the oral hearing in *eDate and Martinez*, 14.12.2010 (on file with author), 56 ('establishment of the website operator').

823 Stone, EU PIL, pp 93-94 (fns omitted, italics in the original). Similarly, see also Nuyts, in: Nuyts, International Litigation, p 121. Cf. Nygh/Pocar Report, p 60 [regarding the place where the act or omission that caused injury occurred or may occur under Art 10(1)(a) and Art 10(3) of the draft Hague Judgments Convention in relation to torts taking place at a distance].

2. The place where the web server, to which the content was uploaded, is located

As *supra* Ch. II.A noted, information uploaded by a publisher to his own or a third party's website is stored on his own or a third party's web server(s) as digital data. Accordingly, the web server maintains the information available to the public. It follows that, from a technical point of view, and in the eyes of the online visitors, it is the device that ensures the availability of the digitalised content, as that content is transmitted from this device through the traceroute to the requesting computer. In addition, the location of the server might be practical in the context of enforcement. If the server is located in the forum state, there is no difficulty in enforcing that judgment within a short time, providing that data are not removed from the server in the meantime.[824] For this and similar reasons, it is occasionally argued that the place where the web server, to which the content was uploaded, is located shall be deemed to be a jurisdictionally relevant place.[825]

3. The place where the content was uploaded

The place where the publisher uploads the content to the Internet, i.e., to the web server, is largely regarded as a jurisdictionally relevant place in legal writing.[826] This solution seems right for reasons exclusively oriented

---

824 See also Svantesson, PIL and the Internet, p 357.

825 On this, see Roth, Die internationale Zuständigkeit, p 184; Germany: Case 2-03 O 366/00 (9.11.2000), *LG Frankfurt/M.* as summarised at the ECJ Website No 2001/28; UK/England: *Football Dataco Ltd & Ors v Sportradar GmbH & Anor* [2010] EWHC 2911 (Ch) (17.11.2010) as referred to and analysed in O'Reilly, EJLT 2011, 1-13; Marly, JurPC 1992, 1442, 1448-1449 ('Knotenrechner'). Marly (*ibid.*, p 1449) also suggests that for systems that hold the content available without directing it to a particular place («bereithaltende Systeme»), e.g. mailbox-systems, solely the place of operation of the system is attributable to the operator (on this, see also Roth, Die internationale Zuständigkeit, p 260).

826 See e.g. Hoare, C.L.Pract. 2004, 4, 9; Spickhoff, IPRax 2011, 131, 132 («Absendeort»); Bachmann, IPRax 1998, 179, 182-183, 187 (regarding newsgroups, she mentions the place where the computer is situated). Cf. Germany: Case 15 U 148/09 (30.3.2010), *OLG Köln* as referred to in case *Seven Days in Moscow* VI ZR 111/10 (29.3.2011), *BGH* (GRUR 2011, 558), 4 (Art 32 of the *ZPO*). Note that in *Hejduk*, 25 the ECJ localised the causal event at the place where the defendant «took and carried out the decision to place photographs online on a par-

towards the perpetrator's act of uploading. According to Peter Mankowski, torts committed on the Internet «display their most relevant activity with the uploading of the incriminated content.»[827] The act of uploading focuses on the publisher's final physical act that belongs to his sphere. Therefore, as Oren Bigos notes, «[t]his approach is sensible because the defendant should face liability for his act in the place where he chooses to act. He cannot legitimately complain about this, because the choice where to act was his own.»[828] At the touch of a button, the content is out of his control and becomes generally available to the public. Thus, from his point of view, he did everything possible that was necessary for the comprehension of the content by third party online visitors.[829] Further successive components of a violation are completed partly automatically on a technical basis and partly contingent on the online visitors' purposeful act by pulling the passively available information from a web server.[830] In addition, the act of uploading is a precondition for the comprehension of the disputed information.[831] However, as Isabel Roth points out, the plaintiff may face difficulties in proving which was the place where the defendant uploaded the disputed material. Therefore, various scholars propose that the defendant legal person's seat or the individual publisher's habitual residence should be presumed as the (regular) place of uploading.[832]

ticular website.» (On this, see also *supra* fns 457 and 571). The act of carrying out the decision could be understood as the act of uploading of the disputed content. For details on this place, see also Roth, Die internationale Zuständigkeit, pp 180-182.

827 Mankowski, in: Magnus/Mankowski, Brussels I Regulation, p 250, para 226 (fn omitted).

828 Bigos, ICLQ 2005, 585, 605.

829 On this, see also Kubis, Internationale Zuständigkeit, p 172; Roth, Die internationale Zuständigkeit, p 181.

830 On this, see *supra* Ch. II.A.

831 See Roth, Die internationale Zuständigkeit, p 180.

832 See Roth, Die internationale Zuständigkeit, p 182. See also von Hinden, Persönlichkeitsverletzungen, pp 71-73 (applicable law); Thorn, FS Bernd von Hoffmann, p 762, point 2 [legal persons: seat, as the centre of their conduct («Verhaltenszentrale»); individuals: place of uploading]. Regarding the localisation of the causal event of individuals as online actors, see also *infra* Ch. VII.D.II.1.

4. Isabel Roth: three places under a rebuttable rule of presumption

Isabel Roth determines the place of the causal event in two steps: first, she identifies jurisdictionally relevant places, and then she proposes a rebuttable presumption.[833]

As far as the first step is concerned, Isabel Roth focuses on three places, namely, on the place where the content was conceptualised and developed («Ort der Angebotskonzeption und -entwicklung»);[834] the place of uploading («Ort des Einspeisens»); and for companies with different departments ('arbeitsteilige Unternehmen'), on the place where the decision on the content and publication of the material is taken.[835, 836] She stresses that these places meet the requirements of procedural valuations listed in *supra* Ch. IV.B.I.1.c), and therefore, they should be regarded as jurisdictionally relevant places. In particular, she argues that these places guarantee proximity and ease of taking evidence, since acts completed therein are significant components of the entire tort, and each was performed by a physical activity of the perpetrator.[837] In addition, they ensure an additional jurisdiction to the defendant's domicile, and thus, they favour the plaintiff.[838] Thirdly, they are attributable to the perpetrator, since he was able to influence their location, and the acts performed therein establish sufficient do-

---

833 Roth, Die internationale Zuständigkeit, pp 193-206, 206-211. Acc. to her opinion, the court shall have jurisdiction to rule on all the damage there (*ibid.*, pp 340-341).

834 This place was also considered by Mankowski, RabelsZ 1999, 203, 262-267 (applicable law). On this, see also Roth, Die internationale Zuständigkeit, pp 183-184.

835 In addition, Roth, Die internationale Zuständigkeit, p 196 identifies this place as the place where the physical act [see *supra* Ch. IV.B.I.1.c)] is performed by such companies. In particular, she specifies e.g. the place where the editorial office or the decision-making body takes the decision, or when one person decides, the place of the instruction. See also *ibid.*, p 198.

836 Similar place (i.e., place where the decision on the publication was taken) was also considered by von Hinden, Persönlichkeitsverletzungen, pp 58-61, 69 (applicable law) (see also Roth, Die internationale Zuständigkeit, pp 182-183). Cf. Case *Seven Days in Moscow* VI ZR 111/10 (29.3.2011), *BGH* (GRUR 2011, 558), 16 in which the *BGH* did not expressly opt for the first two places referred to by Roth but rejected jurisdiction *inter alia* on the basis of the fact that: «Nach dem Vortrag des Klägers hat die Beklagte in den Vereinigten Staaten den Bericht abgefasst und ins Internet gestellt.»

837 Roth, Die internationale Zuständigkeit, pp 198, 193-198.

838 Roth, Die internationale Zuständigkeit, pp 198-199.

mestic connection between the state and the dispute.[839] In this latter regard, she also notes that when the injurious content was prepared at different places and times, the sufficient connection is given at the place where the defendant predominantly acted (centre of gravity of the act).[840] Finally, they meet the interest of the state in restoring legal peace and providing procedural satisfaction for the litigants.[841]

However, Isabel Roth notes that when the court seised expresses doubts, or the defendant contests the jurisdiction, the plaintiff might face significant evidential difficulties in proving that the jurisdictionally relevant acts were performed at those places.[842] This is so because the aforementioned places are not immediately apparent to him. In other words, the plaintiff cannot ascertain from the injurious web content or email where it was created and saved onto the Internet or where the decision about its content and publication was taken. In addition, nor do top-level domain names provide reliable information about the place where the content was conceptualised and developed or uploaded. Moreover, Isabel Roth also questions whether the place of uploading is determinable due to the technical data and whether data protection law does not hinder the plaintiff from obtaining such data. Finally, she expresses doubts about the ascertainability of the place where the content was conceptualised and developed, since the concept belongs to the organisational sphere of the perpetrator into which the plaintiff cannot gain entry. Mindful of these evidential difficulties, Isabel Roth proposes a rebuttable rule of presumption.[843] Hence, for private persons, on the basis of usual daily life experience, it is presumed that the place where the material is created and uploaded to the Internet coincides with the domicile or habitual residence of the tortfeasor.[844] For companies with different departments, it is supposed to be their

---

839 Roth, Die internationale Zuständigkeit, pp 201, 203. For details, see *ibid.*, pp 200-205.

840 Roth, Die internationale Zuständigkeit, p 204.

841 Roth, Die internationale Zuständigkeit, pp 206, 205-206.

842 Roth, Die internationale Zuständigkeit, pp 206-209.

843 Roth, Die internationale Zuständigkeit, pp 209, 209-211.

844 Roth, Die internationale Zuständigkeit, p 209. She proposes defining the term 'domicile' acc. to the *lex fori* due to the relevant rule of Brussels I, the BC, and the 1988 LC (see *ibid.*, fn 1004). It is, however, unclear whether the domicile is a presumed place for jurisdictional purposes, since it is mentioned only on page 209, and it is ignored on pages 211 and 212.

seats, since it is generally acknowledged that the significant decisions regarding the content and the publication of the material are taken there.[845]

II. The place where the damage occurred or may occur

Proposals for localising the place of the damage in online violations of personality rights stretch far beyond the second *Shevill*-criterion: they either emphasise the accessibility of the content in a particular state or regard the direction of the information. Alternatively, it is also possible that they focus on the victim's forum.

1. Accessibility and actual access of the online content

Two essential concepts are crystallised in legal writing and judicial practice; they are built upon the condition that the online content should be accessible in the forum. Their differences lie in the level of the accessibility required.

a) Accessibility of the online content

The concept of mere accessibility confers jurisdiction on the courts of a state where the disputed content is accessible on the basis of the conception that the content uploaded on a web server is generally made available to the public and accessed anywhere in the world.[846] Thus, it is often justified by the finding that «those who make information accessible by a particular method do so knowing of the reach that their information may have. In particular, those who post information on the World Wide Web do so knowing that the information they make available is available to all and sundry without any geographic restriction.»[847] This concept is formu-

845 Roth, Die internationale Zuständigkeit, p 209. She proposes defining the seat of legal persons in accordance with the relevant rule on domicile of legal persons under Brussels I, the BC and the 1988 LC (see *ibid.*, fn 1005).

846 Cf. *infra* Ch. VI.A.II.4.

847 *Dow Jones and Company Inc v Gutnick* [2002] HCA 56; 210 CLR 575; 194 ALR 433; 77 ALJR 255 (10 December 2002), 39 (Gleeson CJ, McHugh, Gummow and Hayne JJ.).

lated both in legal writing[848] and practice[849] mainly on the basis of the *Shevill*-approach.[850] Accordingly, Birgit Bachmann states:

> «Die internationale Zuständigkeit im Internet folgt grundsätzlich den Regeln des Presserechts. Dabei besitzt die Rechtsprechung des EuGH besondere Bedeutung.»[851]

In particular, she proposes that the place of the damage should be the place where the content is accessible, if the interests of the aggrieved person are affected there.[852] Moreover, she adds that the extent of the jurisdiction of the competent court should be limited to the damage that arose in that territory except when the measure claimed is an injunction. In the case of injunctions, the limited extent of jurisdiction should be ignored.[853] Similarly, AG Cruz Villalón submits in his opinion delivered in *eDate and Martinez* in relation to the place of the damage:

> «[I]n principle, a possible connecting factor might be based on the *accessibility* of the information, which would justify an automatic connection with all the Member

---

848 E.g. Coester-Waltjen, FS Rolf A. Schütze, p 184; Schack, MMR 2000, 135, 138 (violations of intellectual property rights). See also Roth, Die internationale Zuständigkeit, p 243.

849 Germany: Case 6 U 9/02 (10.7.2002), *OLG Karlsruhe* as summarised at the ECJ Website No 2003/26 (commercial sign); Sweden: Case M.E. Aktiebolag v Hamar Arbeiderblad AS (4.2.2008), *Svea hovrätt* as summarised at the ECJ Website No 2009/62 (copyright); France: question referred for a preliminary ruling in *eDate and Martinez*, 29, first subpara; France: *Cour de cassation, Société Castellblanch v Société Champagne Louis Roederer*, No 01-03225 (9.12.2003) as summarised at the ECJ Website No 2004/27 (violation of rights); Switzerland: judgment of the Swiss *Bundesgericht* of 6.3.2007 (violation of trade mark by domain names) as referred to in Parker *et al.*, Tenth report, pp 5-6; Italy (law of venue has been influenced by *Shevill* in online defamation cases): Study JLS/C4/2005/03, National Report Italy (Consolo et al) (Questionnaire 3), point 2.2.11, IT-10, available at <ec.europa.eu/civiljustice/news/docs/study_bxl1_italy.pdf>.

850 See observations submitted by the UK and the Greek governments as well as the COM (referring to the criterion 'to be known', on this, see *supra* Ch. V.B.II.2) in Minutes of Proceedings drawn up for the oral hearing in *eDate and Martinez*, 14.12.2010 (on file with author), 50-51, 56, 58-59.

851 Bachmann, IPRax 1998, 179, 187.

852 Bachmann, IPRax 1998, 179, 187. Roth, Die internationale Zuständigkeit, p 270 notes that it is not clear whether Bachmann refers to the violation of the reputational right or of other interests because these interests could be regarded as consequential to the violation of the former right. Although in this respect, the present author agrees with Roth, she underlines that by outlining this concept, Bachmann, IPRax 1998, 179, fns 102, 104 and p 187 refers several times to *Shevill*, and thus, it is supposed that her concept is premised on this judgment.

853 Bachmann, IPRax 1998, 179, 187.

> States, since, in practice, the allegedly harmful information is accessible in all of them.»[854]

Then, he went on to conclude:

> «[I]n the event of an infringement of personality rights by means of information disseminated in a number of Member States via the internet, that the holder of those rights may bring an action for compensation: ... before the courts of each Member State in which the information was published and in which the holder of personality rights claims to have been the victim of an attack on his reputation, which have jurisdiction to hear an action concerning only the damage caused in their respective States».[855]

Finally, Michael Bogdan attributes relevance to the occurrence of real and potential and not symbolical damage at the place where the website can be accessed. He notes:

> «The accessibility of the website from a certain Member State, whether closely related to the plaintiff or not, thus should not per se suffice for jurisdiction of that State's courts, but if combined with the requirement of real or potential damage arising in the forum country (a requirement following from the above-mentioned limitation of jurisdiction to such damage), it seems to constitute a reasonable compromise.»[856]

b) Actual access of the online content

The second variation of the concept of mere accessibility is the actual access approach. It suggests that the content does not cause non-pecuniary harm to the concerned person as long as it is not accessed, read, and comprehended by third party online visitors. Consequently, the jurisdictionally relevant place is where the online content is actually accessed (downloaded), since it is presumably the place where the online visitor also comprehends the disputed content.[857] Viewed in this light, for exam-

---

854 AG in *eDate and Martinez*, 56 (italics in the original).

855 AG in *eDate and Martinez*, 67, second subpara (first subpara omitted). For his alternative test regarding the concept of damage, see *infra* Ch. VI.A.II.2.b)aa).

856 Bogdan, Masaryk U. J.L. & Tech. 2011, 1, 4 (fn omitted). For underlying his notice, he refers (*ibid.*) to a decision of a «Swedish appellate court in RH 2008:4, concerning Swedish jurisdiction to deal with damages for a copyright infringement committed by a Norwegian publisher whose Norwegian website had some 60 subscribers in Sweden.»

857 On this, see similarly, Roth, Die internationale Zuständigkeit, pp 232-233. See also Stone, EU PIL, p 94 (downloaded); Australia: *Dow Jones and Company Inc*

ple, Csongor István Nagy, by maintaining the *Shevill*-test, suggests that «the actual access (number of visitors, downloads, etc) should be the surrogate of distribution.»[858] In addition to the criterion of actual access, he attaches importance to the following factors: whether the parties are domiciled in the same country, whether it is the place of the main directions or the side effects of the publication, and whether the victim has a reputation there. For example, if the litigants are domiciled in different countries, and the plaintiff sues the defendant in the country of main direction, the strong connection between the dispute and the forum exists. The court of the side effect country, however, should have jurisdiction, if the harm that arose there is substantial, i.e., either the circulation of the publication is substantial or the reputation of the allegedly aggrieved person is significant.[859]

c) An adjunct question: the use of geolocation tools

Nevertheless, the accessibility and the actual access tests raise an adjunct question similar to the criterion of intended distribution of offline material and to the targeting test of the online content.[860] Specifically, it is questionable whether the place where the publisher aimed to avoid the accessibility of the content by the use of geolocation tools, but where it became accessible by these tools being circumvented, could be regarded as a jurisdictionally relevant place.[861] Two main positions are taken on this issue. First, academics attach less importance to geolocation tools and state that even if geolocation tools are employed, the content should be regarded as being available worldwide. Isabel Roth, for instance, notes:

> «Das Abrufgebiet ist ... zwar technisch beschränkbar, mangels Zuverlässigkeit und Zumutbarkeit dieser technischen Einrichtungen ist im Rahmen der Erfolgsortan-

---

v Gutnick [2002] HCA 56; 210 CLR 575; 194 ALR 433; 77 ALJR 255 (10 December 2002) and on this case, see *supra* Intr.

858 Nagy, J. Priv. Int. L. 2012, 251, 276 (note that his suggestion is put forward after the delivery of the *eDate and Martinez* judgment). Cf. Bachmann, IPRax 1998, 179, 184-185 considers the place where the content is the most viewed, but she rejects it on the basis of a lack of accurate factors capable of identifying that place.

859 Nagy, J. Priv. Int. L. 2012, 251, 276-277. It is noteworthy that *ibid.*, p 278 submits that if the parties are domiciled in the same state, other Member States should have jurisdiction if substantial harm occurred there.

860 On these two approaches, see *supra* Ch. V.B.II.1.b); *infra* Ch. VI.A.II.2.

861 On this, see *supra* Ch. II.B.

> knüpfung dennoch davon auszugehen, dass die Internetangebote weltweit abrufbar sind.»[862]

By contrast, Michel Reymond militates in favour of geolocation technologies and proposes that they should be taken into account, if they «were reasonably available to the website owner at the time of the offence.»[863] In this respect, he distinguishes between «big-time» and «smaller» publishers. The former group, which already spends funds to employ certain geolocation technologies, has the means of assessing the risks of publishing in a particular territory and of filtering undesired fora. Therefore, they should be held to high standards: for example, if they do not avoid access to their content by the online visitors located in the forum, targeting of that state is possible. Nonetheless, if a jurisdiction is adequately filtered, then, in his opinion, targeting will be rejected «even if a few users located in the forum state manage to slip through the cracks and nonetheless access the website. In order to foster implementation of these filtering schemes, professional media companies should not be held liable for the still existing failings of current technology.»[864] Regarding smaller publishers, he states:

> «[T]hey should be held to a lower standard of scrutiny and should not be found as "targeting" every unfiltered jurisdiction. In these cases, the test should take account of the website owner's financial and technical ability, and accordingly determine if his or her use of geolocation was adequate at the time of the offense. For example, if the defendant is a fairly popular personal blogger, deployment of high-end IP-based geolocation will not be required; however, due to the popularity of the website, use of less onerous methods, such as a low-end statistical determination of the location of its regular readers, should be expected.»[865]

2. The targeting test

The targeting test aims to localise Internet-based activities through complex and occasionally technology-dependent criteria. This test has at-

862 Roth, Die internationale Zuständigkeit, p 248 (emphasis omitted). Cf. Mankowski, in: Magnus/Mankowski, Brussels I Regulation, p 264, para 249d.

863 Reymond, YbPIL 2012/2013, 205, 234 [it was discussed as a part of his targeting test; on this, see *infra* Ch. VI.A.II.2.b)cc)].

864 Reymond, YbPIL 2012/2013, 205, 235.

865 Reymond, YbPIL 2012/2013, 205, 235. Cf. acc. to Marly, JurPC 1992, 1442, 1449, if a header under the title distribution limits the content to a particular region, only this region is regarded as jurisdictionally relevant.

tracted the attention of numerous scholars.[866] Trevor C. Hartley, for example, proposes as an optional connecting factor:

> «In the case of non-contractual obligations arising out of violations of privacy and rights relating to personality, including defamation, article 5(3) shall apply only if —
>
> ...
>
> (b) the defendant has taken significant steps to make the offending material available in the country of the forum and has targeted that country more than any other.»[867]

In addition, this test has also been applied in judicial practice. *OLG München* (Germany), for example, interpreted Art 5(3) of Brussels I in line with the inherent nature of the distribution test established in *Shevill.* It held that the effect of the online publication of a statement is located in Germany «if the web presentation was intended to have effect in that State.»[868] Similarly, the Heidelberg Report, by referring to the Scottish and French judicial practice, states:

> «Especially in internet cases, the courts seem to be on their way to develop reliable criteria for a localisation of torts, e. g. by asking to which country a certain website is directed.»[869]

Two different forms of the targeting test are recognised in legal writing and judicial practice, and thus, these are considered below: one essentially

---

866 For details on this test, see Reymond, YbPIL 2012/2013, 205-246; Smith, CRi 2004, 145-152. See also Roth, Die internationale Zuständigkeit, pp 253-255, 272.

867 Hartley, ICLQ 2010, 25, 36 [fns and emphases omitted; regarding Brussels I; for his alternative test regarding the concept of damage, see *infra* Ch. VI.A.II.3)]. For preferring this test, see also e.g. observations submitted by the MGN Limited and the French government in Minutes of Proceedings drawn up for the oral hearing in *eDate and Martinez*, 14.12.2010 (on file with author), 64, 70; Borchers, NILR 2003, 401, 413; Boskovic, Boskovic on Rome II, 2010. Cf. Hestermeyer, Nw. J. Int'l L. & Bus. 2006, 267, 286 ff. (Internet jurisdiction for torts).

868 Voinov/de Lapasse/Janzen, Twelfth Report, p 12 regarding case 29 U 2713/07 (6.12.2007), *OLG München*, No 2009/33 (fn omitted, unfair competition). On the distribution test in *Shevill*, see *supra* Ch. V.B.II.1.b).

869 Heidelberg Report, para 210 (fn omitted). See also Germany: Case 2-03 O 366/00 (9.11.2000), *LG Frankfurt/M.* as summarised at the ECJ Website No 2001/28 (offer for sale); Case I ZR 24/03 (30.3.2006), *BGH* as summarised at the ECJ Website No 2007/18 (offer for sale); UK/Scotland: *Bonnier Media Limited / Greg Lloyd Smith and Kestrel Trading Corporation* (Court of Session, 1.7.2002), paras 18-20 (trade mark), available at the ECJ Website No 2003/34.

focuses on the subjective intention of the publisher, and the other evaluates objective criteria.[870]

a) The targeting test *à la Pammer and Hotel Alpenhof*

Art 17(1)(c),[871] as interpreted by the ECJ in *Pammer and Hotel Alpenhof* concerning transport and consumer contracts concluded over the Internet, represents the first form of the targeting test. In both jointly decided cases, decisive for the jurisdiction of the Austrian court was whether the company's activity within the meaning of Art 15(1)(c) of Brussels I had been directed towards the Member State of the consumer's domicile. By answering this question, the ECJ essentially identified a non-exhaustive list of criteria capable of demonstrating evidence of the trader's intention to direct an activity to a particular Member State, i.e., to envisage doing business with consumers domiciled in one or more Member States.[872] This list, which is to be examined by the competent national court,[873] includes, possibly in combination with one another, the following items:

> «[T]he international nature of the activity, mention of itineraries from other Member States for going to the place where the trader is established, use of a language or a currency other than the language or currency generally used in the Member State in which the trader is established with the possibility of making and confirming the reservation in that other language, mention of telephone numbers with an international code, outlay of expenditure on an internet referencing service in order to facilitate access to the trader's site or that of its intermediary by consumers domiciled in other Member States, use of a top-level domain name other than that of the Member State in which the trader is established, and mention of an international clientele composed of customers domiciled in various Member States.»[874]

870 On this, see Reymond, YbPIL 2012/2013, 205, 215-217, who differs between subjective and objective targeting requirements.

871 Note that this para was introduced first in Brussels I and 2007 LC within Art 15(1)(c).

872 See *Pammer and Hotel Alpenhof*, 75-76, 92. Cf. targeting test in the case law of the ECJ (substantive law): AG in *Thuiskopie*, 53-54; *Donner*, 27 ff.; *L'Oréal*, 61 ff.; *Blomqvist*, 30 ff. US: 'knowledge-plus' standard as referred to in *supra* fn 22.

873 *Pammer and Hotel Alpenhof*, 85, 93.

874 *Pammer and Hotel Alpenhof*, 93. See also *ibid.*, 75 ff. Acc. to *Pammer and Hotel Alpenhof*, 77, 91 *inter alia* the following factors are irrelevant: display of the email address or geographical address of the intermediary company or of the trader, the use of the German language, and the ability to book a voyage in that language when that is the trader's language. See also Recital 24 of Rome I. In

Numerous views formulated in legal writing and judicial practice orient the meaning of the place of the damage within Art 7(2) towards the concept of directing an activity to a Brussels-Lugano State pursuant to *Pammer and Hotel Alpenhof*.[875] Accordingly, it was applied in *Dataco* concerning the alleged infringement of a *sui generis* right. In particular, the ECJ pointed out that the localisation of the allegedly injurious act depends on evidence that it discloses the defendant's intention to target members of the public in a Member State.[876] In addition, AG Jääskinen in *Pinckney* proposed localising the concept of damage within Art 5(3) of Brussels I in disputes concerning the alleged infringement of certain categorises of exclusive copyright over the Internet in the Member State «at which the website in question aims its activity in order to seek compensation for the damage suffered on that territory.»[877] AG Jääskinen added that for determining whether the activity aims at a particular territory, inspiration might be taken from the non-exhaustive list of criteria identified in *Pammer and Hotel Alpenhof*.[878]

b) *Sui generis* targeting tests

Apart from the previous test, *sui generis* targeting tests seek to ignore the subjective intention of the publisher. Instead, they aim objectively to evaluate the link between the forum and the disputed content on the basis of different criteria, such as the design and structure of the website and/or the nature of the content.[879] They, however, differ to a certain extent, since

---

addition, note that the ECJ pointed out in *Pammer and Hotel Alpenhof*, 79 that the interactivity of the website is not decisive.

875 On this, see also Hess, CML Rev. 2012, 1075, 1089.

876 *Dataco*, 39, 47. For items of evidence, see *Dataco*, 40 ff. Due to the unclear wording of the judgment, it is assumed that it concerned, apart from substantive legal issues, the question of jurisdiction within Art 5(3) of Brussels I. On this, see also AG in *Pinckney*, 63.

877 AG in *Pinckney*, 71. See also *ibid.*, 67.

878 AG in *Pinckney*, 66.

879 See Reymond, YbPIL 2012/2013, 205, 217, 215-217. For this practice in France, see e.g. Reymond (*ibid.*, 216-217); Joubert, ICLQ 2009, 476-484. Cf. observations submitted by the German, Danish, Italian, and Luxembourgian governments in Minutes of Proceedings drawn up for the oral hearing in *eDate and Martinez*, 14.12.2010 (on file with author), 41, 45, 47, 48, 69; Rüßmann, JurPC Web-Dok. 1998, Abs. 49-54 (competition law, consumer protection); Rüßmann, K&R 1998, 422, 424-425 (competition law); AG in *Hejduk*, 14, 28 ff.

they assign different weights to the victim's forum and to other, often technology-specific, factors.

aa) AG Cruz Villalón: the centre of gravity of the dispute

AG Cruz Villalón, in his opinion delivered in *eDate and Martinez*, suggested including an additional approach in the form of the place of the centre of gravity of the dispute under the concept of harmful event in Art 5(3) of Brussels I.[880] In his opinion, this approach would confer jurisdiction on a particular court to hear an action for compensation in respect of all the damage caused by the unlawful act.[881] He argued that the court at that place is foreseeable for the media outlet.[882] In addition, that court «is able to adjudicate on a dispute between freedom of information and the right to one's own image under the most favourable conditions. That situation occurs in the State where the potential for an infringement of the right to one's own reputation or the right to privacy *and* the value inherent in the dissemination of certain information or a particular opinion, as the case may be, may be visualised or are more evident. That is the State where the holder of personality rights will suffer the most extensive and serious harm.»[883]

For determining the concept of the centre of gravity of the dispute, AG Cruz Villalón identified two cumulative elements. The first focuses on the aggrieved person and requires that the place of the centre of gravity of the dispute be situated where that individual has the centre of his interests, i.e., the place where he is known and where «in the enjoyment of his personality rights, essentially carries out his life plan, if this exists.»[884] In addition, the second element focuses on the nature of the information, which «must be expressed in such a way that, in the light of the circumstances surrounding the news item, it constitutes information which arouses interest in a particular territory and, consequently, actively encourages readers

880 AG in *eDate and Martinez*, 55. For his alternative tests, see *supra* Ch. VI.A.II.1.a) (regarding the place of the damage) and *supra* Ch. VI.A.I.1 (regarding the place of the causal event).
881 AG in *eDate and Martinez*, 66.
882 AG in *eDate and Martinez*, 58.
883 AG in *eDate and Martinez*, 58 (italics in the original).
884 AG in *eDate and Martinez*, 59.

in that territory to access it.»[885] The relationship of the two elements is described as follows:

> «[T]he centre of gravity of the potential infringement of personality rights tends to be the same as the centre of gravity or interest of the news item or opinion in question. In short, *because* the news item or opinion may be of particular interest in one place, that is also the place where any infringement of personality rights may inflict the highest level of damage.»[886]

For identifying the territory where the information is objectively relevant, AG Cruz Villalón stressed that the subjective intention of the publisher does not play any role, since it is contrary to the wording of Art 5(3) of Brussels I and gives rise to wide-ranging evidential difficulties. Instead, he preferred to determine the second element due to various objective criteria with the sole aim of establishing a link with a certain territory.[887] In particular, he mentioned first the subject matter of the information: «Thus, the more newsworthy a particular news item is in one national territory, the greater the likelihood that infringements of rights committed there will, in principle, have a connection with the courts of that territory.»[888] Other items of evidence, which aim to confirm whether or not certain information has had an impact in a particular territory, include *inter alia* (1) the top-level domain name of the website that is different from that of the Member State where the publisher is established, (2) the language of the website, (3) any advertising that may be on the website, (4) the section of the website in which the information is published, (5) the keywords supplied to search engines to identify the media outlet's site and finally, and as a purely illustrative source, (6) the website access log.[889]

---

885 AG in *eDate and Martinez*, 60.

886 AG in *eDate and Martinez*, 61 (italics in the original).

887 AG in *eDate and Martinez*, 62, 65. Cf. case *New York Times* VI ZR 23/09 (2.3.2010), *BGH* (BGHZ 184, 313), 18. Contra: *supra* Ch. VI.A.II.2.a). For the various objective criteria, see AG in *eDate and Martinez*, 62 ff.

888 AG in *eDate and Martinez*, 64. He *(ibid.)* explains: information about allegedly criminal activities performed in Austria by an Austrian citizen who resides in Austria is clearly newsworthy in that country, even though it may be published in an online newspaper, whose publisher resides in the UK.

889 AG in *eDate and Martinez*, 65.

bb) Isabel Roth: a qualified domestic connection

Isabel Roth proposes the concept of qualified domestic connection ('qualifizierter Inlandsbezug')[890] for localising the jurisdictionally relevant damage in violations of personality rights committed through the online mass communication.[891] She arrives at this solution by noting that the first three procedural valuations outlined in *supra* Ch. IV.B.I.1.c) require a significant domestic connection between the forum and the dispute, while this requirement also corresponds to the interests of the state.[892] Accordingly, she notes that mere accessibility of the information does not suffice; it should be combined with the requirement to establish a qualified domestic connection between the forum and the controversy. The existence of such a connection is to be determined through a party-neutral assessment of all relevant factors of the dispute, whose weight may vary.[893] Thus, she states:

> «Der qualifizierte Inlandsbezug ist ... ein Zusammenspiel verschiedener Faktoren. Liegt einer der Faktoren nicht vor, so spricht dies zunächst gegen einen qualifizierten Inlandsbezug, es sei denn dieser wird durch die besondere Stärke eines anderen Faktors bedingt.»[894]

---

890 Cf. Germany: Case *New York Times* VI ZR 23/09 (2.3.2010), *BGH* (BGHZ 184, 313) and Case *Seven Days in Moscow* VI ZR 111/10 (29.3.2011), *BGH* (GRUR 2011, 558) regarding Art 32 of the *ZPO*.

891 Roth, Die internationale Zuständigkeit, pp 273-287. For the place of the damage in relation to individual communications, e.g. e-mails, (*ibid.*, pp 223-231), she suggests (*ibid.*, p 231, pp 294-295) the place where the e-mail is accessed, if the sender expected it. In particular, that place generally coincides with the place of the addressee's habitual residence. If the sender is aware of this residence, and the addressee accesses the message at the place other than his habitual residence, this latter place is irrelevant. However, if the sender is not aware of the addressee's habitual residence, the place of access could be jurisdictionally relevant. For the place of the damage in relation to communication between a limited or limitable number of people, e.g. newsletters, mailing lists, or access-restricted web content (*ibid.*, pp 289-294), she proposes (*ibid.*, p 295) that the concept of qualified domestic connection as described for mass communication should determine the jurisdictionally relevant place. However, if the content provider is aware of the place of the addressees' or the Internet users' habitual residence, that place should be regarded as the jurisdictionally relevant place. The court seised at these places has jurisdiction to rule on all the damage caused (*ibid.*, pp 340-341).

892 Roth, Die internationale Zuständigkeit, pp 276-277. In detail, see *ibid.*, pp 273 ff.

893 Roth, Die internationale Zuständigkeit, pp 277-278.

894 Roth, Die internationale Zuständigkeit, p 286 (emphasis omitted).

She categorises these relevant factors, for which she provides extensive guidelines, into two sets of non-exhaustive criteria: those that determine the geographically limited circle of the audience who are possibly interested in the information («qualifizierter Inlandsbezug durch geographisch begrenzten Interessentenkreis»)[895] and those that identify the place where the impairment of the personality is perceptible («Spürbarkeit der Persönlichkeitsbeeinträchtigung»). In particular, the first set of criteria determines the territories where the online information arouses significant interest and thus would presumably be accessed and comprehended the most («Hauptabrufgebiete»).[896] It essentially covers factors relating to the structure («Ausgestaltung») and the subject of the information: (1) its language, (2) its subject (e.g. local, worldwide, or sensational), (3) the degree of the perpetrator's reputation, and (4) the degree of the victim's reputation.[897] The second set of criteria, which exists in addition to or, under certain circumstances, instead of the first one, defines the territory where the personality right is violated in a perceptible manner.[898] It encompasses those factors that help to assess the intensity of the violation in a particular state: (1) the number of times the information has been accessed (i.e., page views), (2) the perpetrator's, and (3) the victim's social position, as well as (4) the high degree of sensationalism («Sensationsgrad») of the information.[899] Isabel Roth adds that if the circle of interested audience is global, the provider is globally known, and the information leads to considerable perceptibility of the violation of the personality on a worldwide basis, then a worldwide jurisdiction is justified.[900]

cc) Michel Reymond: an objective targeting requirement

Michel Reymond submits an objective targeting requirement that is «capable of adapting the jurisdictional ground found at the place of receipt of

895 Roth, Die internationale Zuständigkeit, pp 278-282. Note that under the concept of relevant damage, Roth means (*ibid.*, p 294) the place where the legally protected right is violated («Ort der Rechtsgutverletzung»), i.e., the injurious content is comprehended («Ort der Kenntnisnahme»). On this, see also *ibid.*, pp 214 ff.
896 Roth, Die internationale Zuständigkeit, pp 281, 278-282.
897 Roth, Die internationale Zuständigkeit, pp 279-281.
898 Roth, Die internationale Zuständigkeit, p 282.
899 Roth, Die internationale Zuständigkeit, pp 283-285.
900 Roth, Die internationale Zuständigkeit, p 287.

the communication as defined by the *Shevill* and *eDate* case law to internet situations.»[901] His test evaluates the defendant's conduct due to the factual characteristics of his website and determines if the reputational harm suffered in the chosen state was reasonably foreseeable. In his opinion, this requirement is a unilateral process, since «it only seeks to characterize the link between the offending website and the forum; it cannot and should not be used to determine which State is the most substantially affected by the defendant's conduct.»[902] Accordingly, it encompasses three sets of criteria on which he provides extensive guidelines: general and commercial sets of criteria and those that are relevant to personality torts. He stresses, however, that there is no fixed hierarchy between the sets, and therefore, their relevance varies according to the fact pattern of the dispute. In addition, he also puts forward that these sets encompass elements described by him non-exhaustively.[903] The first set of criteria, the so-called general criteria, is useful for all kinds of websites, whether they are commercial or not. It covers the following factors relating to the website: (1) the access numbers (page views) of the particular website, (2) its language, (3) its presence and position in search engines, (4) its choice of top level domain, (5) the geolocation technologies that were already deployed on the website at the time of the alleged harm or that would have been available to its owner at the time of the alleged harm, and (6) its general structure and nature.[904] The second set of criteria focuses on commercial effects, that is, if the website designed to gain revenue from the forum is poised to obtain a reply from that place and is consequently objectively capable of creating an effect there. This commercial positioning can be evaluated from (1) the possibility for persons situated in the forum to enter into a contractual relationship with the website's owner, (2) the presence of paid advertisements on the website, and (3) the geographical reach of business activities conducted offline by the website's owner.[905] Finally, his third set of criteria is specific to defamation and personality torts and consists of two items: (1) the extent of the plaintiff's reputation in the forum, and (2) the content of the tortious article.[906]

---

901 Reymond, YbPIL 2012/2013, 205, 215 (italics in the original). For details on his test, see *ibid.*, pp 205-246.
902 Reymond, YbPIL 2012/2013, 205, 221.
903 Reymond, YbPIL 2012/2013, 205, 221.
904 Reymond, YbPIL 2012/2013, 205, 221, 222-238.
905 Reymond, YbPIL 2012/2013, 205, 238, 238-240.
906 Reymond, YbPIL 2012/2013, 205, 242, 242-245.

c) An adjunct question: the target of the test

Apart from the elements of the targeting test, an adjunct question is the target of the activity of the website, i.e., who or what the publisher or the online information targets. As the aforementioned suggestions show, the state, or the public of a state, is generally accepted as a target point. However, there are other views that specify the public or define other targets. Amy Kristin Sanders, as referred to and outlined by Stephen W. Bosky, for example, suggests the possibility of regarding the community in a forum to which the victim belongs as a target in defamation cases.[907] In order to determine this community, she offers three solutions. First, she proposes a four-factor concept assessing the following criteria: (1) where the plaintiff lives, (2) where he works, (3) where the information was published, and (4) who was wished for as the target audience. Secondly, she describes a specific community test, where the decision on jurisdiction is made by looking at a certain group of persons, such as the art community. Finally, she considers a plaintiff-centred approach, where a plaintiff has to show the community to which he belongs and the harm to reputation suffered within that community. Besides these community-oriented approaches, the public could also be determined on a basis other than of geographical location, namely, on the basis of nationality. Accordingly, in the *Seven Days in Moscow* dispute, *OLG Köln* referred to German Internet users in general, while in the *New York Times* case, *OLG Düsseldorf* examined whether the content was purposefully targeted at Internet users in Germany.[908] Finally, other views promote that the information is oriented at the aggrieved person. AG Léger, albeit in relation to offline violations in *Shevill*, for example, noted:

> «True, it could be maintained that the victim of a defamatory press article is the target of an act which he neither desired nor sought».[909]

---

907 Sanders, Amy Kristin: Defining Defamation: Community and the Age of the Internet, 15 Comm. L. & Pol'y 231, 233 (2010) as referred to and outlined in Bosky, St. Louis U. L.J. 2012, 587, 602-603.

908 Case 15 U 148/09 (30.3.2010), *OLG Köln* as referred to in case *Seven Days in Moscow* VI ZR 111/10 (29.3.2011), *BGH* (GRUR 2011, 558), 4; Case I-15 U 17/08 (30.12.2008), *OLG Düsseldorf* as referred to in case *New York Times* VI ZR 23/09 (2.3.2010), *BGH* (BGHZ 184, 313), 5. On this, see also Thorn, FS Bernd von Hoffmann, p 761.

909 AG 1995 in *Shevill*, 43. Cf. Smith, CRi 2004, 145, 150 who considers in defamatory and privacy cases whether the naming of an individual could be a possible

Similarly, Burkhard Hess observes:

> «It should not be forgotten that, usually, persons targeted (by the yellow press) are in a weaker position than *vis-à-vis* the general media industry.»[910]

3. The victim's forum

The victim's forum appeared not only as a connecting factor in localising offline violations of personality rights, but also for online violations of privacy and rights relating to personality, including defamation.[911] Trevor C. Hartley, for example, in one of his articles written before the delivery of *eDate and Martinez*, suggests retaining Art 5(3) of Brussels I and limiting it in cases concerning non-contractual obligations arising out of these violations. In particular, he stresses that in relation to these violations Art 5(3) of Brussels I shall apply if the plaintiff is domiciled in the territory of the forum state.[912] In addition, in his comment on *eDate and Martinez*, he prefers the concept of the centre of interests approach.[913] Similarly, Peter Arnt Nielsen suggests maintaining the wording of Art 5(3) of Brussels I and including under this paragraph an additional rule for violations of privacy and rights relating to personality, including defamation. Accordingly, he proposes localising these violations, besides the place of the Member State in which the publisher is established, at the place where the alleged victim has the centre of his interests.[914]

---

factor, which makes it possible to conclude that the publisher targeted the state in which the individual is known.

910 Hess, CML Rev. 2012, 1075, 1090 (italics in the original). See also Hess, in: Pocar/Viarengo/Villata, Recasting Brussels I, p 98. Cf. Hamburg Group for Private International Law, Comments on the Draft Proposal, p 26 (applicable law).

911 For offline violations, see *supra* fn 652. Cf. observation submitted by Mr X in Minutes of Proceedings drawn up for the oral hearing in *eDate and Martinez*, 14.12.2010 (on file with author), 54; US: 'knowledge' test in *supra* fn 22.

912 Hartley, ICLQ 2010, 25, 36 [for his alternative test, see *supra* Ch. VI.A.II.2)]. Note that this proposal could also be categorised under the next subsection dealing with unitary approaches, because Hartley suggests these two approaches (i.e., the plaintiff's domicile and the targeting test) without mentioning the place of the causal event under the concept of harmful event.

913 Hartley, L.Q.R. 2012, 197, 201.

914 Nielsen, J. Priv. Int. L. 2013, 269, 279. Cf. (1) Kessedjian, C.: Private International Law Aspects of Cyberspace: Global Communication, Universal Jurisdiction?, paper presented at ASIL/NVIL Fourth Hague Joint Conference on 5.7.1997 as referred to in Ginsburg, Recueil des Cours 273, p 310 (regarding defamation,

4. The draft Hague Judgments Convention: the place of the injury with special emphasis on the injured person's habitual residence

Besides the place where the act or omission occurred or may occur,[915] the victim may also bring an action in tort or delict in the courts of the state where the injury occurred or may occur pursuant to Arts 10(1)(b) and 10(3) of the draft Hague Judgments Convention.[916] The former provision raises only one condition, namely, that the place of injury is reasonably foreseeable for the defendant. However, by virtue of Art 10(4) of that preliminary draft document, the court seised for the state of the injury has jurisdiction solely to rule on the injury that arose or may arise in the forum state, «unless the injured person has his or her habitual residence in that State.»

As Prel. Doc. No 12 of August 2000 states with regard to the territorially fragmented jurisdiction of the courts in the state in which the injury occurred or may occur, several experts noted that the proof of this provision can never be adduced in the online context. They argue that, similar to the newspapers that are distributed on a worldwide basis, a person who uploads defamatory content onto a site can reasonably foresee that it may be read anywhere in the world.[917] Similarly, another preliminary document states:

> «In the context of the Internet, the issue of foreseeability requires an all or nothing approach. Either every jurisdiction is foreseeable or no jurisdiction is foreseeable.»[918]

---

infringement and other torts committed through the Internet, and Art 5(3) of the BC and the 1988 LC); (2) considering a possibility of centralising a claim concerning violation of the author's moral rights at the victim's forum, see Bogdan, Masaryk U. J.L. & Tech. 2013, 193, 200; Ginsburg/Gauthier, RIDA 1997, 61, 85, 87; Ginsburg, Recueil des Cours 273, pp 307 ff.; (3) Kono/Jurčys, Jurisdiction over Copyright Infringements, 2012, pp 23-25 discussing a possibility of concentrating proceedings at the copyright holder's centre of economic interests.

915 See Art 10(1)(a) and Art 10(3) of the draft Hague Judgments Convention (*supra* fn 823).

916 Nygh/Pocar Report, pp 59-61 identifies this place as the place where the direct effects of the act or omission are felt and states (*ibid.*, p 60) that in most cases, it provides «an alternative to the defendant's forum, since it frequently happens that the place of injury coincides with the domicile of the plaintiff».

917 Prel. Doc. No 12 of August 2000, p 8.

918 Prel. Doc. No 17 of February 2002, p 18.

The number of copies distributed online, however, remains unknown. Therefore, it appears from the discussion of the Working Group that violations committed through the Internet necessitate having an alternative forum with general jurisdiction.[919] Consequently, as Prel. Doc. No 12 of August 2000 notes, Art 10(4) «was ... welcomed as particularly important.»[920] This provision confers an unlimited extent of jurisdiction on the courts in a state where the injured person habitually resides if the injury occurred there.[921] Support of the centralisation of proceedings can also be found in Prel. Doc. No 7 of April 1997, which proposes giving jurisdiction in relation to acts of defamation via the press, television, or the Internet to the court of the victim's domicile at the first place, providing that this was foreseeable to the defendant.[922] In addition, the Nygh/Pocar Report also attributes considerable importance to the concept of habitual residence in tortious jurisdictional issues under Art 10(4):

> «This solution avoids a plurality of different fora, while retaining the option for the plaintiff provided in paragraph 1.»[923]

B. Favouring a unitary approach within Art 7(2)

Several views expressed in legal writing prefer, instead of the twin criteria, a unitary approach within Art 7(2), which localises online violations at the place of the act of infringement, at the place of the collision of interests of the parties, or solely at the place of the causal event.[924]

---

919 Prel. Doc. No 12 of August 2000, p 8. This document also refers to the difficulty, or even impossibility, accompanying the identification of the concept of act or omission that caused the injury under Art 10(1)(a) of the draft Hague Judgments Convention.

920 Prel. Doc. No 12 of August 2000, p 8 (emphasis omitted).

921 Other concepts suggested as possible approaches include the following: the place where the most significant injury occurred, the concept of the centre of gravity or the closest connection (see Prel. Doc. No 7 of April 2000, p 22, para 2.1); the targeting test (Prel. Doc. No 17 of February 2002, p 18).

922 Prel. Doc. No 7 of April 1997, para 122. For considering the concept of the victim's habitual residence, see also e.g. Prel. Doc. No 8 of November 1997, para 78; Prel. Doc. No 7 of April 2000, p 21, para 2.1.

923 Nygh/Pocar Report, p 62.

924 Cf. proposals for localising offline defamation in *supra* fn 656.

I. Sebastian Kubis: the place of uploading and the victim's domicile at the place of distribution

As noted in *supra* Ch. IV.B.I.1.b), Sebastian Kubis regards the place of the act of distribution, i.e., where the defendant physically acted or where the content was intentionally distributed, as the jurisdictionally relevant place where the court should be competent to decide on the totality of damage caused. For online violations, he identifies the former place with the place of uploading, since by making the content available to the public, the publisher did everything necessary on his part to disseminate it.[925] Secondly, he limits the latter place on the basis of different reasons. First, due to the lack of limitation, each place in the world where the disputed content is accessed even once could be jurisdictionally relevant.[926] Moreover, such a minimum contact established between the parties and the forum, which unilaterally favours the plaintiff, would mean a hardly calculable and insurable cost risk for certain publishers, and it could restrict the international exchange of information and views. In addition, he argues that judgments delivered at a place with such a minimum contact could seldom be enforced.[927] As a result, Sebastian Kubis suggests localising online impairment of personality rights at the place of the victim's domicile if the online content was distributed there («Wohnsitz des Opfers im Verbreitungsgebiet»).[928] In his opinion, the concentration of the proceedings at that place is foreseeable, serves the interests of the parties, and ensures the litigants' geographical connection to the forum.[929] At that place, the victim is in a position to litigate in the easiest and most cost-effective way, and it enables the perpetrator to foresee the risk of proceedings. Additionally, it is assumed that at that place, the victim typically has the closest social connection and feels the impact of the violation the most.[930] Finally, he specifies that in the case when there are several places of domicile, each of them should be considered. However, if the domicile is not

925 Kubis, Internationale Zuständigkeit, p 172. See also *ibid.*, pp 171-173 and 177-178.

926 Kubis, Internationale Zuständigkeit, p 176.

927 Kubis, Internationale Zuständigkeit, pp 162-163.

928 Kubis, Internationale Zuständigkeit, pp 176-177. On this, see Roth's view on Kubis' proposal in Roth, Die internationale Zuständigkeit, pp 255-257.

929 Kubis, Internationale Zuständigkeit, p 177.

930 Kubis, Internationale Zuständigkeit, pp 164-165.

determinable, he proposes the concept of habitual residence as a substitute for domicile.[931]

II. Marc Leonhard: accessibility and domicile or certain degree of reputation together with proximity

Similar to Sebastian Kubis, Marc Leonhard opts for a unitary approach that allocates jurisdiction to the court for the place where the content is made available to the public [i.e., the place of intended distribution or accessibility («Abrufort»)].[932] He also emphasises that due to the special feature of the Internet, the content cannot be limited geographically, as it is accessible everywhere.[933] Therefore, Marc Leonhard equips the concept of accessibility with an additional condition by requiring the violation of the personality («Persönlichkeitsverletzung») at that place.[934] Thus, the jurisdictionally relevant place should be the place where the content is accessible and where the aggrieved person has his domicile, irrespective of whether he enjoys a certain degree of reputation there or not.[935] He underscores his view by referring to a decision of the *BGH*[936] in which the court held that the aggrieved person's domicile or permanent residence is to be regarded as the place of the violation of the personality right, since the reputation and the esteem ('Ruf und Achtung') that he enjoys in society are generally located at one of those places. In addition, the interest of the forum state in an efficient settlement of the dispute also militates in favour of such an understanding. This is because only the court at the place of the aggrieved person's domicile is familiar with the local conditions and close to all relevant evidence, whose value on the basis of their proximity to the aggrieved person can be assessed there in a particularly good way.[937] If the

931 Kubis, Internationale Zuständigkeit, p 167.

932 Leonhard, in: Leipold, Rechtsfragen, p 236. He (*ibid.*, pp 239-241) favours the mosaic approach established in *Shevill* for online violations in which the claim is brought for damages. He recognises that an injunction could practically not be limited to a particular territory in general. However, he argues that this latter consideration does not belong to jurisdictional issues.

933 Leonhard, in: Leipold, Rechtsfragen, p 237.

934 Leonhard, in: Leipold, Rechtsfragen, pp 239, 245.

935 Leonhard, in: Leipold, Rechtsfragen, p 238.

936 Case *BGH* 3.5.1977, NJW 1977, 1590, 1591 as referred to in Leonhard, in: Leipold, Rechtsfragen, p 238.

937 Leonhard, in: Leipold, Rechtsfragen, p 238.

plaintiff enjoys an international reputation, it theoretically means that each court in the world is jurisdictionally competent. However, this assumption, in Marc Leonhard's opinion, fails to recognise that the personality right is an inseparable right from the subjective feelings of the right holder. In particular, he argues:

> «Es kommt nicht nur darauf an, dass durch eine bestimmte Mitteilung im Internet das Ansehen einer Person herabgewürdigt wurde, maßgebend ist vielmehr, dass der Rechtsgutsträger dies auch als möglichen Reputationsverlust empfinden konnte.»[938]

Therefore, he suggests that in the absence of domicile at the forum state, the plaintiff should demonstrate a certain degree of reputation in and a certain level of proximity to that state, for example, because he resides there on a regular basis ('regelmäßiger Aufenthalt').[939]

III. Benedikt Buchner: the aggrieved person's centre of life

Benedikt Buchner searches for a party-neutral and dispute-related approach that constitutes a jurisdictional centre («zuständigkeitsrechtliche Mitte») between the parties and guarantees a fair balance between their interests. In other words, the dispute must be heard where the parties or their spheres of interest collide with each other («Treffpunkt»).[940] Although he admits that the place of intentional distribution would be such a place, in his opinion, it is an inappropriate forum. Therefore, he suggests that the place where the aggrieved person's centre of life («Lebensmittelpunkt des Verletzten»)[941] is located should be regarded as a jurisdictionally relevant place, and the court should hear the dispute there with an unlimited extent of jurisdiction. He argues that this place is where the aggrieved person's personality right can largely be located:[942]

> «Gewinn wie Verlust an Ehre und Ansehen in der Gesellschaft verspürt der einzelne in erster Linie dort, wo er zu Hause ist. Charakteristisch für das gesellschaftliche Ansehen ist gerade, daß es nicht durch den einzelnen allein, sondern durch

938 Leonhard, in: Leipold, Rechtsfragen, p 239.
939 Leonhard, in: Leipold, Rechtsfragen, pp 239, 245.
940 Buchner, Kläger- und Beklagtenschutz, pp 128, 130-131, 141.
941 Acc. to Buchner, Kläger- und Beklagtenschutz, p 144, he supposedly means under the term 'centre of life' the aggrieved person's domicile or residence.
942 Buchner, Kläger- und Beklagtenschutz, pp 142-143. In his opinion (*ibid.*, fn 173), this is also true regarding worldwide known actors or politicians.

> dessen Beziehung zu seinem sozialen Umfeld geprägt wird. Es ist daher naheliegend, auch zu Zuständigkeitszwecken das Persönlichkeitsrecht schwerpunktmäßig dem gewöhnlichen sozialen Umfeld des Verletzten zuzuordnen.»[943]

In Benedikt Buchner's opinion, whether or not the defamatory content is intentionally distributed at this place has no importance. Although the publisher establishes a commercial contact through the intentional distribution of its material, the dispute is not about the distribution but about the attack on the social position of a particular person:

> «*Geschäftlich* mag sich der Herausgeber nur zum bestimmungsgemäßen Verbreitungsgebiet in Beziehung gesetzt haben. Damit ist aber der *konkrete Rechtsstreit* noch nicht ausreichend erfaßt. Dieser zeichnet sich nicht durch das – immer gleiche – Verbreitungsgebiet einer Zeitschrift oder Sendung aus, sondern durch den Angriff auf das gesellschaftliche Ansehen einer bestimmten Person.»[944]

By defaming the victim, the publisher directly and intentionally establishes a link with the aggrieved person's social environment. Thus, that place is automatically attributable to him. In addition, he stresses that solely the place of intended distribution would be an improper basis of jurisdiction because the publisher can choose that place. He also argues that the criterion of intended distribution is arbitrary. As *Shevill* indicates, only a few copies suffice for establishing jurisdiction at the place of distribution, even if the aggrieved person is almost unknown there. In addition, it is consistently ignored that defamatory content can reach the public in the state of the aggrieved person's domicile in a way other than the intended distribution and, consequently, it can cause significant injury to his personality right.[945]

Finally, Benedikt Buchner considers three possible criticisms of the localisation of the violation of a personality right in the state where the plaintiff is domiciled, none of which he finds greatly attractive. First, he denies that this place would be unforeseeable for the publisher by arguing that the publisher selects the persons of his report carefully, and thus, he can and must take into account that the distribution of defamatory content primarily leads to loss of reputation in the habitual social environment of the persons concerned. Secondly, he militates against the view according to which the aggrieved person's domicile or habitual residence is the place

943 Buchner, Kläger- und Beklagtenschutz, p 143 (fn omitted).

944 Buchner, Kläger- und Beklagtenschutz, p 143 (italics in the original). Cf. Thorn, FS Bernd von Hoffmann, p 749.

945 Buchner, Kläger- und Beklagtenschutz, pp 143-144. On *Shevill*, see also *supra* Ch. V.B.II.1.b).

where the consequential damage is suffered, and therefore, it is jurisdictionally irrelevant.[946] In particular, if the focus of a personality right is on the individual person as the holder of this right, the distribution of a defamatory fact is regarded as an attack on this person. Thus, the direct effect of the violation is located at the place of the centre of his life. By contrast, if his standing in society is understood as «ein selbständiges Etwas»,[947] which can be present in every state independently from its holder, then the direct effect of the violation occurs there, where the reputation is affected. However, because the personality right can be determined only with difficulty or not at all, such latter hypothetical decision for establishing jurisdiction should not be considered as decisive. Finally, he argues that the plaintiff's forum is justifiable, since it is a jurisdictional centre between the interests of the parties. The fact that it is situated in violations of personality rights at the place of the aggrieved person's centre of life is merely an unremarkable coincidence.[948]

IV. Andrew Dickinson: the place of the causal event

In Andrew Dickinson's opinion, a narrow reading of the concept of harmful event under Art 5(3) of Brussels I could be given in online violations of personality rights «so as to *exclude* the criterion of damage as a connecting factor for jurisdiction purposes».[949] He supports his opinion based on different reasons. First, he refers to paragraphs 45 and 46 of *eDate and Martinez* in which the ECJ noted that the ubiquitous nature of online publications lead to difficulty in applying the concept of damage under Art 5(3) of Brussels I. Secondly, he stresses that «the special rules of jurisdiction are intended to secure "a close link between the court and the action" and/or "to facilitate the sound administration of justice"».[950] Thirdly, he adds that the narrow reading of the concept of harmful event would be

946 On consequential damage, see *supra* Ch. IV.B.I.2.
947 Buchner, Kläger- und Beklagtenschutz, p 145.
948 Buchner, Kläger- und Beklagtenschutz, pp 144-145.
949 Dickinson, By Royal Appointment, 2012 (italics in the original). Note that his view is put forward in relation to *eDate and Martinez* (on this judgment, see *infra* Ch. VII).
950 Dickinson, By Royal Appointment, 2012.

analogous to the *Besix* decision[951] and consistent with «the dominant approach» taken in the case law, like in *Reisch Montage*,[952] regarding the interpretation of those jurisdictional rules, which are exceptions to the general rule in Art 2 of Brussels I.[953]

C. Proposals regardless of Art 7(2)

In addition to the previous groups of views, which aim to maintain the special rule of jurisdiction within Art 7(2) and offer different solutions for the interpretation of the concept of harmful event, there are two proposals that present another way to approach the localisation of online violations of personality rights.

I. European Publishers Council: removing the media from Art 5(3) of Brussels I

On behalf of the European Publishers Council, Angela Mills Wade, in her contribution to an online symposium on Rome II and Defamation, stresses the unsymmetrical legislative practices on defamation and violations of privacy.[954] In particular, she refers to the lack of applicable rules in Rome II and to the rules of jurisdiction under Brussels I together with *Shevill*, which encourage forum shopping and create uncertainty and the disproportionate risk of lawsuits in multiple jurisdictions. She points out that the

951 Dickinson refers to *Besix*, 32 ff. (on this ruling, see *supra* Ch. III.B.I.3). Cf. *infra* fn 956.

952 Dickinson refers to *Reisch Montage*, 22-23, which consider the restrictive method of interpretation of special rules of jurisdiction. On this, see also *supra* Ch. III.B.I.1.

953 Cf. AG in *Hejduk*, 41 ff. (on this case, see *supra* Ch. III.D.II.2; *infra* Ch. VII.B.I; *supra* fn 585) in which AG Cruz Villalón proposed excluding the possibility of bringing an action in the court of the place where the damage occurred under Art 5(3) of Brussels I. He argued that the making online available of the plaintiff's photographs without oriented them towards any state leads to delocalised damage, which cannot be determined territorially on the basis of reliable criteria. Consequently, he localised the online violation of the author's economic rights (on the subject matter of the case, see also *supra* fn 458) solely at the place where the causal event is occurred.

954 Mills Wade, EPC on The Link between Brussels I and Rome II, 2010.

combination of these rules provides an unbalanced advantage to the plaintiff and, consequently, it directly prejudices editorial independence and press freedom in different jurisdictions, often leading to journalists self-censoring, simply to avoid the possibility of proceedings. In addition, she also notes several recent developments, which have appeared since Brussels I and Rome II were enacted, such as the rise in case law regarding electronic and cross-border publications, dissemination of online news on various platforms, or forum shopping in several states. Mindful of these complications and developments, she aims to increase legal certainty for media companies and remove the threat of forum shopping. Therefore, she proposes the following solution regarding Brussels I:

> «The most proportionate solution would be to remove the media from the scope of article 5(3) which, together with *Shevill* gives rise to legal uncertainty and the dangers of both forum shopping and multiple actions. Instead the media should be subject to the general rule in Article 2.1 which allows plaintiffs to bring cases in their home country for cross border claims of defamation and privacy violations.»[955, 956]

---

955 Italics in the original. See also the responses of the European Federation of Journalists (30.6.2009; signed by Arne König, EFJ President), pp 2-3 and the European Newspaper Publishers' Association (30.6.2009; Sophie Scrive, Deputy Executive Director) to the Green Paper on the review of Council Regulation (EC) N° 44/2001 on jurisdiction and the recognition and enforcement of judgements in civil and commercial matters, available at <http://ec.europa.eu/justice/news/consulting_public/news_consulting_0002_en.htm>.

956 Cf. AG in *CDC*, 39-53 (albeit in respect of tort other than violations of personality rights). The case concerned an action for disclosure and damages against companies domiciled in different Member States and having participated in various places and at various times in a cartel that was found incompatible with Art 81 of the EC Treaty (now Art 101 of the TFEU) and Art 53 of the Agreement on the European Economic Area of 2.5.1992 (OJ 1994 L 1/13). AG Jääskinen is «inclined to the view that that provision *[Art 5(3) of Brussels I]* cannot properly be applied in the *particular case* of a horizontal cartel, which has existed for a long time and has restricted competition throughout Union territory and whose structure is highly complex, since it has given rise to a series of agreements and collusive practices, with the result that both the participants in the cartel and the persons sustaining the alleged damage are scattered over a great many Member States.» [AG in *CDC*, 47 (italics in square brackets added, italics in the original).] Among other grounds, he referred to the *Besix* judgment to justify his view (cf. this case was also referred to by Dickinson in *supra* Ch. VI.B.IV). However, note that the exclusion of the application of Art 5(3) of Brussels I is justified solely on the basis of the complexity of the case, and he regarded this provision as being applicable to less complex competition law issues (AG in *CDC*, fn 47). Cf. Art

II. Christopher Kuner: a flexible rule with the possibility of declining jurisdiction

Christopher Kuner draws attention to the fact that, with increasing regularity, courts of states attempt to establish jurisdiction over online actions («Handlungen im Internet»). However, as these actions are practically and simultaneously present in all states in the world, this often leads to conflict of jurisdictions and to legal uncertainty, which could threaten the further advancement of the Internet.[957] Therefore, he militates in favour of flexible rules, which make it possible to establish jurisdiction only in serious cases («in schwerwiegenden Fällen») affecting the important interests of the state and which leave open the possibility of jurisdiction being declined.[958]

10(2) of the draft Hague Judgments Convention, which excludes the application of the place of injury in anti-trust violations.

957 Kuner, CR 1996, 453. It ought to be noted that Kuner considers jurisdiction over actions on the Internet in general, and he focuses explicitly on neither the Brussels-Lugano Regime nor online violations of personality rights. He only notes (*ibid.*, 456) that the determination of the place where the harmful event occurred in Art 5(3) of the BC is very problematic on the Internet, for instance, in defamation cases.

958 Kuner, CR 1996, 453, 458. See also Roth, Die internationale Zuständigkeit, p 267 and Rüßmann, K&R 1998, 422, 424, who mention Kuner's view in relation to the principle of *forum non conveniens*.

Chapter VII: Jurisdiction in online (potential) violations of personality rights: the *eDate and Martinez* judgment

The interpretation of the concept of harmful event in online (potential) violations of personality rights reached a climax in *eDate and Martinez* delivered by the ECJ sixteen years after *Shevill.* In other words, this judgment put an end to the different views expressed in legal theory and national court practices[959] on localising these violations by establishing uniform connecting factors for that purpose. Mindful of the innovative nature of this judgment, the present chapter undertakes a careful and principle-based assessment in order to determine where the special rule of jurisdiction in online (potential) violations of personality rights, specifically defamation and invasion of privacy, under Art 7(2) currently stands. Besides examining the jurisdictionally relevant concepts of causal event and damage as well as the extent of the jurisdiction of the competent court, it also facilitates at least two further aims. It scrutinises whether by establishing the *eDate and Martinez*-approaches, the ECJ resolved the troublesome issues and answered the open questions described in *supra* Ch. V in relation to the localisation of offline violations of personality rights and it asseses whether these approaches are suitable jurisdictional bases for violations of personality rights through the Internet in Europe, where common legal norms, interests, and values increasingly integrate and connect persons.

A. eDate and Martinez in a nutshell

The present section outlines the factual and procedural background of the *eDate and Martinez* joined cases as well as the questions referred for a preliminary ruling by the *BGH* and the *TGI Paris*. Finally, it summarises the judgment of the ECJ.[960]

959 See *supra* Ch. VI.

960 For the national references, see order *eDate Advertising* VI ZR 217/08 (10.11.2009), *BGH* (GRUR 2010, 261); *TGI Paris*, 17ème ch., ord. du 29/03/2010 (08/15331) - *Martinez and Martinez* (request). For a brief outline of the factual background and the judgment of the ECJ, see also *supra* Intr.

I. Factual and procedural background

1. eDate Advertising

In this dispute, the defendant was eDate Advertising, a company established in Austria that operates an Internet portal under the address <www.***.at>. According to its site notice, the portal is a liberal and politically independent medium that is directed at homosexual, bisexual, and transgender groups. In its section 'Info-News', on the pages dedicated to old news, it gave access to a report on criminal proceedings in Germany and fully named Mr X. Mr X, a German individual being domiciled in Germany, called upon the defendant to desist from reporting the matter and to give an undertaking that it would refrain from future publication. eDate Advertising did not reply to this letter but removed the disputed information from its website. The plaintiff sought before the German courts an injunction, to be applied throughout the territory of Germany, ordering eDate Advertising to refrain from using his full name when reporting about him on its Internet portal relating to the crime that he had committed in the past. eDate Advertising contended the competence of the German court and sought to have the action dismissed.[961]

2. Martinez and Martinez

The dispute was raised in proceedings brought by an actor O. Martinez and his father R. Martinez, both French nationals, against the owner of the Sunday Mirror, MGN Limited, a company governed by English law, before the *TGI Paris*. The plaintiffs sought compensation for their non-pecuniary harm, which they claimed to have suffered owing to the posting in English of information and photographs about them on the website published by the defendant and accessible at <www.sundaymirror.co.uk>. They based their claim on the interference with their private lives and on the infringement of the right of O. Martinez to his image. MGN Limited objected to the competence of the French court due to the lack of a sufficient connecting link between the act of placing the text and photographs online and the alleged damage in French territory. By contrast, the plain-

961 *eDate and Martinez*, 15-18; AG in *eDate and Martinez*, 10-14.

tiffs took the view that such a connecting link is unnecessary and that, in any event, there was such a link.[962]

3. Factual differences

There are a number of not entirely insignificant differences between the two cases. In *eDate Advertising*, the victim, an individual, had been convicted for a murder in the past and released on parole, while in *Martinez and Martinez*, the aggrieved persons were also individuals, but one of them, being an actor, supposedly had a greater extent of reputation than Mr X had. Similarly, the *status quo* of the defendants is identical in the sense that they were both legal persons. However, while in the former case, the defendant was a traditional media outlet, in the latter dispute, it was a company in a simple sense. In addition, in the German proceedings, the action concerned allegedly defamatory information[963] and was brought for an injunction, while in the French case, the action concerned damages caused by violations of the right to private life including the right to one's own image. Finally, while the Internet portal operated by the Austrian company is only available online, the Sunday Mirror is a hybrid newspaper having a presence both in the physical and in the virtual world.[964]

---

962 *eDate and Martinez*, 25-26. Note that the question arose from this dispute was first referred for a preliminary ruling in 2009 [*Martinez and Martinez* (I)]. However, the ECJ found it lacked jurisdiction for answering it (order of the court). It is also noteworthy that the *Cour d'appel de Liège* (Appellate Court, Liège/Belgium) requested a preliminary ruling for localising the harm caused by websites within Art 5(3) of Brussels I *(Real Madrid Football Club)* before the *TGI Paris* in 2009. However, this reference was removed from the register of the CJEU.

963 See AG in *eDate and Martinez*, 29. However, note that the *BGH* qualified this violation under German substantive law in case *eDate Advertising* VI ZR 217/08a (8.5.2012), *BGH* (GRUR 2012, 850), 34 as the violation of a personality right and of the right to respect for private life because the report makes Mr X's misconduct public and qualifies him negatively from the outset in the eyes of the addresses. Cf. Hartley, L.Q.R. 2012, 197 identifies the subject matter of the claim as a 'privacy injunction'.

964 For comparison of the factual background of the cases, see also AG in *eDate and Martinez*, 29; Thorn, FS Bernd von Hoffmann, pp 752-753.

II. The questions referred

The President of the CJEU decided to join the two sets of national proceedings for the purposes of the oral hearing and the judgment «because of the objective connection between them.»[965] In particular, so it was held, they «are linked by a common explicit or underlying concern: the scope of the *Shevill* case-law.»[966] Consequently, the ECJ examined the first two questions referred for a preliminary ruling by the *BGH* and the single question referred for the same purpose by the *TGI Paris* together, which is summarised as follows:

> «[T]he national courts ask the Court, in essence, how the expression 'the place where the harmful event occurred or may occur', used in Article 5(3) of the Regulation *[Brussels I]*, is to be interpreted in the case of an alleged infringement of personality rights by means of content placed online on an internet website.»[967]

III. The judgment of the ECJ

The ECJ first extended the application of the *Shevill*-approaches to other media and means of communication. Further, it established that they «may cover a wide range of infringements of personality rights recognised in various legal systems, such as those alleged by the applicants in the main proceedings.»[968] Then, after revising the place of the damage, it went on to rule:

> «[T]he answer to the first two questions in Case C-509/09 and the single question in Case C-161/10 is that Article 5(3) of the Regulation *[Brussels I]* must be interpreted as meaning that, in the event of an alleged infringement of personality rights by means of content placed online on an internet website, the person who considers that his rights have been infringed has the option of bringing an action

965 AG in *eDate and Martinez*, 28. See also *eDate and Martinez*, 30.

966 AG in *eDate and Martinez*, 30 (italics in the original). It appears from the consolidation that privacy rights and the right to reputation are treated equally. Because of the different aim of the claims and popularity of the plaintiffs, Mikola, JeMa 2011, 14, 18 questions *inter alia* the need for consolidation of the two national cases.

967 *eDate and Martinez*, 37 (italics in square brackets added). For the third question of the *BGH*, see *infra* Ch. VII.C.I.2.b). Note that the question of the *TGI Paris* also considered the application of Art 2 of Brussels I (*eDate and Martinez*, 29), which remained unconcerned in the judgment.

968 *eDate and Martinez*, 44.

> for liability, in respect of all the damage caused, either before the courts of the Member State in which the publisher of that content is established or before the courts of the Member State in which the centre of his interests is based. That person may also, instead of an action for liability in respect of all the damage caused, bring his action before the courts of each Member State in the territory of which content placed online is or has been accessible. Those courts have jurisdiction only in respect of the damage caused in the territory of the Member State of the court seised.»[969]

Before moving into a detailed analysis of this ruling, it ought to be noted at the outset that the ruling raises two points of uncertainty.

First, the ECJ remained silent on answering the first set of questions submitted by the *BGH* for a preliminary ruling in *eDate Advertising* regarding the application of the concept of harmful event to potential violations. After upholding the admissibility of these questions disputed by the Italian government, it treated the two national cases, as they would have solely concerned online violations of personality rights already committed. Nevertheless, due to the views expressed in legal theory and practice, *eDate and Martinez* should equally be applicable to potential violations, and thus, preventive actions.[970]

Secondly, the German language version of the judgment shows serious inconsistencies with the other language versions. This is of considerable importance because besides French, German was the other procedure language of the ECJ. In particular, paragraph 52 of *eDate and Martinez* placed great emphasis on the establishment of the author rather than of the publisher: it refers to the Member State in which the author of the disputed content is established (Mitgliedstaat, «in dem der Urheber dieser Inhalte niedergelassen ist»[971]) although the term 'publisher' ('Herausgeber') was employed in paragraph 33 of *Shevill*. Such a substantial change is not noticeable either from the wording and logic of the judgment or from AG Cruz Villalón's opinion.[972] The other language versions of paragraph 52 of the judgment use the word 'publisher' or equivalent terms (e.g. French: 'émmetteur', Spanish: 'emisor', Hungarian: 'közzétevő', Italian: 'emesso'). Thus, it is highly assumable that the German version is a

969 *eDate and Martinez*, 52 (italics in square brackets added). See also *supra* Intr.

970 See Roth, IPRax 2013, 215, 218, 222; Hess, JZ 2012, 189, 191; Case *eDate Advertising* VI ZR 217/08a (8.5.2012), *BGH* (GRUR 2012, 850), 17.

971 See also *eDate and Martinez*, 45, 50.

972 Note that the *BGH* in its reference for a preliminary ruling [order *eDate Advertising* VI ZR 217/08 (10.11.2009), *BGH* (GRUR 2010, 261)] used the term 'operator of the website' («Betreiber der Website»). See also *eDate and Martinez*, 24.

linguistic mistake. Otherwise, it would have a significant impact on the localisation of the causal event: the victim could initiate proceedings against the publisher in the court of the Brussels-Lugano State of the place where the author who created the contested online material is established.[973] Therefore, the present author is inclined to the view that the German language version of this expression should be disregarded. Mindful of this view, she will consistently refer to the publisher's establishment in line with the English language version of the judgment and the wording of *Shevill.*

B. The place of the harmful event à la Shevill between confirmation and revision

As is clear from the ruling, the ECJ generally allowed the victim to bring an action against the publisher for the online violation of his personality rights in the courts of the Brussels-Lugano State where the publisher is established, the victim's centre of interests is located, or the online content is or has been accessible. The present part of this book aims to elicit the interpretation and *de facto* application of these connecting factors.

I. The place of the causal event at the publisher's establishment is confirmed

The ECJ did not place great emphasis on the localisation of the causal event. It solely confirmed, without further explanation, the applicability of the publisher's establishment test ruled in *Shevill*,[974] or, as Wulf-Henning Roth observes, «für den Anknüpfungspunkt des Handlungsorts alles beim Alten bleiben soll».[975] As everything remained unchanged, it is supposed that the finding, which underlined the concept of the publisher's establishment in *Shevill* by identifying specific causal acts that occurred at that

973 Regardless of this observation, the German term has not only appeared in the decision of the *Oberster Gerichtshof* (Austria) in case 4 OB 82/12f (10.7.2012), 1.3 (a), but this court also surreptitiously rewrote the first *Shevill*-test (see in *supra* Ch. V.A.III) by referring to it as the «Niederlassung des Urhebers der Inhalte (*Shevill* Rz 33; *eDate Advertising* Rz 43)».

974 *eDate and Martinez*, 44, 52.

975 Roth, IPRax 2013, 215, 217.

place, is also an appropriate basis of justification for this concept in *eDate and Martinez*. Accordingly, «the place of the event giving rise to the damage ... can only be the place where the publisher ... in question is established, since that is the place where the harmful event originated and from which the libel *[rather: violation of personality rights]* was issued and put into circulation.»[976] These specific causal acts could correspond in an online context to the proposed causal events that were outlined in *supra* Ch. VI.A.I, namely, the creation of the disputed content, the taking of a decision upon its uploading, placing it online, and the storing of the online content at the location of the web server.[977] However, bearing in mind that those acts must occur at the place of the publisher's establishment, any that fall outside of this place are irrelevant for jurisdictional purposes. It follows that the determination of the place of the publisher's establishment is of decisive importance. As noted in *supra* Ch. V.B.I.2, this place often, if not always, coincides with the broadly interpreted place of the defendant's domicile,[978] or it is frequently localised in the same Brussels-Lugano State where the defendant's domicile is based. Viewed in this light, the concept of causal event in the form of the publisher's establishment does not fulfil its function to provide an alternative forum to the general rule of jurisdiction under Art 4, and thus, it loses its effectiveness. Exceptions to this finding are possible, but, since they function only to a limited extent, they are of little use for restoring the usefulness of this concept.[979] Mindful of the judicial practice of the ECJ on the localisation of a

---

976 *Shevill*, 24 (emphases omitted, italics in square brackets added).

977 For questioning which specific act in the chain of successive acts could be regarded as the causal event, cf. Picht, GRUR Int. 2013, 19, 20; Spindler, AfP 2012, 114, 117.

978 For finding that: (1) it is often identical, see Mansel/Thorn/Wagner, IPRax 2012, 1, 12; Garber, ÖJZ 2012, 108, 117 (in most of the cases); (2) always identical, see von Welser, GRUR-Prax 2011, 513. Note that scholars have described the place of the publisher's establishment as the 'defendant's seat' (Wittwer/Fussenegger, ZEuP 2013, 812, 823) or the 'publisher's domicile' (Kuipers, CML Rev. 2012, 1211, 1218), but reference has also been made to the 'seat of the media outlet' (Hess, JZ 2012, 189), or to the 'seat of the publisher' («Herausgeber») (Schnichels/Stege, EuZW 2012, 812, 814). For the meaning of the term 'domicile', see *supra* Ch. III.C.I.

979 Three exceptions were noted in *supra* Ch. V.B.I.2. The first one, concerning the determination of the domicile of the legal person under the BC and the 1988 LC, comes into play rarely. The second one, based on the different time when the domicile must be established, is seriously questioned in *infra* Ch. VII.B.II.1.e).

causal event,[980] this outcome seems, however, to be widely accepted, most recently in AG Cruz Villalón's opinion delivered in *Hejduk*. In particular, he proposed localising an online violation of the author's economic rights solely at the place where the causal event occurred, irrespective of the fact that, as he admitted, in most cases, and in the present case of *Hejduk*, this place coincides with the defendant's place of domicile.[981]

It follows from the practically ineffective nature of the concept of causal event that only the concept of damage functions effectively to localise online violations of personality rights. Although this result is consistent with AG Capotorti's opinion delivered in *Bier*,[982] in its effect, with the views favouring a unitary approach within Art 7(2),[983] and with the reality, that the victim principally avails himself of the place of the damage, the present author feels uneasy about it for no less than six reasons. First, such an artificial interpretation of the concept of causal event seems to be contrary to the restrictive method of interpretation of the special rules of jurisdiction, since it deprives Art 7(2) of its practical effect.[984] To put it differently, the concept of causal event in the form of the publisher's establishment is interpreted too restrictively. Secondly, as become evident from the aim of the drafters of the BC and from the settled case law of the ECJ dating back to *Bier*, the duality of the basis of jurisdiction under Art 7(2) is both desired and firmly enshrined.[985] In addition, if the concept of causal event had been regarded as an unsuitable basis of jurisdiction, the EU legislative authority would have taken the opportunity to change it

---

Thirdly, since the publisher's establishment partly coincides with the connecting factor used in Art 7(5), Art 7(2) is of little use.

980 See *supra* Ch. IV.B.I.1.e) and especially, *supra* fn 571.

981 AG in *Hejduk*, 45 (on this, see cross-references in *supra* fn 953). Contra: Kono/Jurčys in *supra* fn 914. The correctness of AG Cruz Villalón's proposal is questionable on the basis of the pure wording of Art 7(2), which refers to the concept of harmful event and not to the term 'act of infringement' as, for example, Art 93(5) of Reg. (EC) No 40/94 (OJ 1994 L 11/1) does (regarding the interpretation and difference of these connecting factors, see *Coty Germany*, 24-38). In addition, it is doubtful why the damage caused by the online violation of the author's economic rights cannot be localised.

982 AG in *Bier*, 10 (p 1758).

983 See *supra* Ch. VI.B.I-III. However, note that Kubis' and Leonhard's views focus solely on the act of infringement as being the harmful event and deny essentially that violations of personality rights can be localised at the place of the damage.

984 On this effect, see *supra* Ch. III.B.I.1, especially the observation of AG in *Tacconi*.

985 On this, see *supra* Ch. IV.B.I.

during the revision of Brussels I. However, it did not take this advantage and left the wording of this special rule of jurisdiction unchanged in Brussels Ia. Fourthly, special rules of jurisdiction are genuine alternatives to the general basis of jurisdiction laid down in Art 4(1). Consequently, the concept of causal event as an optional connecting factor under Art 7(2) shall also fulfil this function. Fifthly, it is also ruled in *Bier* and in the subsequent decisions of the ECJ that the place of the causal event is, depending on the circumstances, particularly helpful from the point of view of evidence and of the conduct of proceedings.[986] Finally, AG Jääskinen, in his opinion delivered in *CDC*, focused on the places where the unlawful cartel agreement was entered into by its members or was actually put into effect as possible places of the causal event rather than on «the various places where the registered offices of the companies concerned are situated».[987] This opinion could be regarded as an icebreaker of the judicial practice of the ECJ, which, as has just been referred to, consistently identified the place where the act of the defendant and his establishment coincide.

Taking into account all these reasons, the present author is of the opinion that an adequate point in the chain of successive acts, and thus a particular place, should be determined rather than reference being made simply to the place of the publisher's establishment. This solution would put an end to the empty reference to the place of the causal event, and thus, it would restore its function by providing a possibility of locating this connecting factor at a place other than that which is designated by Art 4(1) or 7(5). Based on views expressed in legal theory and practice, *supra* Ch. V.B.I.1 suggested the act of creation or the taking of the decision regarding the publication as reasonable points in the chain of successive acts, which perhaps were what was intended to be meant by the concept of the publisher's establishment in *Shevill*. This automatically poses two interrelated questions. First, it is questionable whether these points, and thus, the places where they were performed, are also suitable in the context of online (potential) violations of personality rights. Secondly, it raises the question of whether those acts and places could meet the objective methods proposed by Isabel Roth and Peter Kaye for determining the jurisdictionally relevant place of the causal event.[988]

986 See e.g. *Bier*, 17; *Melzer*, 26. See also *supra* Ch. IV.B.I.

987 AG in *CDC*, 49.

988 See *supra* Ch. IV.B.I.1.c)-d), and see also *supra* Ch. IV.B.I.1.e).

The present author has no difficulty in agreeing with the latter act, which shall be localised at the place where the main editorial office, other committee, or person competent for taking this decision is based.[989] The decision on making the content online available to the public is actively taken on behalf of the publisher and manifested to the external world. It is a conduct that factually initiates the chain of other events culminating in damage. It is true regardless of the fact that it leads to damage only through a sequence of acts, such as the act of uploading, performed by the employees of the publisher possibly in different places. Thomas Garber also regards as essential the place where the decision on the publication is taken, while the place of uploading is, in his opinion, a subsequent act, which implements that decision:

> «An diesem Ort *[der Ort der Niederlassung des vermeintlichen Schädigers]* wird die Entscheidung über die Veröffentlichung der Information getroffen. Das nach der getroffenen Entscheidung erfolgte Uploading der Information stellt hingegen lediglich den Vollzug einer bereits getroffenen Entscheidung dar; als nachfolgende Handlung ist das Uploading unbeachtlich.»[990]

Furthermore, this place is not only predictable, but it also establishes proximity and facilitates the sound administration of justice and the efficacious conduct of proceedings. Being the place where the initial evaluation of the subject of the online material and its final version are approved, it ensures the collection of evidence for establishing the liability of the publisher over the injurious content. The shortcoming of this place is, however, that it often, if not always, coincides with the place where the publisher is domiciled or where its establishment under Art 7(5) is situated, and therefore, it becomes ineffective.[991]

As far as the act of creation of the contested content is concerned, the present author sympathises with Isabel Roth's view[992] for several reasons, and therefore, she regards the place where it is performed to be plausible for jurisdictional purposes, providing that the said place is predictable and foreseeable for the parties. This condition is of considerable importance because knowledge of this place belongs exclusively to the publisher's organisational sphere, and it is normally not displayed online. By contrast,

989 See also Roth (*supra* Ch. VI.A.I.4); Wagner (*supra* fn 633); the settled case law of the ECJ (see *supra* fn 571).

990 Garber, ÖJZ 2012, 108, 111 (fn omitted, italics in square brackets added).

991 Cf. the identification of the place of central administration as a category of domicile by Hartley in *supra* Ch. III.C.I.1.

992 See *supra* Ch. VI.A.I.4.

the place where, for example, the contested photographs of the victim were taken is evident for both litigants: for the publisher, because its employee acted on its behalf at that place, and for the victim, because he supposedly knows where he was when the photographs were taken. In complex situations, when the publisher acts in different places because, for example, its employees collected sources, drafted reports, and took photographs in different locations, Isabel Roth appears to focus on the place where the defendant predominantly acted. This proposal could work satisfactorily. However, the present author would prefer to regard each place as jurisdictionally relevant, since each place is in a causal connection with the damage, and the publisher unilaterally decided to act at those places. In addition, support for the place of the creation can be drawn from *Kainz*. In this dispute, the ECJ preferred the place where the defective product was manufactured to the place where the manufacturer is established, where the product is put into circulation, or where the user acquired the defective product.[993] By analogy, the place of the creation of the content also serves the requirements of the sound administration of justice and the efficacious conduct of proceedings, that is, the place where significant evidence, like witnesses, relating to the injurious nature of the content could be present, or circumstances in which photographs were taken or other information was acquired. Furthermore, by virtue of an analogous application of *DFDS Torline*,[994] the act of creation could be regarded as a necessary precondition of the decision on its online distribution. Finally, and perhaps more importantly, this place has been regarded as jurisdictionally relevant in several national decisions, such as the decision of the *LG Frankfurt/M.* (regional court of Frankfurt am Main, Germany). In this case, the dispute concerned jurisdiction under Art 5(3) of the 1988 LC for an injunction against a Swiss website of a Swiss professional photographer, which offered also to German newspapers an aerial photograph of the house of a popular German racer living in Switzerland. The court held that the causal event occurred in Switzerland because *inter alia* the contested photograph was taken there.[995]

993 See *supra* Ch. IV.B.I.1.e); *supra* Ch. V.B.I.1.

994 See *supra* Ch. IV.B.I.1.e).

995 Case 2-03 O 471/09 (15.7.2010), *LG Frankfurt/M.* (AfP 2010, 512-514). Cf. finding of the *BGH* in case *Seven Days in Moscow* VI ZR 111/10 (29.3.2011), *BGH* (GRUR 2011, 558), 16; question submitted by the *TGI Paris* in *eDate and Martinez*, 29, second question, fourth indent; US: *Calder v. Jones* 465 U.S. 783 (1984), fn 6 states that the *Court of Appeal of California* suggested that the inves-

Remarkable beyond these acts, and thus, places, is that, as mentioned previously, two further acts, namely, the storing of the online content at the location of the web server and the act of placing it online, could possibly also be regarded as causal events. However, the present author feels uneasy about categorising them as adequate acts; this is due to the following reasons. Attaching significance to the location of the web server on which the content is stored is severely criticised and mostly rejected in legal theory and practice.[996] It is argued that the publisher, either by operating or renting the web server(s), selects the physical location on the basis of different economic, financial, and legal considerations.[997] This place creates, as Conall O'Reilly points out, «a legal loophole and risks fostering illicit behaviour. It allows those involved in dubious practice to benefit from the Internet's wide reaching, communicative nature easily to escape responsibility for the local effects of their actions.»[998] This situation that he describes is exacerbated by the fact that the content «may be stored on more than one web server, and with different web servers at different times. Different parts of a single web page may be stored on different web servers in different jurisdictions.»[999] Premising jurisdiction on the location of each web server on which the disputed content is stored, providing that it is traceable, would lead to an increase in the grounds of jurisdiction, and thus, to an unsatisfactory result. In addition, information can easily be transmitted from one web server to another, and web servers can be relocated without trouble. Helmut Rüßmann properly describes the location of the web server as follows:

> «Wo ein Webserver steht, ist im übrigen technisch völlig willkürlich. Der Betreiber kann ihn von einem beliebigen anderen Ort der Welt aus technisch pflegen

---

tigative activities of one of the petitioners employed by the publisher, «including one visit and numerous phone calls to California, formed an independent basis for an assertion of jurisdiction over him in this action.»

996 E.g. Roth, Die internationale Zuständigkeit, pp 196-197, 201-203; Coester-Waltjen, FS Rolf A. Schütze, p 184; Garber, ÖJZ 2012, 108, 111; case 15 U 148/09 (30.3.2010), *OLG Köln* as referred to in case *Seven Days in Moscow* VI ZR 111/10 (29.3.2011), *BGH* (GRUR 2011, 558), 4, 16. Due to the majority opinion, intermediary stations and access points are also regarded as jurisdictionally irrelevant (see e.g. Bachmann, IPRax 1998, 179, 183-184; Garber, ÖJZ 2012, 108, 111).

997 On this, see *supra* Ch. II.A.

998 O'Reilly, EJLT 2011, 1, 3.

999 *Dow Jones and Company Inc v Gutnick* [2002] HCA 56; 210 CLR 575; 194 ALR 433; 77 ALJR 255 (10 December 2002), 199 (Callinan J.) (Australia).

> und ihn deshalb auch beliebig platzieren. Ein Anbieter, der rechtliche Nachteile gleich welcher Art fürchtete, bräuchte also ohne weitere organisatorische Maßnahmen nur den Server in einem anderen Land aufzustellen oder seine Daten nach dort auf einen anderen Rechner zu übertragen. Schon der Arbeitsplatz, von dem aus er sein Angebot elektronisch pflegte, könnte in seinem Heimatland verbleiben. Irgendwelche Rechtsfolgen von dem Standort eines Servers abhängig zu machen, ist deshalb willkürlich und öffnet dem Mißbrauch Tür und Tor.»[1000]

Mindful of these complications, identifying the real-time location of the web server on which the content is stored might be a delicate, or even an impossible task, for the plaintiff. The unforeseeability of this place also encouraged the ECJ to regard it as jurisdictionally irrelevant in paragraph 36 of *Wintersteiger* concerning the alleged online violation of a trade mark under Art 5(3) of Brussels I:

> «[I]n view of the objective of foreseeability, which the rules on jurisdiction must pursue, the place of establishment of that server cannot, by reason of its uncertain location, be considered to be the place where the event giving rise to the damage occurred».

In addition, this place might withstand any requirements of the principles of sound administration of justice and efficacious conduct of proceedings, since no act attributable to the publisher was physically performed there. Equally, the simple location of the web server cannot be regarded as a factual element of the violation, which would establish a close relationship between this place and the forum or would ease the collection of evidence relating to the violation.[1001] Holding content ready for access is no act at all, and it cannot be regarded as the place where the violation is committed to establish jurisdiction in that forum.[1002]

Similarly, the act, and thus, the place of uploading are also associated with several uncertainties that render them unsuitable for the jurisdictional question.[1003] First, the arguments put forward in their favour in *supra* Ch. VI.A.I.3 principally focus on the publisher's perspective, and therefore, they favour the publisher at the expense of the aggrieved person. In addition, this act is even more independent of a particular territorial location

1000 Rüßmann, JurPC Web-Dok. 1998, Abs. 32. See also Rüßmann, K&R 1998, 422, 423. Cf. *supra* Ch. II.A (regarding territorial independence of the Internet and online information).

1001 See also Roth, Die internationale Zuständigkeit, pp 196-197.

1002 See Bigos, ICLQ 2005, 585, 605 (regarding mere availability of material on a website). See also Roth, Die internationale Zuständigkeit, p 196. Contra: regarding operators, as perpetrators, see *supra* fn 825.

1003 Contra: Picht, GRUR Int. 2013, 19, 20 (regarding *eDate and Martinez*).

than the web server is. Theoretically, the information can be placed online on behalf of the publisher at any desired place where an Internet connection is available. Furthermore, several Internet service providers allow their users flexibility in the form of the so-called scheduled publishing, i.e., scheduling the information to go public at a specified time.[1004] This could lead to an adjunct question regarding which physical place is the place of uploading: the place where the time is scheduled, or alternatively, the place where the web server that makes that information available to the public at a certain time is located. Remarkable beyond these difficulties is the fact that the information about the place where the content is uploaded belongs to the publisher's organisational sphere, and its possible online display depends on his decision. Accordingly, this place might be hidden from online visitors,[1005] or alternatively, it might also be possible to indicate a fictitious place. It follows from all these considerations that the act and the place of uploading are adventitious and opportunistic. The identification of the place of uploading would therefore overburden the victim and, it could be rebutted at any time by the publisher who possesses, or perhaps creates in bad faith, technical information about that location. In addition and closely related to the foregoing discussion, the place of uploading fits uneasily with the principles of sound administration of justice and efficacious conduct of proceedings and might provide no information on the nature of the online content that lies at the heart of the dispute.[1006] It could very well be possible that the computer that uploads the content does not store any further information, which would be useful for deciding upon the injurious nature of the online content because, for example, the information is exclusively saved on an external drive located somewhere else. Furthermore, and perhaps even more importantly, the act of uploading appears from the pure wording of paragraph 45 of *eDate and Martinez* as a kind of substitute for distribution, by stating that «the placing online of content on a website is to be distinguished from the regional distribution of media such as printed matter».

1004 See e.g. Facebook: Updates to Page Composer Make it Easier to Share Great Content <https://www.facebook.com/business/news/Updates-to-Page-Composer-Make-it-Easier-to-Share-Great-Content>; Google – Youtube – Help – Scheduled Publishing <https://support.google.com/youtube/answer/1270709?hl=en>.

1005 See e.g. Facebook: How do I remove my location from a post? <https://www.facebook.com/help/166181076782926>. Cf. many online newspaper articles do not indicate the place of uploading.

1006 On this, see *supra* Ch. V.C.I.1.

However, the act of distribution by which the publisher relinquishes control over the physical content was disregarded as a causal event for offline defamation in *Shevill.*[1007] Why, then, should it be regarded as jurisdictionally relevant for online violations?[1008]

Conclusion and summary

It is respectfully noted that the concept of the publisher's establishment is a highly unsuitable basis for jurisdiction under Art 7(2). It is often, if not always, located in the Brussels-Lugano State in which the defendant's domicile within Art 4(1) is based. Exceptions to this finding are possible, but, since they function only to a limited extent, they are of little use for restoring the usefulness of this concept. Viewed in this light, the concept of causal event in the form of the publisher's establishment does not fulfil its function of providing an alternative forum to the general rule of jurisdiction, and thus, it loses its effectiveness. Hence, after an examination of possible acts in the chain of successive acts culminating in online violations of personality rights, the place where the disputed content was created is preferred.

II. The place of the damage is twice revised

Relying on *Shevill*, the ECJ revised the place of the damage in two respects: besides retaining the mosaic approach in the form of the accessibility test, it centralised that place in the Brussels-Lugano State in which the victim's centre of interests is located.[1009]

1007 It is so because the place of distribution was considered to be the place of the damage. On this, see *supra* Ch. V.B.II.1.b).

1008 Contrary to this latter argument, it could equally be reasoned that there is a spatial distinction between the place of uploading and the place where its consequence is felt, i.e., the place where the content is accessible and causes damage. Viewed in this light, the act of uploading includes both elements of liability (event and damage), which occur at the same time but principally at different locations.

1009 Note that Killias, SZIER 2012, 697, 714 point 12 identifies this newly introduced concept as «ein neues, autonomes Kriterium». This view could be very well supported by the pure wording of *eDate and Martinez*, 48 in which the ECJ held that «[t]he connecting criteria referred to in paragraph 42 of the present judgment

1. Revision no 1: the victim's centre of interests

The ECJ underlined the revision of the second *Shevill*-approach, and consequently, the introduction of the victim's centre of interests, with the following terms:

> «... the placing online of content on a website is to be distinguished from the regional distribution of media such as printed matter in that it is intended, in principle, to ensure the ubiquity of that content. That content may be consulted instantly by an unlimited number of internet users throughout the world, irrespective of any intention on the part of the person who placed it in regard to its consultation beyond that person's Member State of establishment and outside of that person's control.
>
> It thus appears that the internet reduces the usefulness of the criterion relating to distribution, in so far as the scope of the distribution of content placed online is in principle universal. Moreover, it is not always possible, on a technical level, to quantify that distribution with certainty and accuracy in relation to a particular Member State or, therefore, to assess the damage caused exclusively within that Member State.
>
> The difficulties in giving effect, within the context of the internet, to the criterion relating to the occurrence of damage which is derived from *Shevill and Others* contrasts, as the Advocate General noted at point 56 of his Opinion, with the serious nature of the harm which may be suffered by the holder of a personality right who establishes that information injurious to that right is available on a worldwide basis.
>
> The connecting criteria referred to in paragraph 42 of the present judgment must therefore be adapted in such a way that a person who has suffered an infringement of a personality right by means of the internet may bring an action in one forum in respect of all of the damage caused, depending on the place in which the damage caused in the European Union by that infringement occurred. Given that the impact which material placed online is liable to have on an individual's personality

---

must ... be adapted» (emphasis omitted). The reference in plural form to the *Shevill*-approaches mentioned in para 42 of *eDate and Martinez* might lead to the conclusion that the concept of the victim's centre of interests is an independent criterion. However, as is noted in this section, the present author rather shares the view predominantly expressed in legal theory and practice according to which the concept of the victim's centre of interests is a revised place of the damage [cf. Roth, IPRax 2013, 215, 220: «ein einzelner qualifizierter Erfolgsort»; Slonina, ÖJZ 2012, 61, 64: 'ein zentralisierter Erfolgsort am Schwerpunkt der Persönlichkeitsrechte'; Heinze, EuZW 2011, 947, 949: «Verdopplung der Erfolgsorte (einerseits gestreut an jedem Verbreitungsort, andererseits gebündelt am Interessenmittelpunkt)»], and therefore, she proceeds with the analysis of the place of the damage established in *eDate and Martinez* below accordingly.

rights might best be assessed by the court of the place where the alleged victim has his centre of interests, the attribution of jurisdiction to that court corresponds to the objective of the sound administration of justice, referred to in paragraph 40 above.

The place where a person has the centre of his interests corresponds in general to his habitual residence. However, a person may also have the centre of his interests in a Member State in which he does not habitually reside, in so far as other factors, such as the pursuit of a professional activity, may establish the existence of a particularly close link with that State.

The jurisdiction of the court of the place where the alleged victim has the centre of his interests is in accordance with the aim of predictability of the rules governing jurisdiction ... also with regard to the defendant, given that the publisher of harmful content is, at the time at which that content is placed online, in a position to know the centres of interests of the persons who are the subject of that content. The view must therefore be taken that the centre-of-interests criterion allows both the applicant easily to identify the court in which he may sue and the defendant reasonably to foresee before which court he may be sued».[1010]

These findings essentially focus on five issues, which are examined in the present section one by one. Accordingly, after shedding light on the reasons for revising the concept of distribution derived from *Shevill*, the concept of the victim's centre of interests is defined. Finally, the grounds of justification for the introduction of this concept are analysed.

a) Reason no 1: worldwide accessibility

The ECJ highlighted two main differences between the placing online of content and the distribution of offline material. First, the placing online of content is intended in principle to ensure worldwide accessibility. This means, so the ECJ went on to argue, that an unlimited number of Internet users can instantly access that content throughout the world, «irrespective of any intention on the part of the person who placed it in regard to its consultation beyond that person's Member State of establishment and outside of that person's control.»[1011] Secondly, as is stressed in paragraph 46 of *eDate and Martinez*, it is not always possible to quantify on a technical

1010 *eDate and Martinez*, 45-50 (case references and emphases omitted, italics in the original).

1011 *eDate and Martinez*, 45.

level that distribution with certainty and accuracy in respect of a particular Member State.[1012]

Two comments are called for on these differences. First, it is clear from the universal nature of the content that the concept of the victim's centre of interests applies when the content is accessible from the Brussels-Lugano State in which it is based.[1013] This is important, since in the absence of accessible injurious information, damage does not normally occur. Support for this comment can also be drawn from paragraph 48 of the judgment, in which the ECJ put forward considerations underlying the adaption of the *Shevill*-test. In particular, it favoured one forum where the plaintiff may bring proceedings for all of the damage caused, «depending on the place in which the damage caused in the European Union by that infringement occurred.»[1014] As far as the second comment is concerned, it can be safely assumed, subject to the exemption noted in *infra* Ch. VII.B.II.1.d), that the ECJ did not only disregard the subjective intention of the publisher in the form of the targeting test *à la Pammer and Hotel Alpenhof*, but it also appeared to be unsatisfied with the actual access approach.[1015] As the following sections briefly demonstrate, the present author has no difficulty in agreeing with these findings.

1012 On offline distribution, see *supra* Ch. II.D; *supra* Ch. V.B.II.1.b).

1013 See also AG in *Hejduk*, 26; Hungary: *Debreceni Ítélőtábla* (Debrecen Regional Court of Appeal) in case Gf. I. 30 741/3012/3 (BDT 2013.3.50); Ireland: *CSI Manufacturing Ltd v Dun and Bradstreet* [2013] IEHC 547 (29.11.2013), 20. Contra: Reymond, YbPIL 2011, 493, 499-500. In addition, as mentioned previously, the present author regards the place of the victim's centre of interests as a qualified place where the damage, as a result of the accessibility of the content, occurred or may occur. The simple concept of accessibility, as can be seen in *infra* Ch. VII.B.II.2, is applicable if the content is or has been accessible in the forum state. Therefore, the present author also argues that the concept of the victim's centre of interests applies not only when the content complained of *is* but also if it *was* accessible in the state where this centre is based.

1014 Note that it might be possible to interpret this finding as to allow the victim to bring an action against the defendant for the totality of the damage caused in the courts of any Member State where the damage occurred (cf. Hartley's English translation of the French language version of this para in Hartley, L.Q.R. 2012, 197, 199). However, in the present author's opinion, it is clear from the logic of the judgment that this sentence is only a part of the entire reasoning, which is put forward to establish the concept of the victim's centre of interests. Thus, it shall not be interpreted on its own.

1015 See also Hess, JZ 2012, 189, 191-192; Spindler, AfP 2012, 114, 116. By doing so, the ECJ answered in the negative several questions posed by the national

aa) The targeting test

The disregard of the targeting test *à la Pammer and Hotel Alpenhof* seems to be right for the following reasons.

First, this test does not follow clearly from the plain wording of Art 5(3) of Brussels I.[1016]

Secondly, it is also consistent with other judgments of the ECJ, such as *Pinckney*, in which it held that Art 5(3) of Brussels I «does not require, in particular, that the activity concerned to be 'directed to' the Member State in which the court seised is situated.»[1017]

In addition, this test would unilaterally favour the publisher.[1018] He could set up a website in a preferred language equipped, for example, with a domain name and a disclaimer, and with mention of a telephone number of his choice. If he had the free choice to select these and other elements, he would not only be enabled but also encouraged to zone the Internet manipulatively. He could intentionally choose those elements and show an intention not to target the state in which the victim's centre of interests is located, regardless of the fact that the website would be available there and it would be capable of causing harm to the person concerned. Similarly, he could claim to intend that the online content not be accessible in certain states, where the law is tilted towards the holder of the personality rights. Viewed in this light, the targeting test runs counter to several principles, objectives, and aims either regarded as general fundamental values or guaranteed specifically in the EU. In particular, zoning of the Internet may be contrary to the very purpose and nature of this medium, which is to enable anyone to communicate globally and to avail himself of the right to freedom of expression and information as well as of the fundamental freedom to conduct a business.[1019] In addition, Thomas Garber appears to question whether having the targeting test depend on numerous criteria is in the interest of a functioning internal market.[1020] Moreover, Michael

---

courts (see *eDate and Martinez*, 24, second question and 29, second question, first and third indents).

1016 See also the view of the French national court in *eDate and Martinez*, 28.

1017 *Pinckney*, 42. See also *Hejduk*, 31-33; AG in *Hejduk*, 28-31. Contra: proposals in *supra* Ch. VI.A.II.2.a).

1018 Cf. Spindler, AfP 2012, 114, 116.

1019 Cf. Garber, ÖJZ 2012, 108, 112; *Telekabel*, 42 ff. (regarding violation of copyright, blocking measure).

1020 Garber, ÖJZ 2012, 108, 115.

Bogdan explains, in relation to *Pammer and Hotel Alpenhof*, that limitation of the offers on the website to persons in some Member States designated by name may constitute, under certain circumstances, a fragmentation of the internal market and a covert indirect discrimination on grounds of nationality.[1021]

Fourthly, it is also obvious that the non-exhaustively listed criteria, of which the targeting test is composed, have high levels of complexity and flexibility. Accordingly, they turn the targeting test into an open-textured connecting factor, which enables the court seised to weigh and balance them on a case-by-case basis. The present author is, however, unsure whether the intention of the Brussels-Lugano Regime is to bind the court's jurisdiction to a lengthy and complex assessment of combinations of criteria. Rather, she stresses that the regime is based on connecting factors, which are common to all the Brussels-Lugano States and are foreseeable for the parties and to which recourse is certain and rapid.[1022] Thus, a set of criteria of this kind is not conductive to the principle of legal certainty and particularly, foreseeability.[1023] Burkhard Hess is of a similar opinion in relation to the targeting test within Art 15(1)(c) of Brussels I:

> «Allerdings hat dieser Lösungsweg erheblich an „Charme“ verloren, seit der *EuGH* den Begriff des Ausrichtens im Rahmen von Art. 15 lit. c) EuGVO einzelfallbezogen interpretiert mit der Folge, dass die erforderliche Zuständigkeitsklarheit nicht gewährleistet ist.»[1024]

To take an example, several scholars, who prefer the targeting test, militate in favour of the language of the website and of the content as being one of the pivotal factors to decide the state towards which the content is oriented. It is often suggested that contents drafted in exotic languages are predominantly comprehended within their relevant language regions.[1025] However, the importance of this suggestion varies in the light of the different considerations put forward in *supra* Ch. II.A, especially regarding online translation services and non-verbal means of communication, such as photographs. Furthermore, languages are spoken not exclusively in one geographically determinable territory. Although, for example, the Hungarian language could be regarded as an exotic language, as on a worldwide

---

1021 Bogdan, Masaryk U. J.L. & Tech. 2011, 1, 8.
1022 Cf. *supra* Ch. III.B.I.4; Slonina, ÖJZ 2012, 61, 64-65.
1023 See also Garber, ÖJZ 2012, 108, 116.
1024 Hess, JZ 2012, 189, 190 (italics in the original; fns omitted).
1025 Cf. Roth, Die internationale Zuständigkeit, p 279.

scale it is spoken only by a minority, not all content written in Hungarian is directed at Hungary, since this language is also widely spoken in certain parts of Slovakia, Romania, and Serbia. The same holds true in respect of the content written in the German language. It may target Germany or, alternatively, Austria, the German language region of Belgium, the Southern Tyrol of Italy, or Switzerland.[1026] Furthermore, it must be stressed that millions of people avail themselves of the fundamental freedom of the free movement of persons guaranteed within the EU and reside and work in a Member State of which they are not nationals.[1027] Mindful of these observations, language as a criterion for determining a particular state or audience in a state is less appealing.[1028] Similarly, as outlined in *supra* Ch. II.B.I.3, domain names are hardly suitable to conclude a particular territorial confinement. Finally, and perhaps most importantly, the complex set of criteria works ineffectively when the online content targets not a particular state or audience of that state, but rather the general public of the virtual world or a specific section of that public. A plausible example of this is the website in *eDate Advertising*, which was oriented towards homosexual, bisexual, and transgender groups.[1029]

One additional comment is required regarding the preceding discussion. By introducing the concept of the victim's centre of interests and remaining silent on the centre of gravity approach, as proposed by AG Cruz Villalón and outlined in *supra* Ch. VI.A.II.2.b)aa), it becomes evident that the *sui generis* targeting tests are also not taken into consideration for localising online (potential) violations of personality rights within Art 7(2). Although these tests aim objectively to evaluate the link between the forum and the content, the factors on which this evaluation is performed are reminiscent of the subjective criteria on which the targeting test *à la Pammer and Hotel Alpenhof* is based. Indeed, for example, AG Cruz Villalón in his opinion delivered in *eDate and Martinez* expressly referred to certain factors that are equivalent to those items and that actually indicate the subjective intent on the part of the publisher to direct the informa-

---

1026 See also Nagy, J. Priv. Int. L. 2012, 251, 295 (regarding the Hungarian and the German language). Cf. Rüßmann, K&R 1998, 422, 424.

1027 Cf. *supra* fn 34. Note also that EU institutions attract nationalities at least from each Member State.

1028 Cf. Rüßmann, K&R 1998, 422, 424.

1029 See *supra* Ch. VII.A.I.1.

tion to a particular state.[1030] Accordingly, the above-mentioned reasons as possible weaknesses and troublesome features of the targeting test *à la Pammer and Hotel Alpenhof* are basically also valid for the *sui generis* targeting tests, which in turn render them inapt as bases for jurisdiction.

bb) The actual access approach

The disregard of the actual access approach cannot seriously be disputed, and it is also largely accepted in legal thinking and practice.[1031] One of its main drawbacks is that the number of page views is available solely for the publisher, and, in principle, the victim is not aware of them. As Burkhard Hess states:

> «[D]ieser Ansatz leidet vor allem darunter, dass derartige Informationen im Zweifel nur dem beklagten Medienunternehmen zur Verfügung stehen, so dass der Verletzte gar nicht über ausreichende Informationen verfügt, um die Erfolgschance seiner Klage am (Teil-)Erfolgsort einschätzen zu können.»[1032]

In attempting the collection of such (electronically stored) information, the victim can often be trapped in a vicious circle. Although it might be possible to collect such information, if it has not been destroyed or erased,[1033] due to the existence of different data protection laws,[1034] such a task might be time-consuming and seriously burdensome for the aggrieved person. Even if he collects information on simple circulation figures, they may display incorrect data on the number of actual accesses for the following two reasons. First, Internet users may use evasion techniques to travel in the virtual world with the result that they access content as if they were at

1030 See also Thorn, FS Bernd von Hoffmann, p 756, fn 50. Cf. AG in *eDate and Martinez*, 65.

1031 See e.g. AG in *eDate and Martinez*, 47, 50. Contra: Nagy in *supra* Ch. VI.A.II.1.b).

1032 Hess, JZ 2012, 189, 191. See also Bachmann, IPRax 1998, 179, 186 (in relation to Newsgroups). Two more or less reliable means to show that the content has been read: if the online visitor leaves a comment or likes the content (see Gibson, It came from CyberSpace, 2014, pp 10-11). In addition, the redistribution of the content could also be a possible indicator. However, this should be taken into account with certain limitations, since the content could also be automatically redistributed.

1033 See phone hacking scandal and connected privacy cases in the UK as referred to in Gibson, It came from CyberSpace, 2014, pp 14-15.

1034 On this, see *supra* Ch. II.B.I.3.

a place other than where they are physically present.[1035] In addition, as Judith Gibson notes, a separate hit is recorded each time a person visits the website, regardless of whether he has visited it before or not and whether he has read the content or not. In addition, she goes on to notice that, for example, the identification of IP address of the online visitor helps to elaborate a profile of the extent to which online material has been published.[1036] At this point, however, the question of the reliability of technology, especially of the identification of IP addresses, may come into play.[1037] Finally, but perhaps even more importantly, the actual access approach addresses violations of personality rights only after the content has been visited, and therefore, it fits awkwardly with potential violations.[1038]

cc) Two adjunct questions: blocking measures and redistribution

Two adjunct questions closely related to the preceding issues but not discussed in *eDate and Martinez* ought to be indicated that could perhaps be subjects of future preliminary rulings.

First, the ECJ stressed in paragraphs 45 and 46 of *eDate and Martinez* that the content placed online is, in principle, ubiquitous. By using the term 'in principle', it is supposed that the ECJ left open the door for certain situations when the placing online of the content does not initially ensure the universal nature of the content. Currently, such a situation could be imaginable when the publisher blocks public access from certain Brussels-Lugano States.[1039] It is possible to draw support for this view from the finding laid down in paragraph 50 of *eDate and Martinez* according to which the publisher is in the position to know the victim's centre of interests «at the time at which that content is placed online». It follows that at that time, the publisher can foresee where his content is accessible and where it is not. In other words, if the content is blocked in the Brussels-Lugano State in which the victim's centre of interests is based, this con-

1035 On this, see *supra* Ch. II.B.I.2, especially Trimble's opinion.
1036 Gibson, It came from CyberSpace, 2014, p 14.
1037 On this, see *supra* Ch. II.B.I.1.
1038 See also Garber, ÖJZ 2012, 108, 113.
1039 Cf. Ireland: *Coleman v MGN Limited* [2012] IESC 20 (15.3.2012); *CSI Manufacturing Ltd v Dun and Bradstreet* [2013] IEHC 547 (29.11.2013) in which the *High Court of Ireland* held (para 14): «Where a site is a subscription site the information is not readily available across jurisdictions.»

cept supposedly does not apply, since, according to the publisher's best knowledge, it is not accessible in that state. Although this view makes sense, it is equally true that the shortcomings of geolocation tools raise queries regarding the effectiveness of blocking measures. On this, by analogy, Mr Justice Arnold's finding in *Cartier International and Others v. BSkyB and others* shall be invoked:

> «No doubt it is the casual, inexperienced or lazy users who stop visiting those websites, whereas the experienced and determined users circumvent the blocking measures».[1040]

Indeed, blocking would supposedly discourage a certain number of Internet users from accessing the content, and thus, it would lead to a reduction in the overall level of access to the website.[1041] However, a lesson drawn from *Shevill* shows that the allocation of jurisdiction to a court does not depend on the number of readers, i.e., online visitors. A decrease in traffic to blocked websites and contents does not exclude bringing claims in courts, since even if a few people accessed the content, it still suffices for jurisdictional purposes. Moreover, mindful of the fact that reliable blocking measures often represent significant expense and require complex and difficult technical solutions,[1042] online actors, other than those possessing sufficient resources, would be disadvantaged because they could not afford such measures, and therefore, they could easily be sued.[1043]

The second adjunct question concerns the issue of redistribution of the content by third party Internet users to the so-called new public[1044] that is

1040 *Cartier International and Others v. BSkyB and others* [2014] EWHC 3354 (Ch), 236 (regarding violation of trade mark; site blocking order). On the effectiveness of these measures, see also *supra* Ch. II.B.I and *supra* Ch. VI.A.II.1.c).

1041 Cf. by analogy, regarding blocking measures, ECJ: *Telekabel*, 58 ff.; UK/England: *Cartier International and Others v. BSkyB and others* [2014] EWHC 3354 (Ch), 218 ff.

1042 See *Telekabel*, 50.

1043 A possible solution is to require different online actors to take different measures, which do not represent unreasonable sacrifices for them [cf. Reymond in *supra* Ch. VI.A.II.1.c)]. However, it is, in the present author's opinion, seriously disputable. First, it leads to the different treatment of online actors and ensures discretion on the part of the court. Secondly, it is ineffective, since the content may be accessed, and thus, it may cause harm anyway.

1044 By analogy with *Svensson*, 24, a new public is a public that was not considered by the publisher at the time of the initial distribution. The question of redistribution (linking) from a substantive legal aspect has been decided by the ECJ or it has been referred for a preliminary ruling in relation to an alleged violation of copyright, e.g. in *Svensson* (hyperlinks, copyright); *BestWater* (embedded con-

located in the Brussels-Lugano State in which the victim's centre of interests is based. To put it another way, it is questionable whether the original publisher can be sued in the state where he initially has not made his content accessible in order to compensate for the harm caused by a third person publisher's subsequent redistribution.[1045]

Several arguments can be put forward in favour of a negative answer. Beyond the aforementioned argument concerning the time at which the publisher can foresee by the initial online distribution where his content is accessible, it could also be argued that the court is competent for deciding upon the damage that occurred if the disputed content is or was originally accessible there.[1046] Thus, the latter formulation referring to the accessibility of the content in the past suggests that the publisher could subsequently restrict the accessibility of the content or remove it from the Internet. Mindful of the special characteristics of this information medium indicated in *supra* Ch. II, especially the mass redistribution practices, it is evident that without being concerned exclusively with the initial distribution of the content, the subsequent removal or restriction of the access would often be an impossible task. This can also be demonstrated by the decision of the Athens First Instance Court concerning «the application for protective measures of a Greek university Professor against a Greek Wikipedia

---

tent, copyright, order); *Mc Fadden* (copyright infringing music, request); *C More Entertainment* (linking, copyright). Cf. Canada: *Crookes v. Newton* [2011] 3 SCR 269 (whether hyperlink to a defamatory material constitutes publication of that material) as analysed in Radnoff/Archer, Defamation Law in Canada.

1045 Without straying into a discussion, it is worth noting that this adjunct question could be divided into two subsequent areas depending on the method of redistribution. Namely, content can be redistributed intentionally and goal-oriented, e.g. a blogger is aware of and intends the redistribution. Alternatively, online content could be redistributed automatically without any human interaction through the working of Internet intermediaries, such as search engines, by displaying search results (cf. *supra* fn 138). On liability of intermediaries, see e.g. *Google Spain* (regarding data protection), and on the national application of this case, see Spain: Peguera, The right to be forgotten, 2015; the Netherlands: Spauwen, Dutch Google Spain ruling, 2014; Spauwen, Dutch court (II), 2015. Cf. World Intermediary Liability Map <http://cyberlaw.stanford.edu/our-work/projects/world-intermediary-liability-map-wilmap>; Ireland: *CG v Facebook & Anor* [2015] NIQB 11; France: *TGI de Paris* (ord. réf.), 24 novembre et 19 décembre 2014 - *Marie-France M. cl Google France et Google Inc.* and *TGI de Toulouse* (ord. réf.), 21 janvier 201 - *Franck J. c/ Google France et Google Inc.* as referred to in Blocman, The right to be forgotten, 2015.

1046 See *supra* Ch. VII.B.II.1.a).

user, who posted allegedly unflattering statements on the Wikipedia article about him.»[1047] As Apostolos Anthimos explains, the plaintiff was granted a temporary restraining order by virtue of which the Wikipedia user was obliged to remove the disputed phrases until the court delivers its decision in ordinary proceedings. Regardless of this order, as he points out, «dozens of other users uploaded several times the same content which was removed in accordance with the order. This is a demonstrative sign of the ineffectiveness of taking similar measures in cyberspace. In other words, it proved the vanity and futility of coercive measures against Wikipedia users, reminiscent of the notorious labour of Hercules against the Lernaean Hydra.»[1048] Thirdly, *Shevill* was based on the initial distribution of a newspaper article.[1049] Why, then, should its online counterpart be treated differently? Fourthly, the damage caused by redistribution to the new public could be regarded as damage consequential upon the damage that actually arose elsewhere as a result of the initial distribution, and thus, is irrelevant as a basis of jurisdiction.[1050]

Although these arguments for a negative answer might very well be true, the following counterarguments could equally be put forward in favour of allowing the court to assume jurisdiction over the dispute concerning the liability of the initial publisher for the damage (threatened to be) caused by the redistributed content. First, by analogy with *DFDS Torline* outlined in *supra* Ch. IV.B.I.1.e), the initial distribution of the content could be regarded as a necessary precondition of the redistribution, and thus, of the occurrence of harm.[1051] Moreover, the court at the place of redistribution could also assume jurisdiction over the publisher for the harm caused by the redistribution by virtue of the analogous application of the attribution of effect approach laid down in cases concerning co-perpetrators and outlined in *supra* Ch. III.D.II.3. Accordingly, the court at

---

1047 Anthimos, Defamation through Wikipedia postings, 2014 [regarding case *Athens First Instance Court*, Nr. 9118/2014 (unreported)].

1048 Anthimos, Defamation through Wikipedia postings, 2014.

1049 See *supra* Ch. V.B.II.1.b).

1050 On this, see also Nagy, J. Priv. Int. L. 2012, 251, 274-275 (regarding hearsay). On consequential damage, see *supra* Ch. IV.B.I.2.

1051 Cf. UK/England: *Ames & Anor v The Spamhaus Project Ltd & Anor* [2015] EWHC 127 (QB), 45 {noting that «[a] publisher is responsible for damage caused by republications which are the natural and probable or reasonably foreseeable consequence of its own publication»}; Canada: *Breeden v. Black* 2012 SCC 19, [2012] 1 S.C.R. 666, 20 (holding that «the republication is the natural and probable result of the original publication»).

the place of the new public could hear a claim against the original publisher for the harm caused by the redistribution. Thirdly, several scholars argue that violations of personality rights are not dependent on the publisher's intention, but rather, they hinge on the attack on the victim's social position, which could also be caused by the content that reached the territory accidentally.[1052] Consequently, redistribution could be an important issue. In addition, against the validity of the aforementioned argument based on the consequential damage, it could be argued that it was ruled in a case concerning financial loss, but not non-material damage, and that redistribution to the new public could result in direct harm regarding this public. Finally, and perhaps more significantly, it is important not to turn a blind eye to the recent technological developments and new social interactions coupled with permanent postings, which should basically be evident to anybody who uses the Internet. Thus, it is expected that the publisher is aware, or ought to be aware, of the fact that its posts could easily be redistributed.

Regardless of these pros and cons, it remains to be seen how these adjunct questions are dealt with at a European level. Contemporary, Christian Heinze is of the following opinion:

> «Zudem mag man fragen, ob der Gerichtsstand am Interessenmittelpunkt des Betroffenen auch dann greift, wenn die Internetinhalte als Folge technischer Beschränkungen nicht weltweit zugänglich sind, vielleicht nicht einmal in seinem Heimatstaat. Allerdings lassen sich geographische Abrufbeschränkungen umgehen und eine Weiterverbreitung durch andere Nutzer kaum verhindern, so dass technische Beschränkungen den *Gerichtshof* wohl nicht überzeugen werden, den Bündelungsgerichtsstand aufzugeben.»[1053]

b) Reason no 2: serious nature of the harm

After shedding light on the difficulties in giving effect, in the context of the Internet, to the concept of distribution equipped with the mosaic approach, the ECJ went on to put forward another reason in favour of revising this *Shevill*-approach. In particular, it held that these difficulties contend with «the serious nature of the harm which may be suffered by the

1052 In this regard, see also Buchner in *supra* Ch. VI.B.III; Thorn in *supra* fn 944; Huet as referred to in AG 1994 in *Shevill*, 82.

1053 Heinze, EuZW 2011, 947, 950 (fn omitted, italics in the original). Contra: Reymond in *supra* Ch. VI.A.II.1.c).

holder of a personality right who establishes that information injurious to that right is available on a world-wide basis.»[1054] This finding was based on paragraph 56 of AG Cruz Villalón's opinion delivered in *eDate and Martinez*, in which he pointed out:

> «[T]he serious nature of the harm which may be suffered by the holder of the fundamental right to privacy, who observes how the information injurious to his reputation is available anywhere on the planet, must contend with a solution which fragments his right in each Member State where he is known.»[1055]

Mindful of this reasoning, Csongor István Nagy notes that the concept of the victim's centre of interests primarily focuses on persons known in several states. Persons having a reputation in a single state, so he explains, could enforce the main part of their claim in their home state under the mosaic approach, since the bulk of their harm occurred there. Then, he goes on to argue:

> «On the other hand, persons having a reputation in more than one country may have found the mosaic theory particularly disadvantageous, since the loss they allegedly suffered may have been geographically dispersed. Under *Shevill*, they were required to sue in several Member States to collect compensation for the entire loss. In this sense, the "centre-of-interests" doctrine favours celebrities and persons having an international reputation, who often do have the resources to sue outside their country of domicile.»[1056]

The core part of this argument generally makes sense in relation to defamation. The concept of the victim's centre of interests is principally useful for internationally known people who do not have to initiate mosaic proceedings in the courts of different Brussels-Lugano States. Nevertheless, the importance of this argument should not be overstated. As is evident from their findings, both AG Cruz Villalón and Csongor István Nagy attach considerable jurisdictional importance to the requirement that the victim be known in the state in which the violation of his personality rights occurs. However, the existence of and the necessity for this requirement derived from *Shevill* is seriously doubted in the context of offline defamation. Beyond those arguments put forward in *supra* Ch. V.B.II.2, the need for this requirement is even more questionable in online violations of personality rights for the following reasons. First, the ECJ did not adopt the wording of the above-quoted paragraph of AG Cruz Villalón's opinion, in

1054 *eDate and Martinez*, 47.
1055 See also similarly, AG in *eDate and Martinez*, 48, 52.
1056 Nagy, J. Priv. Int. L. 2012, 251, 271 (italics in the original).

which he placed great emphasis on the requirement 'to be known' as a condition for the second *Shevill*-test. Instead, it referred to the occurrence of the injury to a personality right in general without specifying its jurisdictionally relevant meaning or its necessary criteria. Secondly, the existence of online reputation[1057] renders ineffective the function of this requirement, that is, to limit the jurisdictionally relevant places where the aggrieved person may bring an action against the publisher. Since anybody may become internationally known in the virtual world through their online activities, it is not only celebrities in the ordinary meaning of the term who could suffer serious harm but also ordinary persons, provided that the existence of their virtual reputation is obviously manifested to the outside world, and their violations bear relevance for claiming compensation for non-pecuniary harm. Thirdly, it seems particularly questionable how the requirement 'to be known' could fit any prospective defamation, since it excludes possible places where violations threaten to occur because of the establishment of a negative reputation of the person concerned, thus impairing the prospective developments and professional or social opportunities he might reasonably have had.[1058] Would the connecting factor, which requires a reputation at the place of the damage, render justice in this case? Fourthly, it is difficult to reconcile this substantive legal requirement with the nature of privacy rights as guaranteed under Art 7 of the Charter, whose meaning and scope correspond to those afforded within Art 8(1) of the ECHR.[1059] In particular, violations of privacy rights do not automatically depend on the requirement that the victim be known. As is clear from the judicial practice of the ECtHR on the interpretation of Art 8(1) of the ECHR, the right to one's own image, for example, can also be violated if the victim is unknown:

> «For a private individual, unknown to the public, the publication of a photo may amount to a more substantial interference than a written article».[1060]

Mindful of this judicial practice, the victim's privacy rights could also be violated outside the state in which the victim's centre of interests is based

1057 On this, see also *supra* Ch. II.C.

1058 See also Kaye, Law of the European Judgments Convention, p 1471.

1059 See *supra* fn 297 and *supra* fn 770. For the role of the Charter in interpreting EU legislative instruments, see *supra* Ch. III.B.I.1.

1060 *Von Hannover v. Germany (No. 2)* (nos 40660/08, 60641/08), 113. Cf. Roth, Die internationale Zuständigkeit, p 268 argues that regarding injury to the person's intimate sphere, it is irrelevant whether the receiver of the private information or of a naked photograph of the victim knew the victim previously.

even if he is not known there. Two comments are called for on this finding. First, it appears that such an interpretation of the place of the damage under the concept of harmful event within Art 7(2) may be regarded as being inconsistent with the meaning and scope of privacy rights as guaranteed under Art 7 of the Charter. Secondly, by equipping privacy rights with the requirement that the victim be known in the forum state already at the stage of jurisdiction excludes, similar to defamation,[1061] those possible violations that could be compensated for in accordance with substantive legal provisions.

c) Definition: the victim's centre of interests

Taking into account these aforementioned reasons, the ECJ lifted the ban on the extent of jurisdiction of the court seised in the Brussels-Lugano State in which the victim's centre of interests is located. In Peter Mankowski's words, «[d]as Mosaikprinzip bewertet er *[EuGH]* nun bei Internetdelikten als zu nachteilig für Verletzte (Rz. 45-47) und führt deshalb als große Neuerung den Gerichtsstand am „Mittelpunkt der Interessen" ein, an dem der gesamte weltweit entstandene Schaden eingeklagt werden kann (Rz. 48).»[1062] Then, the ECJ went on to define this concept with the following terms:

> «The place where a person has the centre of his interests corresponds in general to his habitual residence. However, a person may also have the centre of his interests in a Member State in which he does not habitually reside, in so far as other factors, such as the pursuit of a professional activity, may establish the existence of a particularly close link with that State.»[1063]

1061 See above and in *supra* Ch. V.B.II.2; *supra* Ch. V.C.II.3.b) (regarding reputation of unknown persons).

1062 Mankowski, EWiR 2011, 743-744 (italics in square brackets added). Cf. Wulf-Henning Roth in *infra* Ch. VII.B.II.1.c)aa).

1063 *eDate and Martinez*, 49. Cf. second question, second indent as referred for a preliminary ruling in *eDate and Martinez*, 29. This concept is reminiscent of the first element of the centre of gravity test [see *supra* Ch. VI.A.II.2.b)aa); AG in *eDate and Martinez*, 59] and of the centre of main interests test (on this, see *infra* Ch. VII.D.II.2) under Reg. (EC) No 1346/2000 (OJ 2000 L 160/1) (in this regard, see Bogdan, YbPIL 2011, 483, 486; Slonina, ÖJZ 2012, 61, 66).

Due to the wording of this paragraph, Michael Bogdan explains that only a single centre of interests exists, since the ECJ referred to 'the' and not 'a' centre of interests.[1064] Laurent Killias is of the same opinion, stressing:

> «Ohne dies ausdrücklich zu sagen, scheint der Gerichtshof davon auszugehen, dass es nur einen Mittelpunkt der Interessen geben kann.»[1065]

As a result, if the victim lives in a Brussels-Lugano State but earns most of his income from activities in another such a state, he might be regarded as having his centre of interests in the latter state. Similarly, if he lives in a non-Brussels-Lugano State and derives his income from activities in a Brussels-Lugano State, he could avail himself of the concept and sue the publisher before the court of the Member State in which he pursues a professional activity.[1066] The choice between these two aspects is basically made from the victim's perspective, providing that they both are located in different Brussels-Lugano States.[1067] Because of its subjective nature, Sandra Schmitz feels uneasy about this concept, which she calls «a subjective interpretation of forum conveniens».[1068] However, the importance of this notice should not be overstated, since, so Michael Slonina points out, the similar subjective character of the place of the causal event preferring the perpetrator is not criticised:

> «Allerdings muss auch berücksichtigt werden, dass dieselbe „Willkürlichkeit" bzw Beeinflussbarkeit bei dem ohnedies auch bisher nicht durch das Mosaikprinzip eingeschränkten Handlungsort kaum als störend empfunden wurde. Auch wenn zweifelhaft ist, ob der Tatortgerichtsstand des Art 5 Nr 3 EuGVVO neben der Sach- und Beweisnähe eine „Privilegierung des Opfers bezweckt, so spricht zumindest wenig dafür, die bei weitem weniger leicht zu manipulierende Anknüpfung am gewöhnlichen Aufenthaltsort ausschließen zu wollen, gleichzeitig aber zu akzeptieren, dass der Täter durch seine Tat zunächst den Handlungsort (letztlich aber ja auch den Erfolgsort) bestimmen kann – wenn man also die Wahl des Auf-

---

1064 Bogdan, YbPIL 2011, 483, 486.

1065 Killias, SZIER 2012, 697, 714 point 10. See also Roth, IPRax 2013, 215, 221; Slonina, ÖJZ 2012, 61, 66.

1066 On this, see also Hartley, L.Q.R. 2012, 197, 199; Mansel/Thorn/Wagner, IPRax 2012, 1, 12.

1067 Thus, it is principally irrelevant what the relationship between the two aspects of the concept is, i.e., they are alternative to each other [e.g. Heinze, EuZW 2011, 947, 949; Wolter, jurisPR-ITR 2012, point, B.1. (2)] or the second aspect suppresses the first one (e.g. Killias, SZIER 2012, 697, 714, point 10; Slonina, ÖJZ 2012, 61, 66).

1068 Schmitz, Masaryk U. J.L. & Tech. 2012, 159, 168. Cf. *Dumez*, 19 (regarding the plaintiff's domicile).

enthaltsorts durch das Opfer als „Gerichtsstandsmanipulation“ ansieht, wieso soll Entsprechendes nicht auch für die „Tat“ des Täters gelten?»[1069]

aa) Forum actoris and actor sequitur forum rei: opposition or justified parallelism?

Through the concept of the victim's centre of interests, the ECJ basically introduced *forum actoris* within Art 5(3) of Brussels I,[1070] which in turn, generated two main objections to this concept in legal theory and practice. These objections, however, do not attract the present author greatly.

First, it is argued that the ECJ introduced a concept that was expressly and repeatedly denied in its settled case law[1071] because of its exorbitant character.[1072] However, it may be countered that these cases dealt exclusively with financial losses. Furthermore, in *Kronhofer*, in which the plaintiff sought to recover damages for his financial loss that he claimed to have suffered as a result of the defendants' act, the ECJ did not completely exclude this criterion from the scope of Art 5(3) of the BC. Rather it left open the door for its possible recognition under certain circumstances.[1073] In particular, it held that the place where the pecuniary damage occurred does not refer to the place where the plaintiff is domiciled or where his assets are centred «*by reason only of the fact* that he has suffered financial damage there resulting from the loss of part of his assets which arose and was incurred in another Contracting State.»[1074] To put it a different way, as the ECJ explained it many years later in *Kolassa*, the courts of the plaintiff's domicile may not assume jurisdiction on the basis of the mere

---

1069 Slonina, ÖJZ 2012, 61, 63-64 (fns omitted).

1070 *Forum actoris* refers to the victim's habitual residence (see also Kuipers, CML Rev. 2012, 1211, fn 21) regardless of the fact that this term might also cover his domicile (e.g. *Group Josi*, 50). For observing that the ECJ basically introduced *forum actoris*, see e.g. Thiede, ecolex 2012, 131, 132; Hess, in: Pocar/Viarengo/Villata, Recasting Brussels I, p 98; Thiede, GPR 2012, 219, 221.

1071 See Kuipers, CML Rev. 2012, 1211, 1220-1221. For cases in which it was denied, see e.g. *Dumez*, 19; *Marinari*, 13. Contra: *forum actoris* was indirectly upheld in *Bier* (in this regard, see AG in *Kronhofer* in the present subsection below), and it was allowed by equipping it with the mosaic approach in *Shevill* and in *eDate and Martinez*.

1072 On exorbitant grounds of jurisdiction, see *supra* Ch. III.C.II.

1073 On this, see also Blobel, EuLF 2004, 187, 191; Kosmehl, FS Thomas Rauscher, pp 87-89.

1074 *Kronhofer*, 21 (author's italics). See also *Kolassa*, 48.

fact that the plaintiff suffered financial consequences there, since both the causal event and the damage occurred in the territory of another Member State.[1075] In *Kolassa*, however, concerning the loss in value of a financial investment through a financial instrument issued by the bank, it could be said the ECJ opened that door wider. It first noted that under Art 5(3) of Brussels I, the attribution of jurisdiction to the courts of the plaintiff's domicile is justified if the plaintiff's domicile is situated, in fact, at the place in which the causal event took place or the damage occurred.[1076] Then, it went on to localise the plaintiff's financial damage as follows:

> «Under Article 5(3) of Regulation No 44/2001, the courts where the applicant is domiciled have jurisdiction, on the basis of the place where the loss occurred, to hear and determine such an action, *particularly when* the damage alleged occurred directly in the applicant's bank account held with a bank established within the area of jurisdiction of those courts.»[1077]

Furthermore, Michael Slonina points out that it is only at a first glance that *eDate and Martinez* contrasts with the previous case law concerning financial loss in which the ECJ refused to localise the damage at the *forum actoris*. In his opinion, the exclusion of the *forum actoris* should not be generalised due to those cases. Instead, its application should be avoided only when the centralisation at that place is fictional and aims to favour the victim without establishing connection between the forum and the tort. Then, he goes on to state:

> «[Z]umal es einer solchen Fiktion schon deswegen kaum bedarf, weil mit dem konkreten Ort der Vornahme einer Vermögensverfügung oder dem „Abflussort" des konkret geschädigten Vermögensgegenstands idR durchaus Anknüpfungspunkte vorliegen werden. Dagegen scheint die Lokalisierung der „Ehre", bzw der Persönlichkeitsrechte einer Person an irgendeinem Ort von vornherein schwieriger; sie dort zu verorten, wo jemand seinen gewöhnlichen Aufenthalt hat oder seiner Tätigkeit nachgeht, ist daher durchaus naheliegend.»[1078]

1075 *Kolassa*, 49.
1076 *Kolassa*, 50.
1077 *Kolassa*, 57 (author's italics). In the present author's view, this ruling is remarkable, since the expression 'particularly when' could be regarded as an attempt to open wider the door left open in *Kronhofer* for a possible recognition of the *forum actoris* under Art 7(2). Cf. Lehmann, Which Court is Competent, 2015 who states that «[r]egrettably, the judgment still leaves room for speculation which court would be competent if the bank account from which the investor paid for the securities were located outside his domicile.»
1078 Slonina, ÖJZ 2012, 61, 64.

Thirdly, the victim's centre of interests shall not be regarded as an exorbitant basis of jurisdiction for the following reason. As AG Léger explained in his opinion delivered in *Kronhofer*, the twin criteria established in *Bier* are based on considerations relating to the sound administration of justice and the efficacious conduct of proceedings. Therefore, so he went on to note, they might not be understood as vesting jurisdiction on the plaintiff's forum in the form of an exorbitant ground of jurisdiction, «even if it is possible that in some cases one or other of the criteria for attributing jurisdiction specified in that case, namely the place where the event which resulted in damage occurred or the place where the resulting damage was sustained, may coincide in practice with the place where the victim is domiciled.»[1079]

Finally and closely related to the preceding, AG Capotorti, in 1976, had already highlighted that the place of the damage tends to coincide with the state in which the plaintiff usually has his residence.[1080] Therefore, the victim-centred forum at the place of the damage should not be looked at with a critical eye.

As far as the second objection to the concept of the victim's centre of interests is concerned, it could possibly be argued that this concept is «the antithesis of the *actor sequitur* principle».[1081] In particular, it could be put forward that this concept not only undermines the general scheme of the rules of jurisdiction hinging on the genuine principle of the defendant's domicile, but it also challenges the protection of the defendant guaranteed under Art 4.[1082] The flaw in this argument, according to the inherent features of the twin criteria of *Bier* and according to other considerations, is obvious. First, the ECJ established the twin criteria in *Bier* under the concept of harmful event on an equal footing, which was overset in *Shevill* by

1079 AG in *Kronhofer*, 35. Cf. *Kolassa*, 50 (see above).

1080 AG in *Bier*, 9 (p 1758).

1081 Gillies, ICLQ 2012, 1007, 1016 (as a possible argument for the unnecessary nature of the plaintiff's centre of interests test; italics in the original).

1082 In this regard, see Dickinson, By Royal Appointment, 2012 who refers to particular sentences of *eDate and Martinez*, 48, 49 in which, in his opinion, the ECJ «repudiates its longstanding principle of avoiding interpretations of the rules of special jurisdiction in Art. 5 which favour the courts of the claimant's domicile in such a way as to undermine to an unacceptable degree the protection which Art. 2 affords to the defendant». Cf. Heinze, EuZW 2011, 947, 949; Nagy, J. Priv. Int. L. 2012, 251, 270. Contra: Verheul in *supra* fn 394 questions the rationale behind the *actor sequitur* principle.

the introduction of the mosaic approach and partly restored in *eDate and Martinez*. In Wulf-Henning Roth's words:

> «In der Sache wird damit durch *eDate Advertising* die Einschränkung der Kognitionsbefugnis der Gerichte am Erfolgsort bei Pressedelikten aufgrund des *Shevill*-Urteils im Hinblick auf das zu schützende Rechtsgut zum Teil wieder rückgängig gemacht; die Ausnahmeregelung des Art. 5 Nr. 3 EuGVVO erhält - soweit es um das Gericht am „Mittelpunkt der Interessen" als Erfolgsort geht - ihren alten Anwendungsbereich wieder.»[1083]

Secondly, numerous views expressed in legal writing appear to hold that by introducing this concept, the ECJ achieved a sufficient balance between the interests of the plaintiff and the defendant, and thus, the concept provides procedural equality.[1084] For instance, Burkhard Hess finds that the victim and the (alleged) perpetrator are placed on equal footing with the effect that the victim can usually initiate proceedings at his habitual residence.[1085]

Thirdly, *forum actoris* does not necessarily favour the aggrieved person, since, as Arthur T. von Mehren notices:

> «Few, if any, jurisdictional bases are ... systemically linked with pro-plaintiff or pro-defendant procedural and substantive rules and principles. In a particular case, the defendant's domicile may well turn out to favour — except with regard to accessibility and familiarity — the plaintiff while the plaintiff's domicile favors the defendant.»[1086]

Indeed, «[t]he party that a given forum advantages depends upon the interaction of the facts of the case with that forum's conflictual, procedural, and substantive law.»[1087] Arthur T. von Mehren further also notes in another context that new technologies, such as e-mail or airplanes, have greatly increased the mobility of litigants. Along with sociological and economic developments that represent a globalising world, such changes have led some jurists to conclude that, as a matter of corrective justice, nowadays, plaintiffs are more likely to be in the right than defendants are. Therefore, they would revoke the premise on which the principle of *actor*

1083 Roth, IPRax 2013, 215, 219 (italics in the original).

1084 See Hess, JZ 2012, 189, 191; Garber, ÖJZ 2012, 108, 117 (partly critical). Contra: Thiede, GPR 2012, 219, 221; Thiede, ecolex 2012, 131, 132.

1085 Hess, in: Pocar/Viarengo/Villata, Recasting Brussels I, p 99.

1086 Von Mehren, Recueil des Cours 295, p 195 (emphases, fn omitted).

1087 Von Mehren, Recueil des Cours 295, p 196. See also *supra* Ch. V.C.II.4.a).

sequitur forum rei rests and principally require that the defendant go to the plaintiff's jurisdiction.[1088]

Finally, and perhaps even more importantly, a connecting factor in the form of *forum actoris* is not uncommon within the special rules of jurisdiction. In particular, jurisdiction in disputes concerning maintenance claims was decided by the drafters of the BC to be conferred on the maintenance creditor's forum under Art 5(2) of the BC for social and practical reasons.[1089] First, the creditor should not be required to bring a claim in a court that is competent for the defendant since, as Jan Kropholler and Jan von Hein explain, *inter alia* he is principally financially disadvantaged.[1090] Secondly, «the court for the place of domicile of the maintenance creditor is in the best position to know whether the creditor is in need and to determine the extent of such need.»[1091] Mindful of these considerations, the present author is of the opinion that similar reasons could perhaps also be valid for underlining the introduction of the concept of the victim's centre of interests. Regarding the second reason expressly mentioned by the ECJ in *eDate and Martinez* and discussed below, the potential adequateness of the first reason lies at the heart of the present succinct consideration; specifically, beyond the principle of sound administration of justice, it could also be argued that jurisdiction could be correctly allocated to the court for the place where the victim has his centre of interests because of his defenceless position. Viewed in this light, the victim, entitled to have free development of his personality in relation with other human beings,[1092] is disadvantaged because of his defenceless position in respect of the publisher, who the Internet empowers to create and distribute at a low cost injurious information unilaterally by simply tapping a button. AG Cruz Villalón appeared to describe the victim's position in a similar way in *eDate and Martinez*:

> «[T]he possible victims of publications which are harmful to personality rights are in a particularly vulnerable position when the medium is provided by the internet. The universal scope of the information contributes to the harm being potentially

1088 Von Mehren, FS Hein Kötz, p 78.

1089 Jenard Report, p 25; Kropholler/von Hein, EuZPR, p 189, para 54. On weaker parties, see *supra* Ch. III.B.II.4.

1090 Kropholler/von Hein, EuZPR, p 189, para 54.

1091 Jenard Report, p 25. See also Kropholler/von Hein, EuZPR, p 189, para 54.

1092 See *Von Hannover v. Germany* (no 59320/00), 50 (regarding the applicability of Art 8 of the ECHR).

more acute than that suffered, for example, by means of a conventional medium.»[1093]

Similarly, and possibly even more evidently, it is also observed in legal writing that «usually, persons targeted (by the yellow press) are in a weaker position than *vis-à-vis* the general media industry.»[1094] By contrast, Csongor István Nagy argues that while «the Brussels I Regulation does contain certain jurisdictional rules that are meant to protect the weaker party (consumers, employees, insured persons, policyholders); the victims of the violations of personality rights are not enumerated there.»[1095] Although it is undoubtedly so, this argument is less appealing in at least two respects. First, precedent shows that it is possible to reshape a special jurisdictional provision into a protective rule of jurisdiction. Specifically, the ground of jurisdiction on individual contracts of employment originally formed one segment of Art 5(1) of the BC, but it has been developed into a separate provision through the case law of the ECJ dating back to *Ivenel*, in which the position of the employees was recognised as being worthy of additional protection *vis-à-vis* the employers. However, it was years before legislative steps followed this judicial activism in Brussels I and in the 2007 LC.[1096] In addition, as was indicated in *supra* Ch. III.B.II.4, Brussels Ia, contrary to the other Brussels-Lugano instruments, somewhat broadens the scope of weaker parties listed by Csongor István Nagy. Indeed, it often provides the same treatment for the injured party as it guarantees for weaker parties. Bearing in mind these challenges, the present author would not absolutely refute the idea of the weaker party protection of victims who claim that their personality rights are violated.[1097] This is even though the time for this view has not yet arrived, since, by analogy, it could be argued that «[t]he transformation ... of the rules of special jurisdiction, aimed at facilitating sound administration of justice,

---

1093 AG in *eDate and Martinez*, 48 (fn omitted).

1094 Hess, CML Rev. 2012, 1075, 1090 (italics in the original, fn omitted). See also *supra* Ch. VI.A.II.2.c).

1095 Nagy, J. Priv. Int. L. 2012, 251, 271. For further reference arguing that Art 7(2) is not aimed to favour or protect the victim, see *supra* fn 529.

1096 Note that the 1989 Accession Convention to the BC already modified the wording of Art 5(1) of the BC in relation to individual contracts of employment. See also Art 5(1) of the 1988 LC.

1097 It is noteworthy that the targeting test is based on weaker party considerations in the field of consumer-friendly special rule of jurisdiction [see *Pammer and Hotel Alpenhof* in *supra* Ch. VI.A.II.2.a)]. Why, then, should *forum actoris* on the same considerations be criticised?

into rules of unilateral jurisdiction protecting the party deemed to be weaker would go beyond the balance of interests which the Community legislature has established in the law as it currently stands.»[1098] Indeed, as noted above and analysed below, due to the underlying principles of Art 7(2) set out in the Brussels-Lugano Regime, the ECJ exclusively referred to the principle of sound administration of justice as one of the two justifications for the introduction of the victim's centre of interests.

d) Justification no 1: sound administration of justice

In the light of the foregoing discussion, it becomes obvious that the ECJ justified the introduction of the concept of the victim's centre of interests by referring to the principle of sound administration of justice. It held:

> «Given that the impact which material placed online is liable to have on an individual's personality rights might best be assessed by the court of the place where the alleged victim has his centre of interests, the attribution of jurisdiction to that court corresponds to the objective of the sound administration of justice».[1099]

In the absence of any reasoning, the precise basis and correctness of this finding is somewhat unclear and gives rise to different scholarly positions. Dissenting opinions centred on the targeting test point out that the victim's centre of interests is not necessarily the most appropriate forum in which to decide upon the online violations of personality rights because certain other factors might establish a particularly closer connection with another state.[1100] In this context, Sandra Schmitz stresses that the concept «alone is not sufficient to establish a domestic connecting factor. Thus, this solution excludes jurisdiction where the victim has a reputation to defend but the information may not raise particular interest of the local readership for example because it is published in a language that is commonly used only by a small number of people in the territory of the court seised.»[1101] She finds it unfortunate that the concept does not consider that, due to issues of language or content, many websites may be oriented towards a more or less

1098 *Glaxosmithkline and Laboratoires Glaxosmithkline*, 32 (emphases omitted). See also AG in *Melzer*, fn 46.

1099 *eDate and Martinez*, 48.

1100 For arguments stating that *forum actoris* is not consistent with the principle of sound administration of justice, see e.g. AG 1994 in *Shevill*, 46; Huber, ZEuP 1996, 295, 309.

1101 Schmitz, Masaryk U. J.L. & Tech. 2012, 159, 170.

regional audience.[1102] Jan-Jaap Kuipers is of a similar opinion, which he demonstrates through the *Martinez and Martinez* case. In particular, he supposes that relatively few people read the report in France, since the disputed content dealing with the reunification of a famous Australian singer with a French person was published in the English language on a UK Internet page. Thus, in his opinion, the case was manifestly more closely connected with England than with France.[1103] These dissenting opinions might very well be true at a first glance. However, for at least three reasons, the present author respectfully disagrees with them, and consequently, supports the finding of the ECJ. First, as noted in *supra* Ch. VII.B.II.1.a)aa), the targeting test with its complex criteria has several drawbacks that render it inappropriate within Art 7(2). In addition, the ECJ appeared to put great emphasis not on the content, but on the person concerned therein:

> «[T]he publisher of harmful content is … in a position to know the centres of interests of the *persons who are the subject of that content*.»[1104]

The ECJ, in the present author's view, correctly focused on the holder of the personality rights and not on the newsworthiness of the online content in a particular state or for a particular audience in that state as the targeting test principally does. It follows from this targeting requirement *in personam* that the concept of the victim's centre of interests aims to establish the closest ties between the holder of the personality right and the forum. In Wulf-Henning Roth's words:

> «Mit dem „Mittelpunkt der Interessen" einer Person wird vom Gerichtshof nicht etwa ein neuer Erfolgsort geschaffen, sondern allein aus den vielen Erfolgsorten, an denen der – nicht auf Individualkommunikation gerichtete – Internetinhalt zugänglich ist ... ein einzelner qualifizierter Erfolgsort bestimmt, der für die Geltendmachung des *Gesamt*schadens im Hinblick auf die Durchführung des Verfahrens wegen seiner Verbundenheit mit dem potentiellen Opfer als besonders geeignet erscheint.»[1105]

Thirdly, and closely related to the preceding discussion, the injurious content is not only an attack on the person concerned and on his personality

1102 Schmitz, Masaryk U. J.L. & Tech. 2012, 159, 175.
1103 Kuipers, CML Rev. 2012, 1211, 1221.
1104 *eDate and Martinez*, 50 (emphases omitted; author's italics). Cf. Hess, CML Rev. 2012, 1075, 1090 cited in *supra* Ch. VI.A.II.2.c) and Ch. VII.B.II.1.c)aa); Buchner in *supra* Ch. VI.B.III. Critically on this: Heinze, EuZW 2011, 947, 949-950 and basically contra of this critique: Picht, GRUR Int. 2013, 19, 22.
1105 Roth, IPRax 2013, 215, 220 (italics in the original; emphases, fn omitted).

rights, but is also an attack on his social position, which is predominantly located in the Brussels-Lugano State in which the place of his centre of interests is based. Two consequences, as adjunct points, of this finding ought to be noted. First, the victim feels the harm the most in his habitual social environment[1106] because, as Peter Picht notes, the injurious content has an effect on his most important living environment where friends and acquaintances look at him askance, or his professional contacts are negatively affected:

> «Er *[der gewöhnliche Aufenthalt]* liegt also dort, wo der Verletzte durch sein soziales Umfeld verankert ist. Gerade an diesem Ort wird aber ein persönlichkeitsrechtsverletzender Internetinhalt den Verletzten am stärksten beeinträchtigen, weil er sich dort auf sein wichtigstes Lebensumfeld auswirkt und von seiner Umgebung auf den Verletzten zurückgeworfen wird – mag es der Verletzte verschmerzen können, wenn sich wegen einer erfundenen Skandalmeldung Passanten in seinem Urlaubsland nach ihm umdrehen, so trifft es ihn ungleich härter, wenn er von Freunden und Bekannten in seiner Heimat scheel angesehen wird oder berufliche Verbindungen leiden.»[1107]

Secondly, the court of the place where the alleged victim has his centre of interests seems to be the best placed to assess the impact which material placed online is liable to have on the aggrieved person's personality right and social position. It is familiar with the local conditions and close to all relevant evidence that is inseparable from the aggrieved person and from his social environment.[1108]

Taking all these findings into account, the justification of the ECJ seems reasonable. The concept of the victim's centre of interests establishes the closest ties between the personality right, its holder, and the forum, and consequently, with the focal point of the dispute, i.e., the alleged

---

1106 Garber, ÖJZ 2012, 108, 117. Cf. Kubis and Buchner in *supra* Ch. VI.B.I and III; Mankowski, EWiR 2011, 743, 744. This finding is reminiscent of the main harm approach of Huet as referred to in AG 1994 in *Shevill*, 82.

1107 Picht, GRUR Int. 2013, 19, 22 (italics in square brackets added). Cf. localising injury to reputation in *supra* Ch. V.B.II.2. In the present author's opinion, this argument has its stand irrespective of the fact that a hobby blogger, who appears online without the use of any identity masks (on this, see *supra* Ch. II.B.I.2), is known in another state where people read his blog the most. His virtual reputation does not establish a profound contact with the society of those Internet users (cf. regarding celebrities, see Leonhard in *supra* Ch. VI.B.II). Furthermore, the publisher might be overburdened, since it can normally not foresee where the hobby blogger's posts are read the most, i.e., the number of page views might only be known by the blogger [cf. vicious circle in *supra* Ch. VII.B.II.1.a)bb)].

1108 Cf. Leonhard in *supra* Ch. VI.B.II.

(threatened) violation of his personality right and the possible impacts on that right and on the holder's social relationship.

e) Justification no 2: predictability

In addition to the principle of sound administration of justice, another justification for introducing the concept of the victim's centre of interests, so the ECJ held, lies in its predictable nature. In particular, this concept enables the plaintiff easily to identify the court in which he may sue and the defendant reasonably to foresee in which court he may be sued.[1109] Although this justification has been widely accepted in legal writing and practice,[1110] two discrete challenges punch a hole in it. While one of them focuses on the concept of the victim's centre of interests, the other challenges the time of causation.[1111]

1109 *eDate and Martinez*, 50.

1110 See e.g. *Wintersteiger*, 23; Spindler, AfP 2012, 114, 121; Wittwer/Fussenegger, ZEuP 2013, 812, 824; Garber, ÖJZ 2012, 108, 117 (in most of the cases); Gillies, ICLQ 2012, 1007, 1016. Contra (regarding *forum actoris*): AG in *Kronhofer*, 50. For predictability in relation to libel tourism, see *infra* Ch. VII.C.I.2.b).

1111 Note that Kuipers, CML Rev. 2012, 1211, 1221 questions the foreseeable nature of the concept from two further perspectives: (1) regarding international celebrities, whose centres of interests are not always determinable, and (2) cases, such as *Martinez and Martinez*, which involve more than one victim, since then the concept could «lead to the competence of different courts, depending upon which person initiates the proceedings.» The present author, however, respectfully disagrees with these perspectives. For the first one, see Leonhard's view in *supra* Ch. VI.B.II. Considering the second perspective, two observations can respectfully be put forward. First, it could always be argued against the concept of damage that a tort involving more than one victim could multiply the number of jurisdictionally relevant places. This would, however, be even further exacerbated by the lack of a centralised place of the damage, since otherwise, not only the number of the victims, but also the mosaic approach would be a multiplication factor of the relevant courts. It would follow that two victims could initiate in sum 56 proceedings in the Member States. Secondly, it is remarkable that the victim's side is criticised without mentioning cases involving more than one perpetrator. Finally, as a kind of improvement of the current rule, the present author would be inclined to recommend a proposal that enables one of the victims to initiate proceedings in the court of the Brussels-Lugano State in which any of the victims' centre of interests is based. This proposal would serve procedural economy similar to Art 8(1).

It is often observed in legal writing that the exact meaning of the concept of the victim's centre of interests remains uncertain, and consequently, it requires further specification.[1112] Such uncertainty is less evident for the determination of the concept of habitual residence, since, as noted in *supra* Ch. III.C.I.1, its common understanding can be derived from the *acquis communautaire*.[1113] Accordingly, by determining the place where a person's professional and/or personal-familial centre of interests is situated, the habitual residence refers to a state with which he has the closest bonds.[1114] By contrast, in relation to the second aspect of the victim's centre of interests Andrew Dickinson notes:

> «It is, however, extremely difficult to reconcile this confident statement *[laid down in the aforementioned paragraph 50]* with the Court's earlier recognition that "a person may also have the centre of his interests in a Member State in which he does not habitually reside, in so far as other factors, such as the pursuit of a professional activity, may establish the existence of a particularly close link with that State" (para. 49). If predictability were the objective, it is hard to see how the Court could have done more to remove it.»[1115]

By agreeing with Andrew Dickinson's view, the present author is of the opinion that this second aspect represents special problems, which raise serious questions about the predictable and foreseeable character of the concept of the victim's centre of interests. First, she argues that it is rather difficult to comprehend why the ECJ simply referred to other factors, which may establish the existence of a particularly close link with the fo-

1112 See e.g. Hess, JZ 2012, 189, 191-192; Mikola, JeMa 2011, 14, 18.

1113 See also Hess, JZ 2012, 189, 192.

1114 On this, see *supra* Ch. III.C.I.1. By virtue of *eDate and Martinez*, the plaintiff's centre of interests was held without difficulty: (1) in Germany by the *BGH* in case *eDate Advertising* VI ZR 217/08a (8.5.2012), *BGH* (GRUR 2012, 850) by holding (para 18, references omitted): «Der Mittelpunkt der Interessen des Klägers befand und befindet sich in Deutschland. Hier hat er seinen gewöhnlichen Aufenthalt und Lebensmittelpunkt. Hier wohnt er und ist sozial und familiär eingebunden ... . Hier wirkt sich eine Verletzung seines Achtungsanspruchs aus.» (2) in France by *TGI Nanterre*, 1ère ch. Ord. de mise en état (11.10.2012) in case *Marion C. / Rossel & Compagnie* dealing *inter alia* with violation of the right to image by ruling that the plaintiff «être contestée être née en France, y résider avec sa famille et y exercer son activité professionnelle. Le centre de ses intérêts est donc situé en France.» (3) in Hungary by the *Debreceni Ítélőtábla* in case Gf. I. 30 741/3012/3 (BDT 2013.3.50), and (4) in Greece by the *Court of Appeal of Dodecanese* [Nr. 220/2013, unreported] as referred to in Anthimos, Online defamation, 2014.

1115 Dickinson, By Royal Appointment, 2012 (italics in square brackets added).

rum. Rather, this second open-textured aspect should be armed with the same features that arm the concept of habitual residence, i.e., it should establish the closest ties between the holder of the personality right, the forum, and the dispute. Otherwise, the two aspects pull the concept of the victim's centre of interests in different directions with the result that it loses its inherent balance and coherency. In this respect, Peter Picht similarly suggests:

> «Der EuGH hat Raum dafür gelassen, dass statt dem gewöhnlichen Aufenthalt andere Orte als Interessenmittelpunkt bestimmt werden. In der Literatur wird zu Recht darauf hingewiesen, dass nunmehr ein Prozess vonnöten ist, in dem Wissenschaft und Rechtspraxis das Wo und Wann solcher abweichender Interessenmittelpunkte ausformen. Im Hinblick auf das soeben Gesagte sollte bei diesem Prozess darauf geachtet werden, dass sich nur alternative Interessenmittelpunkte etablieren, die an Überzeugungskraft und Vorhersehbarkeit dem gewöhnlichen Aufenthalt gleichkommen.»[1116]

Furthermore, it also remains unclear to the present author why the ECJ chose to locate it exemplarily in the state of the pursuit of a professional activity rather than the principal state of the pursuit of a professional activity. It would appear from its sole meaning that if the victim undertakes more than one professional activity or one such activity in more than one state – which is admittedly easy through the Internet – all of them are relevant for jurisdictional purposes, providing that each activity establishes a particularly close connection with the state where it is pursued. However, the concept of the victim's centre of interests designates only a single state, since, as mentioned in *supra* Ch. VII.B.II.1.c), only one centre of interests exists. Secondly, and closely related to this and in particular to the common understanding of the concept of habitual residence under the *acquis communautaire*, it appears unnecessarily obtuse a connection to focus upon the pursuit of a professional activity considering that the concept of habitual residence covers the principal place of the pursuit of a professional activity.[1117] Thirdly, it remains unclear what kind of activity the term 'professional activity' encompasses, since professional activity is, in principle, regarded as being different from business activity in EU PIL instruments. For example, by virtue of Art 23(2) of Rome II, the term 'business activity' encompasses all activities exercised as business activities or liberal professions in a self-employed capacity (i.e., «self-employed busi-

1116 Picht, GRUR Int. 2013, 19, 22-23 (fn omitted; regarding the above-mentioned remarks that he mentions, see *ibid.*, pp 22-23).

1117 On this, see *supra* Ch. III.C.I.1, and especially, see *supra* fn 409.

nesspersons and traders»[1118]), thereby excluding employment activities from its scope.[1119] It follows that the concept of professional activity as different from that of business activity supposedly refers to the occupational activity pursued due to an individual contract of employment. So far so good. This train of thought, however, is seriously disputable on the basis of the two official procedural language versions of *eDate and Martinez*, namely, the German and the French versions, since they both refer to the term 'business activity' ('berufliche Tätigkeit'/'activité professionnelle'). Viewed in this light, the concept is identical to the one just mentioned within Rome II; consequently, it suggests referring to economic activities exercised as liberal professions or business activities pursued in a self-employed capacity. However, this latter understanding of the concept has two shortcomings. First, it disregards the victim's private and social spheres, which are crucial for determining his non-pecuniary harm caused or threatened to be caused by a (potential) violation.[1120] Secondly, and consequently, it is supposed that at the place where the victim pursues a business activity he suffers, similar to legal persons as outlined in *infra* Ch. VII.D.II.2, material rather than non-material loss. Finally, this briefly demonstrated definitional uncertainty is coupled with an adjunct question, that is: How should the professional activity be localised? Michael Slonina notes that this should be answered in the course of a further request for a preliminary ruling:

> «Gerade die im Ausgangsfall zu Grunde liegenden Fälle von Persönlichkeitsverletzungen zulasten bekannter Künstler oder anderer Prominenter zeigen jedoch, wie schwierig es sein kann, einen beruflichen Mittelpunkt der Interessen zu verorten, zumal Art 5 Nr 3 EuGVVO neben der internationalen auch die örtliche Zuständigkeit erfasst. Hier sind bereits künftige Vorlagefragen an den EuGH vorprogrammiert: Wo etwa soll die Zuständigkeit am beruflich begründeten Mittelpunkt der Interessen eines berühmten Sängers liegen: am Sitz seiner Agentur/seines Tonträgerunternehmens oder am häufigsten Auftrittsort?»[1121]

1118 See Altenkirch, in: Huber, Rome II Regulation, p 415, para 10.

1119 See Baetge, in: Calliess, Rome Regulations, p 610, para 18. Cf. Commission Document COM(2003) 427 final, p 27.

1120 On this, see also Hess, JZ 2012, 189, 191-192. Cf. Bogdan, YbPIL 2011, 483, 486 states that besides economic factors, «the determination of the centre of interests in personality infringement cases should reasonably also take into account non-economic factors, such as the habitual residence of the victim's relatives and close friends.»

1121 Slonina, ÖJZ 2012, 61, 66. He also questions the degree of reputation that is required to establish jurisdiction there (on this, cf. Roth, IPRax 2013, 215, 221). In

Beyond the aforementioned special problems in respect of the second aspect of the concept of the victim's centre of interests, it is also seriously questionable whether the time of causation, namely, the time of uploading of the content,[1122] serves the predictable and foreseeable nature of this connecting factor. Although it is very true that at the time of uploading, the defendant can foresee the victim's centre of interests, there are at least three reasons why this finding may be replete with greater than usual complications for the aggrieved person, who relocates his centre of interests. First, concerning prospective violations, the real time at which the online content is or will be uploaded remains unpredictable for him. In addition, as Aron Mefford notes, «documents published on the Net do not remain fixed and therefore original, but adapt and evolve through constant modification and addition. The publication date is therefore never a fixed time because the Internet offers the unique ability to modify endlessly.»[1123] This notice further poses the question of whether the time when the initial content placed online or when it is updated determines the time of uploading, providing that they are both noticeable for the victim. This latter condition regarding the noticeability on the site of the victim bears considerable importance, since the time of uploading is not always automatically displayed online. Indeed, it could very well be possible that the time is hidden from Internet users or it indicates a time other than when it was originally uploaded.[1124] In cases when the time of uploading is hidden or there is a serious doubt that the time is displayed is not the real time, the victim who moved his centre of interests even once – which is eased by the fundamental freedoms in the internal market – is required to find out the real time of uploading. This could overburden him and put him in a similar vicious circle as was briefly described in *supra* Ch.

the present author's opinion, the concept of an employee's habitual working place laid down in Art 21(1)(b)(i) would be a good starting point for localising an individual's occupational activity. For business activity, see principally the market place or country of protection tests as mentioned in *infra* Ch. VII.D.II.2.

1122 *eDate and Martinez*, 50. Regarding the time of causation, see also *supra* Ch. IV.B.III.

1123 Mefford, Ind. J. Global Legal Stud. 1997-1998, 211, 220 (fns omitted).

1124 E.g. the website of a newspaper (on file with author) indicated as the date of uploading 00:00 o'clock on 24.10.2014 when it was visited at 9:39 pm on 23.10.2014. Cf. Facebook: Changing the date of a story on one's timeline <https://www.facebook.com/help/331944693487215/>; Joomla!: Remover of creation date, update <http://docs.joomla.org/Removing_author_name,_creation_date_or_update_date_from_an_article>.

VII.B.II.1.a)bb). Would this result ensure justice? As an alternative solution, would it perhaps not be better to require that the time of the initiation of the proceedings be used? Mindful of the above-described complications, the present author is sympathetic towards this alternative solution,[1125] providing that it would be foreseeable to the publisher.[1126]

2. Revision no 2: the concept of accessibility

The ECJ introduced the second aspect of the concept of the place of the damage by holding that:

> «[T]he criterion of the place where the damage occurred, derived from *Shevill and Others*, confers jurisdiction on courts in each Member State in the territory of which content placed online is or has been accessible. Those courts have jurisdiction only in respect of the damage caused in the territory of the Member State of the court seised.»[1127]

It should be abundantly clear from the pure wording of this ruling that the ECJ simply confirmed the concept of distribution with all its features[1128] in the context of online violations of personality rights in the form of the concept of accessibility, a concept that was consistently refused in legal theory and practice.[1129] Admittedly, the features of these criteria overlap

---

1125 Cf. As Kropholler/von Hein, EuZPR, p 293, para 4 note, in accordance with Art 11(2) of Brussels I the injured party is enabled to bring an action directly against the insurer within Art 9(1)(b) of Brussels I at the place where the plaintiff is domiciled. That place must exist at the time of the commencement of the proceedings («Klageerhebung») and not at the time of injury («Zeitpunkt der Schädigung»).

1126 If the victim moved his centre of interests to another place (this could be important in states where the first instance jurisdiction is scattered throughout the state) or to another Brussels-Lugano State before the initiation of the proceedings with the intention of settling therein, and this was not foreseeable to the publisher, then, in the opinion of the present author, the court of the last centre of interests should determine the jurisdictionally relevant place of centre of interests.

1127 *eDate and Martinez*, 51 (italics in the original).

1128 See *supra* Ch. V.B.II (distribution, injury to reputation; the possible requirement that the victim be known).

1129 These refusals were announced in the context of violations of rights other than personality rights, such as AG in *Wintersteiger*, 22-23; *Pammer and Hotel Alpenhof*, 69-74; *L'Oréal*, 64; Recital 24 of Rome I [this statement was a reply to Recital 13 of Commission Document COM(1999) 348 final, which proposed the concept of accessibility of certain websites for basis of jurisdiction in consumer issues].

as far as the mosaic approach dealt with below is concerned. However, having in mind that the concept of the victim's centre of interests is regarded as a «Bündelungsgerichtsstand»,[1130] it is supposed that the concept of accessibility shares the features of the victim's centre of interests criterion as described in *supra* Ch. VII.B.II.1, apart from the extent of jurisdiction that it confers on particular courts. Accordingly, because of the difficulties in giving effect to the intention of the publisher and in quantifying page views, it is presumed that if the disputed content is accessible in a Brussels-Lugano State, it automatically has a negative impact on the personality right and on its holder's social environment. Furthermore, the jurisdiction of the courts of the Brussels-Lugano States in which the disputed content is or has been accessible depends neither on potential injury to reputation nor on the requirement that the victim be known in the states in which the courts sit. Rather, it hinges on the potential injury to personality rights without the requirement that the victim be known in those states.[1131]

Conclusion and summary

The ECJ adapted the second *Shevill*-approach to online (potential) violations by doubling the jurisdictionally relevant places under the concept of damage. Although the criteria of accessibility and centre of the victim's interests share common features, their differences are significant and lead to tension under the concept of damage. As an in-depth review of the former criterion is conducted below, mindful of the preceding information, the following can be observed regarding the latter criterion. The concept of the victim's centre of interests is understood as a single place within a Brussels-Lugano State where the victim's professional and/or personal-familial centre of interests is located. Therefore, the second aspect of this concept, which refers to the state in which the victim pursues his professional activity, is too vague and deceptive. Furthermore, the time of causation, namely, the time when the disputed content is uploaded, is unsuitable in the light of the constantly changing and changeable nature of

1130 Heinze, EuZW 2011, 947, 950. On this, see also *supra* Ch. VII.B.II.1 and *supra* fn 1009.

1131 See also Garber, ÖJZ 2012, 108, 117-118. Contra (reputation is required): AG in *eDate and Martinez*, 51; Roth, IPRax 2013, 215, fn 40; Kuipers, CML Rev. 2012, 1211, 1218.

the Internet. With these pitfalls in mind, the present author is inclined to the view that a most plausible interpretation of the concept of the victim's centre of interests as the place of the damage is to regard it as the place of the victim's habitual residence,[1132] which should be established at the time of the initiation of the proceedings.

C. The extent of jurisdiction

The connecting factors in *eDate and Martinez* were characterised as being confirmations and revisions of the *Shevill*-approaches. This dichotomy is also true for the extent of jurisdiction. In particular, the ECJ confirmed the unlimited and limited extent of jurisdiction of the courts of the Brussels-Lugano State in which the publisher's establishment is located and the content is or has been accessible. A partial revision took place for the concept of damage by lifting the mosaic approach on the extent of the jurisdiction of the court of the Brussels-Lugano State in which the victim's centre of interests is based.[1133] Thus, this concept, equivalent to the concept of the publisher's establishment, confers an unlimited extent of jurisdiction.

These different extents pose questions and present special problems in respect of the Internet and injunctive reliefs granted to prevent violations. However, before moving into a discussion of these issues, one common feature of allocating jurisdiction ought to be observed. Whilst the sole wording of the concept of causal event in *Shevill* entitles the plaintiff to bring an action «before the courts of the Contracting State *of the place* where the publisher of the defamatory publication is established»,[1134] in *eDate and Martinez*, the ECJ referred only to «the courts of the Member State in which» one of the jurisdictionally relevant factual elements of the violation of a personality right is occurred.[1135] This formulation suggests that the *eDate and Martinez*-approaches allocate solely international jurisdiction regardless of the fact that special rules of jurisdiction also desig-

1132 For similar proposals, see *supra* Ch. VI.A.II.3.

1133 See *eDate and Martinez*, 52. Cf. Roth's view as quoted in *supra* Ch. VII.B.II.1.c)aa).

1134 *Shevill*, 33 (author's italics).

1135 See *eDate and Martinez*, 52. For similar observation regarding the second aspect of the victim's centre of interests in para 49 of *eDate and Martinez*, see Leible, LMK 2012, 329468.

nate venue.[1136] To resolve this uncertainty, it seems reasonable to suppose that the two connecting factors confer an unlimited extent of jurisdiction on the courts for the place where the publisher's establishment and the victim's centre of interests are based,[1137] while for the mosaic approach, the findings put forward in *supra* Ch. V.C.II.2 shall be applicable.

I. Observations complementary to the notes on the mosaic approach

The following observations on the suitability of the mosaic approach for the Internet and for preventive measures in the form of injunctions aim to complement the problematic issues noted in *supra* Ch. V.C regarding the mosaic approach *vis-à-vis* offline violations of personality rights.

1. Practicability

a) Assessment of online violations of personality rights committed

Supra Ch. V.C.I.1 was highly critical of the question of whether the cornerstone elements of the dispute that must be assessed in order to hold the publisher liable for the online content, namely, the act of distribution, liability, and the right to reputation, can be split territorially between the different mosaic jurisdictions. Those findings ought hereby to be supplemented and extended. First, the act of distribution in the context of the Internet can safely be regarded as a single and uniform act, since the publisher taps only once the 'send' button to upload the material to the Internet. Thus, it is supposed that the publisher is held liable for the same content placed online by this single act in each mosaic jurisdiction. Secondly, since *Martinez and Martinez* was concerned with an invasion of privacy, it is necessary to underline that similar to the right to reputation, the right to privacy is regarded as a single ideal right that is enjoyed by and inseparably attached to its right holder.[1138] Thus, the assumption that it can be fragmented along geographical boundaries is erroneous.

1136 See *supra* Intr. to Ch. III.D.II and *supra* Intr. to Ch. IV.
1137 Cf. *eDate and Martinez*, 49 considers the place of the victim's habitual residence.
1138 On this, see *supra* Ch. I.; *supra* Ch. V.C.I.1 and *supra* Ch. VII.C.I.1.a).

b) Measures for (potential) violations of personality rights

As noted in *supra* Ch. V.C.I.2, monetary compensation awarded for the non-pecuniary harm caused by the violation of a personality right is conditional upon the determination of the extent of that harm. Whilst this determination was seriously doubted in disputes concerning offline violations, it is exacerbated in the online context. This is so because, as the ECJ held, «it is not always possible, on a technical level, to quantify that distribution with certainty and accuracy in relation to a particular Member State or, therefore, to assess the damage caused exclusively within that Member State.»[1139]

While monetary compensation is awardable for the harm already caused, an injunction granted by the court in a mosaic jurisdiction aims to prevent a behaviour regarded as wrongful. It follows that if Mr X had been granted this measure in *eDate Advertising*,[1140] the defendant Austrian company would have been obliged to enforce it, as the plaintiff requested it, with the application throughout the territory of Germany. Mindful of the fact, as Michael Bogdan points out, that «there is at present no reliable software making it simple, practical and economically feasible to divide Cyberspace along national boundaries»,[1141] it is highly questionable whether the defendant would have been able to enforce the injunction accordingly. Rather, as is also noted in legal theory, the enforcement of injunctions granted by courts in mosaic jurisdictions may principally amount to the total, that is, Brussels-Lugano States-wide and worldwide, prohibition of the distribution of the content.[1142] In turn, it implies the enforcement of the standard of protection of the forum state over other states often at the expense of the freedom of expression and of the press.[1143]

1139 *eDate and Martinez*, 46. Cf. Slonina, ÖJZ 2012, 61, 63; Wittwer/Müller, Eur. L. Rptr. 2012, 95, 97; Garber, ÖJZ 2012, 108, 117; Spindler, AfP 2012, 114, 117.

1140 See case *eDate Advertising* VI ZR 217/08a (8.5.2012), *BGH* (GRUR 2012, 850), 33 ff.

1141 Bogdan, Masaryk U. J.L. & Tech. 2011, 1, 5. Cf. *supra* Ch. II, especially *supra* Ch. II.B.I.2.

1142 See Bogdan, Masaryk U. J.L. & Tech. 2011, 1, 5; Thiede, ecolex 2012, 131, 133. See also Rüßmann, K&R 1998, 422, 427 (competition law). On the effectiveness of blocking measures, cf. *supra* Ch. VI.A.II.1.c) and *supra* Ch. VII.B.II.1.a)cc).

1143 See Roth, IPRax 2013, 215, 223. Cf. Hartley, L.Q.R. 2012, 197, 201. On the basis of different considerations outlined by Roth, IPRax 2013, 215, 223-224, at least for injunction and removal claims, he appears to prefer to limit the place of

2. Compatibility with the governing objectives and underlying principles

a) Further depriving the twin criteria of their inherent natures

By introducing the accessibility test, the ECJ further deprived the twin criteria of their inherent natures, and thus, created more tension between the approaches adopted under the concept of harmful event for localising online (potential) violations of personality rights than is described in *supra* Ch. V.C.II.3 in respect of offline violations.

Considering the principles of sound administration of justice, proximity, and predictability, on which the rules of special jurisdiction hinge, the following can be ascertained. It appears from *eDate and Martinez* that either these principles became customary, and thus, meaningless means of justification for interpreting the concept of harmful event, or they were applied arbitrarily. Although it is admittedly true that these principles guarantee a flexible interpretation of the concept of harmful event to tailor it to the different nature of tortious acts, the question may arise of whether they are suitable for justifying all three connecting factors of *eDate and Martinez*.[1144] Moreover, should they be referred to four times in a row in order to reach the concept of accessibility?[1145] Even if this question should be answered in the affirmative, an adjunct question is whether this concept is consistent with those principles. To put it differently, does the concept of accessibility as one part of the concept of damage, besides the concept of the victim's centre of interests within the harmful event criterion, meet the requirements of proximity, sound administration of justice, and predictability? The answer is supposedly in the negative. First, it does not set up a particularly close territorial link with the forum.[1146] Rather, it creates an automatic and unqualified link with all Brussels-Lugano States on an equal footing, since the disputed content with a universal nature is or has

---

the damage by virtue of different criteria, such as the degree of reputation, the layout, and the language of the website.

1144 For express or implicit reference to the principle of sound administration of justice, see e.g. *eDate and Martinez*, 41, 44, 48, 51.

1145 I.e., (1) Recital 16 for opening a special rule of jurisdiction; (2) *Bier* for introducing the twin criteria (see *supra* Ch. IV.B.I); (3) *Shevill* for introducing the distribution test (see *supra* Ch. V.C.II.3); (4) *eDate and Martinez* for justifying the concept of accessibility (see *supra* fn 1144).

1146 See also Garber, ÖJZ 2012, 108, 112.

been available in all of them.[1147] Secondly, it does not facilitate predictability, since the publisher cannot foresee in which particular court it can be sued for an alleged violation of personality rights.[1148] Alternatively, does it perhaps facilitate predictability in an abnormal sense by ensuring that the publisher can predict that it can principally be sued in all Brussels-Lugano States?[1149]

Furthermore, it is rather difficult to comprehend why the ECJ upheld the concept of accessibility besides the criterion of the victim's centre of interests under the concept of damage.[1150] Based on their different features, such as the extent of jurisdiction they confer and their personal scope of application (i.e., whether third country plaintiff can avail himself of them), these connecting factors pull the concept of damage in different directions.

b) Libel tourism eased but to a certain extent minimised

The aforementioned automatic link that the concept of accessibility establishes principally with all Brussels-Lugano States where the victim's personality rights are potentially violated admittedly eases the problem of libel tourism. However, the ECJ appears to a certain extent to minimise this tactical incentive of the victim from two aspects: a jurisdictional and a substantive legal aspect.

The combination of the two connecting factors under the place of the damage criterion has divided the views expressed in legal writing on libel tourism. Many scholars suggest that the victim will initiate proceedings in the court of the place where his centre of interests is located, rather than in the Brussels-Lugano State in which the content is or has been accessible for the local harm occurred there. In short, the victim's centre of interests

---

1147 See also Nagy, J. Priv. Int. L. 2012, 251, 269; AG in *eDate and Martinez*, 51, 56. On the requirement that the victim be known, see *supra* Ch. VII.B.II.2.

1148 See also Garber, ÖJZ 2012, 108, 112; Nagy, J. Priv. Int. L. 2012, 251, 270; AG in *eDate and Martinez*, 51. Note that this unpredictability is also inconsistent with Recital 16, which expressly underlines the need for legal certainty and foreseeability in violations of personality rights (on this, see *supra* Ch. III.B.II.1). Cf. *Besix* (lack of territorial limitation of the obligation not to do something) as referred to in *supra* Ch. III.B.I.3; *supra* Ch. VI.B.IV and *supra* fn 956.

1149 See Nagy, J. Priv. Int. L. 2012, 251, 270.

1150 Cf. von Hinden, ZEuP 2012, 940, 950. Contra: Slonina, ÖJZ 2012, 61, 63-64 (listing advantages of the double places of the damage).

approach is more appealing, and consequently, it will mitigate libel tourism.[1151] This suggestion may very well be true.[1152] However, for at least one reason, the importance of this newly introduced connecting factor should not be overstated. In particular, the differing scholarly positions place great emphasis on the importance of the victims' tactical motives to threaten publishers with foreign proceedings and thus with potential procedural costs. Mindful of this finding, they are of the opinion that the concept of accessibility gives rise to libel tourism.[1153] The present author is convinced by the validity of both views for online violations already committed. Therefore, she is in favour of a middle-ground solution, which is, in her opinion, pointed out by Peter Arnt Nielsen as follows:

> «[B]y maintaining that courts of other Member States only have jurisdiction over the "local" damage, the CJEU minimises the incentives to sue in those states. However, for libel tourism to have been completely eliminated, the CJEU ought to have eradicated the possibility to sue in those states.»[1154]

Considering potential violations, she is of the opinion that the mitigating effect of the concept of the victim's centre of interests is principally irrelevant. As noted in *supra* Ch. VII.C.I.1.b), enforcement of an injunction that is granted in a mosaic jurisdiction principally produces a global prohibition. It follows that the victim may shop freely to select the mosaic jurisdiction that guarantees the largest possible extent of protection of his personality rights.

As far as the substantive legal aspect is concerned, the following can be indicated. In *eDate and Martinez*, the ECJ dealt with the character of Art 3(1) and Art 3(2) of Dir. 2000/31/EC (OJ 2000 L 178/1) on e-commerce to answer the third question referred for a preliminary ruling in *eDate Advertising*. The *BGH* essentially asked whether such provisions have the character of a conflict of laws rule or whether they operate as a corrective to the law declared to be applicable pursuant to the national conflict of laws rules. At the outset, it ought to be noted that Art 3 contributes to the proper functioning of the internal market by ensuring the free movement

1151 On this, see e.g. Hess, JZ 2012, 189, 191; Schnichels/Stege, EuZW 2012, 812, 814.

1152 For national cases in which the concept of the victim's centre of interests was a suitable basis of jurisdiction, see *supra* fn 1114.

1153 On this, see e.g. Kuipers, CML Rev. 2012, 1211, 1222; Reymond, YbPIL 2011, 493, 502-503; Wittwer/Müller, Eur. L. Rptr. 2012, 95, 97; Garber, ÖJZ 2012, 108, 117. Cf. AG in *eDate and Martinez*, 56.

1154 Nielsen, J. Priv. Int. L. 2013, 269, 278-279 (fn omitted).

of information society services between the Member States. In particular, the ECJ held that the first paragraph «principally imposes on Member States the obligation to ensure that the information society services provided by a service provider established on their territory comply with the national provisions applicable in the Member States in question which fall within the coordinated field. The imposition of such an obligation is not in the nature of a conflict-of-laws rule designed to resolve a specific conflict between several laws which may be applicable.»[1155] The second paragraph, so the ECJ went on to rule, «prohibits Member States from restricting, for reasons falling within the coordinated field, the freedom to provide information society services from another Member State.»[1156] It «does not require transposition in the form of a specific conflict-of-laws rule.»[1157] Consequently, the forum state may apply its own rules of PIL to settle the conflict of laws.[1158] By ruling in this way, the ECJ put an end to the scholarly discourse on this issue or as Christian Kohler, Sibylle Seyr and Jean-Christophe Puffer-Mariette point out:

> «Diese Entscheidung führt die Diskussion über die Struktur des Herkunftslandprinzips auf ein handhabbares Maß zurück. Der kollisionsrechtlichen Überhöhung des Prinzips wird eine Absage erteilt, Art.3 der Richtlinie 2000/31 wird entmystifiziert.»[1159]

Rather, the ECJ appeared to hold that those provisions operate as a corrective to the law declared to be applicable pursuant to the national conflict of laws rules:

> «[I]n relation to the coordinated field, Member States must ensure that, subject to the derogations authorised in accordance with the conditions set out in Article 3(4) of the Directive, the provider of an electronic commerce service is not made subject to stricter requirements than those provided for by the substantive law applicable in the Member State in which that service provider is established.»[1160]

1155 *eDate and Martinez*, 61. On the coordinated fields, see Art 2(h) of Dir. 2000/31/EC (OJ 2000 L 178/1).

1156 *eDate and Martinez*, 62.

1157 *eDate and Martinez*, 63. Cf. Recital 23 and Art 1(4) of Dir. 2000/31/EC (OJ 2000 L 178/1).

1158 See also Kuipers, CML Rev. 2012, 1211, 1231.

1159 Kohler/Seyr/Puffer-Mariette, ZEuP 2013, 323, 330.

1160 *eDate and Martinez*, 68. It follows that it applies neither to service providers established in one of the Lugano States, nor service providers falling outside of the scope of Dir. 2000/31/EC (OJ 2000 L 178/1), such as printed media (see also Nagy, J. Priv. Int. L. 2012, 251, 292-293). For questioning the meaning of the term 'service provider', see Spindler, AfP 2012, 114, 120. For specifying the

It follows that, as the above-quoted scholars explain, there is a new favourability principle, a so-called «Günstigkeitsprinzip *in favorem offerentis*».[1161] Account shall not be taken of the substantive law designated by the conflict of laws rules of the forum state, which are less favourable to the service provider than is the substantive law of the state in which the service provider is established.[1162] As is clear from the judgment, substantive law requirements cover private law issues, unless they are explicitly excluded.[1163] Moreover, in *Papasavvas*, the ECJ held that Dir. 2000/31/EC (OJ 2000 L 178/1) «does not preclude a Member State from adopting rules of civil liability for defamation, applicable to information society service providers established in its territory.»[1164] Without straying into a detailed discussion of the criticisms of the *eDate and Martinez* ruling, and solely supposing (1) that the reference to the substantive law requirement in the aforementioned quotation of *eDate and Martinez* also encompasses rules of civil liability for defamation and, in general, for violations of personality rights,[1165] and (2) that the application of the rules on personality rights of the state other than the one in which the service provider is established cannot be justified under the concept of public policy and the protection of «human dignity concerning individual persons» listed in Art 3(4)(a)(i) of Dir. 2000/31/EC (OJ 2000 L 178/1), as an exception allowing derogation from Art 3(2),[1166] the ruling has the effect of minimising libel tourism in disputes concerning online violations of personality rights committed by online service provider defendants established within the EU. The substantive private law of the Member State in which the provider of an electronic commerce service is established determines the level of protection of personality rights, and any other stricter national substantive law, which

terms 'information society service' and 'service provider' on the basis of the relevant provisions of Dir. 2000/31/EC (OJ 2000 L 178/1), see *Papasavvas*, 26-30 [cf. *Mc Fadden* (request)].

1161 Kohler/Seyr/Puffer-Mariette, ZEuP 2013, 323, 330 (italics in the original).

1162 For a different understanding, see e.g. Kuipers, CML Rev. 2012, 1211, 1224 ff.

1163 *eDate and Martinez*, 58 ff.

1164 *Papasavvas*, 33. Note that the ECJ did not examine in this case, due to factual reasons, the possible effect of Art 3(2) of Dir. 2000/31/EC (OJ 2000 L 178/1).

1165 For a different approach, cf. Kuipers, CML Rev. 2012, 1211, 1227 ff.

1166 On this, see Spindler, AfP 2012, 114, 120; von Hinden, ZEuP 2012, 940, 953. Note that the above-quoted Art 3(4)(a)(i) concerns only individuals although, under certain circumstances, legal persons may also have personality rights (on this, see *infra* Ch. VII.D.II.2).

would be applicable according to the conflict of laws rules of the forum, must be corrected accordingly.[1167]

c) Even more certain application of rules of *lis pendens* and grounds for refusal

The rules of *lis pendens* more evidently apply to parallel mosaic proceedings initiated for compensating the non-pecuniary harm caused by the online violations of personality rights than to mosaic procedures dealing with offline violations.[1168] Whilst for offline materials, the nature of the act of distribution, and thus, the identical character of the causes of actions, might be a little unclear, the identical character of the causes of actions brought in different mosaic jurisdictions in relation to online violations is evident, since the act of uploading, i.e., tapping a button, is a single act. This is significant for two reasons. First, for applying the rules of *lis pendens*, solely the nature of the subject matter of the actions remains to a certain extent uncertain. Secondly, in line with an even more certain application of rules of *lis pendens*, the risk of irreconcilable judgments delivered in different mosaic jurisdictions is increased.[1169]

Considering preventive actions, the present author is satisfied that the rules of *lis pendens* apply to parallel proceedings initiated in different mosaic jurisdictions for injunctions that cannot be split along geographic boundaries. Such proceedings certainly involve, in addition to the same parties and cause of action, the same subject matter of the actions, since their undividable nature produces a global prohibitory effect. Thus, contrary to the compensation for the mosaic parts of his damage, the plaintiff does not have anything to gain in other parallel mosaic proceedings, and

1167 It also appears to mean that the national judge is regarded as «a superhuman intellectual power and patience», a «Hercules» (terms are used in Dworkin, Law's Empire, p 239), who can compare every aspects of the tortious rules of the *lex cause* and the law of the place of establishment even in complex situations when the claim is not only for injunction but also for compensation for the non-pecuniary harm. Cf. von Hinden, ZEuP 2012, 940, 952 [he questions how the comparison of substantive laws ('sachrechtlicher Günstigkeitsvergleich') could work in practice].

1168 On this, see *supra* Ch. V.C.II.7.

1169 On this, see *supra* Ch. V.C.II.8. For reference to problematic issues attached to the mosaic principle in relation to *lis pendens* and the effect of the judgment, see also Spindler, AfP 2012, 114, 117; Garber, ÖJZ 2012, 108, 117.

by arguing so, the uncertainty attached in *supra* Ch. V.C.II.7.a) to the identity of the subject matter of the actions is resolved. Consequently, judgments delivered in parallel mosaic proceedings cannot be enforced separately; they entail legal consequences that are mutually exclusive.[1170] Therefore, it is safely assumed that they are irreconcilable with each other and the ground for refusal under Art 45(1)(c) or (d) applies.

Conclusion and summary

In sum, the following concluding remarks can be made regarding the mosaic approach. First, it is principally unpractical in respect of substantive legal issues, such as the assessment of violations of personality rights, the determination of the extent of non-pecuniary harm, and the enforcement of preventive measures. In addition, it is also contrary to most of the underlying principles and governing objectives of the Brussels-Lugano Regime and is inconsistent with certain rights guaranteed under the Charter. These challenges render the concept of accessibility a highly unsuitable basis for jurisdiction. Therefore, the present author is of the opinion that the concept of accessibility, and thus, the mosaic approach, should be abolished.[1171] Accordingly, besides the concept of causal event, the concept of damage in the form of the victim's habitual residence should localise online (potential) violations of personality rights.

This solution might be challenged by arguing that if the victim's centre of interests is based outside the territories of the Brussels-Lugano States, he could not sue the publisher at the place of the damage, irrespective of the fact that portions of the damage may have occurred or threaten to occur in different Brussels-Lugano States. Thus, the place of the damage criterion would be disregarded, and possibly, he could be deprived of his right guaranteed under Art 47 of the Charter to bring proceedings in order to determine the merits of his claim.[1172] This challenge, however, does not attract the present author greatly. The establishment of the twin criteria under the concept of harmful event does not mean that the plaintiff can always choose among them. As is evident from *Réunion européenne*, the

1170 By analogy with *Hoffmann*, 22.

1171 Cf. Hartley, L.Q.R. 2012, 197, 201; Garber, ÖJZ 2012, 108, 117; Nielsen, J. Priv. Int. L. 2013, 269, 279-280.

1172 On the protection of this right, see *Hypoteční banka*, 49 ff.; *de Visser*, 48 ff.

ECJ, because of its uncertain character, did not determine the place of the causal event and had recourse only to the place of the damage.[1173] In addition, the victim could bring an action in the court of the Brussels-Lugano State of the place where the disputed content was created, for example, where the photograph of him was taken. Alternatively, he could sue the publisher in accordance with other rules of jurisdiction outlined in *supra* Ch. III.D.[1174] Furthermore, none of the criteria proposed for localising the place of the damage in online (potential) violations of personality rights,[1175] other than the victim's habitual residence, satisfy most of the governing objectives and underlying principles of the Brussels-Lugano Regime. Finally, and closely related to the foregoing, it could be argued that the victim's right to bring actions in the courts of the Brussels-Lugano State where he is not habitually resident is outweighed by the defendant's right to a fair and predictable procedure, as well as to his right to access to justice and his freedom of expression. To put it differently, the abolition of the accessibility criterion equipped with the mosaic approach stems from a compromise, a solution of weighing and balancing exercise. It aims to facilitate predictability by providing at the same time judicial justice, fairness, and convenience to the parties, especially to the defendant.

II. Unlimited extent of jurisdiction: a choice between the Brussels-Lugano States-wide and the worldwide harm

The ECJ failed to bring absolute certainty regarding the scope of the unlimited extent of jurisdiction. To put it another way, there remains uncertainty in relation to what it intended to mean in its reference to 'all the damage caused' by ruling that the aggrieved person «has the option of bringing an action for liability, in respect of all the damage caused, either before the courts of the Member State in which the publisher of that content is established or before the courts of the Member State in which the

1173 On this case, see also *infra* Ch. VII.D.II.1 and *supra* fn 533.

1174 See also a proposal put forward in *supra* fn 1111 for allowing a third state victim to bring an action at the place of the other victim's habitual residence.

1175 See *supra* Ch. VI.A.II.1-2 and their criticism in *supra* Ch. VII.B.II.1.a)aa)-bb), *supra* Ch. VII.B.II.2 and *supra* Ch. VII.C.I.

centre of his interests is based.»[1176] Did the ECJ intend to mean the totality of the harm caused Brussels-Lugano States-wide by online violations of personality rights? Alternatively, did it refer to the worldwide harm?[1177] At the outset, it can safely be assumed from the wording of Art 7(2), especially from its chapeau, that the damage or its portion must have occurred in one or more Brussels-Lugano States:

> «A person domiciled in a Member State may be sued in another Member State:»
>
> «(2) in matters relating to tort, delict or quasi-delict, in the courts for the place where the harmful event occurred or may occur».

Accordingly, if the harm occurred or threatens to occur in none of the Brussels-Lugano States, the concept of damage under Art 7(2) does not apply. Consequently, the aforementioned uncertainty is relevant only if the harm occurred or threatens to occur both within and outside of the territories of those states. Views in legal writing taken on this issue appear principally to prefer either the Brussels-Lugano States-wide or the worldwide understanding without going into great detail.[1178] The present subsection is therefore an attempt to elicit the scope of the unlimited extent of jurisdiction by balancing possible arguments put forward for supporting one view or the other.

It is possible to draw some support for the Brussels-Lugano States-wide understanding on the basis of two main aspects. First, the wording of the aforementioned chapeau of Art 7(2) refers exclusively to harm that has occurred within the territories of the Brussels-Lugano States, and thus, it excludes its extraterritorial application. In addition, such an understanding could also be underpinned by the initial function of the unlimited extent of jurisdiction derived from *Shevill* and upheld in *eDate and Martinez*:

1176 *eDate and Martinez*, 52. This question did not arise in *Shevill* in which the harm occurred solely in different Contracting States of the BC (on this, see *supra* Ch. V.A).

1177 In-depth nature of this question lies in the territorial scope of application of Art 7(2). On this, see e.g. Michaels, in: Nuyts/Watté, International Civil Litigation, pp 129-156.

1178 Regarding principally the concept of the victim's centre of interests, (1) for the EU-wide understanding, see e.g. Schnichels/Stege, EuZW 2012, 812, 814; Schmitz, Masaryk U. J.L. & Tech. 2012, 159, 168; (2) for the worldwide understanding, see e.g. Kuipers, CML Rev. 2012, 1211, 1214 (publisher's establishment), 1218, 1220; Thiede, GPR 2012, 219, 222 («total international damage»); Reymond, YbPIL 2011, 493, 498, 502; Mankowski, EWiR 2011, 743, 744.

> «[W]hile it is true that the limitation of the jurisdiction of the courts in the State of distribution solely to damage caused in that State presents disadvantages, the plaintiff always has the option of bringing his entire claim before the courts either of the defendant's domicile or of the place where the publisher of the defamatory publication is established».[1179]

It follows that the totality of the harm is supposed to be the bundle of the damage caused in each mosaic jurisdiction. In other words, according to this aspect, the aggrieved person must bring proceedings in each mosaic jurisdiction to receive compensation for the full harm. Therefore, the amount of damages awarded in each mosaic jurisdiction basically corresponds to the amount of damages which would be granted for all the harm before a single court of the place where the publisher is established.[1180] Two final arguments about this understanding are also remarkable and, indeed, do not attract the present author greatly. First, the Brussels-Lugano Regime generally aims to develop judicial cooperation in civil matters that have cross-border implications in order to strengthen the legal protection of persons established in the territories of the Brussels-Lugano States as well as the legal and economic cooperation therein.[1181] Admittedly, this is so. However, it is equally correct that, as noted in *supra* Ch. III.C.III, the Brussels-Lugano Regime includes several provisions that are applicable to legal relationships involving one Brussels-Lugano State and one or more third states. Why, then, should Art 7(2) not be understood as one of such rules? As far as the second argument is concerned, it is noteworthy that the fact patterns and AG Cruz Villalón's opinion delivered in *eDate and Martinez* satisfy a Brussels-Lugano States-wide understanding. In particular, as outlined in *supra* Ch. VII.A.I.1-2, in *eDate Advertising*, Mr X sought an injunction to be applied throughout the territory of Germany, while the plaintiffs in *Martinez and Martinez* alleged that the damage occurred in France. Moreover, the question referred by the *TGI Paris* for a preliminary ruling also reflected a Brussels-Lugano States-wide application of Art 5(3) of Brussels I, since it concerned solely the publication of information on an Internet site in another Member State.[1182] Similarly, AG Cruz Villalón proposed that the concept of harmful event must be inter-

---

1179 *Shevill*, 32 as confirmed in *eDate and Martinez*, 43.

1180 On this, cf. *supra* Ch. V.C.II.3.b).

1181 See preamble of 2007 LC; Recitals 1, 3 and the first sentence of Recital 13. Cf. decision of the *Norges Høyesterett*, 20.12.2012, HR-2012-2393-A – Rt-2012 – 1951 as referred to in *supra* fn 396.

1182 *eDate and Martinez*, 29.

preted as meaning that «in the event of an infringement of personality rights by means of information disseminated *in a number of Member States* via the internet, that the holder of those rights may bring an action for compensation»[1183] in the Member States specified therein. These notices may very well be true. However, their importance should not be overstated. Rather, it might be argued that the fact patterns and AG Cruz Villalón's opinion considered only the harm and the measures claimed for in line with *Shevill*, which was concerned purely with the territory of certain Contracting States of the BC.

By contrast, five sets of arguments, which aim for the worldwide understanding of the term 'unlimited extent of jurisdiction', run as follows. First, regarding the meaning of the extent of jurisdiction conferred by the connecting factors at stake separately, the following can be ascertained. The ECJ presumably attributed an unlimited extent of jurisdiction to the court for the place of the publisher's establishment, because the harm caused «is connected in its entirety to that act»[1184] and therefore, it has a particularly close connection with all the harm.[1185] However, why should the harm caused within the territories of the Brussels-Lugano States be closer to the causal event than the harm caused outside of those territories? Ralf Michaels' notice, put forward in 2005 in relation to multiple consecutive places suggests, by analogy, that the reply to this question would be that there are no differences between those losses:

> «[T]he courts of the place of conduct have jurisdiction even over injuries suffered outside of the European Union. ... if a factory owner in Germany pollutes the River Danube in Germany, he can be sued in Germany for injuries caused in Romania, even though Romania is not part of the EU.»[1186]

In addition, the wording of *eDate and Martinez* neither limits the availability of the online content to the (digital) internal market of the EU, nor considers the harm caused solely within the Member States. Instead, the ECJ justified the introduction of the victim's centre of interests by referring to the universal reach of this information medium and to the serious nature of the harm caused by virtue of the globally accessible online con-

1183 AG in *eDate and Martinez*, 67 (author's italics). See similarly, e.g. AG in *eDate and Martinez*, 51.

1184 Lagarde as referred to by AG 1994 in *Shevill*, 62.

1185 On this, see *supra* Ch. V.C.II.3.c).

1186 Michaels, in: Nuyts/Watté, International Civil Litigation, pp 137-138 (a sentence, emphases omitted).

tent.[1187] Moreover, views expressed in legal writing underline the appropriateness of the unlimited extent of the jurisdiction of the competent courts for the place of the victim's centre of interests because of the existence of a link between the forum, the nature of the harm, and the holder of the right.[1188] Consequently, the concept of the publisher's establishment and the victim's centre of interests approach are constructed in a way that supposedly independently of each other, they allocate jurisdiction to the competent court to decide upon the worldwide harm caused by the online violation of a personality right.

Secondly, as aforementioned, the ECJ confirmed in *eDate and Martinez* its finding put forward in *Shevill* according to which the court at the place of the causal event has the same unlimited extent of jurisdiction as the courts of the Member State in which the defendant is domiciled. In short, the aggrieved person can bring his «entire claim» before those courts. As is clear from *supra* Ch. III.C.III, Art 4(1) operates in the international legal order. It is applicable to circumstances involving legal relationships between the courts of a single Brussels-Lugano State and one or more non-Brussels-Lugano States rather than relationships between the courts of different Brussels-Lugano States, providing that the defendant is domiciled in the territory of one of the latter states.[1189] A classic example of this international character is *Owusu*, in which the substance of the dispute concerned a claim brought by the victim against several defendants, one of whom was domiciled in England, for compensation for the harm that occurred because of an accident in Jamaica. It follows that due to the general rule of jurisdiction, the competent court has an unlimited extent of jurisdiction to rule on the entire worldwide harm.[1190] This finding gets the ball rolling on a line of reasoning. Indeed, since the court designated by the defendant's domicile criterion can decide upon the damage that occurred outside the territory of the Brussels-Lugano States, it seems reasonable to

---

1187 *eDate and Martinez*, 45-47. Contra: Roth, IPRax 2013, 215, fn 90 (italics in square brackets added): «Die weltweite Abrufbarkeit des Internetinhalts wird zwar vom Gerichtshof in Rn. 46 *[des eDate Advertising-Urteils]* in Bezug genommen, spielt aber im Rahmen von Art. 5 Nr. 3 EuGVVO natürlich keine Rolle.»

1188 Ginsburg, Recueil des Cours 273, p 311 (regarding certain Internet-generated torts: nature of the harm and the author); Roth, IPRax 2013, 215, 220 (forum and the holder of the personality right). Cf. *supra* Ch. VII.B.II.1.d).

1189 See *Owusu*, 35 (regarding Contracting States of the BC).

1190 Cf. Bogdan, Masaryk U. J.L. & Tech. 2011, 1, 3 («totality of the damage caused»).

suppose that the concept of the publisher's establishment confers jurisdiction to the same extent. In turn, it also appears obvious that the court at the place of the victim's centre of interests also has such an unlimited extent of jurisdiction, since it has the same features as that with which the court at the place of the publisher's establishment is clothed.

Thirdly, it could also be argued that, like the national rules of jurisdiction, which basically confer an unlimited extent of decision-making power on a court, the jurisdictional basis under Art 7(2) should also have the same effect.[1191]

Fourthly, and closely related to the preceding argument, avoiding the fragmentation of the extent of jurisdiction into territories within and outside of the Brussels-Lugano States would be efficient for at least three reasons. First, it would avoid the initiation of possible parallel proceedings on the same dispute in a third state.[1192] Secondly, and closely related to this, it would also protect the interests of the defendant who was established in a Brussels-Lugano State by preventing him from being sued in a third state where European values would possibly not apply. Thirdly, and perhaps most importantly, since the Brussels-Lugano States-wide damage could be regarded as a portion – a mosaic – of the worldwide damage, most of the arguments put forward against the mosaic principle in *supra* Ch. V.C and *supra* Ch. VII.C.I could be used to argue against the Brussels-Lugano States-wide understanding.

Finally, and provided that the conflict of laws rules applicable to violations of privacy and rights relating to personality were harmonised under

---

1191 Cf. (1) US: Ginsburg, Recueil des Cours 273, p 297 notes that due to the Restatement (Second) of Torts §577A (1977) a plaintiff may recover damages for extraterritorial publications, since it declares: «In [plaintiff's] single action he may recover damages for the publication to all persons whom the communication has reached or may be expected to reach ... . This is true even though the publication has crossed state lines and has been read, heard or seen in every state and in foreign countries; and all damages sustained in all jurisdictions may be recovered in the one action.» (2) UK/England: *Ames & Anor v The Spamhaus Project Ltd & Anor* [2015] EWHC 127 (QB), 103 ff. (regarding publication in the US).

1192 This would be advantageous even if (1) Brussels Ia includes rules on *lis pendens* and related actions in respect of third states (see *supra* Ch. III.B.II.2), and (2) the wording of Art 52 allows the Member State addressed for recognition or enforcement to review the judgment of a third state as to its substance (e.g. level of protection of personality rights). This is so because, contrary to Art 36 of Brussels I, which refers to a foreign judgment, the wording of Art 52 refers to a judgment of the Member State.

Rome II, the worldwide understanding would be consistent with the scope of the universal application of this instrument, as defined in its Art 3. Otherwise, the effects of this regulation would go much further than those that stem from the Brussels instruments.

Conclusion and summary

In the light of the foregoing, the present author sympathises with the latter sets of arguments, which are in favour of the understanding according to which the reference to 'all the damage caused' could and should be intended to be meant the worldwide damage.

D. Extending the application of the eDate and Martinez-approaches

As is clear from the foregoing, the *eDate and Martinez* judgment was delivered in two joined cases in which the individual victims sought to establish the liability of the legal person publishers for online (potential) violations of their personality rights. This limited scope of the fact patterns automatically raises two adjunct questions, which are briefly discussed below.

I. Is there a need for technology neutrality?

Although the ECJ held that the *Shevill*-approaches «may, as was noted by the Advocate General at point 39 of his Opinion, also be applied to other media and means of communication»,[1193] as became evident from the analysis laid down in the present chapter, it departed from its finding. Apart from the revision of the concept of distribution, this departure is apparent from the two reasons the ECJ put forward in favour of introducing the concept of the victim's centre of interests exclusively for online violations of personality rights.[1194]

Two comments, of which the second forms the main concern of the present subsection, are called for on this finding. First, although the concept

1193 *eDate and Martinez*, 44.
1194 See *supra* Ch. VII.B.II.1.a)-b).

of the victim's centre of interests is introduced in respect of universally accessible online content, the present author would not reject its application to violations of personality rights that were committed or threatened to be committed through other forms of online communication, such as e-mails or social media platforms.[1195] Secondly, numerous scholars, with whom the present author readily agrees, are of the opinion that the distinction between offline and online violations does not take into account the reality, namely, that many media content is distributed simultaneously via numerous channels, like the Internet, press and/or broadcast media.[1196] It follows that if, for example, the newspaper is a so-called hybrid one appearing both in printed and electronic formats,[1197] the victim is given an excessively wide choice of fora. In particular, he could sue or threaten to sue the publisher for all the damage caused by the online and offline publications at the place of the publisher's establishment, for all the damage caused by the online publication at the place of the victim's centre of interests, or for the territorially restricted damage caused by the content in each mosaic jurisdiction where it is traditionally distributed and where it is or has been accessible online.

Parallel proceedings initiated for monetary compensation for the damage caused by the electronic and printed formats of the content or for preventing the distribution of such versions pose several questions concerning substantive legal and jurisdictional issues. It is seriously questionable how the extent of the damage caused by the online and offline versions could separately be determined in states where both versions of the content are available.[1198] Moreover, jurisdictional uncertainties primarily concern procedural economy,[1199] the application of the rules on *lis pendens* or related actions, the delivery of contradictory[1200] and even irreconcilable decisions regarding the same content and, consequently, difficulties in recognising and enforcing judgments. To solve these complications, different proposals have been put forward in legal writing. Principally, a technologically

---

1195 Cf. Roth's view in *supra* fn 891.

1196 See von Hinden, ZEuP 2012, 940, 950; Kuipers, CML Rev. 2012, 1211, 1223; von Hein, Von Hein on Kate Provence Pictures, 2012; Brand, NJW 2012, 127, 129.

1197 On this, see *supra* Ch. II.C.

1198 See also Slonina, ÖJZ 2012, 61, 66; Heinze, EuZW 2011, 947, 949; Nagy, J. Priv. Int. L. 2012, 251, 266.

1199 See also Heinze, EuZW 2011, 947, 949.

1200 See also von Hein, Von Hein on Kate Provence Pictures, 2012.

neutral criterion is favoured, which treats the online and traditional media alike.[1201] In this regard, Jan-Jaap Kuipers stresses that from a methodological point of view, the distinction between different media introduced by the ECJ leads to friction under the general structure of Brussels I. Specifically, he refers to the solution adopted by the EU legislator and confirmed by the ECJ in *Pammer and Hotel Alpenhof* for localising consumer contracts within Art 15 of Brussels I, which aimed to avoid the adoption of different approaches depending on whether a consumer contract was concluded on the Internet or through different means.[1202] Furthermore, the UK government noted that it follows neither from the wording of Art 5(3) of Brussels I nor from the objectives of this regulation that there should be any differentiation between the distribution of printed materials and the distribution of materials through the Internet for determining the place where the harmful event occurred.[1203] Accordingly, Wulf-Henning Roth is of the opinion that it can be expected that the concept of the centre of interests will be extended to violations of personality rights in print media, at least when parallel publication takes place. However, he stresses that it would be preferable to develop this concept to a technology-neutral criterion in the future.[1204] Others, like Michel Slonina, hope that as a consequence of the increasing online media presence, the concept of the victim's centre of interests becomes generally accepted in disputes concerning violations of personality rights.[1205]

These proposals are appealing. Since the vast majority of communication today is electronic, it may well be true that the concept of the victim's centre of interests will be applied frequently in the future. Support for this finding can also be drawn from the national decisions,[1206] which were delivered on the basis of this concept. However, in situations when the con-

---

1201 On this, see e.g. von Hinden, ZEuP 2012, 940, 950; Nagy, J. Priv. Int. L. 2012, 251, 277. Cf. AG in *eDate and Martinez*, 53, 54 regarding the centre of gravity of the dispute test, see *supra* Ch. VI.A.II.2.b)aa).

1202 Kuipers, CML Rev. 2012, 1211, 1224.

1203 Observation submitted by the UK government in the Minutes of Proceedings drawn up for the oral hearing in *eDate and Martinez*, 14.12.2010 (on file with author), 51 (regarding and by proposing the *Shevill*-test for online violations).

1204 Roth, IPRax 2013, 215, 221. Contra: Junker, FS Helmut Rüßmann, p 821 states (italics in the original): «Auch ergibt es keinen Sinn, die Anwendung (nur) der *Shevill*-Doktrin auf Printveröffentlichungen davon abhängig zu machen, dass der fragliche Inhalt nicht zugleich Online publiziert wurde.»

1205 Slonina, ÖJZ 2012, 61, 66.

1206 See *supra* fn 1114.

tent is available simultaneously in both printed and electronic formats, the present author is of the opinion that since, in principle, the online content has a wider reach than the content of the traditional media, the former should annex the latter with the result that exclusively the *eDate and Martinez*-approaches should apply.[1207]

II. Reversal of the roles: are the *eDate and Martinez*-approaches suitable for individual online actors and legal person victims?

An extension of the application of the *eDate and Martinez*-approaches are not only questionable regarding the medium through which the allegedly injurious content is or has been distributed. The technical developments and new communication practices, which increasingly empower individuals to participate in the creation and distribution of online information,[1208] automatically question whether the concept of the publisher's establishment and the victim's centre of interests approach, originally adjusted to legal person publishers and individual victims, are also suitable for individual online actors and legal person victims.[1209, 1210]

1207 This book does not aim to propose new connecting factors for offline violations of personality rights. However, it could briefly be argued that the concept of the victim's centre of interests should suppress the concept of distribution in cases when the disputed offline material is also distributed in the Brussels-Lugano State of the place where that centre is based (cf. Bogdan, YbPIL 2011, 483, 485 suggests extending under certain circumstances the reasoning of the *eDate and Martinez* judgment to, for example, short-wave radio or satellite television; Hartley, L.Q.R. 2012, 197, 201 appears to propose abolishing the mosaic approach and extending the concept of the victim's centre of interests «to hard-copy claimants»). Alternatively, it could be argued that *Shevill* should belong to the past, since, irrespective of the intentional distribution of the printed material, the printed material could easily be digitalised and uploaded to the Internet. However, this latter solution can be disputed from three main aspects. First, it would go too far in the causal connection between the different acts. Secondly, it would concern the issue of redistribution. Finally, it would also run counter to the separate treatment of activities taking place in the physical and digital world with the result that the Internet would turn upside-down almost all physical activities.

1208 On this, see *supra* Ch. II.C.

1209 Since the concept of accessibility is independent of the litigants' personal view, it does not require further analysis. It should also be recalled that besides Ms Shevill, three French-registered companies were also plaintiffs in the main proceedings in *Shevill* (see *supra* Ch. V.A.I). However, since the concept of the victim's centre of interests was not a connecting factor in that case, the question of its

1. Individuals as online actors

As explained in *supra* Ch. VII.B.I, the concept of the publisher's establishment is an unsuitable and empty basis of jurisdiction for legal person publishers, which essentially coincides with the general rule of jurisdiction laid down in 4(1). Therefore, it was examined whether a specific act in the chain of successive acts would be a reasonable substitute for the concept of the publisher's establishment. For this purpose, the taking of the decision to place of the content online and the creation of the contested content seemed reasonable points, which could amount to the causal event. However, considering that the place where the decision is taken generally coincides with the place that is designated by Art 4(1) or Art 7(5), the place where the disputed content was created was finally regarded as an adequate basis of jurisdiction in disputes involving legal person publishers. Since the interpretation of the concept of the publisher's establishment supposedly leads to the same conclusion in respect of individual online actors, i.e., it refers to their domicile,[1211] it is reasonable to examine

---

suitability to legal persons remains unclear.

1210 Theoretically, the defendant could also be an Internet intermediary (see *supra* fn 1045). However, since the present book is based upon disputes in which the defendant is sued for his own content, it is sufficient to sum up the present author's views as follows. (1) In disputes when the person is sued because of a third person's content, the concept of causal event should not apply; since the defendant cannot be sued at the place where he did not act (on this, see *supra* Ch. III.D.II.3). (2) Based on the attribution of effect test, the concept of damage could be a jurisdictionally relevant concept. (3) Possibly, the place of the web server (cf. Marly in *supra* fn 825) could also determine the competent forum. For cases concerning intermediary liability for jurisdictional purposes, see e.g. Germany: case VI ZR 269/12 (14.5.2013), *BGH* (GRUR 2013, 751) (regarding Art 32 of the *ZPO*), and for comments on this decision, see Gebauer, IPRax 2014, 513 ff.; case references as highlighted in Internet & Jurisdiction Project – Retrospect <http://www.internetjurisdiction.net/observatory/retrospect/>.

1211 The settled case law of the ECJ has rarely dealt with the interpretation of the concept of harmful event, and thus, with the localisation of torts in relation to individual defendants. This was the case, for example, in *Kronhofer* and in *ÖFAB*. However, in both cases, the individuals were sued as directors or investment consultants of a company (*Kronhofer*, 2) and as a member of the board of directors of another company (*ÖFAB*, 9, 55) and not as simple individuals for their own actions. Cf. request of the *Hoge Raad der Nederlanden* (Supreme Court of the Netherlands) for a preliminary ruling in *Holterman Ferho Exploitatie u.a.* (concerning an individual in his capacity as director and employee of a company). A case before the ECJ in which an individual is sued for his own act would have

whether the place where the decision is taken or where the content was created is suitable to be considered the place of the causal event for individual online actors (individual publishers).

While the latter place does not require additional clarification, the former one should further be elaborated upon because individual online actors differ from legal persons in two major aspects. Besides the fact that they are increasingly mobile, they principally act on their own, and their acts are attributable only and exclusively to them. Consequently, the place where the decision on the uploading of the content is taken coincides with the place where the individual taps the button and uploads the content to the Internet. In other words, the place of uploading is the place where the decision on the uploading of the content is manifested to the external world through the act of uploading.[1212] However, as noted in *supra* Ch. VII.B.I, the place of uploading is replete with serious difficulties. It is an opportunistic and unpredictable place, which is often unrelated to the substance of the violation of a personality right, and it extensively handicaps the aggrieved person. To solve this localisation problem, a rebuttable presumption is generally accepted in legal writing. In particular, it is assumed that the place of uploading is the place where the individual online actor is domiciled or habitually resident, providing that he does not prove to the contrary.[1213]

While this rebuttable presumption could undoubtedly be a possible solution, the present author is unconvinced of its adequacy for at least four reasons. First, even if there is no need for recourse to a presumption because the place of uploading is displayed online, as was just noted, this place withstands any reasonable test of predictability and sound administration of justice on which the special rules of jurisdiction hinge.[1214] Furthermore, having in mind that the publisher is granted the freedom to decide what kind of information he posts online, the accuracy of such dis-

---

been *de Visser*, (1) if the referring German court had not withheld its questions relating to Art 5(3) of Brussels I and decided it in the light of *eDate and Martinez* on its own [see case *de Visser* 1 O 1205/09 (2) (24.4.2012), *LG Regensburg*] and (2) if the domicile of *de Visser* had been known (see *supra* Ch. III.C.III).

1212 See also Garber, ÖJZ 2012, 108, 111. Cf. Thorn in *supra* fn 832. Exceptions are possible but rare. It could be, for example, when the individual's decision is manifested previously to the public somewhere else, e.g. when he posts its intention on a website prior to uploading.

1213 On this, see *supra* Ch. VI.A.I.3-4.

1214 On this, see *supra* Ch. III.B.I and II.1, as well as *supra* Ch. VII.B.I.

played information is highly doubtful. Thirdly, presumptions in the forms of the individual publisher's domicile and habitual residence are inadequate. While his domicile usually coincides with the general rule of jurisdiction laid down in Art 4(1), and therefore, it loses its effectiveness,[1215] the defendant's habitual residence is an irrelevant connecting factor within the Brussels-Lugano Regime.[1216] Fourthly, the rebuttable character of this proposal seems also to be problematic. Since the information, which is necessary to rebut the presumption, belongs exclusively to the online actor's individual sphere, he could rebut the jurisdiction of the court seised with real or other manipulated information at any time.[1217] This would be disadvantageous to the victim in at least three respects. It would cause him unnecessary expense, since he supposedly would have hired a lawyer in that jurisdiction and would have had the court documents drafted according to the national procedural law. In addition, it would threaten the legal protection of his personality rights, since it would be possible that the individual publisher would present evidence establishing the competence of the court of a state where the law applicable to the dispute was tilted categorically towards him. Finally, it is also seriously disputable whether this rebuttable presumption, which depends on uncertain and fortuitous factors and thus tends to be reminiscent of the *forum non conveniens* rule,[1218] fits the governing objectives and underlying principles of the Brussels-Lugano Regime, which facilitate certain attributions of jurisdiction, the recourse to which is clear and rapid for the courts.

Mindful of these contradictory and troublesome issues, the present author is of the opinion that the place where the decision upon the uploading is taken should also be disregarded as it is jurisdictionally irrelevant in disputes concerning individual online actors as defendants. It is possible to draw support for this view from the *Réunion européenne* judgment. In this case, the dispute concerned *inter alia* the determination of the place where the harmful event occurred when the damage arose in the course of international transport by sea and road. In essence, a French company

1215 See also Slonina, ÖJZ 2012, 61, fn 22. A possible exception to this coincidence is the case when he relocated his domicile after uploading the disputed content. However, because of the unpredictable nature of the time of causation [i.e., time of uploading, see *supra* Ch. VII.B.II.1.e)], the validity of this exception is seriously questionable.

1216 On this, see *supra* Ch. III.C.I.

1217 On this, see *supra* Ch. VII.B.I.

1218 On this, see *supra* Ch. III.B.I.4.

purchased a large quantity of pears from Australia, which were transported by different persons in refrigerated containers to the Netherlands by sea and then to France by road. At the place of final delivery in France, where the purchaser had its registered office, it discovered damage resulting from a premature ripening of the fruit due to a breakdown in the cooling system. After the company Réunion Européenne and nine other insurance companies had paid compensation for the damage, they subrogated to the rights of the purchaser and brought an action in France against several persons who participated in the transportation. Since the jurisdiction of the French courts was disputed under Art 5(3) of the BC, the third question referred for a preliminary ruling by the French *Cour de Cassation* sought to ascertain whether it was competent to hear the dispute.[1219] Put simply, the ECJ ruled in respect of the place of the causal event as follows:

> «As the Advocate General emphasises in points 54 to 56 of his Opinion, in an international transport operation of the kind at issue in the main proceedings the place where the event giving rise to the damage occurred may be difficult or indeed impossible to determine. In such circumstances, it will be for the consignee of the damaged goods to bring the actual maritime carrier before the courts for the place where the damage occurred.»[1220]

By analogy, it is obvious that since it is difficult or impossible to determine the place where the individual publisher takes the decision on the placing online of the content, it should be regarded as not jurisdictionally relevant. Therefore, and identical to the conclusion drawn in respect of legal person publishers, besides the place of the creation as the place of the causal event, the place of the damage should confer jurisdiction in online (potential) violations of personality rights.

2. Legal persons as victims

Although the concept of the victim's centre of interests was originally established for individual victims, the simple wording of *eDate and Martinez* does not exclude the possibility of applying it to legal person victims whose personality rights are violated. According to several views, such an application could potentially be suggested from the wording of the second aspect of the concept, namely, from the reference to the pursuit of a pro-

1219 For the facts and background procedure, see AG in *Réunion européenne*, 2-6, 37.
1220 *Réunion européenne*, 33.

fessional activity.[1221] Abbo Junker takes an even more confident view by questioning that if an actor at the place of his centre of interests can defend himself against defamation through the digital Yellow Press, why should the same not be allowed for a company that is defamed online by its competitor in an anti-competitive manner. Therefore, in his opinion, «[d]ie Entscheidung des EuGH hat also durchaus das Potenzial für einen wettbewerbsrechtlichen Klägergerichtsstand».[1222]

Even assuming the correctness of these findings, two adjunct issues remain uncertain. First, it remains open how the concept of the victim's centre of interests could be determined for legal persons. As Christian Heinze observes, the determination of a state as the centre of interests is more complicated for legal persons, especially for multinational companies, than for individuals.[1223] Perhaps the concept of the centre of main interests employed in cross-border insolvency law or the concept of the habitual residence of companies and other bodies described in Art 23(1) of Rome II could be helpful starting points.[1224] However, the shortcoming of these determinations as possible meanings of the concept of the victim's centre of interests is that they often coincide with the concept of domicile as defined in Art 63.[1225]

As far as the second adjunct question is concerned, the existence of legal persons' personality rights as distinguished from their intellectual property rights and from competition law aspects is disputable.[1226] The

1221 On this, see Heinze, EuZW 2011, 947, 950; Junker, FS Helmut Rüßmann, p 822. Note that the German language version does not distinguish between professional and business activities [see *supra* Ch. VII.B.II.1.e)]. Cf. Hartley, L.Q.R. 2012, 197, 198-199, who refers besides professional to commercial interests.

1222 Junker, FS Helmut Rüßmann, p 822.

1223 Heinze, EuZW 2011, 947, 950.

1224 Due to Art 75 of the Virgos/Schmit Report, it is presumed that the centre of main interests of companies and legal persons is the registered office [note that the meaning of the concept of the centre of main interests is currently under partial modification, see e.g. Recitals 13a and 13b, Art 3, modification no (22) of Commission Document COM(2012) 744 final], while Rome II principally refers under the concept of habitual residence to the place of the central administration. However, for branch, agency, and any other establishment, see Art 23(1), second indent of Rome II. Cf. Hamburg Group for Private International Law, Comments on the Draft Proposal, p 26 in the context of law applicable to defamation; they propose the central administration or the principal place of business as the geographical centre of the company victim's activities and interests.

1225 On this, see also Heinze, EuZW 2011, 947, 950.

1226 Regarding the question of the existence of legal persons' personality rights, see

importance of this question lies in the fact that different connecting factors, namely, the concepts of country of protection, registration, or possibly the relevant market targeted, localise disputes concerning the latter two fields.[1227] Given the lack of a clear isolation of these three fields of law, the concept of the victim's centre of interests would suppress the latter two connecting factors. This result would, however, not be reasonable, since, contrary to the individuals' professional and/or personal-familial centres of interests,[1228] the centres of interests of legal persons might not refer to the states with which legal persons have their closest (social, economic) bonds.[1229] Support for this view can be drawn from a *BGH* decision, in which the dispute concerned an alleged violation of Art 4(7) of the German *Act against Unfair Competition (Gesetz gegen den unlauteren Wettbewerb)* through a disparaging or defamatory online content. The *BGH* held that the jurisdiction of the court at the place of the damage under Art 5(3) of Brussels I is justified only if the disputed online content is intended to have an impact on the domestic market. By contrast, the German court went on to rule, it does not matter whether the competitor mentioned in the online content has its habitual residence or centre of its life («Lebensmittelpunkt») in Germany.[1230]

In addition, and closely related to the preceding discussion, it is questionable whether legal persons can suffer non-pecuniary harm at all or whether they suffer solely a financial loss as a consequence of violations of their intellectual property rights or as a result of the unfair competition practices of their competitors. Although this is principally a substantive legal question,[1231] it could be argued that a legal person primarily «cannot

---

also Heinze, EuZW 2011, 947, 950; Spindler, AfP 2012, 114, 118.

1227 See e.g. *Wintersteiger* (trade mark), 39; *Pinckney* (copyright), 43, 47; *Coty Germany* (unfair competition, trade mark), 52 ff.; AG in *CDC*, 47 ff. For an overview of the different connecting factors relating to different fields of tort, see AG in *Hejduk*.

1228 I.e., habitual residence. On this, see *supra* Ch. VII.B.II.1.e).

1229 On this, see also Spindler, AfP 2012, 114, 118. E.g. ebay, a US-based multinational e-commerce company offers through <eBay.com>, an online auction and shopping website, different services in several states with which it supposedly establishes stronger economic connections than with the state in which it is based.

1230 Case I ZR 131/12 (12.12.2013), *BGH* (GRUR 2014, 601), summary of the judgment, point a) but see also paras B.II ff.

1231 Cf. the finding of the ECtHR in *Steel and Morris v. The United Kingdom* (no 68416/01), 94 (emphasis omitted): «The State ... enjoys a margin of appreciation as to the means it provides under domestic law to enable a company to challenge the truth, and limit the damage, of allegations which risk harming its reputation».

be injured in its feelings, it can only be injured in its pocket. Its reputation can be injured by a libel but that injury must sound in money.»[1232]

Taking into account all these considerations, the present author agrees with Christian Heinze's view;[1233] she proposes that restraint should be exercised when extending the application of the concept of the victim's centre of interests to violations of legal persons' personality rights.[1234]

Conclusion and summary

The present subsection argued that the recommended reform of the concept of the publisher's establishment and the victim's centre of interests, namely, the place where the contested material was created and where the victim is habitually resident, could be extended to certain factual patterns based on *eDate and Martinez*. In particular, the present author is of the opinion that the proposed connecting factors could be extended to disputes concerning parallel publications and to cases involving individual publishers and legal person victims, albeit to cases involving legal person victims only with certain limitations.

1232 Lord Reid in *Lewis v. Daily Telegraph Ltd.* [1964] A.C. 234, 262 as cited in *Shevill and Others v. Presse Alliance S.A.* [1992] 2 *W.L.R.* 1 (C.A.), p 14/B (regarding companies). Cf. Carter, BYbIL 1993, 519, 521 [regarding the legal person plaintiffs in *Shevill*, he states that they suffered only financial damage and not non-personal (i.e., non-material) damage].

1233 Heinze, EuZW 2011, 947, 950.

1234 However, see the Hungarian and Greek decisions (see *supra* fn 1114) in which victims were (also) legal persons and the national courts assumed their jurisdiction based on the concept of the victim's centre of interests. Cf. *Shevill*, 29, in which the ECJ treated individuals and legal persons on an equal footing.

Chapter VIII: A proposal to reform the *eDate and Martinez* judgment

By analysing the *eDate and Martinez* judgment, *supra* Ch. VII critically described where the special rule of jurisdiction in online (potential) violations of personality rights, specifically defamation and injury to the right to private life, under Art 7(2) currently stands. It was explained that the ECJ neither resolved the troublesome issues nor answered the open questions outlined in *supra* Ch. V in relation to *Shevill*. Above that, it generated additional complications. In particular, except for the concept of the victim's habitual residence as the place of the damage, criticisms focused on the concept of causal event in the form of the publisher's establishment, on the second aspect of the concept of the victim's centre of interests and on the accessibility criterion equipped with the mosaic approach. Moreover, it was noted that the ECJ failed to bring absolute certainty regarding the time of causation and the meaning of the reference to the 'unlimited extent of jurisdiction' of the courts. In addition, it was also noticed that these critical points to some extent outweigh one underlying principle and governing objective of Art 7(2) over the other and essentially render the *eDate and Martinez*-approaches unsuitable jurisdictional bases for disputes concerning violations of personality rights through the Internet in Europe, where common legal norms, interests, and values increasingly integrate and connect persons. Mindful of these observations and other experiences gained from the previous chapters, the present author's proposal embedded in *supra* Ch. VII to reform the *eDate and Martinez* judgment can be summed up as follows:

- The duality of jurisdiction under Art 7(2) should be upheld in disputes concerning online violations of personality rights. Accordingly, in the case where the place in which the event which may give rise to liability occurs and the place where that event results in damage are not identical, the expression 'place where the harmful event occurred' in Art 7(2) must be understood as being intended to cover both the place of the causal event and the place of the damage, with the result that the publisher may be sued, at the option of the person who considers that his personality rights have been violated, in the courts for either of those places.

- The place of the causal event should be the place of a Brussels-Lugano State where the disputed content was created. In situations where it was created in several places, each place should be regarded as jurisdictionally relevant.

- The place of the damage should be the place of a Brussels-Lugano State where the victim's centre of interests in the form of his habitual residence is based, provided that the disputed content is or has been accessible there.

- The relevant time when the causal event and the damage must be established should be the time of the initiation of the proceedings.

- The court of the Brussels-Lugano State, which is designated by the concept of causal event or damage, should have an unlimited, world-wide, extent of jurisdiction to hear the dispute.

- These connecting factors should apply irrespective of the legal status of the litigants to violations of personality rights committed through content universally available online or through other forms of online communications. In addition, they should also apply to violations committed by the simultaneous distribution of the printed and electronic versions of the content.

- These connecting factors should be applicable not only to disputes concerning online violations of personality rights already committed but also to disputes in which persons aim to prevent such violations from occurring.

The virtues of this proposal can be categorised into two groups: those that satisfy the governing objectives and underlying principles of the Brussels-Lugano Regime, as outlined in *supra* Ch. III.B, and those that serve practical purposes.

A. Virtues satisfying the governing objectives and underlying principles

I. Consistency with legal certainty

The proposed connecting factors would allow both the victim easily to identify the court in which he may sue and the publisher reasonably to foresee before which court he may be sued. In addition, recourse to these approaches would be clear and rapid on the part of the court, and they would indirectly enable the litigants to predict the law applicable to their dispute.

1. Guaranteeing equality and uniformity of the rights and obligations

The autonomous interpretation of the proposed connecting factors, which in turn would guarantee the principle of equality and uniformity of the rights and obligations arising out of the Brussels-Lugano Regime, would seldom cause problems. While the creation of the content would be self-evident, the expression 'habitual residence' could be defined by virtue of the *acquis communautaire* as referring to the place where the victim's professional and/or personal-familial centre of interests is based. Furthermore, the proposed connecting factors, as interpretations of the concept of harmful event, would also be consistent with the rights guaranteed under the Charter in no less than two respects. First, the disregard for the disputable requirement that the victim be known at the place of the damage would resolve the inconsistency of the interpretation of Art 7(2) with the common understanding of personality rights afforded in Art 7 of the Charter. Secondly, the concentration of proceedings at one of the places designated by the proposed approaches would facilitate the access to justice of the parties, and by doing so, it would strengthen the protection of the publisher's freedom of expression and the victim's personality rights. Moreover, these autonomous definitions would not give rise to an interpretation that would go beyond the cases expressly envisaged by the Brussels-Lugano Regime and would not deprive Art 7(2) of its practical effect. Rather, these connecting factors would treat equally the twin criteria established in *Bier*. In addition, the concept of the creation of the content would put an end to the empty reference to the concept of causal event by restoring its function to provide a genuine alternative to the general basis of jurisdiction laid down in Art 4(1).

2. Avoiding multiplication of courts and fragmentation of proceedings

The proposal would not lead to a proliferation of new points of connection within Art 7(2). Rather it would avoid the multiplication of courts in cases when the disputed content is simultaneously distributed in both printed and electronic formats. Furthermore, it would avoid the fragmentation of proceedings from several aspects. First, by abolishing the mosaic approach, the proposal would avoid situations in which different courts would have jurisdiction regarding various aspects of one and the same legal relationship. In turn, it would put an end to the problematic issues addressed in *supra* Ch. V.C and *supra* Ch. VII.C.I. In addition, by conferring an unlimited extent of jurisdiction on the competent court, it would concentrate the dispute in a single forum, regardless of whether the non-pecuniary harm caused by the online violation occurred alongside the Brussels-Lugano States-wide damage also outside of the territories of those states.

3. Identifying jurisdiction in a rapid and certain way

The recourse to these connecting factors would be rapid and certain on the part of the court seised, which would only have to identify one of these points of connection with the Brussels-Lugano State in which it sits. It would be abundantly clear, for example, whether a photograph was taken in Paris (France) or in Vilnius (Lithuania). The same is equally true for the concept of habitual residence, which was identified by the national courts without any additional complications in the decisions referred to in *supra* Ch. VII.B.II.1.e).

II. Determining the most appropriate court

The proposed connecting factors would determine which court of a Brussels-Lugano State is the most appropriate to assume jurisdiction for the following reasons.

1. Consistency with the principles of sound administration of justice and proximity

The designated courts would be territorially the best placed to decide most efficiently on the case because they would have the practical advantage of ease of taking of evidence, first-hand knowledge of the facts, and knowledge of the law applicable to the dispute. The place of the creation of the disputed content would be particularly helpful to ensure the possibility of gathering evidence in order to establish the liability of the publisher for the injurious content or to grant preventive measures. The same holds true in respect of the place of the victim's habitual residence, since this place would principally enable the competent court, which is familiar with the local conditions, easily to collect and assess information about the (potential) impacts which material placed online is liable to have on the personality rights and on the individual right holder's social relationships.

2. Supporting that the entire dispute is decided before a single forum

The proposal would make it possible for the entire dispute concerning online and possibly simultaneous offline violations of personality rights to be decided before a single forum of a Brussels-Lugano State for the place where the content was created or the victim's habitual residence is based. In turn, concentration of the dispute in a single court would militate in favour of the certain and simple application of other provisions of the Brussels-Lugano Regime, such as the rules of *lis pendens*.

III. Fostering mutual recognition of judgments

By establishing certain and simple bases of jurisdiction, the proposal would strengthen the degree of trust that the national courts accord to each other's administration of justice, and in turn, it would foster the principle of mutual recognition of judgments. Most importantly, the concentration of the dispute in a single forum would minimise the possibilities of refusing the recognition or enforcement of judgments delivered in another Brussels-Lugano State on the ground of irreconcilability.

IV. Strengthening the legal protection of persons established in the Brussels-Lugano States

The proposed connecting factors would strengthen the protection of persons, particularly the protection of the publishers, established in the Brussels-Lugano States. By avoiding the fragmentation of the same dispute into mosaic proceedings and the multiplication of courts in situations when the contested content is distributed in both printed and electronic formats simultaneously, the proposal would significantly reduce the number and variety of competent fora among which the victim is able to choose. In addition, the place of the damage would only be jurisdictionally relevant if the victim's centre of interests were based in a Brussels-Lugano State. However, this does not mean that the proposal would be disadvantageous to the person who considers that his personality rights have been violated. Rather it would also take into account his interest in no less than two respects. First, the concept of habitual residence is interpreted with a certain amount of flexibility. This flexibility would enable a victim who, for example, lives in a third state and derives his income from activities principally pursued in a Brussels-Lugano State to avail himself of this concept and sue the publisher before the court of that state, providing that that is the place where his professional centre of interests is based. Moreover, even if his habitual residence is based in a third state, he could have recourse to the court of the Brussels-Lugano State of the place where the disputed content was created, for example, where the photograph of him was taken. Alternatively, he could sue the publisher by virtue of other rules of jurisdiction outlined in *supra* Ch. III.D.

B. Virtues serving practical purposes

Two peripheral virtues shall be mentioned, which, although they do not influence jurisdictional considerations, give added value to the proposed connecting factors for practical purposes.

First, the concentration of the dispute in a single forum of a Brussels-Lugano State of the place where the allegedly injurious content was created or the victim's habitual residence is based would be compatible with several substantive legal issues. Accordingly, for example, the proposal would strengthen the legal protection of personality rights. In addition, it would ease the assessment of the violation threatened or committed and the determination of the extent of non-pecuniary harm caused. Finally, it would also be consistent with the contemporary nature of online preventive measures, such as injunctions, whose effect cannot easily be divided along national borders in an economically feasible way.

Secondly, the technology-neutral nature of the proposed connecting factors benefits from the fact that violations of personality rights are strongly connected to the physical world: the creation of the allegedly injurious content and its potential impacts on the personality rights and on the individual right holder's social relationships can principally be linked to physical places and persons. Therefore, they would function effectively in a constantly evolving and rapidly changing online environment without the need to adapt them to new forms of technology and communications.

Conclusions: International jurisdiction of European courts in the digital age - An insight view

The present book has examined how the *eDate and Martinez*-approaches advance administrability, predictability, and litigational justice and assessed whether they are suitable jurisdictional grounds for disputes concerning (potential) violations of personality rights through the Internet in Europe, where common legal norms, interests, and values strongly integrate and connect persons. The key findings can briefly be outlined as follows.

eDate and Martinez is based on Brussels I, a secondary legislative act of the EU, which is part of the Brussels-Lugano Regime. This regime encompasses numerous instruments principally having a different temporal, territorial, and occasionally subject matter scope of application. As far as one instrument partly or completely replaces the other, the interpretation provided by the ECJ in respect of the provisions of the replaced instrument is also valid for the other instruments if their provisions may be considered to be equivalent. Equivalency exists regarding Art 5(3) of Brussels I, on which the *eDate and Martinez*-approaches are based and which has been replaced by Art 7(2) since 10.1.2015 (*supra* Ch. III.A.I-II).

This provision is one of the most important jurisdictional bases, and it enables the person who considers that his personality rights are (threatened to be) violated through the Internet to initiate proceedings against the alleged perpetrator. It is a special rule of jurisdiction in tort that confers international jurisdiction and venue and derogates from the general jurisdictional rule of the courts of the Brussels-Lugano State in which the defendant is domiciled. It is applicable if the defendant is domiciled in the territory of one of the Brussels-Lugano States or if the whereabouts of the defendant, who is probably an EU citizen (?), are unknown, provided that the court seised does not have firm evidence to support the conclusion that the defendant is, in fact, domiciled outside the EU. Art 7(2) compromises two basic elements, namely, a subject matter and a connecting factor, which are interpreted independently and restrictively (*supra* Ch. III.B.I.1; Ch. III.C; Ch. III.D.II; Ch. IV).

In proceedings concerning online (potential) violations of personality rights, the victim seeks to establish the liability of the publisher, and the cause of action is not related to matters relating to a contract within the meaning of Art 7(1)(a), since in a violation, no obligation is freely assumed by one party towards another. Indeed, the defendant unilaterally imposes the actual or potential violation upon the victim. Therefore, online (potential) violations of personality rights are classified as «matters relating to tort, delict or quasi-delict», and thus, they fall under the subject matter of Art 7(2) (*supra* Ch. IV.A).

The connecting factor selected as an element forming one of the facts of «matters relating to tort, delict or quasi-delict» to allocate these matters to a legal system is «the place where the harmful event occurred or may occur». As is held in *Bier*, and as is consistently confirmed in the settled case law of the ECJ, it is intended to cover both the place where the event giving rise to the damage occurred or may occur and the place where the damage occurred or may occur on an equal footing. Accordingly, the perpetrator may be sued at the option of the plaintiff in the courts for either of these places. The interpretation of these dual places is governed by several objectives and underlined by various principles, which, although often competing with each other, aim to promote the universal principle of the Brussels-Lugano Regime, namely, the principle of strengthening the legal protection of persons established in the Brussels-Lugano States. Accordingly, these dual concepts should be highly predictable. In addition, they establish at the time of causation a particularly close (sometimes called the closest) connection between the dispute and the competent courts. The existence of this proximity should ensure legal certainty, and it justifies the attribution of jurisdiction to those courts for reasons relating to the sound administration of justice and the efficacious conduct of proceedings. It follows that these two places are regarded as being particularly helpful in relation to the evidence and the conduct of the proceedings. The courts at these places are objectively the best placed to determine whether the elements constituting the perpetrator's liability exist. By maintaining the principle of legal certainty and the principle that disputes should be decided in an appropriate forum, the dual criteria also facilitate the liberal recognition and enforcement of judgments. Mindful of these governing objectives and underlying principles as well as the legal theory and practice on Art 7(2), the concept of causal event is generally understood as the original act, which factually commences the chain of successive events resulting in damage. The place of the damage is generally viewed as the place other than the place where the indirect or the direct victim suffered consequential harm (*supra* Ch. III.B; Ch. IV.B).

These dual criteria were first applied in *Shevill* to an action seeking to obtain monetary compensation for the non-material harm allegedly caused by a defamatory newspaper article distributed in various Contracting States of the BC. The ECJ identified the place of the causal event with the place where the publisher of the defamatory publication is established. At that place, the competent court has an unlimited extent of jurisdiction to rule on the entire dispute. The place of the damage was held to be the Contracting State where the publication was distributed and where the victim claims to have suffered injury to his reputation. This court has jurisdiction to rule solely in respect of the harm caused in the state of the court seised (so-called mosaic approach). It was stressed that these two criteria withhold practicability in respect of substantive legal considerations and are contrary to the governing objectives and underlying principles of Art 7(2) in different respects. The key criticisms centred on (1) the concept of the publisher's establishment, (2) the disputable requirement that the victim be known at the place where the newspaper complained of is distributed, and (3) the mosaic approach (*supra* Ch. V).

eDate and Martinez partly confirmed and partly revised the *Shevill*-criteria. By doing so, it was respectfully argued that the ECJ failed to resolve the troublesome issues outlined in relation to *Shevill*. Above that, it was noted that the *eDate and Martinez*-approaches generated additional complications. The key criticisms focused on (1) the concept of the publisher's establishment; (2) the concept of the victim's centre of interest; (3) the accessibility criterion equipped with the mosaic approach; (4) the time of causation; (5) the meaning of the reference to the unlimited extent of jurisdiction of the courts designated by the concept of the publisher's establishment and the victim's centre of interests approach; and (6) the restriction of the scope of application of the approaches to online violations. It was also noticed that these critical points to some extent outweigh in an unacceptable manner one underlying principle and governing objective of Art 7(2) over the other. Consequently, they basically turn upside down the balancing exercise not only between ease of administration of justice and predictability *vis-à-vis* litigational justice but also between ease of administration of justice and predictability. By doing so, they also weaken the liberal recognition and enforcement of judgments (*supra* Ch. VII).

These key criticisms strengthened the present author's belief that reform of the *eDate and Martinez*-approaches is necessary. Mindful of the proposals advocated in the legal theory and practice for localising violations of personality rights (*supra* Ch. VI; Ch. VII.B-D), she therefore suggests a solution that can be summed up as follows:

The present author's approaches: the place of the creation of the content and the victim's habitual residence

The present author essentially recommends that by abolishing the concept of accessibility and thus, the mosaic approach, in violations of personality rights through the Internet, the expression «the place where the harmful event occurred or may occur» employed in Art 7(2) be interpreted as meaning, that the victim could bring an action for compensation in respect of all the worldwide damage caused in the courts for either of the following two places. Accordingly, he could bring his action in the court for the place of the Brussels-Lugano State where the content complained of was created. Alternatively, he could sue the publisher in the court for the place of the Brussels-Lugano State where his habitual residence at the time of the initiation of the proceedings is based, provided that the disputed content is or has been accessible there. These connecting factors should apply not only to disputes concerning violations already committed, but also to disputes in which persons aim to prevent such violations from occurring. The application of these approaches could and should also be extended to three situations: (1) to (potential) violations through different forms of online communications, (2) under certain circumstances, to (potential) violations (threatened to be) committed by the simultaneous distribution of the printed and electronic versions of the content, and (3) to disputes involving individuals as defendants and, with certain limitations, to disputes involving legal persons as victims (*supra* Ch. VII; Ch. VIII).

The present author is convinced that the proposed connecting factors essentially satisfy the governing objectives and underlying principles of Art 7(2). They are not only consistent with the principle of legal certainly, but also determine the most appropriate court and foster the liberal recognition and enforcement of judgments. In addition, they are fair to both parties. They strengthen the legal protection of persons, especially the defendants, established in the Brussels-Lugano States without being disadvantageous to the persons who consider that their personality rights have been (threatened to be) violated. Accordingly, they generally restore the balance between ease of administration of justice and predictability and between ease of administration of justice and predictability *vis-à-vis* litigational justice. Furthermore, they also serve other peripheral virtues, which give them added value in no less than two respects. First, they are compatible with the meaning and nature of personality rights and non-pecuniary harm as well as of the enforcement of injunctions (*supra* Ch. I; Ch. V.C.I; Ch.

VII.B.II.1; Ch. VII.C.I.1). Secondly, they are also suitable bases of jurisdiction for the different online actors, various forms of online communication, and the constantly evolving and rapidly changing characteristics of the Internet (*supra* Ch. II).

Two final comments are called for on this proposal. First, it demonstrates the present author's opinion that the localisation of online (potential) violations of personality rights does not require the adoption of technology-specific or even complex connecting factors. Instead, these violations can be localised by having recourse to traditional, technology-neutral, and simple criteria. Secondly, although the recommended connecting factors reflect and give effect to various considerations and interests of the legislator, from a bird's eye view, it could be noted that they come near to the approaches established by certain courts from different corners of the globe in respect of the localisation of violations of personality rights through the Internet (*supra* Intr.).

Bibliography

Books, Book Chapters, Articles, Blog Entries and Studies

A Focus on Efficiency. A whitepaper from Facebook, Ericsson and Qualcomm, September 16, 2013, available at <https://fbcdn-dragon-a.akamaihd.net/hphotos-ak-prn1/851575_520797877991079_393255490_n.pdf> (cited: A Focus on Efficiency, A whitepaper, 2013)

Altenkirch, Markus: Art. 23, in: Huber, Peter (ed.), Rome II Regulation. Pocket Commentary, Munich, sellier. european law publishers GmbH, 2011, pp 410 ff. (cited: Altenkirch, in: Huber, Rome II Regulation)

Anterion, Karine/Moréteau, Olivier: The Protection of Personality Rights against Invasions by Mass Media in France, in: Koziol, Helmut/Warzilek, Alexander (eds.), Persönlichkeitsschutz gegenüber Massenmedien/The Protection of Personality Rights against Invasions by Mass Media, Tort and Insurance Law, Vol. 13, Vienna/New York, Springer, 2005, pp 117, paras 1 ff. (cited: Anterion/Moréteau, in: Koziol/Warzilek, Persönlichkeitsschutz)

Anthimos, Apostolos: Defamation through Wikipedia postings, blog entry posted on 10.9.2014, available at <http://icl-in-greece.blogspot.de/2014/09/defamation-through-wikipedia-postings.html> (cited: Anthimos, Defamation through Wikipedia postings, 2014)

Anthimos, Apostolos: Online defamation: International jurisdiction and applicable law, blog entry posted on 10.4.2014, available at <http://icl-in-greece.blogspot.de/2014_04_06_archive.html> (cited: Anthimos, Online defamation, 2014)

Azar, Deborah: On Selecting Jurisdiction in Internet Defamation, The Dartmouth Law Journal, Spring 2008, Vol. VI:2, pp 161 ff. (cited: Azar, The Dartmouth Law Journal 2008, 161)

Bach, Ivo: Deine Rechtskraft? Meine Rechtskraft!, EuZW 2/2013, pp 56 ff. (cited: Bach, EuZW 2013, 56)

Bachmann, Birgit: Der Gerichtsstand der unerlaubten Handlung im Internet (zu LG München I, 17.10.1996 – 4 HK O 12190/96, unten S. 208, Nr. 19), IPRax 1998, Heft 3, pp 179 ff. (cited: Bachmann, IPRax 1998, 179)

Baetge, Dietmar: Article 23 Rome II (Habitual Residence of Natural Persons), in: Calliess, Gralf-Peter (ed.), Rome Regulations. Commentary on the European Rules of the Conflict of Laws, Alphen aan den Rijn, The Netherlands, Kluwer Law International, 2011, pp 610 ff., paras 17 ff. (cited: Baetge, in: Calliess, Rome Regulations)

Baetge, Dietmar: Auf dem Weg zu einem gemeinsamen europäischen Verständnis des gewöhnlichen Aufenthalts. Ein Beitrag zur Europäisierung des Internationalen Privat- und Verfahrensrechts, in: Baetge, Dietmar/von Hein, Jan/von Hinden, Michael

(Hrsg.), Die richtige Ordnung. Festschrift für Jan Kropholler zum 70. Geburtstag, Tübingen, Mohr Siebeck, 2008, pp 77 ff. (cited: Baetge, FS Jan Kropholler)

Baetge, Dietmar: Habitual Residence, in: Basedow, Jürgen/Hopt, Klaus J./ Zimmermann, Reinhard/Stier, Andreas (eds.), The Max Planck Encyclopedia of European Private Law, Oxford, OUP, 2012, Vol. I, pp 813 ff. (cited: Baetge, in: Basedow *et al.*, Max Planck Encyclopedia)

Barnes, Corinne: Citizen Journalism vs. Traditional Journalism. A Case for Collaboration, Caribbean Quarterly, Vol. 58, No. 2/3, June-September 2012, pp 16 ff. (cited: Barnes, Caribbean Quarterly 2012, 16)

Barnett, Ned: How to make money from your blog, available at <http://www.microsoft businesshub.com/news_and_updates/make_money_from_your_blog> (cited: Barnett, How to make money)

Basedow, Jürgen: The Law of Open Societies: Private Ordering and Public Regulation of International Relations, General Course on Private International Law (volume 360), Collected Courses of the Hague Academy of International Law. The Hague Academy of International Law. Brill Online, 2015. Reference. Saarlandes des Universitat Bibliothek. 14 April 2015 <http://referenceworks.brillonline.com/ entries/the-hague-academy-collected-courses/the-law-of-open-societies-private-ordering-and-public-regulation-of-international-relations-general-course-on-private-international-law-volume-360-ej.9789004255500.009_516> (accessed on 14 April 2015) (cited: Basedow, Recueil des Cours 360)

Bedat, Alexia: Case Law, France: Julie Gayet v Closer, Privacy damages awarded against French tabloid, blog entry posted on 28.3.2014, available at <http://inforrm. wordpress.com/2014/03/28/case-law-france-julie-gayet-v-closer-privacy-damages-awarded-against-french-tabloid-alexia-bedat/> (cited: Bedat, Case Law, France, 2014)

Bennett, William: New Developments in the United Kingdom: The Defamation Act 2013, YbPIL, Vol. 14 (2012/2013), pp 173 ff. (cited: Bennett, YbPIL 2012/2013, 173)

Bertoni, Eduardo: Determining jurisdiction in Internet defamation cases: Insights on Latin America, in: Bertoni, Eduardo (ed.), Towards an Internet Free of Censorship: Proposals for Latin America, available at <http://www.palermo.edu/cele/ english/publication.html> (cited: Bertoni, in: Bertoni, Towards an Internet Free of Censorship)

Beverley-Smith, Huw/Ohly, Ansgar/Lucas-Schloetter, Agnès: Privacy, Property and Personality: Civil Law Perspectives on Commercial Appropriation, Cambridge, CUP, 2005 (cited: Beverley-Smith/Ohly/Lucas-Schloetter, Privacy, Property and Personality)

Bigos, Oren: Jurisdiction over Cross-Border Wrongs on the Internet, ICLQ vol 54, July 2005, pp 585 ff. (cited: Bigos, ICLQ 2005, 585)

BIICL: The Effect in the European Community of Judgments in Civil and Commercial Matters: Recognition, *Res Judicata* and Abuse of Process, Comparative Report, Project Reference: JLS/2006/FPC/21 – 30-CE-00914760055, Jacob van de Velden (Project Director), Justine Stefanelli (Project Research Fellow), Andrew Dickinson

(Project Consultant) (cited: BIICL, Recognition, Res Judicata and Abuse of Process)

Blanco, Pilar Jiménez: Unmarried Fathers and Child Abduction in European Union Law, J. Priv. Int. L., Vol. 8, No. 1, April 2012, pp 135 ff. (cited: Blanco, J. Priv. Int. L. 2012, 135)

Blobel, Felix: Der europäische Deliktsgerichtsstand und reine Vermögensschäden. Eine Anmerkung zur Entscheidung des EuGH vom 10.6.2004, Kronhofer/Maier u.a., EuLF, Heft 3-2004, pp 187 ff. (cited: Blobel, EuLF 2004, 187)

Blocman, Amélie: The right to be forgotten: first decision delivered in application of CJEU jurisprudence, IRIS 2015-4:1/8, available at <http://merlin.obs.coe.int/newsletter.php?year=2015&issue=4&id=15226> (last accessed on 15.4.2015) (cited: Blocman, The right to be forgotten, 2015)

Bogdan, Michael: Defamation on the Internet, *Forum Delicti* and the E-Commerce Directive: Some Comments on the ECJ Judgment in the *eDate* Case, YbPIL, Vol. 13 (2011), pp 483 ff. (cited: Bogdan, YbPIL 2011, 483)

Bogdan, Michael: Jurisdiction in Disputes about Infringements of Intellectual Property Rights on the Internet in View of Recent ECJ Case Law, 7 Masaryk U. J.L. & Tech. 193 2013, pp 193 ff. (cited: Bogdan, Masaryk U. J.L. & Tech. 2013, 193)

Bogdan, Michael: Website Accessibility as Basis for Jurisdiction under the Brussels I Regulation, 5 Masaryk U. J.L. & Tech. 1 2011, pp 1 ff. (cited: Bogdan, Masaryk U. J.L. & Tech. 2011, 1)

Borchers, Patrick J.: Tort and Contract Jurisdiction via the Internet: the 'Minimum Contacts' Test and the Brussels Regulation compared, NILR, 2003, pp 401 ff. (cited: Borchers, NILR 2003, 401)

Boronkay, Miklós: A képmáshoz és a hangfelvételhez fűződő jog, In Medias Res, 2013/1, június, pp 111 ff. (cited: Boronkay, In Medias Res, 2013, 111)

Boskovic, Olivera: Boskovic on Rome II and Defamation, blog entry posted by Cuniberti, Gilles on 20.7.2010, available at <http://conflictoflaws.net/2010/boskovic-on-rome-ii-and-defamation/> (last accessed on 23.4.2015) (cited: Boskovic, Boskovic on Rome II, 2010)

Bosky, Stephen W.: Defamation in the Internet Age: Missouri's Jurisdictional Fight begins with *Baldwin v. Fischer-Smith*, St. Louis U. L.J., Vol. 56:587, 2012, pp 587 ff. (cited: Bosky, St. Louis U. L.J. 2012, 587)

Brand, Peter-Andreas: Persönlichkeitsrechtsverletzungen im Internet, E-Commerce und „Fliegender Gerichtsstand", NJW 3/2012, pp 127 ff. (cited: Brand, NJW 2012, 127)

Brand, Ronald A.: Jurisdictional Developments and the New Hague Judgments Project, in: The Permanent Bureau of the Hague Conference on Private International Law (ed.), A Commitment to Private International Law: Essays in Honour of Hans van Loon, Cambridge – Antwerp – Portland, intersentia, 2013, pp 89 ff. (cited: Brand, FS Hans van Loon)

Brüggemeier, Gert/Colombi Ciacchi, Aurelia/O'Callaghan, Patrick (eds.): Personality Rights in European Tort Law, Cambridge *et al.*, CUP, 2010 (cited: Brüggemeier/Colombi Ciacchi/O'Callaghan, Personality Rights)

Buchner, Benedikt: Kläger- und Beklagtenschutz im Recht der internationalen Zuständigkeit: Lösungsansätze für eine zukünftige Gerichtsstands- und Vollstreckungskonvention, Tübingen, Mohr Siebeck, 1998 (cited: Buchner, Kläger- und Beklagtenschutz)

Calvo Caravaca, Alfonso Luis/Carrascosa González, Javier: Art 24, in: Magnus, Ulrich/Mankowski, Peter (eds.), Brussels I Regulation, Munich, sellier european law publishers GmbH, 2nd edn., 2012, pp 514 ff. (cited: Calvo Caravaca/Carrascosa González, in: Magnus/Mankowski, Brussels I Regulation)

Carter, P.B.: Private International Law - Jurisdiction in defamation cases, Case No. I., The British Yearbook of International Law 1992, Sixty-Third Year of Issue, Oxford, At the Clarendon Press, 1993, pp 519 ff. (cited: Carter, BYbIL 1993, 519)

Chitsa, Sarudzai: Name Calling On The Internet: The Problems Faced By Victims Of Defamatory Content In Cyberspace, Cornell Law School Inter-University Graduate Student Conference Papers, 4-1-2011, Paper 48, pp 1 ff., available at <http://scholarship.law.cornell.edu/lps_clacp/48> (cited: Chitsa, Name Calling On The Internet, 2011)

Coester-Waltjen, Dagmar: Internationale Zuständigkeit bei Persönlichkeitsrechtsverletzungen, in: Geimer, Reinhold (Hrsg.), Wege zur Globalisierung des Rechts. Festschrift für Rolf A. Schütze zum 65. Geburtstag, München, C.H. Beck'sche Verlagsbuchhandlung, 1999, pp 175 ff. (cited: Coester-Waltjen, FS Rolf A. Schütze)

Crespi Reghizzi, Zeno: 'Mutual Trust' and 'Arbitration Exception' in the European Judicial Area: The *West Tankers* Judgment of the ECJ, YbPIL, Vol. 11 (2009), pp 427 ff. (cited: Crespi Reghizzi, YbPIL 2009, 427)

Csehi, Zoltán (Nagy és Trócsányi): Comparative Study of "Residual Jurisdiction" in Civil and Commercial Disputes in the EU, National Report for Hungary, available at <http://ec.europa.eu/justice/civil/document/index_en.htm> (cited: Csehi, Residual Jurisdiction in Hungary)

Cuniberti, Gilles/Rueda, Isabelle: Abolition of Exequatur - Addressing the Commission's Concerns, RabelsZ Bd. 75 (2011), pp 286 ff. (cited: Cuniberti/Rueda, RabelsZ 2011, 286)

De Winter, L. I.: Excessive Jurisdiction in Private International Law, ICLQ vol 17, July 1968, pp 706 ff. (cited: de Winter, ICLQ 1968, 706)

Delany, Hilary/Carolan, Eoin: The Right to Privacy. A Doctrinal and Comparative Analysis, Murphy, Cliodhna (with a contribution on French privacy law), Dublin, Thomson Round Hall, 2008 (cited: Delany/Carolan, The Right to Privacy)

Dickinson, Andrew: By Royal Appointment: No Closer to an EU Private International Law Settlement?, blog entry posted on 24.10.2012, available at <http://conflictoflaws.net/2012/by-royal-appointment-no-closer-to-an-eu-private-international-law-settlement/> (last accessed 23.4.2015) (cited: Dickinson, By Royal Appointment, 2012)

Dietze, Jan: Anmerkung zum Urteil des EuGH vom 16.01.2014 (C-45/13; EuZW 2014, 232) – EuGVVO: Zuständigkeit am Handlungsort in Produkthaftungsfällen, EuZW 6/2014, pp 234 f. (cited: Dietze, EuZW 2014, 234)

DLA Piper (prepared by): EU Study on the Legal analysis of a Single Market for the Information Society. New Rules for a new age?, the study was undertaken by Prof. dr. Patrick Van Eecke and Maarten Truyens, for other members of the study's team, see Chapter 1 (Summary), p 1, Chapter 4 - The future of online privacy and data protection. SMART 2007/0037 November 2009, available at <http://ec.europa.eu/information_society/newsroom/cf/newsletter-item-detail.cfm?item_id=7022> (cited: DLA Piper, New Rules for a new age?, 2009)

Dodge, Martin: Mapping How The Data Flows, blog entry posted at <http://mappa.mundi.net/maps/maps_004/> (cited: Dodge, Mapping How The Data Flows)

Dogpile.com: Different Engines, Different Results. Web Searchers Not Always Finding What They're Looking for Online, A Research Study by Dogpile.com in Collaboration with Researchers from Queensland University of Technology and the Pennsylvania State University, April 2007, available at <csearchcdn1.inspcloud.com/dogpile/9.0.0.170/content/downloads/overlap-differentenginesdifferentresults.pdf> (cited: Dogpile.com, Different Engines, Different Results, 2007)

Dougan, Michael: The Treaty of Lisbon 2007: Winning Minds, not Hearts, CML Rev. 45, 2008, pp 617 ff. (cited: Dougan, CML Rev. 2008, 617)

Down on the server farm. The real-world implications of the rise of internet computing, N.N., The Economist, 22.5.2008, SEATTLE, available at <http://www.economist.com/node/11413148> (cited: Down on the server farm, The Economist, 2008)

Dworkin, Ronald: Law's Empire, Cambridge, *et al.*, The Belknap Press of Harvard University Press, 1986 (cited: Dworkin, Law's Empire)

Eady, David: Injunctions and the protection of privacy, C.J.Q. 2010, 29(4), pp 411 ff. (cited: Eady, C.J.Q. 2010, 411)

Edelman, Benjamin: Running Out of Numbers: Scarcity of IP Addresses and What to Do About It, Harvard Business School, Working Paper 09-091, 2009, pp 1 ff., available at <http://ssrn.com/abstract=1337075> or <http://dx.doi.org/10.2139/ssrn.1337075> (cited: Edelman, Running Out of Numbers, 1)

Edelman, Benjamin: Shortcomings and Challenges in the Restriction of Internet Retransmissions of Over-the-air Television Content to Canadian Internet Users, pp 1 ff., available at <http://cyber.law.harvard.edu/archived_content/people/edelman/pubs/jump-091701.pdf> (cited: Edelman, Shortcomings and Challenges, 1)

EGTL (ed.): Principles of European Tort Law. Text and Commentary, Vienna/New York, Springer, 2005 (cited: EGTL, Principles)

Fallon, Marc/Kinsch, Patrick/Kohler, Christian (eds.): Le droit international privé européen en construction. *Vingt ans de travaux du GEDIP*. Building European Private International Law. *Twenty Years' Work by GEDIP*, Cambridge-Antwerp-

Portland, intersentia, 2011 (cited: Fallon/Kinsch/Kohler, Le droit international privé)

Fawcett, James J./Carruthers, Janeen M./North, Peter: Cheshire, North & Fawcett. Private International Law, Oxford, OUP, 14th edn., 2008 (cited: Fawcett/Carruthers/ North, PIL)

Fawcett, James J./Torremans, Paul: Intellectual Property and Private International Law, Oxford Private International Law Series, Oxford, OUP, 2nd edn., 2011 (cited: Fawcett/Torremans, Intellectual Property and Private International Law)

Fechner, Frank: Medienrecht, Tübingen, Mohr Siebeck, 15. Aufl., 2014 (cited: Fechner, Medienrecht)

Fentiman, Richard: Introduction to Arts. 27-30, Art 27, in: Magnus, Ulrich/ Mankowski, Peter (eds.), Brussels I Regulation, Munich, sellier european law publishers GmbH, 2nd edn., 2012, pp 557 ff. (cited: Fentiman, in: Magnus/Mankowski, Brussels I Regulation)

Ferid, Murad/Sonnenberger, Hans Jürgen: Das Französische Zivilrecht, Band 1/1, Erster Teil: Allgemeine Lehren des Französischen Zivilrechts: Einführung und Allgemeiner Teil des Zivilrechts, Heidelberg, Verlag Recht und Wirtschaft GmbH, 2. Aufl., 1994 (cited: Murad/Sonnenberger, Das Französische Zivilrecht)

Fernández Arroyo, Diego P.: What's New in Latin American Private International Law?, YbPIL, Vol. 7 (2005), pp 85 ff. (cited: Fernández Arroyo, YbPIL 2005, 85)

Fézer, Tamás: A nem vagyoni (erkölcsi) sérelmek megítélése a polgári jogban, Budapest, HVG-ORAC, 2011 [cited: Fézer, A nem vagyoni (erkölcsi) sérelmek megítélése]

Fisher, David I.: Defamation via Satellite. A European Law Perspective, The Netherlands, Kluwer Law International, 1998 (cited: Fisher, Defamation via Satellite)

Forgács, Nóra (interjút készítette): Az új Ptk. koncepcionális kérdései – interjú Székely László miniszteri biztossal, interjú, 14.11.2012, available at <http://ptk2013.hu/ interjuk/az-uj-ptk-koncepcionalis-kerdesei-interju-szekely-laszlo-miniszteri-biztossal/942> (cited: Forgács, Interjú Székely László miniszteri biztossal, 2012)

Forsyth, Christopher: Defamation under the Brussels Convention: A Forum Shopper's Charter?, C.L.J. 1995, pp 515 ff. (cited: Forsyth, C.L.J. 1995, 515)

Forum Shopping Reconsidered, Note, N.N., 103 Harv. L. Rev. 1677 1989-1990, pp 1677 ff. (cited: Forum Shopping, Harv. L. Rev. 1989-1990, 1677)

Fötschl, Andreas: Keine Anwendung des Lugano-Übereinkommens für Kläger aus Drittstaaten – Zur Entscheidung des norwegischen Høyesterett in Raffles Shipping v. Trico Subsea AS (zu Norwegisches Høyesterett, 20.12.2012 – HR-2012-2393-A), IPRax 2014, Heft 2, pp 187 ff. (cited: Fötschl, IPRax 2014, 187)

Gallagher, Louise: Internet Defamation - In what Jurisdiction Can An Action Be Taken? *USA Rugby Football Union Limited -v- Ivan Calhoun*, case report posted on Internet Newsletter for Lawyers, January/February 2003, by Delia Venables, available at <http://www.venables.co.uk/n0301jurisdiction2.htm> (cited: Gallagher, Internet Defamation)

Gampp, Edda: *Perpetuatio fori internationalis* im Zivilprozeß und im Verfahren der freiwilligen Gerichtsbarkeit, Frankfurt am Main *et al.*, Peter Lang, 2010 (cited: Gampp, Perpetuatio fori internationalis)

Garber, Thomas: Die internationale Zuständigkeit für Klagen aufgrund einer Persönlichkeitsrechtsverletzung im Internet, ÖJZ 2012/13, pp 108 ff. (cited: Garber, ÖJZ 2012, 108)

Garnett, Richard/Richardson, Megan: Libel Tourism or Just Redress? Reconciling the (English) Right to Reputation with the (American) Right to Free Speech in Cross-Border Libel Cases, J. Priv. Int. L. Vol. 5, No. 3, December 2009, pp 471 ff. (cited: Garnett/Richardson, J. Priv. Int. L. 2009, 471)

Gebauer, Martin: Persönlichkeitsrechtsverletzung durch Suchergänzungsfunktion bei Google (zu BGH, 14.5.2013 – VI ZR 269/12, unten S. 538, Nr. 46), IPRax 2014, Heft 6, pp 513 ff. (cited: Gebauer, IPRax 2014, 513)

Geuer, Ermano: Verletzung des Persönlichkeitsrechts durch Veröffentlichung privater Facebook-Fotos in Tageszeitung. Orientierungssatz zur Anmerkung, jurisPR-ITR 6/2013 Anm. 4 (cited: Geuer, jurisPR-ITR 2013)

Giannakaki, Maria: The "Right to be Forgotten" in the Era of Social Media and Cloud Computing, in: Akrivopoulou, Christina M./Garipidis, Nicolaos (eds.), Human Rights and Risks in the Digital Era: Globalization and the Effects of Information Technologies, Hershey, PA, Information Science Reference (an imprint of IGI Global), 2012, Chapter 2, pp 10 ff. (cited: Giannakaki, in: Akrivopoulou/Garipidis, Human Rights and Risks)

Gibson, Judith: It came from CyberSpace: Defamation Law and the Internet, NSW State Legal Conference: Session 16, Thursday 28 August 2014, available at <https://inforrm.files.wordpress.com/2014/09/it-came-from-cyberspace-judith-gibson.pdf> (cited: Gibson, It came from CyberSpace, 2014)

Giliker, Paula: The Europeanisation of English Tort Law, Oxford and Portland, Oregon, Hart Publishing, 2014 (cited: Giliker, The Europeanisation of English Tort Law)

Gillies, Lorna: Jurisdiction for Cross-Border Breach of Personality and Defamation: *eDate Advertising and Martinez*, ICLQ vol 61, 4/2012, pp 1007 ff. (cited: Gillies, ICLQ 2012, 1007)

Ginsburg, Jane C./Gauthier, Myriam: The Celestial Jukebox and Earthbound Courts: Judicial Competence in the European Union and the United States Over Copyright Infringements in Cyberspace, RIDA 173, Juillet 1997, pp 61 ff. (cited: Ginsburg/Gauthier, RIDA 1997, 61)

Ginsburg, Jane C.: The Private International Law of Copyright in an Era of Technological Change (volume 273), Collected Courses of the Hague Academy of International Law. The Hague Academy of International Law. Brill Online, 2015. Reference. Saarlandes des Universitat Bibliothek. 14 April 2015 <http://referenceworks.brillonline.com/entries/the-hague-academy-collected-courses/the-private-international-law-of-copyright-in-an-era-of-technological-change-volume-273-ej.9789041112514.239_405> (accessed on 14 April 2015) (cited: Ginsburg, Recueil des Cours 273)

Gócza, Éva (felelős szerk.): Polgári Törvénykönyv. Civil Code, Budapest, Wolters Kluwer, 2013 (cited: Gócza, Civil Code)

Halpern, Joseph: "Exorbitant Jurisdiction" and the Brussels Convention: Toward a Theory of Restraint, 9 Yale J. World Pub. Ord. 369 1982-1983, pp 369 ff. (cited: Halpern, Yale J. World Pub. Ord. 1982-1983, 369)

Hamburg Group for Private International Law: Comments on the European Commission's Draft Proposal for a Council Regulation on the Law Applicable to Non-Contractual Obligations, available at <http://ec.europa.eu/justice/news/consulting_public/rome_ii/contributions/max_planck_en.pdf> (cited: Hamburg Group for Private International Law, Comments on the Draft Proposal)

Harmathy, Attila: On certain Aspects of Privacy, Annales Universitatis Scientiarum Budapestinensis de Rolando Eötvös Nominatae, Sectio Iuridica, Tomus XLVI, Budapest, 2005, pp 5 ff. (cited: Harmathy, Annales Univ. Sci. Budapest., Sec. Iur. 2005, 5)

Harsági, Viktória/Kengyel, Miklós: Anwendungsprobleme des Europäischen Zivilverfahrensrechts in Mittel- und Osteuropa, IPRax 2009, Heft 6, pp 533 ff. (cited: Harsági/Kengyel, IPRax 2009, 533)

Hartley, Trevor C.: 'Libel Tourism' and Conflict of Laws, ICLQ vol 59, January 2010, pp 25 ff. (cited: Hartley, ICLQ 2010, 25)

Hartley, Trevor C.: Choice-of-court Agreements under the European and International Instruments, Oxford Private International Law Series, Oxford, OUP, 2013 (cited: Hartley, Choice-of-court Agreements)

Hartley, Trevor C.: The Modern Approach to Private International Law: International Litigation and Transactions from a Common-Law Perspective (volume 319), Collected Courses of the Hague Academy of International Law. The Hague Academy of International Law. Brill Online, 2015. Reference. Saarlandes des Universitat Bibliothek. 14 April 2015 <http://referenceworks.brillonline.com/entries/the-hague-academy-collected-courses/the-modern-approach-to-private-international-law-international-litigation-and-transactions-from-a-common-law-perspective-volume-319-ej.9789004153783.009_324> (accessed on 14 April 2015) (cited: Hartley, Recueil des Cours 319)

Hartley, Trevor: *Article* 5(3) *of the Brussels Convention. Shevill v. Presse Alliance S.A.* [1992] 2 W.L.R. 1 (C.A.), E.L.Rev., Vol. 17, 1992, pp 274 ff. (cited: Hartley, E.L.Rev. 1992, 274)

Hartley, Trevor: Convention on Jurisdiction and the Enforcement of Judgments in Civil and Commercial Matters – *Article 5 (3): the place of commission of a tort*, European Court, Judgment of November 30, 1976, Case 21/76, *Handelskwekerij G. J. Bier & Stichting Reinwater* v. *Mines de Potasse d'Alsace* (not yet reported) (Dutch), E.L.Rev., Vol. 2, 1977, pp 143 ff. (cited: Hartley, E.L.Rev. 1977, 143)

Hartley, Trevor: Cross-border privacy injunctions: the EU dimension, L.Q.R., 2012, 128(Apr), pp 197 ff. (cited: Hartley, L.Q.R. 2012, 197)

Heinze, Christian: Surf global, sue local! Der europäische Klägergerichtsstand bei Persönlichkeitsrechtsverletzungen im Internet, EuZW 24/2011, pp 947 ff. (cited: Heinze, EuZW 2011, 947)

Hergenröder, Curt Wolfgang: Anmerkung zu EuGH, Urteil vom 5.2.2004, C-18/02 – *Danmarks Rederiforening, handelnd für DFDS Torline A/S*, GPR 1/05, pp 33 ff. (cited: Hergenröder, GPR 2005, 33)

Hess, Burkhard: Der Schutz der Privatsphäre im Europäischen Zivilverfahrensrecht. Besprechung von EuGH, Urteil v. 25.10.2011, verb. Rs. C-509/09 und C-161/10 (eDateAdvertising u. a.), JZ 4/2012, pp 189 ff. (cited: Hess, JZ 2012, 189)

Hess, Burkhard: Mutual Recognition in the European Law of Civil Procedure, ZVglRWiss 111 (2012), pp 21 ff. (cited: Hess, ZVglRWiss 2012, 21)

Hess, Burkhard: The Brussels I Regulation: Recent case law of the Court of Justice and the Commission's proposed recast, CML Rev. 49, 2012, pp 1075 ff. (cited: Hess, CML Rev. 2012, 1075)

Hess, Burkhard: The Proposed Recast of the Brussels I Regulation: Rules on Jurisdiction, in: Pocar, Fausto/Viarengo, Ilaria/Villata, Francesca Clara (eds.), Recasting Brussels I, Padova, Cedam, 2012, pp 91 ff. (cited: Hess, in: Pocar/Viarengo/Villata, Recasting Brussels I)

Hestermeyer, Holger P.: Personal Jurisdiction for Internet Torts: Towards an International Solution?, (2006) 26 Nw. J. Int'l L. & Bus., pp 267 ff. (cited: Hestermeyer, Nw. J. Int'l L. & Bus. 2006, 267)

Hilbig-Lugani, Katharina: Divergenz und Transparenz: Der Begriff des gewöhnlichen Aufenthalts der privat handelnden natürlichen Person im jüngeren EuIPR und EuZVR, GPR 1/2014, pp 8 ff. (cited: Hilbig-Lugani, GPR 2014, 8)

Hoare, Aram: Following on from the Australian Dow Jones decision on jurisdiction in Internet defamation, do compelling reasons exist for legislating for a new approach to this issue?, C.L.Pract., January 2004, pp 4 ff. (cited: Hoare, C.L.Pract. 2004, 4)

Hobér, Kaj: Res Judicata and Lis Pendens in International Arbitration (volume 366), Collected Courses of the Hague Academy of International Law. The Hague Academy of International Law. Brill Online, 2015. Reference. Saarlandes des Universitat Bibliothek. 14 April 2015 <http://referenceworks.brillonline.com/entries/the-hague-academy-collected-courses/res-judicata-and-lis-pendens-in-international-arbitration-volume-366-ej.9789004263956.099_406> (accessed on 14 April 2015) (cited: Hobér, Recueil des Cours 366)

Hohloch, Gerhard: Gerichtsstand der unerlaubten Handlung gem. Art. 5 Nr. 3 EuGVÜ, JuS 1995, Heft 10, pp 928 f. (cited: Hohloch, JuS 1995, 928)

House of Commons, Culture, Media and Sport Committee: Press standards, privacy and libel, Second Report of Session 2009-10, Vol. I, Report, together with formal minutes, Ordered by the House of Commons to be printed 9 February 2010, available at <http://www.publications.parliament.uk/pa/cm200910/cmselect/cmcumeds/362/362i.pdf> (cited: House of Commons, Press standards, privacy and libel)

Huber, Peter: Persönlichkeitsschutz gegenüber Massenmedien im Rahmen des Europäischen Zivilprozeßrechts. *Entscheidung des Europäischen Gerichtshofs vom 7.März*

1995 (Rechtssache C-68/93 – Fiona Shevill u.a./Presse Alliance SA), Anmerkung, ZEuP 2/1996, pp 295 ff. (cited: Huber, ZEuP 1996, 295)

Husovec, Martin: Comment on "Pinckney". Council Regulation (EC) No. 44/2001 of 22 December 2000 on Jurisdiction and the Recognition and Enforcement of Judgments in Civil and Commercial Matters, Art. 5(3) – *Peter Pinckney v. KDG Mediatech AG*, IIC (2014) 45:370–374 (cited: Husovec, IIC 2014, 370)

IPI: Out of Balance: Defamation Law in the European Union: A Comparative Overview for Journalists, Civil Society and Policymakers, Griffen, Scott (lead author), Trionfi, Barbara/Ellis, Steven M./Griffen, Scott (eds.), January 2015, available at <http://www.freemedia.at/ecpm/international-standards.html> (cited: IPI, Defamation Law in the European Union, 2015)

IPI: Principles on Freedom of Expression and Protection of Reputation [adapted from the the original Principles developed by ARTICLE 19 (ARTICLE 19: Defining Defamation, Principles on Freedom of Expression and Protection of Reputation, July 2000)], available at <http://www.freemedia.at/ecpm/international-standards.html> (cited: IPI, Principles on Freedom of Expression and Protection of Reputation)

Jaeger-Fine, Desiree/Reidenberg, Joel R./Debelak, Jamela/Kovnot, Jordan: Internet Jurisdiction: A Survey of German Scholarship and Cases (June 30, 2013). Fordham Law Legal Studies Research Paper No. 2309575, Jaeger-Fine, Desiree (principal study author), Reidenberg, Joel R./Debelak, Jamela/Kovnot, Jordan (CLIP study team), available at SSRN: <http://ssrn.com/abstract=2309575> or <http://dx.doi.org/10.2139/ssrn.2309575> (cited: Jaeger-Fine *et al.*, Internet Jurisdiction, 2013)

Jayme, Erik/Kohler, Christian: Das Internationale Privat- und Verfahrensrecht der EG – Stand 1989, IPRax 1989, Heft 6, pp 337 ff. (cited: Jayme/Kohler, IPRax 1989, 337)

Jayme, Erik/Kohler, Christian: Das Internationale Privat- und Verfahrensrecht der EG auf dem Wege zum Binnenmarkt, IPRax 1990, Heft 6, pp 353 ff. (cited: Jayme/Kohler, IPRax 1990, 353)

Jayme, Erik/Kohler, Christian: Das Internationale Privat- und Verfahrensrecht der EG 1993 – Spannungen zwischen Staatsverträgen und Richtlinien, IPRax 1993, Heft 6, pp 357 ff. (cited: Jayme/Kohler, IPRax 1993, 357)

Jayme, Erik/Kohler, Christian: Europäisches Kollisionsrecht 1995 – Der Dialog der Quellen, IPRax 1995, Heft 6, pp 343 ff. (cited: Jayme/Kohler, IPRax 1995, 343)

Jayme, Erik/Kohler, Christian: Europäisches Kollisionsrecht 1998: Kulturelle Unterschiede und Parallelaktionen, IPRax 1998, Heft 6, pp 417 ff. (cited: Jayme/Kohler, IPRax 1998, 417)

Jayme, Erik/Kohler, Christian: Europäisches Kollisionsrecht 1999: Die Abendstunde der Staatsverträge, IPRax 1999, Heft 6, pp 401 ff. (cited: Jayme/Kohler, IPRax 1999, 401)

Jayme, Erik/Kohler, Christian: Europäisches Kollisionsrecht 2000: Interlokales Privatrecht oder universelles Gemeinschaftsrecht?, IPRax 2000, Heft 6, pp 454 ff. (cited: Jayme/Kohler, IPRax 2000, 454)

Jayme, Erik/Kohler, Christian: Europäisches Kollisionsrecht 2001: Anerkennungsprinzip statt IPR?, IPRax 2001, Heft 6, pp 501 ff. (cited: Jayme/Kohler, IPRax 2001, 501)

Jayme, Erik/Kohler, Christian: Europäisches Kollisionsrecht 2002: Zur Wiederkehr des Internationalen Privatrechts, IPRax 2002, Heft 6, pp 461 ff. (cited: Jayme/Kohler, IPRax 2002, 461)

Jayme, Erik/Kohler, Christian: Europäisches Kollisionsrecht 2003: Der Verfassungskonvent und das Internationale Privat- und Verfahrensrecht, IPRax 2003, Heft 6, pp 485 ff. (cited: Jayme/Kohler, IPRax 2003, 485)

Jayme, Erik/Kohler, Christian: Europäisches Kollisionsrecht 2004: Territoriale Erweiterung und methodische Rückgriffe, IPRax 2004, Heft 6, pp 481 ff. (cited: Jayme/Kohler, IPRax 2004, 481)

Jayme, Erik/Kohler, Christian: Europäisches Kollisionsrecht 2005: Hegemonialgesten auf dem Weg zu einer Gesamtvereinheitlichung, IPRax 2005, Heft 6, pp 481 ff. (cited: Jayme/Kohler, IPRax 2005, 481)

Jayme, Erik/Kohler, Christian: Europäisches Kollisionsrecht 2006: Eurozentrismus ohne Kodifikationsidee?, IPRax 2006, Heft 6, pp 537 ff. (cited: Jayme/Kohler, IPRax 2006, 537)

Jones, Michael A. (general ed.)/Dugdale, Anthony M. (consultant ed.)/Simpson, Mark (associate ad.) *et al.*: Clerk & Lindsell on Torts, Sweet & Maxwell (UK), Thomson Reuters, 20th edn., 2010 (cited: Jones *et al.*, Clerk & Lindsell on Torts)

Joubert, Natalie: Cyber-Torts and Personal Jurisdiction: The Paris Court of Appeal Makes a Stand, ICLQ vol 58, April 2009, pp 476 ff. (cited: Joubert, ICLQ 2009, 476)

Jump in defamation cases driven by celebrities, press release issued by Mattison Public Relations on behalf of Sweet & Maxwell, September 2010, section 'New Media Cases', Press enquiries: Duodu, Korieh/ Mattison, Nick/ Forsey, Sarah, available at <http://www.sweetandmaxwell.co.uk/content/HomePage/SM%20-%20Jump%20in%20defamation%20cases.pdf> (cited: Jump in defamation cases, 2010)

Junker, Abbo: Der Gerichtsstand des Deliktsortes nach der Brüssel I-Verordnung bei der Verletzung von Persönlichkeitsrechten im Internet, in: Stamm, Jürgen (Hrsg.), Festschrift für Helmut Rüßmann, Saarbrücken, juris GmbH Saarbrücken, 2013, pp 811 ff. (cited: Junker, FS Helmut Rüßmann)

Kaye, Peter: Civil Jurisdiction and Enforcement of Foreign Judgments, The application in England and Wales of the Brussels Convention of 1968 on Jurisdiction and the Enforcement of Judgments in Civil and Commerical Matters under the Civil Jurisdiction and Judgments Act 1982, Abingdon, Oxon, Professional Books Limited, 1987 (cited: Kaye, Civil Jurisdiction)

Kaye, Peter: Law of the European Judgments Convention, Chichester, Barry Rose Law Publishers Ltd, Vol. 2 (Article 5(1) to (3)), 1999 (cited: Kaye, Law of the European Judgments Convention)

Kengyel, Miklós/Harsági, Viktória: Európai Polgári Eljárásjog, Budapest, Osiris Kiadó, 2009 (cited: Kengyel/Harsági, Európai Polgári Eljárásjog)

Kengyel, Miklós: Ungarn innerhalb des Tors des Lugano-Übereinkommens, in: Geimer, Reinhold/Schütze, Rolf A. (Hrsg.), Recht ohne Grenzen. Festschrift für Athanassios Kaissis zum 65. Geburtstag, München, sellier european law publishers GmbH, 2012, pp 469 ff. (cited: Kengyel, FS Athanassios Kaissis)

Kengyel, Miklós: Ungarn vor dem Tor des Lugano-Übereinkommens, in: Geimer, Reinhold (Hrsg.), Wege zur Globalisierung des Rechts. Festschrift für Rolf A. Schütze zum 65. Geburtstag, München, C.H. Beck'sche Verlagsbuchhandlung, 1999, pp 347 ff. (cited: Kengyel, in: FS Rolf A. Schütze)

Killias, Laurent: Rechtsprechung zum Lugano-Übereinkommen (2011), SZIER 4/2012, pp 697 ff. (cited: Killias, SZIER 2012, 697)

King, Kevin F.: Personal Jurisdiction, Internet Commerce, and Privacy: The Pervasive Legal Consequences of Modern Geolocation Technologies, Alb. L.J. Sci. & Tech., Vol. 21, 2011, pp 61 ff. (cited: King, Alb. L.J. Sci. & Tech. 2011, 61)

Kohler, Christian/Seyr, Sibylle/Puffer-Mariette, Jean-Christophe: Unionsrecht und Privatrecht. Zur Rechtsprechung des EuGH im Jahre 2011, ZEuP 2/2013, pp 323 ff. (cited: Kohler/Seyr/Puffer-Mariette, ZEuP 2013, 323)

Kohler, Christian: Abschied von der autonomen Auslegung des Begriffs „Zivil- und Handelssachen“ in Art. 1 EuGVVO? (zu EuGH, 12.9.2013 – Rs. C-49/12 – The Commissioners for Her Majesty's Revenue & Customs ./. Sunico ApS e. a., unten S 84, Nr. 1), IPRax 2015, Heft 1, pp 52 ff. (cited: Kohler, IPRax 2015, 52)

Kohler, Christian: Adhäsionsverfahren und Brüsseler Übereinkommen 1968, in: Will, Michael R. (Hrsg.), Schadensersatz im Strafverfahren. Rechtsvergleichendes Symposium zum Adhäsionsprozeß, Kehl am Rhein *et al.*, Engel, 1990, pp 74 ff. (cited: Kohler, in: Will, Schadensersatz)

Kohler, Christian: Balancing the judicial dialogue in Europe: some remarks on the interpretation of the 2007 Lugano Convention on jurisdiction and judgments, in: Forner Delaygua, Joaquim/González Beilfuss, Cristina/Viñas Farré, Ramón (coords.), Entre Bruselas y La Haya: Estudios sobre la unificación internacional y regional del Derecho internacional privado: Liber Amicorum Alegría Borrás, Madrid *et al.*, Marcial Pons, 2013, pp 565 ff. (cited: Kohler, FS Alegría Borrás)

Kohler, Christian: Beyond Brussels: The wide reach of the European Court's case law on the Jurisdiction and Judgments Convention, in: Brand, Ronald A./Walter, Mark (eds.), Private Law, Private International Law, & Judicial Cooperation in the EU-US Relationship, CILE Studies, Vol. II, Eagan, MN *et al.*, Thomson/West, 2005, pp 227 ff. (West 2005) (cited: Kohler, in: Brand/Walter, Private Law)

Kohler, Christian: Das Prinzip der gegenseitigen Anerkennung in Zivilsachen im europäischen Justizraum, ZSR, 2005 II, pp 263 ff. (cited: Kohler, ZSR 2005, 263)

Kohler, Christian: Der europäische Justizraum für Zivilsachen und das Gemeinschaftskollisionsrecht, IPRax 2003, Heft 5, pp 401 ff. (cited: Kohler, IPRax 2003, 401)

Kohler, Christian: Ein Nachtstück: Die Geltung des EuGVÜ in Berlin, IPRax 1989, Heft 2, pp 75 ff. (cited: Kohler, IPRax 1989, 75)

Kohler, Christian: Erstreckung der europäischen Zuständigkeitsordnung auf drittstaatsverknüpfte Streitigkeiten. Tagung der Europäischen Gruppe für Internationales Privatrecht in Bergen, IPRax 2009, Heft 3, pp 285 ff. (cited: Kohler, IPRax 2009, 285)

Kohler, Christian: Fortbildung des Brüsseler Gerichtsstands- und Vollstreckungsübereinkommens durch den Europäischen Gerichtshof: Freizügigkeit oder effektiver Rechtsschutz?, in: Schwind, Fritz (Hrsg.), Europarecht, Internationales Privatrecht, Rechtsvergleichung, Verlag der Österreichischen Akademie der Wissenschaften, Wien, 1988, pp 125 ff. (cited: Kohler, in: Schwind, Europarecht)

Kohler, Christian: Gemeinschaftsrecht und Privatrecht: Zur Rechtsprechung des EuGH im Jahre 1995, ZEuP 3/1996, pp 452 ff. (cited: Kohler, ZEuP 1996, 452)

Kohler, Christian: Homogeneity or Renationalisation in the European Judicial Area? Comments on a Recent Judgment of the Norwegian Supreme Court, in: EFTA Court (ed.), The EEA and the EFTA Court – Decentred Integration, Oxford *et al.*, Hart Publishing Ltd, 2014, Chapter 20, pp 237 ff. (cited: Kohler, in: EFTA Court, Decentred Integration)

Kohler, Christian: Internationale Gerichtsstandsvereinbarungen: Liberalität und Rigorismus im EuGVÜ, IPRax 1983, Heft 6, pp 265 ff. (cited: Kohler, IPRax 1983, 265)

Kohler, Christian: Kodifikation und Reform des Internationalen Privatrechts in Liechtenstein, IPRax 1997, Heft 5, pp 309 ff. (cited: Kohler, IPRax 1997, 309)

Kohler, Christian: Kollisionsrechtliche Anmerkungen zur Verordnung über die Gemeinschaftsmarke, in: Due, Ole/Lutter, Marcus/Schwarze, Jürgen (Hrsg.), Festschrift für Ulrich Everling, Baden-Baden, Nomos, 1995, Band I, pp 651 ff. (cited: Kohler, FS Ulrich Everling)

Kohler, Christian: L'autonomie de la volonté en droit international privé: un principe universel entre libéralisme et étatisme (volume 359), Collected Courses of the Hague Academy of International Law. The Hague Academy of International Law. Brill Online, 2015. Reference. Saarlandes des Universitat Bibliothek. 14 April 2015 <http://referenceworks.brillonline.com/entries/the-hague-academy-collected-courses/lautonomie-de-la-volonte-en-droit-international-prive-un-principe-universel-entre-liberalisme-et-etatisme-volume-359-ej.9789004255418.285_478> (accessed on 14 April 2015) (cited: Kohler, Recueil des Cours 359)

Kohler, Christian: Pathologisches im EuGVÜ: Hinkende Gerichtsstandsvereinbarungen nach Art. 17 Abs. 3, IPRax 1986, Heft 6, pp 340 ff. (cited: Kohler, IPRax 1986, 340)

Kohler, Christian: Practical Experience of the Brussels Jurisdiction and Judgments Convention in the Six Original Contracting States, ICLQ vol 34, July 1985, pp 563 ff. (cited: Kohler, ICLQ 1985, 563)

Kohler, Christian: Status als Ware: Bemerkungen zur europäischen Verordnung über das internationale Verfahrensrecht für Ehesachen, in: Mansel, Heinz-Peter (Hrsg.), Vergemeinschaftung des Europäischen Kollisionsrechts, Vorträge aus Anlaß des fünfzigjährigen Bestehens des Instituts für internationales und ausländisches Privatrecht der Universität zu Köln, Köln *et al.*, Carl Heymans Verlag, 2001, pp 41 ff. (cited: Kohler, in: Mansel, Vergemeinschaftung)

Kohler, Christian: The Case Law of the European Court on the Judgments Convention – Part I, E.L.Rev. 1982, pp 3 ff. (cited: Kohler, E.L.Rev. 1982, Part I, 3)

Kohler, Christian: The Case Law of the European Court on the Judgments Convention – Part II, E.L.Rev. 1982, pp 103 ff. (cited: Kohler, E.L.Rev. 1982, Part II, 103)

Kohler, Christian: The Interpretation of the Lugano Convention of 2007 and the Brussels Instruments on Jurisdiction and Judgments in Civil and Commercial Matters, in: EFTA Court (ed.), Judicial Protection in the European Economic Area, Stuttgart, German Law Publishers, 2012, pp 218 ff. (cited: Kohler, in: EFTA Court, Judicial Protection)

Kohler, Christian: Vom EuGVÜ zur EuGVVO: Grenzen und Konsequenzen der Vergemeinschaftung, in: Schütze, Rolf A. (Hrsg.), Einheit und Vielfalt des Rechts. Festschrift für Reinhold Geimer zum 65. Geburtstag, München, Verlag C.H. Beck, 2002, pp 461 ff. (cited: Kohler, FS Reinhold Geimer)

Kohler, Christian: Vom Markt zum Menschen: Das internationale Familienrecht der Europäischen Union nach dem Vertrag von Lissabon, in: Meng, Werner/Ress, Georg/Stein, Torsten (Hrsg.), Europäische Integration und Globalisierung. Festschrift zum 60-jährigen Bestehen des Europa-Instituts, Baden-Baden, Nomos Verlag, 2011, pp 309 ff. (cited: Kohler, FS Europa-Institut)

Kono, Toshiyuki/Jurčys, Paulius: Jurisdiction over Copyright Infringements in the Cloud, (25.12.2012), pp 1 ff., available at SSRN: <http://ssrn.com/abstract=2181671> (cited: Kono/Jurčys, Jurisdiction over Copyright Infringements, 2012)

Kosmehl, Guido: Welchen Wert hat der Gerichtsstand der unerlaubten Handlung im europäischen Zivilprozeßrecht?, in: Kosmehl, Guido/Pabst, Steffen (Hrsg.), Liber Amicorum. Thomas Rauscher zum 50. Geburtstag, Leipzig, Verlag Ille & Riemer, 2005, pp 79 ff. (cited: Kosmehl, FS Thomas Rauscher)

Koziol, Helmut/Warzilek, Alexander (eds.): Persönlichkeitsschutz gegenüber Massenmedien / The Protection of Personality Rights against Invasions by Mass Media, Vol. 13, Wien/New York, Springer, 2005 (cited: Koziol/Warzilek, Persönlichkeitsschutz)

Kreuzer, Karl/Klötgen, Paul: Die *Shevill*-Entscheidung des EuGH: Abschaffung des Deliktsortsgerichtsstands des Art. 5 Nr. 3 EuGVÜ für ehrverletzende Streudelikte (zu EuGH, 7.3.1995 – Rs. C-68/93 – Shevill u.a./Presse Alliance S. A., unten S. 111, Nr. 9), IPRax 1997, Heft 2, pp 90 ff. (cited: Kreuzer/Klötgen, IPRax 1997, 90)

Krog, Georg Philip: Determination of Jurisdiction for Defamatory Statements in TV Broadcasting, Norway, IRIS 2002-3:10/18, available at <http://merlin.obs.coe.int/iris/2002/3/article18.en.html> (cited: Krog, Determination of Jurisdiction, 2002)

Krog, Georg Philipp: Jurisdiction pursuant to the Lugano Convention art. 5.3 applied on defamatory statements in TV broadcasting, IPRax 2004, Heft 2, pp 154 ff. (cited: Krog, IPRax 2004, 154)

Kropholler, Jan/von Hein, Jan: Europäisches Zivilprozessrecht, Frankfurt am Main, Verl. Recht und Wirtschaft, 9. Aufl., 2011 (cited: Kropholler/von Hein, EuZPR)

Kubis, Sebastian: Internationale Zuständigkeit bei Persönlichkeits- und Immaterialgüterrechtsverletzungen, Bielefeld, Verlag Ernst und Werner Gieseking GmbH, 1999 (cited: Kubis, Internationale Zuständigkeit)

Kühn Baca, Werner Miguel: The Principle of Mutual Recognition of Judicial Decisions in EU Law in the light of the 'Full Faith and Credit' Clause of the US Constitution, Secretaría General de la Comunidad Andina, pp 1 ff., available at <http://www.comunidadandina.org/bda/FichaObra.aspx?cm=1922> (cited: Kühn Baca, The Principle of Mutual Recognition)

Kuipers, Jan-Jaap: Joined Cases C-509/09 & 161/10, *eDate Advertising* v. *X* and *Oliver Martinez and Robert Martinez* v. *MGN Limited*, Judgment of the Court of Justice (Grand Chamber) of 25 October 2011, nyr., CML Rev. 49, 2012, pp 1211 ff. (cited: Kuipers, CML Rev. 2012, 1211)

Kuipers, Jan-Jaap: Towards a European Approach in the Cross-Border Infringement of Personality Rights, GLJ, Vol. 12, No. 08, 2011, pp 1681 ff. (cited: Kuipers, GLJ 2011, 1681)

Kuner, Christopher: Internationale Zuständigkeitskonflikte im Internet, CR 8/1996, pp 453 ff. (cited: Kuner, CR 1996, 453)

Layton, Alexander/Mercer, Hugh (general eds.): European Civil Practice, London, Thomson/Sweet & Maxwell Limited, Vol. 1, 2nd edn., 2004 (cited: Layton/Mercer, European Civil Practice)

Lehmann, Matthias: Which Court is Competent for Prospectus Liability Cases? The CJEU Rules in Kolassa (Case C-375/13), blog entry posted by Marta Requejo on 31.1.2015, available at <http://conflictoflaws.net/2015/which-court-is-competent-for-prospectus-liability-cases-the-cjeu-rules-in-kolassa-case-c-37513/> (last accessed on 23.4.2015) (cited: Lehmann, Which Court is Competent, 2015)

Leible, Stefan: EuGH: Internationale Zuständigkeit und anwendbares Recht bei Persönlichkeitsverletzungen im Internet, Anmerkung, LMK 2012, 329468 (cited: Leible, LMK 2012, 329468)

Leonhard, Marc: Persönlichkeitsverletzungen im Internet – Internationale Zuständigkeit und anwendbares Recht, in: Leipold, Dieter (Hrsg.), Rechtsfragen des Internet und der Informationsgesellschaft, Heidelberg, C.F. Müller Verlag, 2002, pp 233 ff. (cited: Leonhard, in: Leipold, Rechtsfragen)

Lessig, Lawrence: The Zones of Cyberspace, 48 Stan. L. Rev. 1403 1995-1996, pp 1403 ff. (cited: Lessig, Stan. L. Rev. 1995-1996, 1403)

Leurdijk, Andra/Slot, Mijke/Nieuwenhuis, Ottilie: Statistical, Ecosystems and Competitiveness Analysis of the Media and Content Industries: The Newspaper Publishing Industry, Simon, Jean Paul (ed.), JRC Technical Reports, Report EUR 25277 EN, 2012, available at <http://is.jrc.ec.europa.eu/pages/ISG/documents/FINALNewsreportwithcovers.pdf> (cited: Leurdijk/Slot/Nieuwenhuis, The Newspaper Publishing Industry, 2012)

Levi, Lili: The Problem of Trans-National Libel, Am. J. Comp. L., Vol. 60, No. 2 (Spring 2012), pp 507 ff. (cited: Levi, Am. J. Comp. L. 2012, 507)

Lipton, Jacqueline D.: Mapping Online Privacy, 104 NWULR 477, Spring 2010, pp 477 ff. (cited: Lipton, NWULR 2010, 477)

Little, Laura E.: Internet Defamation, Freedom of Expression, and the Lessons of Private International Law for the United States, YbPIL, Vol. 14 (2012/2013), pp 181 ff. (cited: Little, YbPIL 2012/2013, 181)

Löffler, Severin: Mediendelikte im IPR und IZPR, Persönlichkeitsverletzungen durch Medien im Spiegel des deutschen, französischen, schweizerischen und österreichischen Rechts unter besonderer Berücksichtigung des Internets und des Gegendarstellungsanspruchs, Frankfurt am Main *et al.*, Peter Lang, 2000 (cited: Löffler, Mediendelikte)

Löser, Arne: Zuständigkeitsbestimmender Zeitpunkt und perpetuatio fori im internationalen Zivilprozess, JWV Jenaer Wissenschaftliche Verlagsgesellschaft, 2008 (cited: Löser, Zuständigkeitsbestimmender Zeitpunkt)

Mádl, Ferenc/Vékás, Lajos: Nemzetközi magánjog és nemzetközi gazdasági kapcsolatok joga, Budapest, ELTE Eötvös Kiadó, Eötvös Loránd Tudományegyetem, 2012 (cited: Mádl/Vékás, Nemzetközi magánjog)

Mádl, Ferenc/Vékás, Lajos: The Law of Conflicts and Foreign Trade, Budapest, Akadémia Kiadó, 1987 (cited: Mádl/Vékás, The Law of Conflicts)

Magnus, Ulrich/Mankowski, Peter (eds.): Brussels I Regulation, Munich, sellier european law publishers GmbH, 2nd edn., 2012 (cited: Magnus/Mankowski, Brussels I Regulation)

Magnus, Ulrich: Art 23, in: Magnus, Ulrich/Mankowski, Peter (eds.), Brussels I Regulation, Munich, sellier european law publishers GmbH, 2nd edn., 2012, pp 436 ff. (cited: Magnus, Art 23, in: Magnus/Mankowski, Brussels I Regulation)

Magnus, Ulrich: Introduction, in: Magnus, Ulrich/Mankowski, Peter (eds.), Brussels I Regulation, Munich, sellier european law publishers GmbH, 2nd edn., 2012, pp 4 ff. (cited: Magnus, Intr., in: Magnus/Mankowski, Brussels I Regulation)

Mankowski, Peter: Art 5, in: Magnus, Ulrich/Mankowski, Peter (eds.), Brussels I Regulation, Munich, sellier european law publishers GmbH, 2nd edn., 2012, pp 88 ff. (cited: Mankowski, in: Magnus/Mankowski, Brussels I Regulation)

Mankowski, Peter: Das Internet im Internationalen Vertrags- und Deliktsrecht, RabelsZ Bd. 63 (1999), pp 203 ff. (cited: Mankowski, RabelsZ 1999, 203)

Mankowski, Peter: Der gewöhnliche Aufenthalt eines verbrachten Kindes unter der Brüssel IIa-VO. Anmerkung zu EuGH, Urt. v. 22.12.2010 – Rs. C-497/10 PPU, GPR 4/11, pp 209 ff. (cited: Mankowski, GPR 2011, 209)

Mankowski, Peter: Internationale Zuständigkeit, Gerichtsstand, Erfolgsort, Persönlichkeitsrecht, Internet/„eDate Advertising“, EuGVVO Art. 5 Nr. 3; RL 2000/31/EG Art. 3, EuGH EWiR 5/11, pp 743 f. (cited: Mankowski, EWiR 2011, 743)

Mansel, Heinz-Peter/Thorn, Karsten/Wagner, Rolf: Europäisches Kollisionsrecht 2011: Gegenläufige Entwicklungen, IPRax 2012, Heft 1, pp 1 ff. (cited: Mansel/Thorn/Wagner, IPRax 2012, 1)

Mansel, Heinz-Peter/Thorn, Karsten/Wagner, Rolf: Europäisches Kollisionsrecht 2009: Hoffnungen durch den Vertrag von Lissabon, IPRax, 2010, Heft 1, pp 1 ff. (cited: Mansel/Thorn/Wagner, IPRax 2010, 1)

Marly, Jochen P.: Die Verteilung von Artikeln und Programmen in Datennetzen aus urheber- und wettbewerbsrechtlicher Sicht, JurPC 2/1992, pp 1442 ff. (cited: Marly, JurPC 1992, 1442)

McDonald, Henry: Google, Facebook and Twitter may 'face EU defamation and privacy cases', The Guardian, edn.: UK, 24.1.2013 (15:09 GMT), available at <http://www.guardian.co.uk/media/2013/jan/24/google-facebook-twitter-eu-privacy> (cited: McDonald, The Guardian 2013)

McGonagle, Marie: Jurisdiction in Television Libel Cases, Ireland, IRIS 1998-3:8/12, available at <http://merlin.obs.coe.int/iris/1998/3/article12.en.html> (cited: McGonagle, Jurisdiction in Television Libel, 1998)

McMahon, Maryann: Defamation Claims in Europe: A Survey of the Legal Armory, 19 Comm. Law. 24 2001-2002, pp 24 ff. (cited: McMahon, Comm. Law. 2001-2002, 24)

Mefford, Aron: Lex Informatica: Foundations of Law on the Internet, 5 Ind. J. Global Legal Stud. 211 1997-1998, pp 211 ff. (cited: Mefford, Ind. J. Global Legal Stud. 1997-1998, 211)

Mendes, Aluisio Gonçalves de Castro/Tiburcio, Carmen: Jurisdiction over Torts with Foreign Elements according to Brazilian Law, International Journal of Procedural Law, Vol. 3 (2013), No. 2, pp 223 ff. (cited: Mendes/Tiburcio, IJPL 2013, 223)

Michaels, Ralf: Re-placements. Jurisdiction for contracts and torts under the Brussels I Regulation when Arts. 5 (1) and 5 (3) do not designate a place in a Member State, in: Nuyts, Arnaud/Watté, Nadine (eds.), International Civil Litigation in Europe and Relations with Third States, Bruxelles, Bruylant, 2005, pp 129 ff. (cited: Michaels, in: Nuyts/Watté, International Civil Litigation)

Mikola, Orsolya Irén: Az Európai Bíróság ítélete internetes személyiségi jogi jogsértésekről. Két ügy, egy precedensértékű döntés, JeMA hallgatói különszám 2011, pp 14 ff. (cited: Mikola, JeMa 2011, 14)

Mills Wade, Angela: EPC on The Link between Brussels I and Rome II in Cases Affecting the Media, blog entry posted by George, Martin on 25.7.2010, available at <http://conflictoflaws.net/2010/epc-on-the-link-between-brussels-i-and-rome-ii-in-cases-affecting-the-media/> (last accessed on 23.4.2015) (cited: Mills Wade, EPC on The Link between Brussels I and Rome II, 2010)

Milo, Dario: Defamation and Freedom of Speech, Oxford, OUP, 2008, Chapter II: The Right to Reputation, pp 1-38, available at <www.oxfordscholarship.com> DOI:10.1093/acprof:oso/9780199204922.003.0002 (cited: Milo, Defamation and Freedom of Speech)

Mondoloni, Dominique: France, in: Glasser Jr., Charles J. (ed.), International Libel & Privacy Handbook, New York, Bloomberg Press, 2nd edn., 2009, pp 285 ff. (cited: Mondoloni, in: Glasser, International Libel & Privacy)

Morse, Robin: Rights Relating to Personality, Freedom of the Press and Private International Law: Some Common Law Comments, CLP (2005) 58 (1), pp 133 ff. (cited: Morse, CLP 2005, 133)

Mortensen, Reid: The Hague and the Ditch: The Trans-Tasman Judicial Area and the Choice of Court Convention, J. Priv. Int. L., Vol. 5, No. 2, August 2009, pp 213 ff. (cited: Mortensen, J. Priv. Int. L. 2009, 213)

Mortensen, Reid: Woodhouse Reprised: Accident Compensation and Trans-Tasman Integration, J. Priv. Int. L., Vol. 9, No. 1, April 2013, pp 1 ff. (cited: Mortensen, J. Priv. Int. L. 2013, 1)

Nagy, Csongor István: The Word is a Dangerous Weapon: Jurisdiction, Applicable Law and Personality Rights in EU Law – Missed and New Opportunities, J. Priv. Int. L., Vol. 8, No. 2, pp 251 ff. (cited: Nagy, J. Priv. Int. L. 2012, 251)

Nielsen, Peter Arnt: Brussels I and Denmark, IPRax 2007, Heft 6, pp 506 ff. (cited: Nielsen, IPRax 2007, 506)

Nielsen, Peter Arnt: Libel Tourism: English and EU Private International Law, J. Priv. Int. L., Vol. 9, No. 2, 2013, pp 269 ff. (cited: Nielsen, J. Priv. Int. L. 2013, 269)

Nielsen, Peter Arnt: The new Brussels I Regulation, CML Rev. 50, 2013, pp 503 ff. (cited: Nielsen, CML Rev. 2013, 503)

Norris, Erin F.: Why the Internet Isn't Special: Restoring Predictability to Personal Jurisdiction, Arizona Law Review, Vol. 53:1013, 2011, pp 1013 ff. (cited: Norris, Arizona Law Review 2011, 1013)

Nuyts, Arnaud: Suing At the Place of Infringement: The Application of Article 5(3) of Regulation 44/2001 to IP Matters and Internet Disputes, in: Nuyts, Arnaud (ed.), International Litigation in Intellectual Property and Information Technology. European Commission Research Project on Judicial Cooperation in Matters of Intellectual Property and Information Technology, The Netherlands, Kluwer Law International, 2008, Chapter 6, pp 105 ff. (cited: Nuyts, in: Nuyts, International Litigation)

O'Reilly, Conall: Finding jurisdiction to regulate Google and the Internet, EJLT, Vol. 2, Issue 1, 2011, pp 1 ff. (cited: O'Reilly, EJLT 2011, 1)

Ollier, Pierre-Dominique/Le Gall, Jean-Pierre: Various Damages. III. Violation of the Rights of the Personality, in: Tunc, André (chief ed.), International Encyclopedia of Comparative Law, Vol. XI, Tübingen, J. C. B. Mohr (Paul Siebeck), Dordrecht, Boston, Lancaster, Martinus Nijhoff Publishers, 1986, Part 2, Chapter 10, ss.10-70 ff. (cited: Ollier/Le Gall, in: Tunc, IECL)

Parker, Oliver/Terry, Regina/Onaca, Viviana/Burduf, Ioana: Tenth report on national case law relating to the Lugano Convention, available at <www.ejpd.admin.ch/content/dam/data/bj/wirtschaft/privatrecht/lugjurispr-10-e.pdf> (cited: Parker *et al.*, Tenth report)

Parkers, Richard, QC/Mullis, Alastair (joint eds.)/Busuttil, Godwin (senior contributing ed.)/Speker, Adam/Scott, Andrew (contributing eds.)/Strong, Chloe (precedents and damages awards): Gatley on Libel and Slander, UK, Sweet & Maxwell, Thomson Reuters, 12th edn., 2013, Common Law Library Series (cited: Parkers *et al.*, Gatley on Libel and Slander)

PCMLP, Centre for Socio-Legal Studies, University of Oxford: A Comparative Study of Costs in Defamation Proceedings Across Europe, December 2008, available at <http://pcmlp.socleg.ox.ac.uk/research/project/comparative-study-costs-defamation-proceedings-across-europe> (cited: PCMLP, Costs in Defamation Proceedings)

Peguera, Miquel: Spain: The right to be forgotten does not apply to blogger, posted on 4.3.2015 at 9:01 am, available at <https://cyberlaw.stanford.edu/blog/2015/03/spain-right-be-forgotten-does-not-apply-blogger> (cited: Peguera, The right to be forgotten, 2015)

Petrik, Ferenc: Személyhez fűződő jogok védelme, in: Petrik, Ferenc (szerk.), Polgári jog: Kommentár a gyakorlat számára, Budapest, HVG-ORAC, I. kötet, 2012, pp 160/35 (26. pótlás) ff. (cited: Petrik, in: Petrik, Polgári Jog)

Petrik, Ferenc: Személyiségi Jogok, in: Petrik, Ferenc (szerk.), Kommentár a gyakorlat számára (a 2013. évi V. törvény, az új Ptk. kommentárja), Budapest, HVG-ORAC, 3. kiadás, 1. kötet, Harmadik Rész, 2013, pp 77 ff. (cited: Petrik, in: Petrik, Kommentár a gyakorlat számára)

Pichler, Paul: Forum-Shopping für Opfer von Persönlichkeitseingriffen im Internet? - Das EuGH-Urteil eDate Advertising gegen X und Martinez gegen MGN (C-509/09 und C-161/10), MR 7-8/11, pp 365 ff. (cited: Pichler, MR 2011, 365)

Picht, Peter: Von *eDate* zu *Wintersteiger* – Die Ausformung des Art. 5 Nr. 3 EuGVVO für Internetdelikte durch die Rechtsprechung des EuGH, GRUR Int. 1/2013, pp 19 ff. (cited: Picht, GRUR Int. 2013, 19)

Pontier, Jannet A./Burg, Edwige: EU Principles on Jurisdiction and Recognition and Enforcement of Judgments in Civil and Commercial Matters according to the case law of the European Court of Justice, The Hague, T.M.C. Asser Press, 2004 (cited: Pontier/Burg, EU Principles)

Pulkowski, Florian: Außervertragliche Forderungen „aus dem Betrieb einer Zweigniederlassung“ im Sinne von Art. 5 Nr. 5 Luganer Übereinkommen (zur Entscheidung des englischen Court of Appeal (Civil Division) vom 3. 2. 2003 - *Dürbeck GmbH* v. *Den Norske Bank ASA* [2003] EWCA Civ 147, [2003] 2 W.L.R. 1296), IPRax 2004, Heft 6, pp 543 ff. (cited: Pulkowski, IPRax 2004, 543)

Queirolo, Ilaria: Art 26, in: Magnus, Ulrich/Mankowski, Peter (eds.), Brussels I Regulation, Munich, sellier european law publishers GmbH, 2nd edn., 2012, pp 540 ff. (cited: Queirolo, in: Magnus/Mankowski, Brussels I Regulation)

Radnoff, Brian N./Archer, Amy: Defamation Law in Canada in an Electronic World, posted on 16.10.2014, available at <http://www.lexpert.ca/directory/feature-articles/defamation-law-in-canada-in-an-electronic-world-23/> (cited: Radnoff/Archer, Defamation Law in Canada)

Rauscher, Thomas: Unzulässigkeit einer *anti-suit injunction* unter Brüssel I (zu EuGH, 27.4.2004 – Rs. C-159/02 – Gregory Paul Turner ./. Felix Fareed Ismail Grovit u.a., unten S. 425, Nr. 30), IPRax 2004, Heft 5, pp 405 ff. (cited: Rauscher, IPRax 2004, 405)

Reinmüller, Bernd: Gesamtschaden und internationale Deliktszuständigkeit nach dem EuGVÜ (zu Cour d'appel Paris v. 19. 3. 1984 – RG n° K 12.158 – *Prinzessin Caroline von Monaco* c. *Burda GmbH*), IPRax 1985, Heft 4, pp 233 ff. (cited: Reinmüller, IPRax 1985, 233)

Reymond, Michel: Jurisdiction in Case of Personality Torts committed over the Internet: A Proposal for a Targeting Test, YbPIL, Vol. 14 (2012/2013), pp 205 ff. (cited: Reymond, YbPIL 2012/2013, 205)

Reymond, Michel: The ECJ *eDate* Decision: A Case Comment, YbPIL, Vol. 13 (2011), pp 493 ff. (cited: Reymond, YbPIL 2011, 493)

Rhinehart, Erin: Did SCOTUS Recently Hint at How It Will Consider Personal Jurisdiction Issues in Internet Defamation Cases?, posted on 22.5.2014 at 2:36 pm, Business Litigation, available at <http://businesslitigationinfo.com/business-litigation/archives/did-scotus-recently-hint-at-how-it-will-consider-personal-jurisdiction-issues-in-internet-defamation-cases/> (cited: Rhinehart, Internet Defamation Cases, 2014)

Robertson, Rhory/Double, Tom: Ten Years of Facebook: Where is the "Twibel" equivalent and why Zuckerberg's creation is different (if, indeed, it is)?, blog entry posted on 8.3.2014, available at <http://inforrm.wordpress.com/2014/03/08/ten-years-of-facebook-where-is-the-twibel-equivalent-and-why-zuckerbergs-creation-is-different-if-indeed-it-is-rhory-robertson-and-tom-double/> (cited: Robertson/ Double, Ten Years of Facebook, 2014)

Rogers, W.V. Horton (ed.): Damages for Non-Pecuniary Loss in a Comparative Perspective, Tort and Insurance Law, Vol. 2, Vienna/New York, Springer, 2001 (cited: Rogers, Damages for Non-Pecuniary Loss)

Rogers, W.V. Horton: The Protection of Personality Rights against Invasions by Mass Media in England, in: Koziol, Helmut/Warzilek, Alexander (eds.), Persönlichkeitsschutz gegenüber Massenmedien/The Protection of Personality Rights against Invasions by Mass Media, Tort and Insurance Law, Vol. 13, Vienna/New York, Springer, 2005, pp 59 ff., paras 1 ff. (cited: Rogers, in: Koziol/Warzilek, Persönlichkeitsschutz)

Rolph, David: Teacher defamation highlights social media's legal perils, blog entry posted on 10.3.2014 (reproduction), available at <http://inforrm.wordpress.com/2014/03/10/teacher-defamation-highlights-social-medias-legal-perils-david-rolph/> (cited: Rolph, Teacher defamation highlights, 2014)

Rosas, Allan: When is the EU Charter of Fundamental Rights Applicable at National Level?, Jurisprudencija/Jurisprudence, 2012, 19(4), pp 1269 ff. (cited: Rosas, Jurisprudence 2012, 1269)

Roth, Isabel: Die internationale Zuständigkeit deutscher Gerichte bei Persönlichkeitsrechtsverletzungen im Internet, Frankfurt am Main, Peter Lang, 2007 (cited: Roth, Die internationale Zuständigkeit)

Roth, Wulf-Henning: Persönlichkeitsschutz im Internet: Internationale Zuständigkeit und anwendbares Recht (zu EuGH, 25.10.2011 – verb. Rs. C-509/09 und C-161/10, eDate Advertising GmbH./. X und Olivier Martinez, Robert Martinez ./. MGN Limited, unten S. 247, Nr. 12; und BGH, 8.5.2012 – VI ZR 217/08, unten S. 252, Nr. 13), IPRax 2013, Heft 3, pp 215 ff. (cited: Roth, IPRax 2013, 215)

Rüßmann, Helmut: Internationale Zuständigkeit für die Durchsetzung von Ansprüchen aus Geschäfts- und Wettbewerbshandlungen im Internet, JurPC Web-Dok. 108/1998, Abs. 1-56, available at <http://www.jurpc.de/jurpc/show?id=19980108> (cited: Rüßmann, JurPC Web-Dok. 1998)

Rüßmann, Helmut: Wettbewerbshandlungen im Internet – Internationale Zuständigkeit und andwendbares Recht, K&R, Heft 10/1998, pp 422 ff. (cited: Rüßmann, K&R 1998, 422)

Schack, Haimo: Internationale Urheber-, Marken- und Wettbewerbsrechtsverletzungen im Internet – Internationales Zivilprozessrecht, MMR 2000, pp 135 ff. (cited: Schack, MMR 2000, 135)

Schack, Haimo: Rechtsschutz gegen grenzüberschreitende Persönlichkeitsverletzungen durch Rundfunksendungen, in: Hübner, Heinz/Glotz, Peter/Pohl, Ottmar/ Henneberg, Claus H./Tercier, Pierre/Kötz, Hein/Schack, Haimo, Das Persönlichkeitsrecht im Spannungsfeld zwischen Informationsauftrag und Menschenwürde, München, C.H.Beck'sche Verlagsbuchhandlung, 1989, pp 113 ff. (cited: Schack, in: Hübner *et al.*, Das Persönlichkeitsrecht)

Schmitz, Sandra: From where are they Casting Stones? – Determining Jurisdiction in Online Defamation Claims, 6 Masaryk U. J.L. & Tech. 159 2012, pp 159 ff. (cited: Schmitz, Masaryk U. J.L. & Tech. 2012, 159)

Schnichels, Dominik/Stege, Ulrich: Die Entwicklung des europäischen Zivilprozessrechts im Bereich der EuGVVO im Jahr 2011, EuZW 21/2012, pp 812 ff. (cited: Schnichels/Stege, EuZW 2012, 812)

Simon, Károly László: A jogellenes károkozásból származó kártérítési perek joghatósági szabályának gyakorlata a Shevill-ítélet tükrében, Európai Jog, 2010/4. szám, pp 15 ff. (cited: Simon, Európai Jog 2010, 15)

Simon, Károly László: Új fejezet a Brüsszel-I. rendelet 5. cikk 3. pontjának értelmezésében: a Shevill-ügy, in: Kengyel, Miklós/Simon, Károly László (szerk.), Tanulmányok az európai polgári eljárásjog köréből, Tanulmánykötet, [közread. a] Pécsi Tudományegyetem Állam- és Jogtudományi Kar, Pécs, PTE ÁJK Dialóg Campus, 2005, pp 93 ff. (cited: Simon, in: Kengyel/Simon, Tanulmányok)

Siry, Lawrence/Schmitz, Sandra: A Right to Be Forgotten? - How Recent Developments in Germany May Affect the Internet Publishers in the US, EJLT, Vol. 3, No. 1, 2012, pp 1 ff. (cited: Siry/Schmitz, EJLT 2012, 1)

Slane, Andrea: Tales, Techs and Territories: Private International Law, Globalization, and the Legal Construction of Borderlessness on the Internet, 71 Law & Contemp. Probs. 129 2008, pp 129 ff. (cited: Slane, Law & Contemp. Probs. 2008, 129)

Slonina, Michael: Erfolgsortsgerichtsstand nach Art 5 Nr 3 EuGVVO bei Persönlichkeitsrechtsverletzungen im Internet (auch) am Mittelpunkt der Interessen des Opfers, ÖJZ 2012/8, pp 61 ff. (cited: Slonina, ÖJZ 2012, 61)

Smith, Graham: Directing and Targeting – the Answer to the Internet's Jurisdiction Problems?, CRi 5/2004, pp 145 ff. (cited: Smith, CRi 2004, 145)

Spauwen, Joran: Dutch court (II): Google Spain Ruling Not Meant to Suppress News Reporting, 3 maart 2015, Media Report 2015-012, available at <http://www.mediareport.nl/persrecht/03032015/dutch-court-ii-google-spain-ruling-not-meant-to-suppress-news-reporting-2/> [cited: Spauwen, Dutch court (II), 2015]

Spauwen, Joran: Dutch Google Spain ruling: More Freedom of Speech, Less Right To Be Forgotten For Criminals, 26 september 2014, Media Report 2014-067, available at <http://www.mediareport.nl/persrecht/26092014/google-spain-judgment-in-the-netherlands-more-freedom-of-speech-less-right-to-be-forgotten-for-criminals/> (cited: Spauwen, Dutch Google Spain ruling, 2014)

Spickhoff, Andreas: Persönlichkeitsverletzungen im Internet: Internationale Zuständigkeit und Kollisionsrecht (zu EuGH, 20.11.2009 – Rs. C-278/09 – Oliver Martinez, Robert Martinez ./. MGN Ltd, unten S. 166, Nr. 12; BGH, 2.3.2010 – VI ZR 23/09, unten S. 167, Nr. 13; LG Köln, 26.8.2009 – 28 O 478/08, unten S. 170, Nr. 14; und OGH, 8.9.2009 – 4 Ob 138/09m, unten S. 174, Nr. 15), IPRax 2011, Heft 2, pp 131 ff. (cited: Spickhoff, IPRax 2011, 131)

Spindler, Gerald: Kollisionsrecht und internationale Zuständigkeit bei Persönlichkeitsrechtsverletzungen im Internet - die eDate-Entscheidung des EuGH, AfP, Heft 2 vom 24.04.2012, pp 114 ff. (cited: Spindler, AfP 2012, 114)

Sprau, Hartwig, § 823, in: Palandt, Otto (begründet von): Bürgerliches Gesetzbuch. Kommentar, Band 7, 74. Aufl., Verlag C.H.Beck München 2015, pp 1365 ff. (cited: Sprau, in: Palandt, BGB)

Stone, Peter: EU Private International Law. Harmonization of Laws, Cheltenham, UK - Northampton, MA, USA, Edward Elgar, 2006 (cited: Stone, EU PIL)

Struycken, Antoon (Teun) Victor Marie: Co-ordination and co-operation in respectful disagreement. General Course on Private International Law, Recueil des Cours, Collected Courses of the Hague Academy of International Law (2004), Vol. 311, Leiden/Boston, Martinus Nijhoff Publishers, 2009 (cited: Struycken, Recueil des Cours 311)

Struyven, Olivia: Exorbitant Jurisdiction in the Brussels convention, Jura Falconis, Jg 35, 1998-1999, Nr 4, pp 521 ff., available at <http://www.law.kuleuven.be/jura/art/35n4/struyven.htm> (cited: Struyven, Jura Falconis 1998-1999, 521)

Svantesson, Dan Jerker Börje: Private International Law and the Internet, The Netherlands, Kluwer Law International, 2nd edn., 2012 (cited: Svantesson, PIL and the Internet)

Svantesson, Dan Jerker B.: The right of reputation in the Internet era, IRLCT, Vol. 23, No. 3, November 2009, pp 169 ff. (cited: Svantesson, IRLCT 2009, 169)

Székely, László/Vékás, Lajos: Személyiségi jogok, in: Vékás, Lajos (szerk.), A Polgári Törvénykönyv magyarázatokkal, a szerk. munkatársa: Gárdos, Péter, Budapest,

Complex, 2013, pp 55 ff. (cited: Székely/Vékás, in: Vékás, A Polgári Törvénykönyv magyarázatokkal)

Thiede, Thomas: Aktivgerichtsstand für Betroffene von Persönlichkeitsrechtsverletzungen im Onlinebereich, ecolex 2/2012, pp 131 ff. (cited: Thiede, ecolex 2012, 131)

Thiede, Thomas: Bier, Shevill und eDate – Aegrescit medendo? Anmerkung zum Urteil des EuGH in den Rechtssachen C-509/09 und C-161/10, GPR 4/2012, pp 219 ff. (cited: Thiede, GPR 2012, 219)

Thiede, Thomas: Online Medien, Persönlichkeitsrechtsschutz und Internationale Zuständigkeit. Anmerkung zu den Schlussanträgen des GA Cruz Villalón in den Rechtssachen C-509/09 und C-161/10 (eDate Advertising GmbH gegen X (C-509/09) und Oliver Martinez, Robert Martinez gegen Société MGN Limited (C-161/10)), GPR 5/11, pp 259 ff. (cited: Thiede, GPR 2011, 259)

Thorn, Karsten: Internationale Zuständigkeit bei Persönlichkeitsverletzungen durch Massenmedien, in: Kronke, Herbert/Thorn, Karsten (Hrsg.), Grenzen überwinden - Prinzipien bewahren: Festschrift für Bernd von Hoffmann zum 70. Geburtstag, Bielefeld, Gieseking Verlag, 2011, pp 746 ff. (cited: Thorn, FS Bernd von Hoffmann)

Tomlinson QC, Hugh: Privacy and Defamation, Strasbourg blurs the boundaries, blog entry posted on 23.1.2014, available at <http://inforrm.wordpress.com/2014/01/23/privacy-and-defamation-strasbourg-blurs-the-boundaries-hugh-tomlinson-qc/> (cited: Tomlinson, Privacy and Defamation, 2014)

Torremans, Paul L.C.: Intellectual Property puts art.6(1) Brussels I Regulation to the Test, I.P.Q. 2014, Issue 1, pp 1 ff. (cited: Torremans, I.P.Q. 2014, 1)

Trimble, Marketa: The Future of Cybertravel: Legal Implications of the Evasion of Geolocation, Fordham Intell. Prop. Media & Ent. L.J., Vol. 22, 2012, pp 567 ff. (cited: Trimble, Fordham Intell. Prop. Media & Ent. L.J. 2012, 567)

Van Bockel, Bas/Wattel, Peter: New Wine into Old Wineskins: The Scope of the Charter of Fundamental Rights of the EU after *Åkerberg Fransson*, European Current Law, Issue 3, 2014, pp 273 ff. (cited: van Bockel/Wattel, ECL 2014, 273)

Van Dam, Cees: European Tort Law, Oxford, OUP, 2nd edn., 2013 (cited: van Dam, European Tort Law)

Vékás, Lajos: Die Reform des internationalen Zivilverfahrensrechts in Ungarn, IPRax 2002, Heft 2, pp 142 ff. (cited: Vékás, IPRax 2002, 142)

Vékás, Lajos: Hungary and the Lugano Convention, Eur. J.L. Reform 2002, Vol. 4, No. 1, pp 135 ff. (cited: Vékás, Eur. J.L. Reform 2002, 135)

Verheul, J.P.: The Forum Actoris and International Law, in: T.M.C. Asser Instituut, Essays on International & Comparative Law in Honour of Judge Erades, Presented by the Board of the Netherlands International Law Review, The Netherlands, Martinus Nijhoff Publishers, 1983, pp 196 ff. (cited: Verheul, FS Judge Erades)

Vick, Douglas W./Macpherson, Linda: Anglicizing Defamation Law in the European Union, 36 Va. J. Int'l L. 933 1995-1996, pp 933 ff. (cited: Vick/Macpherson, Va. J. Int'l L. 1995-1996, 933)

Vischer, Frank: Connecting Factors, in: Lipstein, Kurt (chief ed.), International Encyclopedia of Comparative Law: Private International Law, Vol. III, Part I, Tübingen, Mohr Siebeck, Leiden, Boston, Martinus Nijhoff Publishers, 2011, Chapter 4 (cited: Vischer, in: Lipstein, IECL)

Vlas, P.: The EEC Convention on Jurisdiction and Judgments, NILR, 1995, pp 413 ff. (cited: Vlas, NILR 1995, 413)

Vlas, Paul: Art 59, in: Magnus, Ulrich/Mankowski, Peter (eds.), Brussels I Regulation, Munich, sellier european law publishers GmbH, 2nd edn., 2012, pp 807 ff. (cited: Vlas, in: Magnus/Mankowski, Brussels I Regulation)

Voinov, Krasimir/de Lapasse, Pierre/Janzen, Ulrike: Twelfth Report on national Case Law relating to the Lugano Convention, available at <www.ejpd.admin.ch/content/dam/data/bj/wirtschaft/privatrecht/lugjurispr-12-e.pdf> (cited: Voinov/de Lapasse/Janzen, Twelfth Report)

Volken, Paul: Rechtsprechung zum Lugano-Übereinkommen (1995), SZIER 1/96, pp 69 ff. (cited: Volken, SZIER 1996, 69)

Von Bar, Christian (prepared by with advice from the Advisory Council and the Drafting Committee approved by the Co-ordinating Group): Principles of European Law, Non-Contractual Liability Arising out of Damage Caused to Another, Study Group on a European Civil Code, Munich, sellier. european law publishers GmbH, [Brussels] Bruylant, Stämpfli Publishers Ltd. Berne, Vol. 7, 2009 (cited: PEL/von Bar, Liab. Dam.)

Von Bar, Christian/Clive, Eric (eds.): Principles, Definitions and Model Rules of European Private Law. Draft Common Frame of Reference (DCFR), Prepared by the Study Group on a European Civil Code and the Research Group on EC Private Law (Acquis Group), Munich, sellier.european law publishers GmbH, 2009, Full edn., Vol. 4, Book VI (cited: von Bar/Clive, Principles, Definitions and Model Rules)

Von Danwitz, Thomas/Paraschas, Katherina: A Fresh Start for the Charter: Fundamental Questions on the Application of the European Charter of Fundamental Rights, 35 Fordham Int'l L.J. 1396 2011-2012, pp 1396 ff. (cited: von Danwitz/Paraschas, Fordham Int'l L.J. 2011-2012, 1396)

Von Hein, Jan: Markenrecht: Internationale Zuständigkeit bei Markenverletzung durch mehrere Beteiligte, EuZW 17/2014, pp 664 ff. (cited: von Hein, EuZW 2014, 664)

Von Hein, Jan: Von Hein on Kate Provence Pictures, blog entry posted by Cuniberti, Gilles on 27.9.2012, available at <http://conflictoflaws.net/2012/von-hein-on-kate-provence-pictures/> (last accessed on 23.4.2015) (cited: Von Hein, Von Hein on Kate Provence Pictures, 2012)

Von Hinden, Michael: Internationale Zuständigkeit und anwendbares Recht bei Persönlichkeitsverletzungen im Internet, *Entscheidung des Europäischen Gerichtshofs vom 25. Oktober 2011*, Anmerkung, ZEuP 4/2012, pp 940 ff. (cited: von Hinden, ZEuP 2012, 940)

Von Hinden, Michael: Persönlichkeitsverletzungen im Internet. Das anwendbare Recht, Tübingen, Mohr Siebeck, 1999 (cited: von Hinden, Persönlichkeitsverletzungen)

Von Mehren, Arthur T.: Should Plaintiffs or Defendants Be Jurisdictionally Preferred? Herein of the *Actor Sequitur Rei* Maxim, The Hague Conference's Service Convention of 1965, and the Brussels Regulation of 2002, in: Faust, Florian/Thüsing, Gregor (Hrsg.), Beyond Borders: Perspectives on International and Comparative Law, Symposium in Honour of Hein Kötz, München *et al.*, Carl Heymanns Verlag, 2006, Band I/6, pp 75 ff. (cited: von Mehren, FS Hein Kötz)

Von Mehren, Arthur Taylor: Theory and Practice of Adjudicatory Authority in Private International Law: A Comparative Study of the Doctrine, Policies and Practices of Common- and Civil-Law Systems, General Course on Private International Law (1996) (volume 295), Collected Courses of the Hague Academy of International Law. The Hague Academy of International Law. Brill Online, 2015. Reference. Saarlandes des Universitat Bibliothek. 14 April 2015 <http://referenceworks.brillonline.com/entries/the-hague-academy-collected-courses/theory-and-practice-of-adjudicatory-authority-in-private-international-law-a-comparative-study-of-the-doctrine-policies-and-practices-of-common-and-civil-law-systems-general-course-on-private-international-law-1996-volume-295-ej.9789041118578.009_431> (accessed on 14 April 2015) (cited: von Mehren, Recueil des Cours 295)

Von Welser, Marcus: EuGH: Persönlichkeitsrechtsverletzung im Internet – Geschädigter kann gesamten Schaden an seinem gewöhnlichen Aufenthaltsort einklagen, Anmerkung, GRUR-Prax 2011, pp 513 ff. (cited: von Welser, GRUR-Prax 2011, 513)

Wagner, Gerhard: Article 6 of the Commission Proposal: Violation of Privacy – Defamation by Mass Media, ERPL, 1-2005, pp 21 ff. (cited: Wagner, ERPL 2005, 21)

Wagner, Gerhard: Ehrenschutz und Pressefreiheit im europäischen Zivilverfahrens- und Internationalen Privatrecht, RabelsZ Bd. 62 (1998), pp 243 ff. (cited: Wagner, RabelsZ 1998, 243)

Wagner, Gerhard: The Protection of Personality Rights against Invasions by Mass Media in Germany, in: Koziol, Helmut/Warzilek, Alexander (eds.), Persönlichkeitsschutz gegenüber Massenmedien/The Protection of Personality Rights against Invasions by Mass Media, Tort and Insurance Law, Vol. 13, Vienna/New York, Springer, 2005, pp 137 ff., paras 1 ff. (cited: Wagner, in: Koziol/Warzilek, Persönlichkeitsschutz)

Wagner, Rolf/Janzen, Ulrike: Das Lugano-Übereinkommen vom 30.10.2007, IPRax 2010, Heft 4, pp 298 ff. (cited: Wagner/Janzen, IPRax 2010, 298)

Warren, Samuel D./Brandeis, Louis D.: The Right to Privacy, 4 Harv. L. Rev. 193 1890-1891, pp 193 ff. (cited: Warren/Brandeis, Harv. L. Rev. 1890-1891, 193)

Weiler, Joseph: In the Dock, in Paris – The Judgment, published on 4.3.2011 on EJIL: *Talk!*, available at <http://www.ejiltalk.org/in-the-dock-in-paris-%E2%80%93-the-judgment-by-joseph-weiler-2/> (cited: Weiler, The Judgment, 2011)

Weller, Matthias: Mutual Trust: In Search of the Future of European Private International Law (December 12, 2014). Journal of Private International Law, Issue 1, 2015 Forthcoming, available at SSRN: <http://ssrn.com/abstract=2538389>, pp 1 ff. (cited: Weller, Mutual Trust, 2014, 1)

Weller, Matthias: Persönlichkeitsrechtsverletzungen im Internet, Internationale Zuständigkeit am „Ort der Interessenkollision"?, in: Geimer, Reinhold/Schütze, Rolf A. (Hrsg.), Recht ohne Grenzen: Festschrift für Athanassios Kaissis zum 65. Geburtstag, München, sellier european law publishers GmbH, 2012, pp 1039 ff. (cited: Weller, FS Athanassios Kaissis)

Wendenburg, Albrecht/Schneider, Maximilian: Vertraglicher Gerichtsstand bei Ansprüchen aus Delikt?, NJW, 23/2014, pp 1633 ff. (cited: Wendenburg/Schneider, NJW 2014, 1633)

Wittwer, Alexander/Fussenegger, Andreas: EuGH-Rechtsprechung zur EuGVVO aus den Jahren 2011 und 2012, ZEuP 4/2013, pp 812 ff. (cited: Wittwer/Fussenegger, ZEuP 2013, 812)

Wittwer, Alexander/Müller, Julia: Internationale Zuständigkeit bei Persönlichkeitsverletzungen im Internet (eDate Advertising GmbH ./. X und Martinez ./. MGN Ltd, EuGH (Grosse Kammer), Urteil vom 25. Oktober 2011, verbundene Rs. C-509/09 und C-161/10), Eur. L. Rptr. 3/2012, pp 95 ff. (cited: Wittwer/Müller, Eur. L. Rptr. 2012, 95)

Witzleb, Normann: Interim injunctions for invasions of privacy: challenging the rule in *Bonnard* v. *Perryman*?, in: Witzleb, Normann/Lindsay, David/Paterson, Moira/Rodrick, Sharon (eds), Emerging Challenges in Privacy Law. Comparative Perspectives, Cambridge, CUP, 2014, pp 407 ff. (cited: Witzleb, in: Witzleb *et al.*, Emerging Challenges in Privacy Law)

Wolter, Kathleen Maja: Rund um die Privatsphäre im Internet - Gerichtszuständigkeit, anwendbares Recht und Reichweite des Persönlichkeitsschutzes, jurisPR-ITR 18/2012 Anm. 3 (cited: Wolter, jurisPR-ITR 2012)

Wurmnest, Wolfgang: Non-Pecuniary Loss, in: Basedow, Jürgen/Hopt, Klaus J./Zimmermann, Reinhard/Stier, Andreas (eds.), The Max Planck Encyclopedia of European Private Law, Oxford, OUP, 2012, Vol. II, pp 1204 ff. (cited: Wurmnest, in: Basedow *et al.*, Max Planck Encyclopedia)

Yale Law School Supreme Court Advocacy Clinic: Roberts v. Kauffman Racing Equipment, L.L.C., On Petition for a Writ of Certiorari to the Supreme Court of Ohio, Kahan, Dan M./Kepko, William J./Pincus, Andrew J./Rothfeld, Charles A. (Counsel for Petitioner), November 2010, available at <http://www.law.yale.edu/documents/pdf/Roberts_Cert_Petition_Brief_Final.pdf> (cited: Yale Supreme Court Clinic, Petition, 2010)

List of Websites

Anonymizer <https://www.anonymizer.com/>

Anonymouse <http://anonymouse.org/>

Assises de la Justice: Shaping Justice policies in Europe for the years to come at <http://ec.europa.eu/justice/events/assises-justice-2013/index_en.htm>

Bing <https://www.bing.com/>

Choice of Court Section of the HCCH <http://www.hcch.net/index_en.php?act=text.display&tid=134>

Chronological overview of the Judgments Project with related documents is available at <http://www.hcch.net/index_en.php?act=text.display&tid=149>

Conflict of Laws.net <http://conflictoflaws.net/>

Disconnect <https://disconnect.me/>

Dogpile <http://www.dogpile.com/>

eBay <eBay.com>

ECJ Website for case references <http://curia.europa.eu/common/recdoc/convention/en/tableau/tableau.htm>
Cases accessed: No 2001/28; No 2003/26; No 2003/34; No 2004/27; No 2007/18; No 2009/33; No 2009/62

Encyclopaedia Britannica – Internet – Origin and development <http://www.britannica.com/EBchecked/topic/291494/Internet>

English translation of the BGB <http://www.gesetze-im-internet.de/englisch_bgb/>. Translation provided by the Langenscheidt Translation Service. Translation regularly updated by Neil Mussett and most recently by Samson Übersetzungen GmbH, Dr. Carmen v. Schöning. Version information: The translation includes the amendment(s) to the Act by Article 4 para. 5 of the Act of 1.10.2013 (Federal Law Gazette I p. 3719). 2014 juris GmbH, Saarbrücken

English translation of the CC <www.legifrance.gouv.fr/content/download/1950/13681/version/3/file/Code_22.pdf>. Translated by Georges Rouhette, Professor of Law, with the assistance of Dr Anne Rouhette-Berton, Assistant Professor of English

English translation of the ZPO <http://www.gesetze-im-internet.de/englisch_zpo/englisch_zpo.html>. Translation provided by Samson-Übersetzungen GmbH, Dr. Carmen von Schöning. Version information: The translation includes the amendment(s) to the Act by Article 1 of the Act of 10.10.2013 (Federal Law Gazette I p. 3786). 2014 juris GmbH, Saarbrücken.

European E-Justice portal <https://e-justice.europa.eu>

European Judicial Network in civil and commercial matters <http://ec.europa.eu/civiljustice/comp_crime_victim/comp_crime_victim_ec_en.htm>

EuropeanDaily <http://europeandaily.com/>

Eurostat Statistics <http://epp.eurostat.ec.europa.eu/tgm/table.do?tab=table&init=1&language=en&pcode=tin00092&plugin=1>

Eurostat Statistics <http://epp.eurostat.ec.europa.eu/tgm/table.do?tab=table&plugin=1&language=en&pcode=tin00127>

Facebook <www.facebook.com/>

Facebook Company Info <http://newsroom.fb.com/company-info/>

Facebook Newsroom <http://newsroom.fb.com/download-media/4227> via <https://archive.org>

Facebook: Changing the date of a story on one's timeline <https://www.facebook.com/help/331944693487215/>

Facebook: How do I remove my location from a post? <https://www.facebook.com/help/166181076782926>

Facebook: Updates to Page Composer Make it Easier to Share Great Content <https://www.facebook.com/business/news/Updates-to-Page-Composer-Make-it-Easier-to-Share-Great-Content>

Faculty of Law and Political Science of Eötvös Loránd University, Budapest (Hungary) <www.ajk.elte.hu>

Flickr <www.flickr.com/>

Frankfurter Allgemeine <http://www.faz.net/>

Frankfurter Allgemeine on Twitter <@FAZ_Topnews>

GEDIP Document <http://www.gedip-egpil.eu/gedip_documents.html>

Geotool from Flagfox at <http://geoip.flagfox.net/>

Ghostery <https://addons.mozilla.org/de/firefox/addon/ghostery/>

Global Social Media Prism by ethority, German Edition V6.0 <http://www.ethority.de/weblog/social-media-prisma/>

Google – About – Company – Facts – Locations <http://www.google.com/about/company/facts/locations/>

Google – Youtube – Help – Scheduled Publishing <https://support.google.com/youtube/answer/1270709?hl=en>

Google <https://www.google.com/>

Google Analytics <https://www.google.com/intl/en/analytics/>

Google Developers – Google Maps API <https://developers.google.com/maps/articles/geolocation>

Google Translate <http://translate.google.de/>

Heti Világgazdaság <http://hvg.hu/>

Internet & Jurisdiction Project – Retrospect <http://www.internetjurisdiction.net/observatory/retrospect/>

Internet Archive <http://archive.org/>

Internet Memory Foundation <http://internetmemory.org/en/>

Internet World Stats, Usage and Population Statistics <http://www.internetworldstats.com/stats.htm>

Joomla!: Remover of creation date, update <http://docs.joomla.org/Removing_author_name,_creation_date_or_update_date_from_an_article>

Journal of Intellectual Property, Information Technology and E-Commerce Law <http://www.jipitec.eu/>

JURE collection <http://eur-lex.europa.eu/collection/n-law/jure.html>

MaxMind, GeoIP <http://www.maxmind.com/en/geolocation_landing?pkit_lang=en>

MetaGer <https://metager.de/>

Mirror Online <www.sundaymirror.co.uk>

Official Statistics on privacy injunctions dealt with at hearings at the High Court or Court of Appeal at the Royal Courts of Justice in London <https://www.gov.uk/government/collections/statistics-on-privacy-injunctions>

Overview: Get Ready for the Next Big.Thing <http://newgtlds.icann.org/en/announcements-and-media/video/overview-en>

Reputation.com <http://www.reputation.com/>

Reputations Verteidiger <http://www.reputationsverteidiger.de/>

Residual jurisdictional rules of the Member States, see Nuyts Report and national reports, available at <http://ec.europa.eu/justice/civil/document/index_en.htm>

Talk of Eli Praiser at <http://www.thefilterbubble.com/ted-talk>

The Economist on Facebook <https://www.facebook.com/TheEconomist>

Tumblr – About <http://www.tumblr.com/about>

Twitter <https://twitter.com>

United States – Census Bureau – U.S. and World Population Clock <http://www.census.gov/popclock/>

Webopedia – Domain name <http://www.webopedia.com/TERM/D/domain_name.html>

Wikipedia Statistics <http://en.wikipedia.org/wiki/Special:Statistics>

Word Lens <http://questvisual.com>

WordPress – About <https://wordpress.com/about/>

World Intermediary Liability Map <http://cyberlaw.stanford.edu/our-work/projects/world-intermediary-liability-map-wilmap>

Youtube – Statistics <http://www.youtube.com/t/press_statistics?hl=en>

List of Other Materials

Doc. on Support of the Republic of Serbia to the initiative of the Republic of Slovenia related to accession of West Balkan Countries to Lugano Convention and other regional initiatives, 2011 (on file with author)

Doc. on the Regional Conference of the Ministers of Interior and Ministers of Justice, Belgrade, 11-12.4.2013, point 6 (on file with author)

English translation of Act No IV of 1959 on the civil code (1959. évi IV. törvény a Polgári Törvénykönyvről): Complex Jogtár Plusz express, Hatály 2009.VII.1.-

(on file with author)

Facebook's Oculus

Google Glass

Integrated automated translation tools (e.g. in Facebook)

Jibbigo Translator

News from 24.4.2013 – Christa Jessel-Holst coordinates preparation of parallel agreement to the Lugano Convention, available at <http://www.mpipriv.de/en/pub/news/institute_snapshots.cfm>

Open Regional Fund for South-East Europe: Cross-Border Jurisdiction, January 2011, available at <http://www.giz.de/expertise/downloads/giz2012-en-orf-cross-border-juristiction-southeasteurope.pdf>

Project on the drafting of Principles of Transnational Civil Procedure for Europe, see <http://www.unidroit.org/work-in-progress-studies/current-studies/transnational-civil-procedure>

Quick Translator 1.0

Responses of the European Federation of Journalists (30.6.2009; signed by Arne König, EFJ President), pp 2-3 and European Newspaper Publishers' Association (30.6.2009; Sophie Scrive, Deputy Executive Director) to the Green Paper on the review of Council Regulation (EC) N° 44/2001 on jurisdiction and the recognition and enforcement of judgements in civil and commercial matters <http://ec.europa.eu/justice/news/consulting_public/news_consulting_0002_en.htm>

Table of Cases

Argentina

J.G.R v Google Inc, Federal Court of Appeal of Salta [Cámara Federal de Apelaciones de Salta], July 4, 2011, LA LEY 7/19/01, fn 32

Australia

Dow Jones and Company Inc v Gutnick [2002] HCA 56; 210 CLR 575; 194 ALR 433; 77 ALJR 255 (10 December 2002), pp 29-30; fns 11-15, 124, 196, 847, 857, 999

Austria

Case 4 NC 3/08s (20.2.2008), Oberster Gerichtshof, fn 724

Case 4 OB 82/12f (10.7.2012), Oberster Gerichtshof, fn 973

Order Hejduk 10 Cg 180/11t (3.7.2013), Handelsgericht Wien (GRUR Int. 2013, 1171-1172), fn 458

Brazil

Superior Court of Justice, Recurso Especial no 1.168.547/RJ, Rel. Min. Luis Felipe Salomão, Quarta Turma, DJe 07.02.2011, fn 32

Canada

Breeden v. Black 2012 SCC 19, [2012] 1 S.C.R. 666, fns 12, 1051

Crookes v. Newton [2011] 3 SCR 269, fn 1044

European Union

European Court of Justice (Alphabetical)

A *see* A (Case C-523/07), 2 April 2009, ECLI:EU:C:2009:225

Åkerberg Fransson *see* Åklagaren v Hans Åkerberg Fransson (Case C-617/10), 26 February 2013, ECLI:EU:C:2013:105

Apostolides *see* Meletis Apostolides v David Charles Orams and Linda Elizabeth Orams (Case C-420/07), 28 April 2009, ECLI:EU:C:2009:271

B and Others *see* A v B and Others (Case C-112/13), 11 September 2014, ECLI:EU:C:2014:2195

Barbara Mercredi v Richard Chaffe (Case C-497/10 PPU), 22 December 2010, ECLI:EU:C:2010:829

Besix SA v Wasserreinigungsbau Alfred Kretzschmar GmbH & Co. KG (WABAG) and Planungs- und Forschungsgesellschaft Dipl. Ing. W. Kretzschmar GmbH & KG (Plafog) (Case C-256/00), 19 February 2002, ECLI:EU:C:2002:99

BestWater International GmbH v Michael Mebes and Stefan Potsch (Case C-348/13), Order of the Court (Ninth Chamber), 21 October 2014, ECLI:EU:C:2014:2315

Bier *see* Handelskwekerij G. J. Bier BV v Mines de potasse d'Alsace SA (Case 21-76), 30 November 1976, ECLI:EU:C:1976:166

Blomqvist *see* Martin Blomqvist v Rolex SA and Manufacture des Montres Rolex SA (Case C-98/13), 6 February 2014, ECLI:EU:C:2014:55

Brogsitter *see* Marc Brogsitter v Fabrication de Montres Normandes EURL and Karsten Fräßdorf (Case C-548/12), 13 March 2014, ECLI:EU:C:2014:148

C More Entertainment AB v Linus Sandberg (Case C-279/13), 26 March 2015, ECLI:EU:C:2015:199

Cartier parfums – lunettes SAS, Axa Corporate Solutions assurances SA v Ziegler France SA, Montgomery Transports SARL, Inko Trade s. r. o., Jaroslav Matěja, Groupama Transport (Case C-1/13), 27 February 2014, ECLI:EU:C:2014:109

Cassis de Dijon *see* Rewe-Zentral AG v Bundesmonopolverwaltung für Branntwein (Case 120/78), 20 February 1979, ECLI:EU:C:1979:42

Color Drack GmbH v Lexx International Vertriebs GmbH (Case C-386/05), 3 May 2007, ECLI:EU:C:2007:262

Coreck Maritime GmbH v Handelsveem BV and Others (Case C-387/98), 9 November 2000, ECLI:EU:C:2000:606

Coty Germany (anciennement Coty Prestige Lancaster Group) v First Note Perfumes NV (Case C-360/12), 5 June 2014, ECLI:EU:C:2014:911

Dataco *see* Football Dataco Ltd and Others v Sportradar GmbH et Sportradar AG (Case C-173/11), 18 October 2012, ECLI:EU:C:2012:642

De Cavel (2) *see* Louise de Cavel v Jacques de Cavel (Case 120/79), 6 March 1980, ECLI:EU:C:1980:70

De Visser *see* G v Cornelius de Visser (Case C-292/10), 15 March 2012, ECLI:EU:C:2012:142

DFDS Torline *see* Danmarks Rederiforening, acting on behalf of DFDS Torline A/S v LO Landsorganisationen i Sverige, acting on behalf of SEKO Sjöfolk Facket för Service och Kommunikation (Case C-18/02), 5 February 2004, ECLI:EU:C:2004:74

Di Paolo *see* Silvana di Paolo v Office national de l'emploi (Case 76-76), 17 February 1977, ECLI:EU:C:1977:32

Donner *see* Criminal proceedings against Titus Alexander Jochen Donner (Case C-5/11), 21 June 2012, ECLI:EU:C:2012:370

Duijnstee *see* Ferdinand M.J.J. Duijnstee v Lodewijk Goderbauer (Case 288/82), 15 November 1983, ECLI:EU:C:1983:326

Dumez France SA and Tracoba SARL v Hessische Landesbank and others (Case C-220/88), 11 January 1990, ECLI:EU:C:1990:8

eDate Advertising GmbH v X (Case C-509/09) and Olivier Martinez and Robert Martinez v MGN Limited (Case C-161/10), 25 October 2011, ECLI:EU:C:2011:685

eDate Advertising *see* Case C-509/09, eDate and Martinez joined judgment

Effer SpA v Hans-Joachim Kantner (Case 38/81), 4 March 1982, ECLI:EU:C:1982:79

Elefanten Schuh GmbH v Pierre Jacqmain (Case 150/80), Judgment of the Court of 24 June 1981, ECLI:EU:C:1981:148

ERTA *see* Commission of the European Communities v Council of the European Communities - European Agreement on Road Transport (Case 22-70), 31 March 1971, ECLI:EU:C:1971:32

Eurocontrol *see* LTU Lufttransportunternehmen GmbH & Co. KG v Eurocontrol (Case 29-76), 14 October 1976, ECLI:EU:C:1976:137

Eurofood IFSC Ltd (Case C-341/04), 2 May 2006, ECLI:EU:C:2006:281

Falco Privatstiftung and Thomas Rabitsch v Gisela Weller-Lindhorst (Case C-533/07), 23 April 2009, ECLI:EU:C:2009:257

Folien Fischer AG and Fofitec AG v Ritrama SpA (Case C-133/11), 25 October 2012, ECLI:EU:C:2012:664

Gantner Electronic GmbH v Basch Exploitatie Maatschappij BV (Case C-111/01), 8 May 2003, ECLI:EU:C:2003:257

Gasser *see* Erich Gasser GmbH v MISAT Srl (Case C-116/02), 9 December 2003, ECLI:EU:C:2003:657

Glaxosmithkline and Laboratoires Glaxosmithkline v Jean-Pierre Rouard (Case C-462/06), 22 May 2008, ECLI:EU:C:2008:299

Google Spain SL and Google Inc. v Agencia Española de Protección de Datos (AEPD) and Mario Costeja González (Case C-131/12), 13 May 2014, ECLI:EU:C:2014:317

Gothaer Allgemeine Versicherung AG and Others v Samskip GmbH (Case C-456/11), 15 November 2012, ECLI:EU:C:2012:719

GREP GmbH v Freitstaat Bayern (Case C-156/12), Order of the Court (Sixth Chamber), 13 June 2012, ECLI:EU:C:2012:342

Group Josi Reinsurance Company SA v Universal General Insurance Company (UGIC) (Case C-412/98), 13 July 2000, ECLI:EU:C:2000:399

Gubisch Maschinenfabrik KG v Giulio Palumbo (Case 144/86), 8 December 1987, ECLI:EU:C:1987:528

Handte *see* Jakob Handte & Co. GmbH v Traitements Mécano-chimiques des Surfaces SA (Case C-26/91), 17 June 1992, ECLI:EU:C:1992:268

Hejduk *see* Pez Hejduk v EnergieAgentur.NRW GmbH (Case C-441/13), 22 January 2015, ECLI:EU:C:2015:28

Henkel *see* Verein für Konsumenteninformation v Karl Heinz Henkel (Case C-167/00), 1 October 2002, ECLI:EU:C:2002:555

Hi Hotel HCF SARL v Uwe Spoering (Case C-387/12), 3 April 2014, ECLI:EU:C:2014:215

Hoffmann *see* Horst Ludwig Martin Hoffmann v Adelheid Krieg (Case 145/86), 4 February 1988, ECLI:EU:C:1988:61

Hypoteční banka a.s. v Udo Mike Lindner (Case C-327/10), 17 November 2011, ECLI:EU:C:2011:745

Ivenel *see* Roger Ivenel v Helmut Schwab (Case 133/81), 26 May 1982, ECLI:EU:C:1982:199

Kainz *see* Andreas Kainz v Pantherwerke AG (Case C-45/13), 16 January 2014, ECLI:EU:C:2014:7

Kalfelis *see* Athanasios Kalfelis v Bankhaus Schröder, Münchmeyer, Hengst and Co. and others (Case C-189/87), 27 September 1988, ECLI:EU:C:1988:459

Kolassa *see* Harald Kolassa v Barclays Bank PLC (Case C-375/13), 28 January 2015, ECLI:EU:C:2015:37

Kongress Agentur Hagen GmbH v Zeehaghe BV (Case C-365/88), 15 May 1990, ECLI:EU:C:1990:203

Krombach *see* Dieter Krombach v André Bamberski (Case C-7/98), 28 March 2000, ECLI:EU:C:2000:164

Kronhofer *see* Rudolf Kronhofer v Marianne Maier and Others (Case C-168/02), 10 June 2004, ECLI:EU:C:2004:364

L'Oréal SA and Others v eBay International AG and Others (Case C-324/09), 12 July 2011, ECLI:EU:C:2011:474

Land Berlin v Ellen Mirjam Sapir and Others (Case C-645/11), 11 April 2013, ECLI:EU:C:2013:228

Lechouritou *see* Eirini Lechouritou and Others v Dimosio tis Omospondiakis Dimokratias tis Germanias (Case C-292/05), 15 February 2007, ECLI:EU:C:2007:102

Lindqvist *see* Criminal proceedings against Bodil Lindqvist (Case C-101/01), 6 November 2003, ECLI:EU:C:2003:596

Lloyd's Register of Shipping v Société Campenon Bernard (Case C-439/93), 6 April 1995, ECLI:EU:C:1995:104

Mærsk Olie & Gas A/S v Firma M. de Haan en W. de Boer (Case C-39/02), 14 October 2004, ECLI:EU:C:2004:615

Mahamdia *see* Ahmed Mahamdia v République algérienne démocratique et populaire (Case C-154/11), 19 July 2012, ECLI:EU:C:2012:491

Maletic *see* Armin Maletic, Marianne Maletic v lastminute.com GmbH, TUI Österreich GmbH (Case C-478/12), 14 November 2013, ECLI:EU:C:2013:735

Marinari *see* Antonio Marinari v Lloyds Bank plc and Zubaidi Trading Company (Case C-364/93), 19 September 1995, ECLI:EU:C:1995:289

Martinez and Martinez (I) *see* Olivier Martinez and Robert Martinez v MGN Ltd. (Case C-278/09), Order of the Court (Eighth Chamber), 20 November 2009, ECLI:EU:C:2009:725

Martinez and Martinez *see* Case C-161/10, eDate and Martinez joined judgment

McB *see* J. McB. v L. E. (Case C-400/10 PPU), 5 October 2010, ECLI:EU:C:2010:582

Melloni *see* Stefano Melloni v Ministerio Fiscal (Case C-399/11), 26 February 2013, ECLI:EU:C:2013:107

Melzer v MF Global UK Ltd (Case C-228/11), 16 May 2013, ECLI:EU:C:2013:305

Mulox IBC Ltd v Hendrick Geels (Case C-125/92), 13 July 1993, ECLI:EU:C:1993:306

ÖFAB, Östergötlands Fastigheter AB v Frank Koot and Evergreen Investments BV (Case C-147/12), 18 July 2013, ECLI:EU:C:2013:490

Overseas Union Insurance Ltd and Deutsche Ruck Uk Reinsurance Ltd and Pine Top Insurance Company Ltd v New Hampshire Insurance Company (Case C-351/89), 27 June 1991, ECLI:EU:C:1991:279

Owusu *see* Andrew Owusu v N. B. Jackson, trading as "Villa Holidays Bal-Inn Villas" and Others (Case C-281/02), 1 March 2005, ECLI:EU:C:2005:120

Painer *see* Eva-Maria Painer v Standard VerlagsGmbH and Others (Case C-145/10), 1 December 2011, ECLI:EU:C:2011:798

Pammer and Hotel Alpenhof *see* Peter Pammer v Reederei Karl Schlüter GmbH & Co. KG (C-585/08) and Hotel Alpenhof GesmbH v Oliver Heller (Case C-144/09), 7 December 2010, ECLI:EU:C:2010:740

Papasavvas *see* Sotiris Papasavvas v O Fileleftheros Dimosia Etairia Ltd (Case C-291/13), 11 September 2014, ECLI:EU:C:2014:2209

Peters *see* Martin Peters Bauunternehmung GmbH v Zuid Nederlandse Aannemers Vereniging (Case 34/82), 22 March 1983, ECLI:EU:C:1983:87

Pinckney *see* Peter Pinckney v KDG Mediatech AG (Case C-170/12), 3 October 2013, ECLI:EU:C:2013:635

Real Madrid Football Club and Others (Case C-584/08), Order of the President of the Court, 24 March 2009, ECLI:EU:C:2009:187

Reisch Montage AG v Kiesel Baumaschinen Handels GmbH (Case C-103/05), 13 July 2006, ECLI:EU:C:2006:471

Réunion européenne SA and Others v Spliethoff's Bevrachtingskantoor BV and the Master of the vessel Alblasgracht V002 (Case C-51/97), 27 October 1998, ECLI:EU:C:1998:509

Rinkau *see* Criminal proceedings against Siegfried Ewald Rinkau (Case 157/80), 26 May 1981, ECLI:EU:C:1981:120

Roche Nederland BV and Others v Frederick Primus and Milton Goldenberg (Case C-539/03), 13 July 2006, ECLI:EU:C:2006:458

Shenavai *see* Hassan Shenavai v Klaus Kreischer (Case 266/85), 15 January 1987, ECLI:EU:C:1987:11

Shevill *see* Fiona Shevill, Ixora Trading Inc., Chequepoint SARL and Chequepoint International Ltd v Presse Alliance SA (Case C-68/93), 7 March 1995, ECLI:EU:C:1995:61

Solvay SA v Honeywell Fluorine Products Europe BV and Others (Case C-616/10), 12 July 2012, ECLI:EU:C:2012:445

Somafer SA v Saar-Ferngas AG (Case 33/78), 22 November 1978, ECLI:EU: C:1978:205

Svensson *see* Nils Svensson and Others v Retriever Sverige AB (Case C-466/12), 13 February 2014, ECLI:EU:C:2014:76

Swaddling *see* Robin Swaddling v Adjudication Officer (Case C-90/97), 25 February 1999, ECLI:EU:C:1999:96

Tacconi *see* Fonderie Officine Meccaniche Tacconi SpA v Heinrich Wagner Sinto Maschinenfabrik GmbH (HWS) (Case C-334/00), 17 September 2002, ECLI:EU:C:2002:499

Tatry *see* The owners of the cargo lately laden on board the ship "Tatry" v the owners of the ship "Maciej Rataj" (Case C-406/92), 6 December 1994, ECLI:EU:C:1994:400

Telekabel *see* UPC Telekabel Wien GmbH v Constantin Film Verleih GmbH and Wega Filmproduktionsgesellschaft mbH (Case C-314/12), 27 March 2014, ECLI:EU:C:2014:192

Tessili *see* Industrie Tessili Italiana Como v Dunlop AG (Case 12-76), 6 October 1976, ECLI:EU:C:1976:133

Trade Agency Ltd v Seramico Investments Ltd (Case C-619/10), 6 September 2012, ECLI:EU:C:2012:531

Turner *see* Gregory Paul Turner v Felix Fareed Ismail Grovit, Harada Ltd and Changepoint SA (Case C-159/02), 27 April 2004, ECLI:EU:C:2004:228

Weber *see* Herbert Weber v Universal Ogden Services Ltd (Case C-37/00), 27 February 2002, ECLI:EU:C:2002:122

West Tankers *see* Allianz SpA, formerly Riunione Adriatica di Sicurtà SpA and Generali Assicurazioni Generali SpA v West Tankers Inc. (Case C-185/07), 10 February 2009, ECLI:EU:C:2009:69

Wintersteiger AG v Products 4U Sondermaschinenbau GmbH (Case C-523/10), 19 April 2012, ECLI:EU:C:2012:220

Zelger *see* Siegfried Zelger v Sebastiano Salinitri (Case 129/83), 7 June 1984, ECLI:EU:C:1984:215

Zuid-Chemie BV v Philippo's Mineralenfabriek NV/SA (Case 189/08), 16 July 2009, ECLI:EU:C:2009:475

Opinions of Advocates General (Alphabetical)

AG 1994 in Marinari *see* Antonio Marinari v Lloyds Bank plc and Zubaidi Trading Company (Case C-364/93), Opinion of Advocate General Darmon delivered on 21 September 1994, ECLI:EU:C:1995:146

AG 1994 in Shevill *see* Fiona Shevill, Ixora Trading Inc., Chequepoint SARL and Chequepoint International Ltd v Presse Alliance SA (Case C-68/93), Opinion of Advocate General Darmon delivered on 14 July 1994, ECLI:EU:C:1994:303

AG 1995 in Marinari *see* Antonio Marinari v Lloyds Bank plc and Zubaidi Trading Company (Case C-364/93), Opinion of Advocate General Léger delivered on 18 May 1995, ECLI:EU:C:1995:146

AG 1995 in Shevill *see* Fiona Shevill, Ixora Trading Inc., Chequepoint SARL and Chequepoint International Ltd v Presse Alliance SA (Case C-68/93), Opinion of Advocate General Léger delivered on 10 January 1995, ECLI:EU:C:1994:303

AG in A *see* Opinion of Advocate General Kokott delivered on 29 January 2009 (Case C-523/07), ECLI:EU:C:2009:39

AG in Bier *see* Handelskwekerij G. J. Bier BV v Mines de potasse d'Alsace SA (Case 21-76), Opinion of Advocate General Capotorti delivered on 10 November 1976, ECLI:EU:C:1976:147

AG in CDC *see* CDC Cartel Damage Claims Hydrogen Peroxide SA v Evonik Degussa GmbH, Akzo Nobel NV, Solvay SA, Kemira Oyj, Arkema France SA, FMC Foret SA, Chemoxal SA, Edison SpA (Case C-352/13), Opinion of Advocate General Jääskinen delivered on 11 December 2014, ECLI:EU:C:2014:2443

AG in Coty Germany *see* Coty Germany (anciennement Coty Prestige Lancaster Group) v First Note Perfumes NV, (Case C-360/12), Opinion of Advocate General Jääskinen delivered on 21 November 2013, ECLI:EU:C:2013:764

AG in DFDS Torline *see* Danmarks Rederiforening, acting on behalf of DFDS Torline A/S v LO Landsorganisationen i Sverige, acting on behalf of SEKO Sjöfolk Facket för Service och Kommunikation (Case C-18/02), Opinion of Advocate General Jacobs delivered on 18 September 2003, ECLI:EU:C:2003:482

AG in Diageo Brands *see* Diageo Brands BV v Simiramida-04 EOOD (Case C-681/13), Opinion of Advocate General Szpunar delivered on 3 March 2015, ECLI:EU:C:2015:137

AG in Dumez *see* Dumez France SA and Tracoba SARL v Hessische Landesbank and others (Case C-220/88), Opinion of Advocate General Darmon delivered on 23 November 1989, ECLI:EU:C:1989:595

AG in eDate and Martinez *see* eDate Advertising GmbH v X (Case C-509/09) and Olivier Martinez and Robert Martinez v Société MGN Limited (Case C-161/10), Opinion of Advocate General Cruz Villalón delivered on 29 March 2011, ECLI:EU:C:2011:192

AG in Folien Fischer *see* Folien Fischer AG and Fofitec AG v Ritrama SpA (Case C-133/11), Opinion of Advocate General Jääskinen delivered on 19 April 2012, ECLI:EU:C:2012:226

AG in Gazprom *see* Gazprom OAO, other party to the proceedings: Republic of Lithuania (Case C-536/13), Opinion of Advocate General Wathelet delivered on 4 December 2014, ECLI:EU:C:2014:2414

AG in Google Spain *see* Google Spain SL Google Inc. v Agencia Española de Protección de Datos (AEPD) Mario Costeja González (Case C-131/12), Opinion of Advocate General Jääskinen delivered on 25 June 2013, ECLI:EU:C:2013:424

AG in Hejduk *see* Pez Hejduk v EnergieAgentur.NRW GmbH (Case C-441/13), Opinion of Advocate General Cruz Villalón delivered on 11 September 2014, ECLI:EU:C:2014:2212

AG in I. Weber *see* Irmengard Weber v Mechthilde Weber (Case C-438/12), Opinion of Advocate General Jääskinen delivered on 30 January 2014, ECLI:EU:C:2014:43

AG in Kalfelis *see* Athanasios Kalfelis v Bankhaus Schröder, Münchmeyer, Hengst and Co. and others (Case C-189/87), Opinion of Advocate General Darmon delivered on 15 June 1988, ECLI:EU:C:1988:312

AG in Kronhofer *see* Rudolf Kronhofer v Marianne Maier and Others (Case C-168/02), Opinion of Advocate General Léger delivered on 15 January 2004, ECLI:EU:C:2004:24

AG in Land Berlin *see* Land Berlin v Ellen Mirjam Sapir and Others (Case C-645/11), Opinion of Advocate General Trstenjak delivered on 28 November 2012, ECLI:EU:C:2012:757

AG in Mærsk *see* Mærsk Olie & Gas A/S v Firma M. de Haan en W. de Boer (Case C-39/02), Opinion of Advocate General Léger delivered on 13 July 2004, ECLI:EU:C:2004:430

AG in Melzer *see* Melzer v MF Global UK Ltd (Case C-228/11), Opinion of Advocate General Jääskinen delivered on 29 November 2012, ECLI:EU:C:2012:766

AG in Painer *see* Eva-Maria Painer v Standard VerlagsGmbH and Others (Case C-145/10), Opinion of Advocate General Trstenjak delivered on 12 April 2011, ECLI:EU:C:2011:239

AG in Pinckney *see* Peter Pinckney v KDG Mediatech AG (Case C-170/12), Opinion of Advocate General Jääskinen delivered on 13 June 2013, ECLI:EU:C:2013:400

AG in Réunion européenne *see* Réunion européenne SA and Others v Spliethoff's Bevrachtingskantoor BV and the Master of the vessel Alblasgracht V002 (Case C-51/97), Opinion of Advocate General Cosmas delivered on 5 February 1998, ECLI:EU:C:1998:45

AG in Roche *see* Roche Nederland BV u. a. gegen Frederick Primus und Milton Goldenberg (Case C-539/03), Opinion of Advocate General Léger delivered on 8 December 2005, ECLI:EU:C:2005:749

Requests for a preliminary ruling (Alphabetical)

Other materials

Minutes of Proceedings drawn up for the oral hearing in eDate and Martinez, 14.12.2010, fns 822, 850, 867, 879, 911, 1203

European Court of Human Rights

Axel Springer AG v. Germany (no 39954/08), fns 36, 680

Karakó v. Hungary (no 39311/05), fns 36, 39

Reklos and Davourlis v. Greece (no 1234/05), fn 36

Steel and Morris v. The United Kingdom (no 68416/01), fn 1231

Times Newspapers Ltd (nos 1 and 2) v. United Kingdom (nos 3002/03 and 23676/03), fn 141

Ungváry and Irodalom Kft v. Hungary (no 64520/10), fn 680

Von Hannover v Germany (No. 3) (no 8772/10), fn 36

Von Hannover v. Germany (no 59320/00), fn 1092

Von Hannover v. Germany (No. 2) (nos 40660/08, 60641/08), fns 36, 773, 1060

Węgrzynowski and Smolczewski v. Poland (no 33846/07), fn 141

France

Cour de cassation, Société Castellblanch v Société Champagne Louis Roederer, No 01-03225, (9.12.2003), fn 849

TGI de Paris (ord. réf.), 24 novembre et 19 décembre 2014 - Marie-France M. cl Google France et Google Inc., fn 1045

TGI de Toulouse (ord. réf.), 21 janvier 201 - Franck J. c/ Google France et Google Inc., fn 1045

TGI Nanterre, 1ère ch. du 27/03/2014 (14/02736) - Julie Gayet c/ Société Mondadori Magazines France, fns 79, 80, 86

TGI Nanterre, 1ère ch. Ord. de mise en état (11.10.2012) - Marion C. / Rossel & Compagnie, fn 1114

TGI Nanterre, (jugement de référé) 18/09/2012 - Catherine Elisabeth Middleton et a. c/ Sas Mondadori Magazine France et a., fn 92

TGI Paris, 17ème ch., ord. du 29/03/2010 (08/15331) - Martinez and Martinez (request), fn 960

TGI Paris, 17ème chamber, N° d'affaire: 0718523043 (3.3.2011) - Ministére Public c/ Weiler, fns 85, 665

Germany

Case 1 U 511/13 (7.11.2013), OLG Jena (AfP 2014, 75-76), fn 646
Case 15 U 148/09 (30.3.2010), OLG Köln, fns 826, 908, 996
Case 158 C 28716/11 (15.6.2012), AG München (ZUM 2013, 159), fn 452
Case 2-03 O 366/00 (9.11.2000), LG Frankfurt/M., fns 825, 869
Case 2-03 O 471/09 (15.7.2010), LG Frankfurt/M. (AfP 2010, 512-514), fn 995
Case 29 U 2713/07 (6.12.2007), OLG München, fns 664, 868
Case 324 S 1/14 (19.9.2014), LG Hamburg (AfP 2015, 183-184), fn 646
Case 6 U 9/02 (10.7.2002), OLG Karlsruhe, fn 849
Case BGH 3.5.1977, NJW 1977, 1590, 1591, fn 936
Case de Visser 1 O 1205/09 (2) (24.4.2012), LG Regensburg, pp 44-45; fns 74, 1211
Case eDate Advertising VI ZR 217/08a (8.5.2012), BGH (GRUR 2012, 850), fns 963, 970, 1114, 1140
Case Ginsengwurzel VI ZR 259/60 (19.9.1961), BGH (BGHZ 35, 363), p 44; fn 72
Case Herrenreiter I ZR 151/56 (14.2.1958), BGH (BGHZ 26, 349), p 44; fn 71
Case I ZR 131/12 (12.12.2013), BGH (GRUR 2014, 601), fns 753, 1230
Case I ZR 24/03 (30.3.2006), BGH, fn 869
Case I-15 U 17/08 (30.12.2008), OLG Düsseldorf, fns 30, 908
Case Leserbrief I ZR 211/53 (25.5.1954), BGH (BGHZ 13, 334), fn 64
Case New York Times VI ZR 23/09 (2.3.2010), BGH (BGHZ 184, 313), pp 32-33; fns 25, 27-29, 31, 887, 890, 908
Case Seven Days in Moscow VI ZR 111/10 (29.3.2011), BGH (GRUR 2011, 558), fns 25, 26, 31, 826, 836, 890, 908, 995, 996
Case VI ZR 211/12 (17.12.2013), BGH (BGHZ 199, 237), fns 65, 68, 139
Case VI ZR 269/12 (14.5.2013), BGH (GRUR 2013, 751), fns 25, 1210
Order eDate Advertising VI ZR 217/08 (10.11.2009), BGH (GRUR 2010, 261), fns 960, 972
Order VI ZR 135/13 (28.10.2014), BGH (GRUR 2015, 192), fn 165

Greece

Athens First Instance Court, Nr. 9118/2014 (unreported), fn 1047
Court of Appeal of Dodecanese, Nr. 220/2013 (unreported), fn 1114

Hungary

Case 2 Pf. 20.658/2012/5, Fővárosi Ítélőtábla (ÍH2013.60), fn 54

Case 2 Pf. 21 008/2013/6, Fővárosi Ítélőtábla (BDT 2014.6.92), fns 51, 53, 56
Case BH2002.261, fn 51
Case Gf. I. 30 741/3012/3, Debreceni Ítélőtábla (BDT 2013.3.50), fns 1013, 1114
Case Gfv. VII. 30.112/2012, Kúria (BH 2013.4.98), fn 60
Case Gfv. X. 31.666/2002. sz., Legf. Bír. (BH 2004.9.376), fn 318
Case Pfv. III. 24313/1998, LB (BH 2001.1.12), fn 60
Decision 28/2014 (IX.29.) AB, fn 53
Decision 8/1990 (IV.23.), AB, fn 49

Ireland

CG v Facebook & Anor [2015] NIQB 11, fns 181, 1045
Coleman v MGN Limited [2012] IESC 20 (15.3.2012), fn 1039
CSI Manufacturing Ltd v Dun and Bradstreet [2013] IEHC 547 (29.11.2013), fns 1013, 1039
Ewins v Carlton [1997] 2 ILRM 223, Irish High Court, 3.3.1997, fns 705, 815
USA Rugby Football Union Limited v Ivan Calhoun (High Court, unreported, 2002), fn 15

Norway

Case of the Supreme Court of Norway (Norges Høyesterett), 17.10.2001, HR-2000-00799 – Rt-2001 – 1322 (240-2001), fn 815
Case of the Supreme Court of Norway (Norges Høyesterett), 20.12.2012, HR-2012-2393-A – Rt-2012 – 1951 (Trico Subsea AS v Raffles Shipping Projects Pte Ltd), fns 396, 1181

Sweden

Case M.E. Aktiebolag v Hamar Arbeiderblad AS (4.2.2008), Svea hovrätt, fn 849
Case RH 2008:4, Swedish Appellate Court, fn 856

Switzerland

Bundesgericht 18.12.2008, BGE 135 III 185, fn 396
Judgment of the Swiss Bundesgericht of 6.3.2007, fn 849

Tribunal fédéral (Bundesgericht), Banque Bruxelles Lambert (Suisse)/République du Paraguay e.a., ATF 124 III 382, fn 248

United Kingdom: England and Wales / Scotland

Ames & Anor v The Spamhaus Project Ltd & Anor [2015] EWHC 127 (QB), fns 97, 101, 102, 106, 680, 1051, 1191

Anton Durbeck v. Den Norske Bank [2003] 2 WLR 1296 (CA), fn 477

Bonnard v. Perryman [1891] 2 Ch 269, p 51; fn 108

Bonnier Media Limited / Greg Lloyd Smith and Kestrel Trading Corporation (Court of Session, Scotland, 1.7.2002), fn 869

Campbell v MGN Ltd [2004] UKHL 22, [2004] 2 AC 457, pp 51-52; fn 115

Canada Trust Company v. Stolzenberg and Gamba [2000] UKHL 51, fn 402

Cartier International and Others v. BSkyB and others [2014] EWHC 3354 (Ch), p 255; fns 1040, 1041

Cooke & Anor v MGN Ltd & Anor [2014] EWHC 2831 (QB), p 50; fns 102, 103, 105, 106, 595

Douglas v Hello! (No 3) [2006] QB 125, fn 122

Football Dataco Ltd & Ors v Sportradar GmbH & Anor [2010] EWHC 2911 (Ch) (17.11.2010), fn 825

Google Inc v Vidal-Hall & Ors [2015] EWCA Civ 311, p 53; fns 121-123

Jameel v Dow Jones & Co [2005] EWCA Civ 75, fn 104

King v Lewis [2004] EWCA Civ 1329, affirming: King v Lewis [2004] EWHC 168 (QB), fn 15

Lewis v. Daily Telegraph Ltd. [1964] A.C. 234, fn 1232

Lillie & Reed v Newcastle City Council & Others [2002] EWHC 1600 (QB), fn 107

Mosley v News Group Newspapers Ltd [2008] EWHC 1777 (QB), p 52; fn 120

OBG Ltd v Allan and Douglas v Hello! [2008] 1 AC 1, fn 116

Olafsson v Gissurarson [2008] EWCA Civ 152, fn 762

Shevill and Others v. Presse Alliance S.A. [1992] 2 W.L.R. 1 (C.A.), fns 615-617, 672, 1232

Shevill and Others v. Presse Alliance S.A. [1995] 2 W.L.R. 499 (E.C.J.), fns 629, 667, 670, 689, 721

Shevill and Others v. Presse Alliance S.A. [1996] 3 W.L.R. 420 (H.L.(E.)), fn 617

Thornton v Telegraph Media Group Ltd [2010] EWHC 1414 (QB), fns 104, 668

Vidal-Hall & Ors v Google Inc [2014] EWHC 13 (QB), fns 115-116, 121-123

United States of America

Table of Legislation

European Union

Treaties

Regulations

Rome II *see* Regulation (EC) No 864/2007 of the European Parliament and of the Council of 11 July 2007 on the law applicable to non-contractual obligations (OJ 2007 L 199/40), pp 185, 229, 230, 274, 275, 295, 303; fns 277, 409, 602, 753, 1224

Directives

Dir. 2000/31/EC (OJ 2000 L 178/1) *see* Directive 2000/31/EC of the European Parliament and of the Council of 8 June 2000 on certain legal aspects of information society services, in particular electronic commerce, in the Internal Market (OJ 2000 L 178/1), pp 284-286; fns 1155, 1157, 1160, 1164

Dir. 95/46/EC (OJ 1995 L 281/31) *see* Directive 95/46/EC of the European Parliament and of the Council of 24 October 1995 on the protection of individuals with regard to the processing of personal data and on the free movement of such data (OJ 1995 L 281/31), fn 165

Council Decisions and Other Documents

CONVENT 49, Explanations relating to the Charter of Fundamental Rights of the European Union (2010), available at <http://www.europarl.europa.eu/charter/convent 49_en.htm>, fn 770

Council, 7700/99, LIMITE JUSTCIV 60 (30.4.1999), fn 239

Dec. 2003/93/EC (OJ 2003 L 48/1) *see* Council Decision of 19 December 2002 authorising the Member States, in the interest of the Community, to sign the 1996 Hague Convention on jurisdiction, applicable law, recognition, enforcement and cooperation in respect of parental responsibility and measures for the protection of children (OJ 2003 L 48/1), fn 275

Dec. 2006/719/EC (OJ 2006 L 297/1) *see* Council Decision 2006/719/EC of 5 October 2006 on the accession of the Community to the Hague Conference on Private International Law, fns 275-277

Dec. 2009/397/EC (OJ 2009 L 133/1) *see* Council Decision 2009/397/EC of 26 February 2009 on the signing on behalf of the European Community of the Convention on Choice of Court Agreements, fn 267

Dec. 2010/718/EU (OJ 2010 L 325/4) *see* European Council Decision of 29 October 2010 amending the status with regard to the European Union of the island of Saint-Barthélemy (2010/718/EU) (OJ 2010 L 325/4), fn 218

Dec. 2012/419/EU (OJ 2012 L 204/131) *see* European Council Decision of 11 July 2012 amending the status of Mayotte with regard to the European Union (2012/419/EU) (OJ 2012 L 204/131), fn 218

Hague Programme (OJ 2005 C 53/1), fn 381

Information of the Council (OJ 2007 L 94/70) *see* Information concerning the date of entry into force of the Agreement between the European Community and the

France

Germany

Hungary

2392/1997 (XII.3.) Government Decision [2392/1997 (XII.3.) Kormányhatározat], p 80

Act No CIV of 2010 on the freedom of the press and the fundamental rules on media content (2010. évi CIV. törvény a sajtószabadságról és a médiatartalmak alapvető szabályairól), p 42

Act No CLXXVII of 2013 (2013. évi CLXXVII. törvény a Polgári Törvénykönyvről szóló 2013. évi V. törvény hatálybalépésével összefüggő átmeneti és felhatalmazó rendelkezésekről), fn 47

Act No CX of 2000 on the amendments to certain provisions of the Law-decree No 13 of 1979 on International Private Law (2000. évi CX. törvény a joghatóságra és külföldi határozatok elismerésére és végrehajtására vonatkozó egyes jogszabályok módosításáról), fns 257, 391

Act No IV of 1977 (1977. évi IV. törvény a Magyar Népköztársaság Polgári Törvénykönyvéről szóló 1959. évi IV. törvény módosításáról és egységes szövegéről), p 41

Be. *see* Act No XIX of 1998 on the Code of Criminal Procedure (1998. évi XIX. törvény a büntetőeljárásról), pp 122, 123; fn 472

Btk. *see* Act No C of 2012 on the Criminal Code (2012. évi C. törvény a Büntető Törvénykönyvről), p 122

Nmj. *see* Law-Decree No 13 of 1979 on International Private Law (A nemzetközi magánjogról szóló 1979. évi 13. törvényerejű rendelet), pp 80-81, 113; fns 257, 318, 391, 429

Pp. *see* Act No III of 1952 on the Code of Civil Procedure (1952. évi III. törvény a polgári perrendtartásról), pp 42, 80, 81, 123; fn 229

Ptk. *see* Act No IV of 1959 on the civil code (1959. évi IV. törvény a Polgári Törvénykönyvről), pp 39-42, 53; fns 50, 51, 55, 54, 56, 59

új Ptk. *see* Act No V of 2013 on the new civil code (2013. évi V. törvény a Polgári Törvénykönyvről), pp 39-42, 54; fns 48, 50, 51, 54, 55, 59, 607

Vht. *see* Act No LIII of 1994 on Court Litigation (1994. évi LIII. törvény a bírósági végrehajtásról), pp 80-81

United Kingdom

Defamation Act 1952, p 49

Defamation Act 1996, pp 49, 51

Defamation Act 2013, pp 49, 54; fns 15, 97, 99, 101, 102, 106, 595, 759

Explanatory Notes to the Defamation Act 2013, fns 104-105

HRA *see* Human Rights Act 1998, pp 51-53

Protection from Harassment Act 1997, fn 112

Private International Law (Miscellaneous Provisions) Act 1995, p 53

United States of America

Restatement (Second) of Torts §577A (1977), fn 1191

Libel Terrorism Protection Act (New York), fn 799

SPEECH Act *see* Securing the Protection of our Enduring and Established Constitutional Heritage (SPEECH) Act (10.8.2010), fn 799

Table of International Treaties, Conventions and Other Documents

Table of Documents of the Hague Conference on Private International Law

Prel. Doc. No 8 of November 1997, Synthesis of the Work of the Special Commission of June 1997 on International Jurisdiction and the Effects of Foreign Judgments in Civil and Commercial Matters drawn up by Catherine Kessedjian Deputy Secretary General, fn 922

Process Paper on the Continuation of the Judgments Project drawn up by the Permanent Bureau, August 2013, fns 272-273

Table of Official Studies and Reports

Pocar Report *see* Convention on jurisdiction and the recognition and enforcement of judgments in civil and commercial matters, signed in Lugano on 30 October 2007 - Explanatory Report by Professor Fausto Pocar (Holder of the Chair of International Law at the University of Milan) (OJ 2009 C 319/1), p 122; fns 240, 243, 246, 305, 397, 405, 444, 470, 483, 524, 590, 592

Schlosser Report *see* Report by Professor Dr. Peter Schlosser on the Convention of 9 October 1978 on the Association of the Kingdom of Denmark, Ireland and the United Kingdom of Great Britain and Northern Ireland to the Convention on jurisdiction and the enforcement of judgments in civil and commercial matters and to the Protocol on its interpretation by the Court of Justice (OJ 1979 C 59/71), p 148; fns 211, 316, 329, 344, 400

Study JLS/C4/2005/03, National Report Italy (Consolo et al) (Questionnaire 3), point 2.2.11, IT-10, available at <ec.europa.eu/civiljustice/news/docs/study_bxl1_italy.pdf>, fn 849

Virgos/Schmit Report *see* Report by Miguel Virgos and Etienne Schmit on the Convention on Insolvency Proceedings (1996), European Union, The Council, 6500/96, fn 1224

Explanatory Memoranda to Regulation Proposals

Bataller Opinion and Report (5.5.2011) *see* Opinion of the European Economic and Social Committee on the Proposal for a Regulation of the European Parliament and of the Council on jurisdiction and the recognition and enforcement of judgments in civil and commercial matters, COM(2010) 748 final/2 / 2010/0383 (COD) INT/566 – Jurisdiction in civil and commercial matters / Brussels, 5 May 2011 / CES 0795/2011 / Rapporteur-general: Mr Hernández Bataller, fn 348

Commission Document COM(1999) 348 final *see* Proposal for a Council Regulation (EC) on jurisdiction and the recognition and enforcement of judgments in civil and commercial matters Brussels, 14.07.1999 / COM(1999) 348 final / 99/0154 (CNS), fns 405, 720, 1129

Commission Document COM(2003) 427 final *see* Proposal for a Regulation of the European Parliament and of the Council on the Law Applicable to Non-Contractual Obligations ("Rome II") Brussels, 22.7.2003 / COM (2003) 427 final / 2003/0168 (COD), fns 436, 522, 662, 666, 1119

Commission Document COM(2006) 346 final *see* Communication from the Commission to the European Parliament, the Council, the European Economic and Social Committee, the Committee of the Regions and the Court of Justice of the European Communities. Adaptation of the provisions of Title IV of the Treaty establishing the European Community relating to the jurisdiction of the Court of Justice with a view to ensuring more effective judicial protection. 28.6.2006 / COM(2006) 346, fn 230

Commission Document COM(2009) 174 final *see* Report from the Commission to the European Parliament, the Council, the European Economic and Social Committee on the application of Council Regulation (EC) No 44/2001 on jurisdiction and the recognition and enforcement of judgments in civil and commercial matters, Brussels, 21.4.2009 / COM(2009) 174 final, fn 433

Commission Document COM(2010) 748 final *see* Proposal for a Regulation of the European Parliament and of the Council on jurisdiction and the recognition and enforcement of judgments in civil and commercial matters, (Recast) Brussels, 14.12.2010 / COM(2010) 748 final / 2010/0383 (COD), fns 364, 505, 801

Commission Document COM(2012) 744 final *see* Proposal for a Regulation of the European Parliament and of the Council amending Council Regulation (EC) No 1346/2000 on insolvency proceedings, Strasbourg, 12.12.2012 / COM(2012) 744 final / 2012/0360 (COD), fn 1224

Commission Document COM(2013) 627 final *see* Proposal for a Regulation of the European Parliament and the Council laying down measures concerning the European single market for electronic communications and to achieve a Connected Continent, and amending Directives 2002/20/EC, 2002/21/EC and 2002/22/EC and Regulations (EC) No 1211/2009 and (EU) No 531/2012, Brussels, 11.9.2013 / COM(2013) 627 / 2013/0309 (COD), fn 34

Commission Document COM(2014) 144 final *see* Communication from the Commission to the European Parliament, the Council, the European Economic and Social Committee, the Committee of the Regions. The EU Justice Agenda for 2020 – Strengthening Trust, Mobility and Growth within the Union, Strasbourg, 11.3.2014 / COM(2014) 144 final, fns 34, 381

Commission Document COM(97) 609 final *see* Commission Communication to the Council and the European Parliament "Towards greater efficiency in obtaining and enforcing judgments in the European Union." Proposal for a Council Act establishing the Convention on jurisdiction and the recognition and enforcement of judgments in civil and commercial matters in the Member States of the European Union, Brussels, 26.11.1997 / COM(97) 609 final / 97/0339 (CNS) (OJ 1998 C 33/3), fns 214, 524, 719

Commission Document COM_SEC(2010) 1547 *see* Impact Assessment. Accompanying document to the Proposal for a Regulation of the European Parliament and the Council on jurisdiction and the recognition and enforcement of judgments in civil and commercial matters (Recast), Brussels, 14.12.2010 / SEC(2010) 1547 final, fn 433

Consultation on a preliminary draft proposal for a council regulation on the law applicable to non-contractual obligations, available at <http://ec.europa.eu/justice/news/consulting_public/rome_ii/news_hearing_rome2_en.htm>, fn 602

EP Resolution, P7_TA(2012)0200 (10.5.2012) *see* European Parliament resolution of 10 May 2012 with recommendations to the Commission on the amendment of Regulation (EC) No 864/2007 on the law applicable to non-contractual obligations (Rome II) (2009/2170(INI)) / P7_TA(2012)0200 / A7-0152/2012, fns 746, 753, 759, 761

EP Resolution, P7-TA(2010)0304 (7.9.2010) *see* European Parliament resolution of 7 September 2010 on the implementation and review of Council Regulation (EC) No

44/2001 on jurisdiction and the recognition and enforcement of judgments in civil and commercial matters (2009/2140(INI), fns 263, 399

Zwiefka Draft Report (28.6.2011) *see* Draft Report on the proposal for a regulation of the European Parliament and of the Council on jurisdiction and the recognition and enforcement of judgments in civil and commercial matters (recast). COM(2010)0748 – C7-0433/2010 – 2010/0383(COD)) Committee on Legal Affairs / Rapporteur: Tadeusz Zwiefka / 28.6.2011 / PE467.046v01-00, fns 351, 433, 801

Appendices

*Appendix 1: Traceroute: Saarbrücken – Hungary – Saarbrücken**

* This traceroute was carried out by using the command 'tracert' of the Microsoft Windows System. The decoded version is on file with author. Geotool from Flagfox (<http://geoip.flagfox.net/>) was used to localise IP addresses. Note that although Geotool indicated the EU as the location under nos 7-11, it pointed at the territory of Switzerland on the map.

1.	1 ms	1ms	1ms	Starting point	x.x.x.x	Germany
2.	21 ms	21 ms	21 ms	x.x.x.net	x.x.x.229	Germany
3.	20 ms	20 ms	20 ms	x.x.x.net	x.x.13.x	Germany
4.	20 ms	20 ms	19 ms	x.x.x.net	x.x.12.x	Germany
5.	23 ms	23 ms	23 ms	x.x.x.net	x.x.2.x	Germany
6.	24 ms	24 ms	23 ms	x.x.x.net	x.x.x.137	Spain
7.	24 ms	23 ms	24 ms	x.x.net	x.x.x.37	EU (Switzerland)
8.	24 ms	24 ms	29 ms	x.x.net	80.x.x.x	EU (Switzerland)
9.	44 ms	36 ms	36 ms	x.x.net	80.x.xx.x	EU (Switzerland)
10.	46 ms	47 ms	48 ms	x.x.net	80.x.x.x	EU (Switzerland)
11.	58 ms	58 ms	58 ms	x.x.x.net	213.x.x.x	EU (Switzerland)
12.	60 ms	58 ms	59 ms	x.x.x.hu	x.111.x.x	Hungary
13.	58 ms	58 ms	57 ms	x.x.hu	x.111.x.x	Hungary
14.	62 ms	62 ms	62 ms	x.x.elte.hu	x.x.x.13	Hungary
15.	60 ms	58 ms	58 ms	x.x.elte.hu	x.x.x.30	Hungary
16.	58 ms	57 ms	57 ms	University	x.x.24.x	Hungary

Appendix 2: Selected social media traffic

World population: approx. 7.233 billion people[1]	
Facebook[2]	1.39 billion monthly active users (31.12.2014)
	1.19 billion mobile monthly active users (31.12.2014)
Facebook[3]	more than 4.75 billion content items (every day)
	more than 4.5 billion 'likes' (every day)
	more than 10 billion messages (every day)
	more than 250 billion photos
WordPress.com[4]	more than 409 million people view more than 15.5 billion pages (each month)
	about 41.7 million new user-posts (each month)
	60.5 million new user-comments (each month)
Tumblr[5]	267.7 million blogs
	125.3 billion posts
YouTube[7]	more than 1 billion users
	300 hours of video are uploaded (every minute)
Wikipedia[8]	35.898.656 pages (all pages in the wiki, incl. talk pages, redirects, etc.)
	763.477.492 page edits since Wikipedia was set up

1 Approx. 7.233.698.722. United States – Census Bureau – U.S. and World Population Clock <http://www.census.gov/popclock/> (last accessed on 30.3.2015, 3:23 pm UTC).

2 Facebook Company Info <http://newsroom.fb.com/company-info/>.

3 A Focus on Efficiency, A whitepaper, 2013, p 6.

4 WordPress – About <https://wordpress.com/about/>.

5 Tumblr – About <http://www.tumblr.com/about> (last accessed on 10.12.2015).

7 Youtube – Statistics <http://www.youtube.com/t/press_statistics?hl=en>.

8 Wikipedia Statistics <http://en.wikipedia.org/wiki/Special:Statistics>.

*Appendix 3: Correlation Table**

* The correlation table lists those provisions that are referred to in this book. If necessary, additional information is given in the footnotes. Cf. Correlation Table annexed to Brussels Ia (Annex III, regarding Brussels I and Brussels Ia); Layton/Mercer, European Civil Practice, pp ccv-ccvii (Table of Destinations, regarding Brussels I – BC – 1988 LC). Symbols are used as follows:
'-': no identical or similar provision exists;
'≈': provisions with (minor) differences.

Brussels Ia	BC	Brussels I	1988 LC	2007 LC
Recital 1	cf. preamble	-	cf. preamble	cf. preamble
Recital 3	-	-	-	-
Recital 6	-	Recital 6	-	-
Recital 8	-	-	-	-
Recital 10	-	≈ Recital 7	-	-
Recital 11	-	-	-	-
Recital 13	-	Recital 8	-	-
Recital 14, first indent	-	≈ Recital 9, first subsentence	-	-
Recital 14, second indent	-	-	-	-
Recital 15	-	≈ Recital 11	-	-
Recital 16	-	≈ Recital 12 (no second sentence)	-	-
Recital 18	-	≈ Recital 13	-	-
Recital 20	-	-	-	-
Recital 21	-	≈ Recital 15	-	-
Recital 22	-	-	-	-
Recital 26, first sentence	-	≈ Recital 16 (no second sentence)	-	-
Recital 34	-	≈ Recital 19	-	-
Recital 38	-	-	-	-
Recital 40	-	≈ Recital 20 (no second sentence)	-	-
Recital 41	-	cf. Recital 21	-	-
Art 1(1)	≈ Art 1(1)	≈ Art 1(1)	≈ Art 1(1)	≈ Art 1(1)
Art 1(2) introductory words	Art 1(2) introductory words	Art 1(2) introductory words	Art 1(2) introductory words	Art 1(2) introductory words

Brussels Ia	BC	Brussels I	1988 LC	2007 LC
Art 1(2) points (a) and (f)	≈ Art 1, point 1	≈ Art 1(2), point (a)	≈ Art 1, point 1	≈ Art 1(2), point (a)
Art 1(2) points (b) to (d)	Art 1, points 2-4	Art 1(2) points (b)-(d)	Art 1, points 2-4	Art 1(2) points (b) to (d)
Art 1(2) points (e)	-	since 18.6.2011	-	-
Art 3	cf. Protocol, Art Va	≈ Art 62	cf. Protocol 1, Art Va	cf. Art 62
Art 4	Art 2	Art 2	Art 2	Art 2
Art 5	≈ Art 3	Art 3	≈ Art 3	Art 3
Art 6	≈ Art 4	≈ Art 4	≈ Art 4	≈ Art 4
Art 7 introductory words	Art 5 introductory words	Art 5 introductory words	Art 5 introductory words	Art 5 introductory words
Art 7(1)(a)	Art 5(1), first subsentence	Art 5(1)(a)	Art 5(1), first subsentence	Art 5(1)(a)
Art 7(1)(b)-(c)	-	Art 5(1)(b)-(c)	-	Art 5(1)(b)-(c)
-	Art 5(2)	Art 5(2) until 18.6.2011	Art 5(2)	Art 5(2) (a)-(b) but not (c)
Art 7(2)	≈ Art 5(3)	Art 5(3)	≈ Art 5(3)	Art 5(3)
Art 7(3)	Art 5(4)	Art 5(4)	Art 5(4)	Art 5(4)
Art 7(5)	Art 5(5)	Art 5(5)	Art 5(5)	Art 5(5)
Art 8 introductory words	Art 6 introductory words	Art 6 introductory words	Art 6 introductory words	Art 6 introductory words
Art 8(1)	≈ Art 6(1)	Art 6(1)	≈ Art 6(1)	Art 6(1)
Art 9	Art 6a	Art 7	Art 6A	Art 7
Art 11	≈ Art 8	Art 9	≈ Art 8	Art 9
Art 17(1) introductory words	Art 13, first indent, introductory words	Art 15(1) introductory words	Art 13, first indent, introductory words	Art 15(1) introductory words
Art 17(1)(c)	cf. Art 13, point 3	Art 15(1)(c)	cf. Art 13, point 3	Art 15(1)(c)
Art 17(2)	Art 13, second indent	Art 15(2)	Art 13, second indent	Art 15(2)
Art 18(1)	≈ Art 14, first indent	≈ Art 16(1)	≈ Art 14, first indent	≈ Art 16(1)
Art 21(1)	≈ Art 5(1), second indent	≈ Art 19	≈ Art 5(1), second indent	≈ Art 19

Brussels Ia	BC	Brussels I	1988 LC	2007 LC
Art 21(2)	-	-	-	-
Art 24	≈ Art 16	≈ Art 22	≈ Art 16	≈ Art 22
Art 25(1) introductory words	≈ Art 17, first indent, introductory words	≈ Art 23(1) introductory words	≈ Art 17, first indent, introductory words	≈ Art 23(1) introductory words
Art 25(1), points (a)-(c)	Art 17, first indent, points (a)-(c)	Art 23(1), points (a)-(c)	Art 17, first indent, points (a)-(c)	Art 23(1), points (a)-(c)
Art 25(2)	-	Art 23(2)	-	Art 23(2)
-	Art 17, se-cond indent	Art 23(3)	Art 17(1), se-cond indent	Art 23(3)
Art 25(3)	Art 17, third indent	Art 23(4)	Art 17(2)	Art 23(4)
Art 25(4)	≈ Art 17, fourth indent	Art 23(5)	≈ Art 17(3)	Art 23(5)
Art 25(5)	-	-	-	-
Art 26(1)	≈ Art 18	Art 24	≈ Art 18	Art 24
Art 26(2)	-	-	-	-
Art 29(1)	≈ Art 21, first indent	≈ Art 27(1)	≈ Art 21, first indent	≈ Art 27(1)
Art 29(2)	-	-	-	-
Art 29(3)	Art 21, se-cond indent	Art 27(2)	Art 21, se-cond indent	Art 27(2)
Art 30(1)	Art 22, first indent	Art 28(1)	Art 22, first indent	Art 28(1)
Art 30(2)	≈ Art 22, se-cond indent	≈ Art 28(2)	≈ Art 22, se-cond indent	≈ Art 28(2)
Art 30(3)	Art 22, third indent	Art 28(3)	Art 22, third indent	Art 28(3)
Art 31(1)	Art 23	Art 29	Art 23	Art 29
Art 31(2)-(4)	-	-	-	-
Art 32(1) points (a)-(b)	-	Art 30	-	Art 30
Art 32(1), 2nd subpar	-	-	-	-
Art 32(2)	-	-	-	-
Art 33	-	-	-	-
Art 34	-	-	-	-
Art 35	≈ Art 24	≈ Art 31	≈ Art 24	≈ Art 31
Art 45(1) introductory words	cf. Art 27 introductory words	cf. Art 34 introductory words	cf. Art 27 introductory words	cf. Art 34 introductory words

Brussels Ia	BC	Brussels I	1988 LC	2007 LC
Art 45(1)(a)	Art 27, point 1	Art 34, point 1	Art 27, point 1	Art 34, point 1
Art 45(1)(b)	≈ Art 27, point 2	Art 34, point 2	≈ Art 27, point 2	Art 34, point 2
Art 45(1)(c)	Art 27, point 3	Art 34, point 3	Art 27, point 3	Art 34, point 3
-	Art 27, point 4	-	Art 27, point 4	-
Art 45(1)(d)	≈ Art 27, point 5	Art 34, point 4	≈ Art 27, point 5	Art 34, point 4
Art 45(1)(e)	≈ Art 28, first indent	≈ Art 35(1)	≈ Art 28, first indent	≈ Art 35(1)
Art 45(2)	Art 28, second indent	Art 35(2)	Art 28, second indent	Art 35(2)
Art 45(3)	Art 28, third indent	Art 35(3)	Art 28, fourth indent	Art 35(3)
Art 52	≈ Art 29	≈ Art 36	≈ Art 29	≈ Art 36
Art 62	Art 52	Art 59	Art 52	Art 59
Art 63(1)	cf. Art 53, first indent	Art 60(1)	cf. Art 53, first indent	Art 60(1)
Art 63(3)	Art 53, second indent	Art 60(3)	Art 53, second indent	Art 60(3)
Art 63(2)	-	≈ Art 60(2)	-	≈ Art 60(2)
Art 64	Protocol, Art II	Art 61	Protocol 1, Art II	Art 61
Art 66(1)	cf. Art 54, first indent	cf. Art 66(1)	cf. Art 54, first indent	cf. Art 63(1)
Art 68	-	Art 68	-	cf. Art 69(6)
Art 71 (1)	≈ Art 57(1)	Art 71(1)	≈ Art 57(1)	≈ Art 67(1)
Art 72	-	Art 72	-	≈ Art 68(1)
-	Art 59	-	Art 59	Art 68(1) last part of the sentence and Art 68(2)
Art 76(1) point (a) OJ 2015 C 4/2	≈ Art 3, second indent	≈ Annex I	≈ Art 3, second indent	≈ Annex I
Art 80	-	-	-	-
Art 81	-	cf. Art 76		-